FRENCH-ENGLISH
ENGLISH-FRENCH
DICTIONARY

FRENCH-ENGLISH
ENGLISH-FRENCH
DICTIONARY

ENGLISH-FRENCH

DICTIONARY

ABBREVIATIONS

adj. adjective	*pron*. pronoun
adv. adverb	*qch*. quelque chose
art. article	*qn*. qulqu'un
conj. conjunction	*rel*. relative
dem. demonstrative	*s*. substantive
f. feminine	*sing*. singular
fig. figurative	*s.o.* someone
impers. impersonal	*sth*. something
inf. infinitive	*v.a.* active verb
int. interjection	*v.a. & n*. active and neuter
m. masculine	verb
pers. person	*v. aux*. auxiliary verb
pl. plural	*v.n.* neuter verb
poss. possessive	* irregular verb
pp. past participle	*prep*. preposition

Pronunciation

We give below a short, simple guide to French pronunciation, giving the French sounds and their description. Vowels or consonants that are equivalent to the English ones are not indicated in this list.

Letters	French key word	Description
a, à, â	la, là, bâtir	between *bag* and *bug*
ai, aî	chaise, maîtr	resembles *ai* in *chair*
an	dans	between the vowels of *ah* and *oh* with *n* nasalised
au	pause	as in *oh* but with no final *u*
c	a) café	before *a, o, u* pronounced as *k*
	b) ici	before *e, i, y* pronounced *s* as in *say*
ç	français	as *s* in *say*
ch	chambre	as *sh* in *she*
e	a) le, petit	as the unstressed vowel of *the, standard*
	b) derriere, m	(in a closed syllable) as *e* i *deck*
é	été	as in *day* but with no final *i*

è, ê	père, fête	resembles the vowels in *pear* or *mare* without diphthongization
eau	eau	as in *oh* but with no final *u*
en	enfant	between *ah* and *oh* with *n* nasalized
er	donner	as in *day* but with no final
eu	jeudi, leur	closer than *earth* or *sir* pronounced with the lips pouted
g	a) rouge	before *e*, *i*, *y* pronounced as *s* in *measure*, *usual*
	b) grand	as *g* in *grand*, *good*
gn	signe	as in *new* or *lenient*
h	homme	it is never pronounced in French
i	a) ici	tenser than English short *i*
	b) mise	as *ee* in *meet*
î	île	as *ee* in *meet*
ille	fille	as in *key* with *y* at the end
in	vin	resembles the sound in *tan* pronounced through the nose
o	jour	as *s* in *usual*
jð	mot, côte	as in *oh* but with no final *u*
œ	œil	closer than *earth* pronounced with the lips pouted
oi	moi	as in *memoir* (memwaa¹)
on	non, son	between *ah* and *oh* with *n* nasalized
ou, oû	rouge, goûter	short or long *oo* as in *foot* or
qu	quand, question	as *k* in English
r	rare	as a slightly rolled English *r*
s	a) son	usually *s* as in *say*
	b) maison	(between two vowels) *z* as in *zero*
th	thé	as *t* in English
tion	nation	always *sio* + nasal *n*
u, û	sur, sûr	no equivalent in English: round lips for *oo* and try to pronounce *ee*
un	brun	the vowel of *her*, *earth* with a nasal *n*
w	wagon	as *v* in English
x	a) deuxième	as *z* in *zero*
	b) six	as *s* in *say*
y	y	as short *i* in English

FRENCH GRAMMAR

L i a i s o n.—Final consonants are not usually pronounced, but in most cases, when a word begins with a vowel (or the mute *h*), it is linked with the last consonant of the preceding word. In such cases final *c* and *g* are pronounced as *k*, final *s* and *x* as *z*, e.g. les⌣Anglais (lezangle). **S t r e s s.**—In polysyllabic words stress usually falls on the last pronounced syllable, e.g. plusieurs, le docteur, la société.

The Article

The definite article is *le* (m.), *la* (f.), *les* (m. f. pl.). *Le, la* are shortened to *l'* before a vowel or mute *h*.

The indefinite article is *un* (m.), *une* (f.).

The Noun

The **p l u r a l** is generally formed in *s*. Nouns in *s, x,* and *z* do not change in the plural. Nouns in *au* and *eu* form their plurals in *x*, e.g. *joyau, joyaux, jeu, jeux*. Nouns in *al*, form their plurals in *aux*, e.g. *cheval, chevaux*.

There are two *genders* in French. Nearly all nouns ending in *e* mute are feminine, except those in *isme, age* and *iste*. Nearly all nouns ending in a consonant or a vowel other than *e* mute are masculine, except nouns in *tion* and *té*. Nouns in *er* form their f. in *ère* e.g. *laitier, laitière*. Nouns

in *en, on* form their f. in *enne, onne*, e.g. *chien, chienne, lion, lionne*. Nouns in *eur* form their 'f. in *euse* except those in *ateur* which have *atrice*, e.g. *admirateur, admiratrice*.

The Adjective

The **p l u r a l** is generally formed in *s*. Adjectives in *s* or *x* do not change. Those in *al* usually form their plurals in *aux*, e.g. *principal, principaux*.

The **f e m i n i n e** is generally formed by adding *e* to the masculine form, e.g. *élégant, élégante*. Adjectives in *f* change *f* into *ve*, e.g. *vif, vive*. Those in *x* change *x* into *se*, e.g. *heureux, heureuse*. Adj. in *er* form their f. in *ère*, e.g. *amer, amère*. Those in *el, eil, en, et, on* double the final consonant before adding *e*, e.g. *bel, belle, bon, bonne*.

C o m p a r a t i v e.—'more ... than' or '... er than' is to be translated by 'plus ... que'; 'less ... than' by 'moins ... que'.

S u p e r l a t i v e.—'the most...' or 'the ... st' is to be translated by 'le plus ...', 'la plus ... ' or 'les plus ...'

The Pronoun

P e r s o n a l p r o n o u n s: je, tu, il, elle; nous, vous, ils, elles.—*Accusative:* me, te, le, la; nous, vous, les. *Dative:* me, te, lui; nous, vous, leur.—

After prep.. moi, toi, lui, elle; nous, vous, eux, elles.

Reflexive pronouns: me, te, se; nous, vous, se.

Possessive pronouns: le mien (la mienne, les miens, les miennes), le tien (la tienne, les tiens, les tiennes), le sien (la sienne, les siens, les siennes); le nôtre (la nôtre, les nôtres), le vôtre (la vôtre, les vôtres), le leur (la leur, les leurs).

Relative pronouns: who = qui, whom = que, whose = dont, which = qui or que, to whom = a qui.

Interrogative pronoun: who, whom = qui; what = que.

The Adverb

Most French adverbs are formed by adding *ment*, to the feminine form of the corresponding adjective, e.g. *facile*, *facile+ment*, *heureux*, *heureuse + ment*. Those in *ant* and *ent* form their adverbs in *amment* and *emment*, respectively, e.g. *patient—patiemment*.

The Verb

We give here the conjugation of the two auxilliaries (*avoir*, *être*) and of the verbs in -er, -ir, and -re, giving only the principal simple forms:

avoir *Pres. Ind.* j'ai, tu as, il a, nous avons, vous avez, ils ont; *Impf.* j'avais, tu avais, il avait, nous avions, vous aviez, ils avaient; *Fut.* j'aurai, tu auras, il aura, nous aurons, vous aurez, ils auront; *Cond.* j'aurais, tu aurais, il aurait, nous aurions, vous auriez, ils auraient; *Pres. Subj.* que j'aie, que tu aies, qu'il ait, que nous ayons, que vous ayez, qu'ils aient; *Imp.* aie, ayons, ayez; *Pres. Part.* ayant; *Past.Part.* eu.

être *Pres. Ind.* je suis, tu es, il est, nous sommes, vous êtes, ils sont; *Impf.* j'étais, tu étais, il était, nous étions, vous étiez, ils étaient; *Fut.* je serai, tu seras, il sera, nous serons, vous serez, ils seront; *Cond.* je serais, tu serais, il serait, nous serions, vous seriez, ils seraient; *Pres. Subj.* que je sois, que tu sois, qu'il soit, que nous soyons, que vous soyez, qu'il soient; *Imp.* sois, soyons, soyez; *Pres. Part.* étant; *Past. Part.* été.

donner *Pres. Ind.* je donne, tu donnes, il donne, nous donnons, vous donnez, ils donnent; *Impf.* je donnais, tu donnais, il donnait, nous donnions, vous donniez, ils donnaient; *Fut.* je donnerai, tu donneras, il donnera, nous donnerons, vous donnerez, ils donneront; *Cond.* je donnerais, tu donnerais, il donnerait, nous donnerions, vous donneriez, ils donneraient; *Pres. Subj.* que je donne, que tu donnes, qu'il donne, que nous donnions, que vous donniez, qu'ils donnent; *Imp.* donne, donnons, donnez; *Pres. Part.* donnant; *Past. Part.* donné.

finir *Pres. Ind.* je finis, tu finis, il finit, nous finissons, vous finnissez, ils finissent; finis, il finit, nous finissons, vous finissez, ils finissent; *Impf.* je finissais, tu finissais, il finissait, nous finissions, vous finissiez, ils finissaient; *Fut.* je finirai, tu finiras, il finira, nous finirons, vous finirez, ils finiront; *Cond.* je finirais, tu finirais, il finirait, nous finirions, vous finiriez, ils finiraient; *Pres. Subj.* que je finisse, que tu finisses, qu'il finisse, que nous finissions, que vous finissiez, qu'ils finissent; *Imp.* finis, finissons, finissez; *Pres. Part.* finissant; *Past Part.* fini.

rendre *Pres. Ind.* je rends, tu rends, il rend, nous rendons, vous rendez, ils rendent; *Impf.* je rendais, tu rendais, il rendait, nous rendions, vous rendiez, ils rendaient; *Fut.* je rendrai, tu rendras, il rendra, nous rendrons, vous rendrez, ils rendront; *Cond.* je rendrais, tu rendrais, il rendrait, nous rendrions, vous rendriez, ils rendraient; *Pres. Subj.* que je rende, que tu rendes, qu'il rende, que nous rendions, que vous rendiez, qu'ils rendent; *Imp.* rends, rendons, rendez; *Pres. Part.* rendant; *Past. Part.* rendu.

Irregular Verbs

Verbs in *-ger* add *e* before endings in *a* and *o*. Verbs in *-eler*, *-eter* double the *l* or *t* before a mute *e*. Verbs having an acute *é* in the last syllable but one change for a grave *e* when the ending begins with a mute *e*. Verbs in *-yer* change *y* into *i* before a mute *e*.

In the following list of the most frequent French irregular verbs (the root verbs only) the numbers indicate the principal tenses and forms in a fixed order: 1. Present Indicative; 2. Imperfect; 3. Future; 4. Present Subjunctive; 5. Imperative; 6. Present Participle; 7. Past Participle. (+ *être*, if *être* is used to form the past tenses e.g. je suis allé.)

absoudre 1. j'absous, tu absous, il absout, nous absolvons, vous absolvez, ils absolvent; 2. j'absolvais; 3. j'absoudrai; 4. que j'absolve; 5. absous, absolvons, absolvez; 6. absolvant; 7. absous, absoute.

acquérir 1. j'acquiers, tu acquiers, il acquiert, nous acquérons, vous acquérez, ils acquièrent; 2. j'acquérais; 3. j'acquerrai; 4. que j'acquière; 5. acquiers, acquérons, acquérez; 6. acquérant; 7. acquis.

aller 1. je vais, tu vas, il va, nous allons, vous allez, ils vont; 2. j'allais; 3. j'irai; 4. que j'aille, que nous allions, qu'ils aillent; 5. va, allons, allez; 6. allant; 7. allé (être).

assaillir 1. j'assaille, tu assailles, il assaille, nous assaillons, vous assaillez, ils assaillent; 2. j'assaillais; 3. j'assaillerai; 4. que j'assaille; 5. assaille, assaillons, assaillez; 6. assaillant; 7. assailli.

asseoir 1. j'assieds, tu assieds, il assied, nous asseyons, vous asseyez, ils asseyent or j'assois, tu assois, il assoit, nous assoyons, vous assoyez, ils assoient; 2. j'assayais or j'assoyais; 3. j'assiérai or j'assoierai; 4. que j'asseye or que j'assoie; 5. assieds, asseyons or assoyons, asseyez or assoyez; 6. asseyant or assoyant; 7. assis.

atteindre as **peindre**.

battre 1. je bats, tu bats, il bat, nous battons, vous battez, ils battent; 2. je battais; 3. je battrai; 4. que je batte; 5. bats, battons, battez; 6. battant; 7. battu.

boire 1. je bois, tu bois, il boit, nous buvons, vous buvez, ils boivent; 2. je buvais; 3. je boirai; 4. que je boive; 5. bois, buvons, buvez; 6. buvant; 7. bu.

bouillir 1. je bous, tu bous, il bout, nous bouillons, vous bouillez, ils bouillent; 2. je bouillais; 3. je bouillirai; 4. que je bouille; 5. bous, bouillons, bouillez; 6. bouillant; 7. bouilli.

clore 1. je clos, tu clos, il clôt; 3. je clorai; 4. que je close; 7. clos.

concevoir 1. je conçois, tu conçois, il conçoit, nous concevons, vous concevez, ils conçoivent; 2. je concevais; 3. je concevrai; 4. que je conçoive; 5. conçois, concevons, concevez; 6. concevant; 7. conçu.

conclure 1. je conclus, tu conclus, il conclut, nous concluons, vous concluez, ils concluent; 2. je concluais; 3. je conclurai; 4. que je conclue; 5. conclus, concluons, concluez; 6. concluant; 7. conclu.

conduire 1. je conduis, tu conduis, il conduit, nous conduisons, vous conduisez, ils conduisent; 2. je conduisais; 3. je conduirai; 4. que je conduise; 5. conduis, conduisons, conduisez; 6. conduisant; 7. conduit.

connaître 1. je connais, tu connais, il connaît, nous connaissons, vous connaissez, ils connaissent; 2. je connaissais; 3. je connaîtrai; 4. que je connaisse; 5. connais, connaissons, connaissez; 6. connaissant; 7. connu.

conquérir as **acquérir**.

construire as **conduire**.

contraindre 1. je contrains, tu contrains, il contraint, nous contraignons, vous contraignez, ils contraignent; 2. je contraignais; 3. je contraindrai; 4. que je contraigne; 5. contrains, contraignons, contraignez; 6. contraignant; 7. contraint.

coudre 1. je couds, tu couds, il coud, nous cousons, vous cousez, ils cousent; 2. je cousais; 3. je coudrai; 4. que je couse; 5. couds, cousons, cousez; 6. cousant; 7. cousu.

courir 1. je cours, tu cours, il court, nous courons, vous courez, ils courent; 2. je courais; 3. je courrai; 4. que je coure; 5. cours, courons, courez; **6.** courant; **7.** couru.

couvrir *as* **ouvrir**.

croire 1. je crois, tu crois, il croit, nous croyons, vous croyez, ils croient; **2.** je croyais; **3.** je croirai; **4.** que je croie; **5.** crois, croyons, croyez; **6.** croyant; **7.** cru.

croître 1. je crois, tu crois, il croit, nous croissons, vous croissez, ils croissent; **2.** je croissais; **3.** je croîtrai; **4.** que je croisse; **5.** crois, croissons, croissez; **6.** croissant; **7.** crû, crue.

cueillir 1. je cueille, tu cueilles, il cueille, nous cueillons, vous cueillez, ils cueillent; **2.** je cueillais; **3.** je cueillerai; **4.** que je cueille; **6.** cueillant; **7.** cueilli.

cuire 1. je cuis, tu cuis, il cuit, nous cuisons, vous cuisez, ils cuisent; **2.** je cuisais; **3.** je cuirai; **4.** que je cuise; **5.** cuis, cuisons, cuisez; **6.** cuisant; **7.** cuit.

déchoir 1. je déchois, tu déchois, il déchoit, nous déchoyons, vous déchoyez, ils déchoient; **2.** je déchoyais; **3.** je décherrai; **4.** que je déchoie; **7.** déchu.

déconfire *as* **confire**.

découvrir *as* **ouvrir**.

déduire, détruire *as* **conduire**.

devoir 1. je dois, tu dois, il doit, nous devons, vous devez, ils doivent; **2.** je devais; **3.** je devrai; **4.** que je doive; **5.** dois, devons, devez; **6.** devant; **7.** dû, due.

dire 1. je dis, tu dis, il dit, nous disons, vous dites, ils disent; **2.** je disais; **3.** je dirai; **4.** que je dise; **5.** dis, disons, dites; **6.** disant **7.** dit.

dissoudre 1. je dissous, tu dissous, il dissout, nous dissolvons, vous dissolvez, ils dissolvent; **2.** je dissolvais; **3.** je dissoudrai; **4.** que je dissolve; **5.** dissous, dissolvons, dissolvez; **6.** dissolvant; **7.** dissous, dissoute.

dormir 1. je dors, tu dors, il dort, nous dormons, vous dormez, ils dorment; **2.** je dormais; **3.** je dormirai; **4.** que je dorme; **5.** dors dormons, dormez; **6.** dormant; **7.** dormi.

échoir *or* **échoir 1.** il échoit *or* il échet, ils échoient; **2.** il échoyait; **3.** il écherra, ils écherront; **4.** qu'il échoie; **6.** échéant; **7.** échu.

écrire 1. j'écris, tu écris, il écrit, nous écrivons, vous écrivez, ils écrivent; **2.** j'écrivais; **3.** j'écrirai; **4.** que j'écrive; **5.** écris, écrivons, écrivez; **6.** écrivant; **7.** écrit.

envoyer, 1. j'envoie, tu envoies, il envoie, nous envoyons, vous envoyez, ils envoient; **2.** j'envoyais; **3.** j'enverrai; **4.** que j'envoie; **5.** envoie, envoyons, envoyez; **6.** envoyant; **7.** envoyé.

éteindre *as* **peindre**.

étreindre *as* **peindre**.

exclure *as* **conclure**.

faire 1. je fais, tu fais, il fait, nous faisons, vous faites, ils font; **2.** je faisais; **3.** je ferai; **4.** que je fasse; **5.** fais, faisons, faites; **6.** faisant; **7.** fait.

falloir 1. il faut; 2. il fallait; 3. il faudra; 4. qu'il faille; 7. fallu.

feindre *as* **peindre.**

frire 1. je fris, tu fris, il frit; 3. je frirai; 5. fris; 7. frit.

fuir 1. je fuis, tu fuis, il fuit, nous fuyons, vous fuyez, ils fuient; 2. je fuyais; 3. je fuirai; 4. que je fuie; 5. fuis, fuyons, fuyez; 6. fuyant; 7. fui.

gésir 1. il git, nous gisons, vous gisez, ils gisent; 2. je gisais; 6. gisant.

haïr 1. je hais, tu hais, il hait, nous haïssons, vous haïssez, ils haïssent; 2. je haïssais; 3. je haïrai; 4. que je haïsse; 5. hais, · haïssons, haïssez; 6. haïssant, 7. haï.

instruire *as* **conduire.**

joindre 1. je joins, tu joins, il joint, nous joignons, vous joignez, ils joignent; 2. je joignais; 3. je joindrai; 4. que je joigne; 5. joins, joignons, joignez; 6. joignant; 7. joint.

lire 1. je lis, tu lis, il lit, nous lisons, vous lisez, ils lisent; 2. je lisais; 3. je lirai; 4. que je lise; 5. lis, lisons, lisez; 6. lisant; 7. lu.

luire *as* **nuire.**

maudire 1. je 'maudis, tu maudis, il maudit, nous maudissons, vous maudissez, ils maudissent; 2. je maudissais; 3. je maudirai; 4. que je maudisse; 5. maudis, maudissons, maudissez; 6. maudissant; 7. maudit.

mentir *as* **sentir.**

mettre 1. je mets, tu mets, il met, nous mettons, vous mettez, ils mettent; 2. je mettais; 3. je mettrai; 4. que je mette; 5. mets, mettons, mettez; 6. mettant; 7. mis.

moudre 1. je mouds, tu mouds, il moud, nous moulons, vous moulez, ils moulent; 2. je moulais; 3. je moudrai; 4. que je moule; 5. mouds, moulons, moulez; 6. moulant; 7. moulu.

mourir 1. je meurs, tu meurs, il meurt, nous mourons, vous mourez, ils meurent; 2. je mourais; 3. je mourrai; 4. que je meure; 5. meurs, mourons, mourez; 6. mourant; 7. mort (être.)

mouvoir 1. je meus, tu meus, il meut, nous mouvons, vous mouvez, ils meuvent; 2. je mouvais; 3. je mouvrai; 4. que je meuve; 5. meus, mouvons, mouvez; 6. mouvant; 7. mû, mue.

naître 1. je nais, tu nais, il nait, nous naissons, vous naissez, ils naissent; 2. je naissais; 3. je naîtrai; 4. que je naisse; 5. nais, naissons, naissez; 6. naissant; 7. né, née (être.)

nuire 1. je nuis, tu nuis, il nuit, nous nouisons, vous nuisez, ils nuisent; 2. je nuisais; 3. je nuirai; 4. que je nuise; 5. nuis, nuisons, nuisez; 6. nuisant; 7. nui.

offrir *as* **ouvrir.**

ouvrir 1. j'ouvre, tu ouvres, il ouvre, nous ouvrons, vous ouvrez, ils ouvrent; 2. j'ouvrais; 3. j'ouvrirai; 4. que j'ouvre; 5. ouvre, ouvrons, ouvrez; 6. ouvrant; 7. ouvert.

paître 1. je pais, tu pais, il paît, nous paissons, vous paissez, ils paissent; 2. je paissais; 3. je paîtrai; 4. que je paisse; 5. pais, paissons, paissez; 6. paissant.

paraître 1. je parais, tu parais, il paraît, nous paraissons, vous páraissez, ils paraissent; 2. je paraissais; 3. je paraîtrai; 4. que je paraisse; 5. parais, paraissons, paraissez; 6. paraissant; 7. paru.

partir 1. je pars, tu pars, il part, nous partons, vous partez, ils partent; 2. je partais; 3. je partirai; 4. que je parte; 5. pars, partons, partez; 6. partant; 7. parti (être.)

peindre 1. je peins, tu peins, il peint, nous peignons, vous peignez, ils peignent; 2. je peignais; 3. je peindrai; 4. que je peigne; 5. peins, peignons, peignez; 6. peignant; 7. peint.

plaire 1. je plais, tu plais, il plaît, nous plaisons, vous plaisez, ils plaisent; 2. je plaisais; 3. je plairai; 4. que je plaise; 5. plais, plaisons, plaisez; 6. plaisant; 7. plu.

pouvoir 1. je peux *or* je puis, tu peux, il peut, nous pouvons, vous pouvez, ils peuvent; 2. je pouvais; 3. je pourrai; 4. que je puisse; 6. pouvant; 7. pu.

prendre 1. je prends, tu prends, il prend, nous prenons, vous prenez, ils prennent; 2. je prenais; 3. je prendrai; 4. que je prenne; 5. prends, prenons, prenez; 6. prenant; 7. pris.

prescrire *as* écrire.
produire *as* conduire.
proscrire *as* écrire.
recevoir *as* concevoir.
reconstruire *as* conduire.
réduire *as* conduire.
repartir *as* partir.
reproduire *as* conduire.

résoudre 1. je résous, tu résous, il résout, nous résolvons, vous résolvez, ils résolvent; 2. je résolvais; 3. je résoudrai; 4. que je résolve; 5. résous, résolvons, résolvez; 6. résolvant; 7. résolu.

restreindre *as* peindre.

rire 1. je ris, tu ris, il rit, nous rions, vous riez, ils rient; 2. je riais; 3. je rirai; 4. que je rie; 5. ris, rions, riez; 6. riant; 7. ri.

savoir 1. je sais, tu sais, il sait, nous savons, vous savez, ils savent; 2. je savais; 3. je saurai; 4. que je sache; 5. sais, sachons, sachez; 6. sachant; 7. sus.

sentir 1. je sens, tu sens, il sent, nous sentons, vous sentez, ils sentent; 2. je sentais; 3. je sentirai; 4. que je sente; 5. sens, sentons, sentez; 6. sentant; 7. senti.

servir 1. je sers, tu sers, ils sert, nous servons, vous servez, ils servent; 2. je servais; 3. je servirai; 4. que je serve; 5. sers, servons, servez; 6. servant; 7. servi.

sortir 1. je sors, tu sors, il sort, nous sortons, vous sortez, ils sortent; 2. je sortais;

3. je sortirai; 4. que je sorte; 5. sors, sortons, sortez; 6. sortant; 7. sorti (être).

souffrir as **ouvrir.**

se souvenir as **venir.**

suffire 1. je suffis, tu suffis, il suffit, nous suffisons, vous suffisez, ils suffisent; 2. je suffisais; 3. je suffirai; 4. que je suffise; 5. suffis, suffisons, suffisez; 6. suffisant; 7. suffi.

suivre 1. je suis, tu suis, il suit, nous suivons, vous suivez, ils suivent; 2. je suivais; 3. je suivrai; 4. que je suive; 5. suis, suivons, suivez; 6. suivant; 7. suivi.

surseoir 1. je sursois, tu sursois, il sursoit, nous sursoyons, vous sursoyez, ils sursoient; 2. je sursoyais; 3. je surseoirai; 4. que je sursoie; 5. sursois, sursoyons, sursoyez; 6. sursoyant; 7. sursis.

taire as **plaire.**

teindre as **peindre.**

tenir 1. je tiens, tu tiens, il tient, nous tenons, vous tenez, ils tiennent; 2. je tenais; 3. je tiendrai; 4. que je tienne; 5. tiens, tenons, tenez; 6. tenant; 7. tenu.

traduire as **conduire.**

traire 1. je trais, tu trais, il trait, nous trayons, vous trayez, ils traient; 2. je trayais; 3. je trairai; 4. que je traie; 5. trais, trayons, trayez; 6. trayant; 7. trait.

vaincre 1. je vaincs, tu vaincs, il vainc, nous vainquons, vous vainquez, ils vainquent; 2. je vainquais; 3. je vaincrai; 4. que je vainque; 5. vaincs, vainquons, vainquez; 6. vainquant; 7. vaincu.

valoir 1. je vaux, tu vaux, il vaut. nous valons, vous valez, ils valent; 2. je valais, 3. je vaudrai; 4. que je vaille; 6. valant; 7. valu.

venir 1. je viens, tu viens, il vient, nous venons, vous venez, ils viennent; 2. je venais; 3. je viendrai; 4. que je vienne; 5. viens, venons, venez; 6. venant; 7. venu (être.)

vêtir 1. je vêts, tu vêts, il vêt, nous vêtons, vous vêtez, ils vêtent; 2. je vêtais; 3. je vêtirai; 4. que je vête; 5. vêts, vêtons, vêtez; 6. vêtant; 7. vêtu.

vivre 1. je vis, tu vis, il vit, nous vivons, vous vivez, ils vivent; 2. je vivais; 3. je vivrai; 4. que je vive; 5. vis, vivons, vivez; 6. vivant; 7. vécu.

voir 1. je vois, tu vois, il voit, nous voyons, vous voyez, ils voient; 2. je voyais; 3. je verrai; 4. que je voie; 5. vois, voyons, voyez; 6. voyant; 7. vu.

vouloir 1. je veux, tu veux, il veut, nous voulons, vous voulez, ils veulent; 2. je voulais; 3. je voudrai; 4. que je veuille, que nous voulions; 5. veuille, veuillions, veuillez or voulez; 6. voulant; 7. voulu.

PHRASES

Good morning. Good evening. Good-bye.	Bonjour. Bonsoir. Au revoir.
I beg your pardon. Excuse me.	Je vous demande pardon. Pardon.
How are you? Very well — and you?	Comment allez-vous? Très bien — et vous?
How do you do (delighted to meet you).	Enchanté (de faire votre connaissance) monsieur (madame, mademoiselle).
Allow me! You are very kind.	Permettez-moi! Vous étes très gentil.
It's all the same to me.	Cela m'est égal.
Your good health.	A votre santé.
Allow me to introduce you to . . .	Permettez-moi de vous présenter à . . .
It is fine (bad) weather.	Il fait beau (mauvais) temps.
You are right. You are wrong.	Vous avez raison. Vous avez tort.
It is not my fault.	Ce n'est pas ma faute.
To do one's best.	Faire son possible.
It is very annoying.	C'est très ennuyeux.
You're pulling my leg.	Vous vous moquez de moi.
So much the better (worse).	Tant mieux (pis).
He's a jolly nice fellow.	C'est un chic type.
To put one's foot in it.	Mettre les pieds dans le plat.
Things are going badly.	Rien ne va bien. Tout va mal.
I am an Englishmen (Englishwoman).	Je suis anglais (anglaise).
I cannot speak French.	Je ne parle pas français.
I am looking for . . .	Je cherche . . .
I don't understand you.	Je ne vous comprends pas.
Please speak slowly!	Parlez lentement, s'il vous plait!
Is there anyone here who speaks English?	Y-a-t-il quelque'un qui parle anglais?
Where is the British Consulate?	Où est le consulat britannique?
It is wonderful, splendid!	C'est épatant, formidable!
No . . . Trespassers will be prosecuted.	Défense de . . . sous peine d'amende.

No entry.	Entrée interdite.
Lavatory.	Les toilettes, les lavabos, les cabinets.
What time is it?	Quelle heure est-il?
It is five past one.	Il est une heure cinq.
We are in a hurry.	Nous sommes pressés.
How long does it take to . . . ?	Combien de temps faut-il pour . . . ?
This evening, tonight. Last night.	Ce soir. Hier soir.
How long have you been here?	Depuis quand êtes-vous ici?
I have been here a month.	Je suis ici depuis un mois.
Can we lunch (dine) here?	Est-ce qu'on peut déjeuner (dîner) ici?
There are four of us.	Nous sommes quatre.
We only want a snack.	Nous voudrions seulement un casse-croûte.
Please give us the menu.	Voulez-vous nous donner le menu, s'il vous plaît.
Bring us the wine list, please.	Apportez-nous la carte des vins, s'il vous plaît.
We would like black coffee (white coffee).	Nous voudrions du café noir (café au lait).
The bill, please.	L'addition, s'il vous plaît.
I want some petrol (oil, water).	Je voudrais de l'essence (de l'huile, de l'eau).
I have had a breakdown.	Je suis en panne.
My car is on the road two kilometres from here.	Mon auto est sur la route à deux kilomètres d'ici.
Do you know the road to . . . ?	Connaissez-vous a route de . . . ?
Is the post office (bank) near here?	Y a-t-il un bureau de poste (bureau de change) près d'ici?
Are there any letters for me?	Y a-t-il des lettres pour moi?
Do you sell . . . ?	Est-ce que vous vendez...?
You have given me the wrong change.	Vous vous êtes trompé en me rendant la monnaie
Have you anything to declare?	Avez-vous quelque chose à déclarer?
I cannot find my ticket.	Je ne peux pas trouver mon billet.
I have left something in the train.	J'ai laissé quelque chose dans le train.
I have a train to catch.	J'ai un train à prendre.
What time is the first (last) train for . . . ?	A quelle heure est le premier (dernier) train pour . . . ?

From which platform?	Sur quel quai?
Where do I change for . . .?	Où est-ce que je change pour . . .?
Is there a hotel where I can stay the night?	Est-ce qu'il y a un hôtel où je peux passer la nuit?
The last train has gone	Le dernier train est parti.
I do not feel well.	Je ne me sens pas bien.
I want to get off at . . .	Je veux descendre à . . .
Do you go near . . .?	Allez-vous près de . . .?
Can I have a room for the night?	Puis-je avoir une chambre pour la nuit?
I am only staying for two or three days.	Je reste deux ou trois jours seulement.
I want a room with a double bed.	Je désire une chambre avec un grand lit.
Can you put me up for the night?	Pouvez-vous me donnez une chambre pour la nuit?
I shall be back at three.	Je serai de retour à trois heures.
Have you any English newspapers?	Avez-vous des journaux anglais?
What does it cost to send a letter to . . .?	Combien met-on sur une lettre pour . . .?
Where can I buy . . .?	Où puis-je acheter . . .?
Will you reserve this place for me?	Voulez-vous me reserver cette place?
Will you take a traveller's cheque?	Acceptez-vous un cheque de voyage?
Will you have letters sent on to this address?	Voulez-vous faire suivre mon courrier à cette adresse?
I need a guide who speaks English.	J'ai besoin d'un guide qui parle anglais.
Is this the right road for . . .?	Est-ce bien la route pour . . .?
How far is it from here to . . . ?	Combien de kilomètres d'ici à . . .?
Have you any post-cards?	Avez-vous des cartes postales?
Have you a map (plan)?	Avez-vous une carte (un plan)?
Do you know what is on at the cinema (theatre)?	Savez-vous ce qu'on donne au cinéma (Théatre)?
Where does this road lead?	Ce chemin, ou mène-t-il?

Can you recommend a cheap restaurant?	Pouvez-vous recommander un restaurant pas trop cher?
It is too dear. Have you anything cheaper?	C'est trop cher. Avez-vous quelque chose de meilleur marché?
We are lost.	Nous sommes perdus.
Have you any identification papers?	Avez-vous une pièce d'identite?
Have you a carrier bag?	Avez-vous un sac en papier?
Here is my address.	Voici mon adresse.
That's all right.	Je vous en prie.
Don't mention it.	Il n'y a pas de quoi.
Take my seat, madame.	Prenez ma place, madame.
Can I help you?	Puis-je vous aider?
Am I disturbing you?	Est-ce que je vous dérange?
I am terribly sorry.	Je suis navré (désolé).
Thank you for your hospitality.	Je vous remercie de votre hospitalité.
We had a very good time.	Nous nous sommes bien amusés.
It's too much. It's too dear.	C'est trop. C'est trop cher.
Look out!	Attention!
You are right. You are wrong.	Vous avez raison. Vous avez tort.
Listen. Look.	Ecoutez. Regardez.
What is the matter?	Qu'est-ce qu'il y a?
Please speak slowly.	Parlez lentement, s'il vous plait.
Wait, I am looking for the phrase in this book.	Attendez, je cherche la phrase dans ce livre.
I have already paid you.	Je vous ai déjà payé.
It's terribly funny.	C'est tordant, c'est rigolo.
You don't say!	Sans blague!
You are joking. Joking apart.	Vous plaisantez. Blague à part.
Agreed. O.K.	Entendu. D'accord.
What a pity!	Quel dommage!
Do not touch.	Ne pas toucher.
Wet paint.	Prenez garde à la peinture.
You have plenty of time.	Vous avez tout le temps.
I have no time.	Je n'ai pas le temps.
The day before yesterday.	Avant-hier.
The day after tomorrow.	Après-demain.

Waiter, bring us some bread, please.	Garçon apportez-nous du pain, s'il vous plaît.
A little more . . .	Encore un peu de . . .
What would you like to drink?	Que désirez-vous boire (comme boisson)?
Is the service (the cover charge) included?	Le service (le couvert), est-il compris?
Keep the change.	Vous pouvez garder la monnaie.
There is a mistake in the bill.	Il y a une erreur dans l'addition.
Please don't mention it.	Je vous en prie.
Is the garage open all night?	Est-ce que le garage est ouvert la nuit?
I want to leave early tomorrow.	Je veux partir demain de bonne heure.
How long shall I have to wait?	Combien de temps faut-il attendre?
Can you lend me . . . ?	Pouvez-vous me prêter . . . ?
How much do I owe you?	Combien est-ce que je vous dois?
I have two first class (second class) seats reserved.	J'ai deux places réservées en première (en seconde).
Excuse me, sir, that seat is mine.	Pardon monsieur, cette place est à moi.
Porter I want to put this luggage in the cloakroom (left-luggage office).	Porteur, je veux mettre ces bagages à la consigne.
I am coming with you.	Je vous suis.
Is there a porter from the . . . Hotel here?	Est-ce qu'il y a un porter de l'hôtel . . . ici?
Where is the enquiry office?	Où est le bureau de renseignements?
When do we get to . . . ?	A quelle heure arrive-t-on à . . . ?
How long does the train stop here?	Combien de temps le train s'arrête-t-il ici?
The plane for . . . is twenty minutes late already.	L'avion pour . . . a déjà vingt minutes de retard.
The . . . plane is announced.	L'avion de . . . est signalé.
Where is the Airline Office?	Où est le bureau de la compagnie aérienne?
I want to reserve a seat on the plane leaving tomorrow for . .	Je voudrais réserver une place dans l'avion qui part demain pour . .

Is there a plane for . . . today?	Est-ce qu'il y a un avion pour . . . audjourd'hui?
I do not feel well.	Je ne me sens pas bien.
Bring me some coffee (brandy, a glass of water), please.	Apportez-moi du café (cognac, un verre d'eau), s'il vous plait.
Put out your cigarettes and fasten your seat-belts, please.	Eteignez vos cigarettes et attachez vos ceintures, s'il vous plait.
Call me a taxi.	Appelez-moi un taxi.
Go quickly, I am in a great hurry.	Dépêchez-vous, je suis très pressé.
Please wait here for a few minutes.	Attendez-moi ici quelques minutes, s'il vous plait.
Where is the office?	Où est le bureau?
Have you a room with a private bathroom?	Avez-vous une chambre avec salle de bains?
What is the price of a room per night?	Quel est le prix d'une chambre par nuit?
I am expecting a gentleman (a lady, a young lady).	J'attends un monsieur (une dame, une demoiselle).
Give me two 25 centime stamps and two at 15 centimes.	Donnez-moi deux timbres de vingt-cinq centimes et deux de quinze.
I want to send a telegram.	Je voudrais envoyer une dépêche.
Have you the time-table of trains for . . . ?	Avez-vous l'horaire des trains pour . . . ?
Can we have an English breakfast?	Peut-on avoir un petit déjeuner anglais?
Order a taxi for 9.30, please.	Commandez un taxi pour neuf heures et demie, s'il vous plait.
Please have my bill made out.	Préparez la note, s'il vous plait.
We want to be together.	Nous voudrions être ensemble.
How far it to . . . ?	Quelle distance d'ici à . . . ?
What is the name of this town· (village)?	Quel est le nom de cette ville (ce village)?
Where is the market place?	Où est le marché?
Weather permitting, we hope to leave at dawn.	Si le temps le permet, nous comptons partir à l'aube.
Get me Molitor 44—94,	Voulez-vous me demander

please.

Molitor quarante-quatre, quatre-vingt quatorze, s'il vous plait.

How much do I owe you for the call?

Combien vous dois-je pour la communication?

Can I make an appointment?

Puis-je prendre un rendezvous?

Can I have something to read?

Puis-je avoir de la lecture?

Can you make up this prescription, please?

Pouvez-vous faire cette ordonnance, s'il vous plaît?

Can you give me something for insect (ant, mosquito) bites?

Pouvez-vous me donner quelque chose pour les piqûres d'insects (de fourmis, de moustiques)?

My skin is smarting; have you anything to soothe it?

La peau me cuit; avez-vous quelque-chose de calmant?

For external use.

Pour l'usage externe.

I want a reversal (negative) colour film.

Je voudrais un film en couleur inversible (negatif).

Do you sell ...?

Est-ce que vous vendez ...?

Have you anything cheaper (better)?

Avez-vous quelque chose de moins cher (de meilleure qualité)?

I want something like this (that).

Je voudrais quelque chose comme ceci (cela).

Can you order it for me?

Pouvez-vous le (la) commander?

Will you send it to this address?

Voulez-vous l'envoyer à cette adresse?

That's exactly what I want.

Voilà ce qu'il me faut.

You have given me the wrong change.

Vous vous êtes trompé en me rendant la monnaie.

Can you change it?

Pouvez-vous le changer?

Do you sell English cigarettes (tobacco)?

Est-ce que vous vendez des cigarettes anglaises (du tabac anglais)?

There has been an accident.

Il y a eu un accident.

Is there a doctor near here?

Y a-t-il un médecin près d'ici?

Welcome to England (France).

Je vous souhaite la bienvenue en Angleterre

(France).	
Avez-vous fait un bon voyage?	Did you have a good journey?
A quelle heure est le petit déjeuner (le déjeuner, le goûter, le diner)?	What time is breakfast (lunch, tea, dinner)?

NUMBERS

1 *one*, un.	1st *first*, premier.
2 *two*, deux.	2nd *second*, deuxième.
3 *three*, trois.	3rd *third*, troisième.
4 *four*, quatre.	4th *fourth*, quatrième.
5 *five*, cinq.	5th *fifth*, cinquième.
6 *six*, six.	6th *sixth*, sixième.
7 *seven*, sept.	7th *seventh*, septième.
8 *eight*, huit.	8th *eighth*, huitième.
9 *nine*, neuf.	9th *ninth*, neuvième.
10 *ten*, dix.	10th *tenth*, dixième.
11 *eleven*, onze.	11th *eleventh*, onzième.
12 *twelve*, douze.	12th *twelfth*, douzième.
13 *thirteen*, treize.	13th *thirteenth*, treizième.
14 *fourteen*, quatorze.	14th *fourteenth*, quatorzième.
15 *fifteen*, quinze.	15th *fifteenth*, quinzième.
16 *sixteen*, seize.	16th *sixteenth*, seizième.

A

a, an, *art.* un, -e.

abandon, *v. a.* abandonner.

abate, *v. a. & n.* diminuer; se calmer, s'apaiser.

abbey, *s.* abbaye *f.*

abbot, *s.* abbé *m.*

abbreviate, *v. a.* abréger.

abbreviation, *s.* abréviation *f.*

abdicate, *v.a. & n.* abdiquer.

abdomen, *s.* abdomen *m.*

abhor, *v. a.* détester, abhorrer.

ability, *s.* capacité *f.*, habilité *f.*

able, *adj.* capable.

aboard, *adv.* à bord.

abode, *s.* demeure *f.*

abolish, *v.a.* abolir; supprimer.

abominable, *adj.* abominable.

abound, *v.n.* abonder (de).

about, *adv. & prep.* autour (de); environ, presque; au sujet de.

above, *adv. & prep.* au-dessus (de); *(in book)* ci-dessus.

abroad, *adv.* à l'étranger.

absence, *s.* absence *f.*, éloignement *m.*

absent, *adj.* absent.

absolute, *adj.* absolu.

absolve, *v.a.* absoudre; relever de; remettre, pardonner.

absorb, *v. a.* absorber.

abstain, *v.n.* s'abstenir de.

abstract, *adj.* abstrait.

abstraction, *s.* abstraction *f.*

absurd, *adj.* absurde; ridicule.

abundance, *s.* abondance *f.*

abundant, *adj.* abondant.

abusive, *adj.* abusif; injurieux; offensant.

academic, *adj.* académique.

academy, *s.* académie *f.*

accelerate, *v.a.* accélérer; *v.n.* s'accélérer.

accent, *s.* accent *m.*

accept, *v.a.* accepter

access, *s.* accès *m.*

accessible, *adj.* accessible.

accessory, *s. & adj.* accessoire *(m.).*

accident, *s.* accident *m.*

accidental, *s.* accidentel.

accommodate, *v.a.* accommoder; loger; ~ *oneself to* s'accommoder à.

accommodation, *s.* ajustement *m.*, adaptation *f.;* commodité *f.;* logement *m.*

accompany, *v.a.* accompagner.

accomplish, *v.a.* accomplir, achever.

accomplishment, *s.* accomplissement *m.;* talent *m.*

accord, *s.* accord *m.*, consentement *m.*

according: ~ *to* selon, d'après.

accordingly, *adv.* donc; en conséquence.

account, *s.* compte *m.;* *(narration)* récit *m.;* *on* ~ *of* à cause de; *on no* ~ dans aucun cas; *take into* ~ tenir compte de; — *v.n.* ~ *for* expliquer; rendre compte de.

accuracy, *s.* exactitude *f.*

accusation, *s.* accusation *f.*

accuse, *v.a.* accuser; incriminer.

accustom, *v.a.* accoutumer (à).

ache, *s.* douleur *f.*

achieve, *v.a.* accomplir, achever; atteindre.

acknowledge, *v.a.* reconnaître; accuser réception de.

acquaint, *v.a.* informer (de); faire part à.

acquaintance, *s.* connaissance *f.*

acquire, *v.a.* acquérir.

acre, *s.* arpent *m.*

across, *prep.* à travers; en croix.

act, *s.* action *f.*; *(law)* loi *f.*; *(theatre)* acte *m.*; — *v.n.* agir; *v.a.* jouer.

action, *s.* action *f.*; acte *m.*; *(war)* combat *m.*

active, *adj.* actif.

activity, *s.* activité *f.*

actor, *s.* acteur *m.*

actress, *s.* actrice *f.*

actual, *adj.* réel.

actually, *adv.* en fait.

adapt, *v.a.* adapter.

add, *v.a.* ajouter; additionner.

addition, *s.* addition *f.*; *in ~ to* en plus de.

additional, *adj.* additionnel; supplémentaire.

address, *s.* adresse *f.*; — *v.a.* adresser.

adequate, *adj.* suffisant.

adjust, *v.a.* ajuster, régler.

administer, *v.a. & n.* administrer.

administration, *s.* administration *f.*

admirable, *adj.* admirable.

admiral, *s.* amiral *m.*

admiration, *s.* admiration *f.*

admire, *v.a.* admirer.

admission, *s.* admission *f.*; entrée *f.*

admit, *v.a.* admettre; laisser entrer.

adopt, *v.a.* adopter.

adoption, *s.* adoption *f.*

adore, *v.a.* adorer.

adult, *adj. & s.* adulte *(m.f.)*

advance, *v. n.* avancer; — *s.* avance *f.*; progrès *m.*

advantage, *s.* avantage *m.*

adventure, *s.* aventure *f.*

adversary, *s.* adversaire *m.*

adverse, *adj.* adverse.

adversity, *s.* adversité *f.*

advertise, *v.a.* annoncer; faire de la réclame (pour).

advertisement, *s.* annonce *f.*; réclame *f.*

advice, conseil *m.*; avis *m.*

advise, *v.a.* conseiller.

aerial, *s.* antenne *f.*

aerodrome, *s.* aérodrome *m.*

aeroplane, *s.* avion *m.*

affair, *s.* affaire *f.*

affect, *v.a.* affecter.

affection, *s.* affection *f.*

affectionate, *adj.* affectueux.

affirmative, *adj.* affirmatif; — *s.* affirmative *f.*

afford, *v.a.* donner, fournir, accorder; *can ~* avoir les moyens de.

afraid, *adj.* effrayé; *be ~ of* avoir peur de.

African, *adj.* africain; — *s.* Africain, -e.

after, *prep. & adj.* après.

afternoon, *s.* après-midi *m.* or *f.*

afterwards, *adv.* après, ensuite.

again, *adv.* encore une fois, de nouveau.

against, *prep.* contre.

age, *s.* âge *m.*

agency, s. agence f.

agent, s. agent m.

aggression, s. agression f.

ago, adv. il y a.

agony, s. agonie f.

agree, v.n. s'accorder, être d'accord; ~ (up-) on convenir sur; ~ to consentir à; ~ with entrer dans les idées de.

agreeable, adj. agréable.

agreement, s. accord m.

agricultural, adj. agricole.

agriculture, s. agriculture f.

ahead, adv. en avant.

aid, s. aide f.; — v.a. aider, assister.

aim, s. but m.; objectif m.; visée f.; — v.a. & n. viser.

air. s. air m.

air-conditioning, s. conditionnement d'air m.; climatisation f.

aircraft, s. avion m.

air-line, s. ligne f. aérienne.

air-mail s. poste aérienne; by ~ par avion.

airport, s. aéroport m.,

alarm, v.a. alarmer; —s. alarme f.

alcoholic, adj. alcoolique.

ale, s. bière (f.) anglaise.

alike, adj. semblable; — adv. également.

alive, adj. vivant.

all, pron. s., adv. & adj. tout; not at ~ pas du tout.

allege, v.a. alléguer.

alley, s. ruelle f.

allow, v.a. permettre; laisser; admettre.

allude, v.n. faire allusion.

ally, v.a. allier; v.n.

s'allier; — s. allié, -e.

almost, adv. presque; à peu près.

alone, adj. & adv. seul.

along, prep. le long de.

aloud, adv. à haute voix.

already, adv. déjà.

also, adv. aussi.

altar, s. autel m.

alter, v.a.&n. changer.

alternate, adj. alternatif; — v.n. alterner.

although, conj. quoique; bien que.

altitude, s. altitude f., élévation f.

altogether, adv. tout à fait; entièrement.

always, adv. toujours.

amaze, v.a. frapper d'étonnement, frapper de stupeur.

amazing, adj. étonnant.

ambassador, s. ambassadeur m.

ambassadress, s. ambassadrice f.

ambition, s ambition f.

ambitious, adj. ambitieux.

ambulance, s. ambulance (automobile) f.

amend, v.a. amender.

amends: make ~ for dédommager de.

American, adj. américain; — s. Américain, -e.

among, prep. parmi; chez.

amount, s. somme f.; (total) montant m.; — v.n. ~ to monter à.

ample, adj. ample.

amplifier, s. amplificateur m.

amuse, v.a. amuser; divertir.

amusement, s. amusement m.; divertissement m.

an see a.

analogy, s. analogie f.

analyse, *v.a.* analyser.

analysis, analyse *f.*

anarchy, *s.* anarchie *f.*

anatomy, *s.* anatomie *f.*

ancestor, *s.* ancêtre *m. f.*

anchor, *s.* ancre *f.*

ancient, *adj.* ancien; antique.

and, *conj.* et.

anecdote, *s.* anecdote *f.*

angel, *s.* ange *m.*

anger, *s.* colère, *f.*

angle, *s.* angle *m.*

angler, *s.* pêcheur *m.*

Anglican, *adj.* anglican.

angry, *adj.* fâché, irrité.

animal, *s.* animal *m. (pl. -aux).*

ankle, *s.* cheville *f.*

anniversary, *s.* anniversaire *m.*

announce, *v.a.* annoncer.

announcement, *s.* annonce.

announcer, *s.* speaker *m.*

annoy, *v.a.* ennuyer; contrarier; gêner.

annoying, *adj.* contrariant; ennuyeux.

annual, *adj.* annuel.

annul, *v.a.* annuler.

another, *pron. & adj.* un autre, une autre.

answer, *s.* réponse *f.;* — *v.a.&n.* répondre.

ant, *s.* fourmi *f.*

antelope, *s.* antilope *f.*

antibiotic, *s.* antibiotique *m.*

anticipate, *v.a.* anticiper.

antipathy, *s.* antipathie *f.*

antiquated, *adj.* vieilli.

antiquity, *s.* antiquité *f.*

anvil, *s.* enclume *f.*

anxiety, *s.* anxiété *f.*

anxious, *adj.* inquiet; désireux; be ～ to désirer faire qch.

any, *adj. & pron.* quelque; *(at all)* n'importe quoi/qui/quel; *(some, in*

question) du, de la; *have you* ～? en avez vous; *not* ～ ne ... pas de; ～ *more* encore du.

anybody, *pron.* quelqu'un; *(at all)* n'importe qui.

anyhow, *adv.* n'importe comment.

anyone *see* anybody.

anything, *pron.* quelque chose; *(at all)* n'importe quoi.

anyway, *see* anyhow.

anywhere, *adv.* n'importe où.

apart, *adv.* à part; de côté; ～ *from* en dehors de.

apartment, *s.* logement *m.;* appartement *m.*

apologize, *v.n.* faire des excuses, s'excuser.

apology, *s.* excuse *f.*

apostle, *s.* apôtre *m.*

appalling, *adj.* épouvantable.

apparatus, *s.* appareil *m.*

apparent, *adj.* manifeste.

appeal, *s.* appel *m.;* — *v.n.* en appeler (à).

appear, *v.n.* (ap)paraître; *(seem)* sembler.

appearance, *s.* apparition *f.; (look)* air *m.*

appendicitis, *s.* appendicite *f.*

appendix, *s.* appendice *m.*

appetite, *s.* appétit *m.*

applaud, *v.n.* applaudir.

applause, *s.* applaudissement *m.*

apple, *s.* pomme *f.*

appliance, *s.* appareil *m.*

applicant, *s.* postulant, -e.

application, *s.* demande *f.; (use)* application *f.*

apply, *v.a.* appliquer; — *v.n.* avoir rapport à; ～ *for* solliciter.

appoint, *v.a.* nommer; désigner.

appointment, *s.* nomination *f.;* emploi *m.;* rendez-vous *m.*

appreciate, *v.a.* apprécier.

appreciation, *s.* appréciation *f.*

apprehend, *v.a.* appréhender; *(understand)* comprendre.

apprentice, *s.* apprenti *m.*

approach, *s.* approche *f.;* — *v. a. & n.* (s')approcher (de).

appropriate, *adj.* approprié, convenable.

approval, *s.* approbation *f.*

approve, *v.a. & n.* approuver.

approximate, *adj.* approximatif.

approximation, approximation *f.*

apricot, *s.* abricot *m.*

April, *s.* avril *m.*

apron, *s.* tablier *m.*

aptitude, *s.* aptitude *f.*

Arab, *s.* Arabe *m.*

Arabian, *adj.* arabe.

arbitrary, *adj.* arbitraire.

arcade, *s.* arcade *f.*

arch, *s.* arche *f.;* arc *m.*

archaeology, *s.* archéologie *f.*

archbishop, *s.* archevêque *m.*

architect, *s.* architecte *m.*

architecture, *s.* architecture *f.*

area, *s.* surface *f.;* aire *f.*

Argentine, *adj.* argentine.

argue, *v.n.* argumenter; *v.a.* discuter.

argument, *s.* argument *m.;* discussion *f.*

arise, *v. n.* se lever; *(emerge)* surgir; *(come from)* résulter de.

aristocratic, *adj.* aristocratique.

arm[1], *s.* bras *m.*

arm[2], *s.(pl).* arme(s) *f.*

armament, *s.* armement *m.*

armchair, *s.* fauteuil *m.*

armour, *s.* armure *f.*

army, *s.* armée *f.*

around, *adv. & prep.* autour (de).

arouse, *v.a.* réveiller.

arrange, *v.a.* arranger.

arrangement, *s.* arrangement *m.;* ~s mesures *f. pl.*

array, *s.* ordre *m.*

arrears, *s. pl.* arriéré *m.*

arrest, *v.a.* arrêter; — *s.* arrestation *f.*

arrival, *s.* arrivée *f.*

arrive, *v.n.* arriver.

arrow, *s.* flèche *f.*

art, *s.* art *m.*

artery, *s.* artère *f.*

article, *s.* article *m.*

artificial, *adj.* artificiel.

artillery, *s.* artillerie *f.*

artist, *s.* artiste *m.*

artistic, *adj.* artistique.

as, *adv. & conj.* comme; *(like a)* en; *(when)* comme; ~ ... ~ aussi ... que.

ascend, *v.n.* monter.

ash(es), *s. (pl.)* cendre *f.*

ashamed, *adj.* honteux; be ~ of avoir honte de.

ashore, *adv.* à terre.

ash-tray, *s.* cendrier *m.*

Asiatic, *adj.* asiatique.

aside, *adv.* de côté.

ask, *v. a.* demander (à + qn., de + *inf.*); ~ about se renseigner sur; ~ for demander.

asleep, *adj.* endormi; *fall* ~ s'endormir.

aspect, *s.* aspect *m.;* *(look)* air *m.*

aspire, *v.n.* aspirer à.

ass, s. âne m.
assail, v. a. assaillir.
assault, s. assaut m.
assemble, v. a. assembler;
v.n. s'assembler.
assembly, s. assemblée f.;
~ hall halle f. de
montage; ~ line chaine
f. de montage.
assert, v.a. affirmer.
assess, v.a. cotiser.
assets, s. pl. actif m.
assign, v. a. assigner;
céder.
assignment, s. cession f.
assist, v.a. aider.
assistance, s. aide f.
associate, v.a. associer;
— s. associé, -e m. f.
association, s. association
f.
assume, v.a. prendre;
assumer; supposer.
assumption, s. supposi-
tion f.
assurance, s. assurance f.
assure, v.a. assurer.
astonish, v. a. étonner.
astonishment, s. étonne-
ment m.
astronomy, s. astronomie
f.
at, prep. (place, time) à;
(house, shop) chez.
athletic, adj. athlétique.
athletics, s. athlétisme m.
at-home, s. réception f.
atlas, s. atlas m.
atmosphere, s. atmos-
phère f.
atom, s. atome m.
atomic, adj. atomique; ~

bomb bombe f. atomi-
que; ~ energy énergie
f. atomique.
attach, v.a. attacher.
attaché, s. attaché m.;
~ case petite valise f.
attachment, s. attache-
ment m.
attack, v.a. attaquer; —

s. attaque f.
attain, v.a. atteindre.
attainment, s. réalisa-
tion f.; connaissances
f. pl.
attempt, s. tentative f.;
— v.a. tenter; entre-
prendre.
attend, v.a. suivre; (look
after) soigner; — v.i.
faire attention à; as-
sister.
attendance, s. présence f.;
(persons present) as-
sistance f.
attendant, s. serviteur m.;
employé m.; ouvreuse
f.
attention, s. attention f.
attitude, s. attitude f.
attorney, s. avoué m.
attract, v.a. attirer.
attraction, s. attraction f.
attractive, adj. attrayant.
attribute, v.a. attribuer.
auction, s. vente f.
audience, s. auditoire m.
audio-visual, adj. audio-
visuel.
auditorium, s. salle f. (de
cours).
August, s. août m.
aunt, s. tante f.
Australian, adj. australien
— s. Australien, -ne m.
f.
Austrian, adj. autrichien;

— s. Autrichien, -enne
m. f.
authentic, adj. authen-
tique.
author, s. auteur m.
authority, s. autorité f.
authorize, v.a. autoriser·
automatic, adj. automa-
tique.
autonomy, s. autonomie
f.
autumn, s. automne m.
avail, s. be of no ~ ne
servir à rien; — v.a.

~ *oneself of* profiter de.

available, *adj*. disponible; sous la main.

avalanche, *s*. avalanche *f*.

avenge, *v.a*. venger.

avenue, *s*. avenue *f*.

average, *s*. moyenne *f*.; — *adj*. moyen.

aversion, *s*. aversion *f*.

avoid, *v.a*. éviter.

await, *v.a*. attendre.

awake, *v. a*. éveiller; *v. n*. s'éveiller; — *adj*. éveillé.

awaken, *v.a*. éveiller.

award, *v.a*. accorder.

aware, *adj. be* ~ *of* avoir conscience de, savoir bien.

away, *adv*. (au) loin; *carry* ~ enlever; *go* ~ partir.

awful, *adj*. terrible.

awhile, *adv*. pendant quelque temps, un moment.

awkward, *adj*. *(pers.)* gauche; maladroit; *(things)* gênant, embarrassant.

axe, *s*. hache *f*.

axis, *s*. axe *m*.

axle, *s*. essieu *m*.

B

babble, *s*. babil *m*.; — *v.n*. babiller.

baby, *s*. bébé *m*.

baby-sitter, *s*. garde-bébé *m*.

bachelor, *s*. célibataire; *(arts)* licencié *m*.

back, *s*. dos *m*.; *(hand)* revers *m*.; *(football)* arrière *m*.; — *adj*. de derrière; arriéré; — *adv*. en arrière; *be* ~ être de retour; — *v.a*. soutenir, seconder; *(bet)* parier pour; *v.η*.

reculer.

background, *s*. fond *m*.; arrière-plan *m*.

backstairs, *s. pl*. escalier *m*. de service.

backward, *adj*. arriéré.

backwards, *adv*. en arrière; à reculons.

bacon, *s*. lard *m*.

bad, *adj*. mauvais.

badge, *s*. insigne *m*.

badger, *s*. blaireau *m*.

badly, *adv*. mal.

bag, *s*. sac *m*.; *(large)* valise *f*.

baggage, *s*. bagage *m*.

bait, *s*. amorce *f*.

bake, *v.a*. cuire; faire cuire.

baker, *s*. boulanger *m*.

bakery, *s*. boulangerie *f*.

balance, *s*. *(weighing, account)* balance *f*.; *(bank)* solde *m*.; *(equilibrium)* équilibre *m*.; — *v.a*. balancer; *v.n*. se balancer.

balcony, *s*. balcon *m*.

bald, *adj*. chauve; plat.

ball, *s*. *(games)* balle *f*. ballon *m*.; *(bowl)* boule *f*.; *(dance)* bal *m*.

ball-bearings, *s. pl*. roulement *m*. à billes.

ballet, *s*. ballet *m*.

balloon, *s*. ballon *m*.

ball(-point) pen, *s*. stylo *m*. à bille.

bamboo, *s*. bambou *m*.

banana, *s*. banane *f*.

band, *s*. *(people)* troupe *f*.; bande *f*.; orchestre *m*.; *(ribbon, tie)* ruban *m*.; lien *m*.

bandage, *s*. bandage *m*.

bandit, *s*. bandit *m*.

bang, *s*. coup *m*.; claquement *m*.

banish, *v.a*. bannir.

banister, rampe *f*.

bank¹, *s*. *(river)* rive *f*.;

(earth) talus *m.*

bank³, *s.* banque *f.*

bank-holiday, *s.* (jour *m.* de) fête *f.* légale.

banknote, *s.* billet *m.* (de banque).

bankruptcy, *s.* banque-route *f.;* faillite *f.*

banner, *s.* bannière *f.*

banquet, *s.* banquet *m.*

baptism, *s.* baptême *m.*

baptize, *v.a.* baptiser.

bar, *s.* *(iron, tribunal, music)* barre *f.;* *(rail-way)* barrière *f.;* *(obstacle)* obstacle *m.;* *(lawyers)* barreau *m.;* *(counter place for drink)* comptoir *m.,* débit *m.* (de boissons), bar *m.*

barber, *s.* coiffeur *m.*

bare, *adj.* nu; *(mere)* seul.

barefoot, *adj.* nu-pieds.

barely, *adv.* à peine.

bargain, *s.* marché *m.;* — *v.n.* marchander.

bark, *s.* aboiement *m.;* — *v.n.* aboyer.

barley, *s.* orge *f.*

barmaid, *s.* demoiselle *f.* de comptoir, barmaid *f.*

barman, *s.* garçon *m.* de comptoir, barman *m.*

barn, *s.* grange *f.*

barometer, *s.* baromètre *m.*

baron, *s.* baron *m.*

baroness, *s.* baronne *f.*

barracks, *s. pl.* caserne *f.*

barrel, *s.* tonneau *m.*

barren, *adj.* stérile.

barrier, *s.* barrière *f.*

barrister, *s.* avocat *m.*

bartender *see* **barman.**

barter, *s.* échange *m.;* — *v.a.* échanger.

base, *s.* fondement *m.;* base *f.*

basement, *s.* sous-sol *m.*

bashful, *adj.* timide.

basic, *adj.* fondamental; basique.

basin, *s.* bassin *m.;* cuvette *f.*

basis, *s.* base *f.*

basket, *s.* panier *m.*

basket-ball, *s.* basket-ball *m.*

bass, *s.* basse *f.*

bat¹, *s.* chauve-souris *f.*

bat², *s.* batte *f.*

bath, *s.* bain *m.;* *(tub)* baignoire *f.*

bathe, *v.n.* se baigner; *v.a.* baigner.

bathing-costume, *s.* costume *m.* de bain(s).

bathroom, *s.* salle *f.* de bain.

battery, *s.* *(military)* batterie *f.;* *(electr.)* pile *f.*

battle, *s.* bataille *f.*

bay, *s.* baie *f.*

be, *v. n.* être; *(be situated)* se trouver; *there is* il y a.

beach, *s.* plage *f.*

bead, *s.* *(string of)* collier *m.*

beak, *s.* bec *m.*

beam, *s.* *(timber)* poutre *f.;* *(light)* rayon *m.*

bean, *s.* fève *f.*

bear¹, *s.* ours *m.*

bear², *v.a.* porter; soutenir; supporter.

beard, *s.* barbe *f.*

bearing, *s.* rapport *m.*

beast, *s.* bête *f.*

beat, *v.a.* battre; frapper; — *s.* battement *m.*

beautiful, *adj.* beau, bel, belle.

beauty, *s.* beauté *f.*

beaver, *s.* castor *m.*

because, *conj.* parce que; ~ *of* à cause de.

beckon, *v.n.* faire signe (à).

become, *v. n.* devenir.

bed, *s.* lit *m.*

bed-clothes, *s. pl.* couvertures *f. pl.*

bedroom, *s.* chambre *f.* à coucher.

bee, *s.* abeille *f.*

beech, *s.* hêtre *m.*

beef, *s.* bœuf *m.*

beef-steak, *s.* bifteck *m.*

beer, *s.* bière *f.*

beetle, *s.* scarabée *m.*

beetroot, *s.* betterave *f.*

before, *prep.(time)* avant; *(space)* devant; — *adv.* avant; *(in front)* en avant.

beforehand, *adv.* d'avance; en avance.

beg, *v.a.* demander, prier; *v. n.* mendier; *I ~ your pardon!* excusez-moi!; pardon!

beget, *v.a.* engendrer.

beggar, *s.* mendiant, -e.

begin, *v. a. & n.* commencer.

beginner, *s.* commençant, -e *m. f.*

beginning, *s.* commencement *m.*

behalf, *s. on ~ of* de la part de; *in ~ of* en faveur de.

behave, *v.n.* se conduire.

behaviour, *s.* conduite *f.*

behind, *prep.* derrière.

Belgian, *adj.* belge; — *s.* Belge *m. f.*

belief, *s.* croyance *f.*

believe, *v.a. & n.* croire.

bell, *s.* cloche *f.*

belly, *s.* ventre *m.*

belong, *v.n. ~ to* appartenir à.

belongings, *s. pl.* effets *m.*; biens *m.*

below, *adv.* au-dessous; en bas; — *prep.* au-dessous de.

belt, *s.* ceinture *f.*

bench, *s.* banc *m.*; *(working)* établi *m.*

bend, *v. a.* courber; tendre

fléchir; *v.n.* se courber; — *s.* courbure *f.*; *(road)* tournant *m.*

beneath *see* **below.**

benefit, *s.* bienfait *m.*; *(gain)* bénéfice *m.*

bent, *s.* penchant *m.*

berry, *s.* baie *f.*; *(coffee)* grain *m.*

berth, *s.* couchette *f.*; *(for ship)* mouillage *m.*

beseech, *v. a.* supplier.

beside, *prep.* auprès de, à côté de.

besides, *adv.* en outre.

best, *adj.* le meilleur; *do one's ~* faire tout son possible (pour).

bestow, *v. a.* conférer (à).

bet, *v.a.* parier.

betray, *v. a.* trahir.

better, *adj.* meilleur; *adv.* mieux.

between, *prep.* entre.

beyond, *prep.* au delà de.

bias, *s.* biais *m.*; *(fig.)* préjugé *m.*

Bible, *s.* bible *f.*

bibliography, *s.* bibliographie *f.*

bicycle, *s.* bicyclette *f.*

big, *adj.* grand; gros.

bill, *s. (hotel)* note *f.*; *(restaurant)* addition *f.*; *(invoice)* facture *f.*; *(of exchange)* lettre *f.* de change; *(of fare)* carte *f.*, menu *m.*; *(poster)* affiche *f.*; *(parliament)* projet *m.* de loi.

bin, *s.* huche *f.*, coffre *m.*

bind, *v.a.* lier; *(book)* relier.

biological, *adj.* biologique.

biology, *s.* biologie *f.*

birch, *s.* bouleau *m.*

bird, *s.* oiseau *m.*

birth, *s.* naissance *f.*

birthday, *s.* anniversaire *m.*

birth-place, s. lieu m. de
naissance.

biscuit, s. biscuit m.

bishop, s. évêque m.

bit¹, s. morceau m.;
(drill) mèche f.; a ~ un
peu (de).

bit², s. *(horse)* mors m.

bite, v. a. & n. mordre.

bitter, adj. amer; mor-
dant; *(cold)* âpre.

bitterness, s. amertume f.

black, adj. noir.

blackbird, s. merle m.

blackmail, s. chantage m.

blacksmith, s. forgeron m.

bladder, s. vessie f.

blade, s. lame f.

blame, s. blâme m.; — v.
a. blâmer, accuser qn.

blameless, adj. innocent.

blank, adj. blanc; nu; —
s. blanc m.

blanket, s. couverture f.

blast, s. rafale f.; coup m.
de vent; souffle m.; —
v.a. faire sauter; dé-
truire.

blaze, s. flamme f.; —
v.n. flamber.

bleak, adj. lugubre.

bleed, v.a. & n. saigner.

blend, s. mélange m.; —
v.a. fondre; mêler.

bless, v.a. bénir.

blessing, s. bénédiction f.

blind¹, adj. aveugle.

blind², s. store m.

blindness, s. cécité f.

blink, v. n. clignoter.

bliss, s. félicité f.

blister, s. ampoule f.

block, s. bloc m.; *(wood)*
billot m.; *(buildings)*
pâté m.; *(traffic)* en-
combrement m.

blond adj. blond.

blood, s. sang m.

bloody, adj. sanglant.

bloom, s. fleur f.; — v. n.
fleurir.

blossom, s. fleur f.

blot, s. tache f.; pâté m.

blouse, s. blouse f.

blow¹, v. a. *(trumpet)* sonner; *(glass)* souffler; ~
out éteindre; ~ up
faire sauter; v.n.
(wind) souffler.

blow², s. coup m.

blue, adj. bleu.

blunder, s. bévue f.; —
v. n. faire une bévue

blunt, adj. émoussé; *(person)* brusque.

blush, v.n. rougir.

board, s. planche f.;
(meals) pension f.;
(council) conseil m.;
(paper) carton m.;
(theatre) ~s planches;
~ and lodging pension
f. et chambre(s); on ~
(ship) à bord d'un na-
vire; — v.n. prendre
pension chez; v.a. mon-
ter à bord de.

boarder, s. pensionnaire
m. f.

boarding-house, s. pension f.

boarding-school, s. pensionnat m.

boast, s. vanterie f.; —
v. n. se vanter (de).

boat, s. bateau m.

body, s. corps m.

bog, s. marécage m.

boil¹, v.a. faire bouillir;
(cook) faire cuire; v. n.
bouillir.

boil², s. furoncle m.

boiler, s. chaudière f.

bold, adj. hardi; effronté.

boldness, s. hardiesse f.;
effronterie f.

bolt, s. verrou m.; — v. a.
verrouiller; v. n. filer.

bomb, s. bombe f.

bond, s. lien m.

bone, s. os m.; *(fish)*

arête *f.*

bonnet, *s.* chapeau *m.*; bonnet *m.*; *(motor)* capot *m.*

bony, *adj.* osseux; maigre.

book, *s.* livre *m.*; — *v.a* prendre (un billet); retenir.

bockcase, *s.* bibliothèque *f.*

booking-office, *s.* guichet *m.*

book-keeper, *s.* teneur *m.* de livres.

book-keeping, *s.* comptabilité *f.*

booklet, *s.* livret *m.*

bookseller, *s.* libraire *m.*

bookshelf, *s.* rayon *m.*

bookshop, *s.* librairie *f.*

book-stall, *s.* bibliothèque (de gare) *f.*

boot, *s.* bottine *f.*; brodequin *m.*

booth, *s.* baraque *f.*

booty, *s.* butin *m.*

border, *s.* bord *m.*; frontiere *f.*

bore, *v. a.* ennuyer, raser; —*s.* raseur *m.*

boring, *adj.* ennuyeux, assommant.

born, *pp.* né; *be* ~ naître.

borrow, *v. a.* emprunter.

bosom, *s.* sein *m.*

boss, *s.* patron *m.*

botanical, *adj.* botanique.

botany, *s.* botanique *m.*

both, *pron. & adj.* l'un(e) et l'autre; tous (les) deux; ~ ... *and* et ... et ...

bother, *v.a.* tracasser.

bottle, *s.* bouteille *f.*

bottom, *s.* bas *m.*; fond *m.*; derrière *m.*

bough, *s.* rameau *m.*

bound, *pp.* ~ *for* à destination de, en route pour.

boundary, *s.* borne *f.*

bounty, *s.* générosité *f.*

bouquet, *s.* bouquet *m.*

bow[1], *s.* arc *m.*; *(violin)* archet *m.*; *(knot)* nœud *m.*

bow[2], *v.a.* incliner; courber; *v.n.* s'incliner; se courber; — *s.* salut *m.*; *(ship)* avant *m.*

bowels, *s. pl.* entrailles *f.*

bowl, *s.* bol *m.*, jatte *f.*

box, *s.* boîte *f.*, caisse *f.*; *(horse)* stalle *f.*; *(theatre)* loge *f.*; *(on the ears)* soufflet *m.*; — *v. n.* boxer.

box-office, *s.* bureau *m.* de location.

boy, *s.* garçon *m.*; ~ *scout* boy-scout *m.*, éclaireur *m.*

bra, *s.* soutien-gorge *m.*

brace, *s.* couple *f.*; lien *m.*; ~*s* bretelles *f. pl.*

bracelet, *s.* bracelet *m.*

brain, *s.* cerveau *m.*; ~*s* cervelle *f.*

brainy, *adv.* intelligent.

brake, *s.* frein *m.*

branch, *s.* branche *f.*

brand, *s.* tison *m.*; marque *f.*; — *v.a.* marquer.

brandy, *s.* cognac *m.*

brass, *s.* cuivre jaune *m.*

brave, *adj.* brave.

brawl, *s.* querelle *f.*

bread, *s.* pain *m.*

breadth, *s.* largeur *f.*

break, *v.a.* briser, casser; *(law)* violer; *(promise)* manquer; *(news)* apprendre à; *v. n.* se casser; se briser; ~ *down* abattre; s'effondrer; *(motor)* avoir une panne; ~ *in* dresser; ~ *up* lever; — *s.* interruption *f.*; pause *f.*

break-down, *s.* *(motor)* panne *f.*; *(health)* débâcle; ~ *lorry* dépanneuse *f.*

breakfast, *s.* déjeuner *m.*

breast, *s.* poitrine *f.*, sein *m.*

breath, *s.* haleine *f.*; souffle *m.*

breathe, *v.a.* & *n.* respirer.

breathless, *adj.* essoufflé; sans souffle.

breeches, *s. pl.* culotte *f.*

breed, *s.* race *f.*; — *v.a.* élever.

breeze, *s.* brise *f.*

breezy, *adj.* venteux.

brew, *v.a.* brasser.

bribe, *s.* pot-de-vin *m.*; — *v.a.* corrompre.

brick, *s.* brique *f.*

bricklayer, *s.* maçon *m.*

bride, *s.* mariée *f.*

bridegroom, *s.* marié *m.*

bridge, *s.* pont *m.*

bridle, *s.* bride *f.*

brief, *adj.* bref.

briefcase, *s.* serviette *f.*

briefly, *adv.* brièvement.

briefs, *s. pl.* slip *m.*

bright, *adj.* brillant; vif; clair; éclatant.

brighten, *v.a.* faire briller; égayer.

brightness, *s.* éclat *m.*

brilliant, *s.* brillant *m.*

brim, *s.* bord *m.*

bring, *v.a.* amener; apporter; ~ *about* amener; ~ *back* rapporter; ~ *forth* produire; ~ *up* élever.

brink, *s.* bord *m.*

brisk, *adj.* vif; actif.

bristle, *s. (brush)* poil *m.*

British, *adj.* britannique.

brittle, *adj.* cassant.

broad, *adj.* large; vaste.

broadcast, *v.a.* radiodiffuser.

broadcasting, *s.* radiodiffusion *f.*

broken, *adj.* brisé.

bronze, *s.* bronze *m.*

brooch, *s.* broche *f.*

brood, *s.* couvée *f.*; — *v.n.* couver.

brook, *s.* ruisseau *m.*

broom, *s.* balai *m.*

brother, *s.* frère *m.*

brother-in-law, *s.* beau-frère *m.*

brow, *s.* sourcil *m.*

brown, *adj.* brun.

bruise, *s.* contusion *f.*; — *v.a.* meurtrir.

brush, *s.* brosse *f.*; pinceau *m.*; balai *m.*; — *v.a.* brosser; ~ *up* donner un coup de brosse à.

brutal, *adj.* brutal, cruel.

brutality, *s.* brutalité *f.*

bubble, *s.* bulle *f.*; — *v. n.* bouillonner.

buck, *s.* daim *m.*

bucket, *s.* seau *m.*

buckle, *s.* boucle *f.*

bud, *s.* bourgeon *m.*

budget, *s.* budget *m.*

buffet, *s.* soufflet *m.*

bug, *s.* punaise *f.*

build, *v.a.* bâtir; construire; sur; ~ *up* établir.

builder, *s.* entrepreneur *m.* de bâtiments; constructeur *m.*

building, *s.* bâtiment *m.*

bulb, *s.* bulbe *m.*; *(lamp)* ampoule *f.*

bulge, *v.n.* bomber.

bulk, *s.* masse *f.*; volume *m.*

bull, *s.* taureau *m.*

bullet, *s.* balle *f.*

bulletin, *s.* bulletin *m.*

bump, *s.* bosse *f.*; collision *f.*; coup *m.*

bumper, *s.* parc-choc *m.*

bun, *s.* brioche *f.*

bunch, *s.* bouquet *m.*; botte *f.*; grappe *f.*

bundle, *s.* botte *f.*; paquet

m.; fagot m.

bunk, s. couchette f.

buoy, s. bouée f.

burden, s. charge f.; fardeau m.

burglar, s. cambrioleur m.

burial, s. enterrement m.

burn, v.a. & n. brûler.

bursary, s. bourse f.

burst, v.n. éclater; crever; exploser; v.a. faire éclater; rompre; crever; — s. éclat m.; explosion f.

bury, v.a. enterrer.

bus, s. autobus m.

bush, s. buisson m.

business, s. affaires f. pl.;

profession f.; on ~ pour affaires; ~ hours heures (f. pl.) d'ouverture.

businessman, s. homme m. d'affaires.

bus-stop, s. arrêt m. d'autobus.

busy, adj. occupé, affairé.

but, conj. mais.

butcher, s. boucher m.; ~'s (shop) boucherie f.

butter, s. beurre m.

butterfly, s. papillon m.

buttock, s. fesse f., derrière m.

button, s. bouton m.

buy, v.a. acheter.

buyer, s. acheteur m.

by, prep. par; de; ~ Monday d'ici à lundi.

bystander, s. spectateur, -trice m. f.

C

cab, s. taxi m.; fiacre m.

cabbage, s. chou m.

cabin, s. cabane f.; (ship) cabine f.

cabinet, s. (politics) cabinet m.

cable, s. câble m.

cablegram, s. câblo-

gramme m.

café, s. café(-restaurant) m.

cage, s. cage f.

cake, s. gâteau m.

calculate, v.a.&n. calculer.

calculation, s. calcul m.

calendar, s. calendrier m.

calf, s. veau m.; (leg) mollet m.

call, v. a. & n. appeler; ~ for, réclamer; ~ on faire visite à; — s. appel m.; cri m.; (visit) visite f.

call-box, s. cabine f. téléphonique.

calm, adj. calme.

calorie, s. calorie f.

camel, s. chameau, -elle m. f.

camera, s. appareil m. (photographique).

camp, s. camp m.

campaign, s. campagne f.

camping, s. camping m.

can¹, s. broc m.; pot m.

can², v. aux. pouvoir; savoir.

canal, s. canal m.

canary, s. canari m.

cancel, v.a. annuler.

cancer, s. cancer m.

candle, s. chandelle f.; bougie f.

cannon, s. canon m.

canoe, e s. canoë m.

canteen, s. cantine f.

canvas, s. toile f.

cap, s. bonnet m.; casquette f.

capable, adj. capable (de).

capacity, s. capacité f.

cape, s. (land) cap m.; (cloak) pèlerine f.; cape f.

capital, s. (city) capitale f.; (letter) majuscule f. (commerce) capital m;

capsule, s. capsule f.

captain, *s.* capitaine *m.*

caption, *s.* sous-titre *m.*

captivate, *v.a.* captiver.

capture, *v.a.* capturer; — *s.* capture *f.*

car, *s.* voiture *f.*, auto *f.*

caravan, *s.* roulotte *f.* (de camping), caravane *f.*

carbon-paper, *s.* papier *m.* carbone.

carburetter, *s.* carburateur *m.*

card, *s.* carte *f.*

cardboard, *s.* carton *m.*

cardinal, *adj. m.* cardinal *m.*

care, *s.* attention *f.;* soin *m.;* souci *m.;* ~ *of* aux bons soins de; *take* ~ *of* prendre soin de; — *v.n.* ~ *for* se soucier de; ~ *to* aimer.

career, *s.* carrière *f.*

careful, *adj.* soigneux.

careless, *adj.* insouciant, négligent.

caress, *v.a.* caresser.

cargo, *s.* cargaison *f.*

caricature, *s.* caricature *f.*

carnation, *s.* œillet *m.*

carpenter, *s.* charpentier *m.*

carpet, *s.* tapis *m.*

carriage, *s.* voiture *f.; (transport)* transport *m.*

carriage-way, *s.* chaussée *f.*

carrier, *s.* voiturier *m.*

carrot, *s.* carotte *f.*

carry, *v.a.* porter; transporter; ~ *on* exercer; ~ *out* mettre à exécution.

cart, *s.* charrette *f.*

cartridge, *s.* cartouche *f.*

carve, *v. a.& n.* sculpter; *(meat)* découper.

case, *s. (box)* étui *m.*, caisse *f.; (instance)* cas *m.; cause f.*

casement, *s.* croisée *f.*

cash, *s.* espèces *f. pl.*

cash-book, *s.* livre *m.* de caisse.

cashier, *s.* caissier, -ère *m. f.*

cash-register, *s.* caisse *f.* enregistreuse.

cask, *s.* tonneau *m.*

cast, *v.a.* jeter; *(metal)* fondre; — *s.* coup *m.; (theatre)* distribution *f.*

castle, *s.* château *m.*

casual, *adj.* casuel.

casualty, *s.* accident *m.*

cat, *s.* chat, -te *m. f.*

catalogue, *s.* catalogue *m.*

catastrophe, *s.* catastrophe *f.*

catch, *v.a.* saisir; attraper; *(eye)* frapper; ~ *up* rattraper; — *s.* prise *f.;* attrape *f.*

category, *s.* catégorie *f.*

cater, *v.n.* pourvoir à.

caterpillar, *s.* chenille *f.*

cathedral, *s.* cathédrale *f.*

catholic, *adj.* catholique.

catholicism, *s.* catholicisme *m.*

cattle, *s.* bétail *m. (pl.* bestiaux).

cauliflower, *s.* chou-fleur *m.*

cause, *s.* cause *f.;* motif *m.;* — *v.a.* causer.

caution, *s.* prudence *f.*

cautious, *adj.* prudent.

cave, *s.* caverne *f.*

cavity, *s.* cavité *f.*

cease, *v.a. & n.* cesser.

ceiling, *s.* plafond *m.*

celebrate, *v.a.* célébrer.

celebration, *s.* célébration *f.;* commémoration *f.*

celery, *s.* céleri *m.*

cell, *s.* cellule *f.*

cellar, *s.* cave *f.*

cello, *s.* violoncelle *m.*

cellophane, *s.* cellophane

f.

cement, *s.* ciment *m.;* — *v.a.* cimenter.

cemetery, *s.* cimetière *m.*

centenary, *s.* centenaire *m.*

central, *adj.* central.

centre, *s.* centre *m.*

century, *s.* siècle *m.*

cereal, *s.* céréale *f.*

ceremony, *s.* cérémonie *f.*

certain, *adj.* certain.

certainly, *adj.* certainement; sans doute

certainty, *s.* certitude *f.*

certificate, *s.* certificat *m.*

certify, *v.a.* certifier.

chain, *s.* chaîne *f.*

chair, *s.* chaise *f.; (professorship)* chaire *f.; take the ~* présider.

chairman, *s.* président *m.*

chalk, *s.* craie *f.*

challenge, *s.* défi *m.;* — *v.a.* défier; provoquer.

chamber, *s.* chambre *f.;* ~s étude *f.;* appartement *m.*

champagne, *s.* champagne *m.*

champion, *s.* champion *m.*

championship, *s.* championnat *m.*

chance, *s.* chance *f.; bv ~* par hasard.

chancellor, *s.* chancelier *m.*

chancery, *s.* chancellerie *f.*

change, *s.* changement *m.; (money)* monnaie *f.;* — *v.a.&n.* changer.

channel, *s.* canal *m.; m.; the English Channel* la Manche.

chap, *s.* type *m.*

chapel, *s.* chapelle *f.*

chaplain, *s.* chapelain *m.*

chapter, *s.* chapitre *m.*

character *s.* caractère *m.; (theatre)* personnage

m.

characteristic, *adj.* caractéristique; — *s.* trait *m.* caractéristique.

charcoal, *s.* charbon *m.* de bois

charge, *s.* charge *f.; (price)* prix *m.; (accusation)* accusation *f.;* — *v.a.* charger (de); *(price)* demander; faire payer; *(accuse)* accuser (de).

charity, *s.* charité *f.*

charm, *s.* charme *m.*

charming, *adj.* charmant.

chart, *s.* carte *f.* marine.

charter, *s.* charte *f.*

charwoman, *s.* femme *f.* de ménage.

chase, *v.a.* chasser; poursuivre; — *s.* chasse *f.*

chassis, *s.* châssis *m.*

chat, *s.* causette *f.;* — *v. n.* causer.

chatter, *v.n.* babiller; *(teeth)* claquer.

cheap, *adj.* bon marché.

cheat, *v.a.* tromper; tricher; — *s.* tromperie *f.;* tricherie; *(pers.)* fourbe *m.*

check, *v.a.* contrôler, vérifier; *(stop)* arrêter; — *s.* vérification *f.,* contrôle *m.*

checkmate, *s.* échec et mat *m.*

check-up, *s.* examen *m.* médical.

cheek, *s.* joue *f.*

cheeky, *adj.* impertinent.

cheer, *v.a.* réjouir, encourager; acclamer; *v.n.* ~ *up* reprendre sa gaieté; courage!; — *s.* joie *f.;* ~s acclamations *f.*

cheerful, *adj.* joyeux.

cheese, *s.* fromage *m.*

chemical, *adj.* chimique.

chemist, *s.* chimiste *m.;*

pharmacien *m.;* ~'s
(shop) pharmacie *f.*
chemistry, *s.* chimie *f.*
cheque, *s.* chèque *m.;*
traveller's ~ chéque
m. de voyage.
cheque-book, *s.* carnet
m. de chèques.
cherish, *v. a.* soigner;
(hope) caresser.
cherry, *s.* cerise *f.*
chess, *s.* échecs *m. pl.*
chess-board, *s.* échiquier
m.
chest, *s.* coffre *m.; (part
of body)* poitrine *f.;*
~ *of drawers* commode
f.
chestnut, *s.* châtaigne *f.*
chew, *v.a.* mâcher.
chicken, *s.* poulet *m.*
chief, *adj.* principal; —
s. chef *m.*
chiefly, *adv.* principa-
lement.
child, *s.* enfant *m.f.*
childhood, *s.* enfance *f.*
childish, *adj.* enfantin.
childless, *adj.* sans enfant.
chill, *s.* coup *m.* de
froid; — *v.a.* refroi-
dir, glacer.
chilly, *adj. (weather)* frais;
(un peu) froid.
chimney, *s.* cheminée *f.*
chin. *s.* menton *m.*
china, *s.* porcelaine *f.*
Chinese, *adj.* chinois; —
s. Chinois, -e.
chip, *s.* éclat *m.;* copeau
m.; ~s frites *f. pl.*
chirp, *v.n.* gazouiller.
chisel, *s.* ciseau *m.;* —
v.a. ciseler.
chivalry, *s.* chevalerie *f.*
chocolate, *s.* chocolat *m.*
choice, *s.* choix *m.*
choir, *s.* chœur *m.*
choke, *v.a. & n.* étouffer.
choose, *v.a.* choisir.
chop, *s.* côtelette *f.*

chorus, *s.* chœur *m.*
Christian, *adj.* chrétien;
~ *name* prénom *m.*
Christianity, *s.* christianisme *m.*
Christmas, *s.* Noël *m.;*
~ *eve* veille *f.* de Noël.
chuckle, *v.n.* rire tout
bas; — *s.* rire étouffé.
church, *s.* église *f.*
churchyard, *s.* cimetière
m.
cider, *s.* cidre *m.*
cigar, *s.* cigare *m.*
cigarette, *s.* cigarette *f.*
cigarette-case, *s.* étui *m.*
à cigarettes.
cigarette-holder, *s.* porte-
cigarette *m.*
cinders, *s.pl.* cendres *f.*
cine-camera, *s.* camera *f.*
cinema, *s.* cinéma *m.*
cinerama, *s.* cinérama *m.*
circle, *s.* cercle *m.*
circuit, *s.* circuit *m.;*
détour *m.;* tournée *f.*
circular, *adj.* circulaire.
circulate, *v.n.* circuler;
v.a. faire circuler.
circulation, *s.* circulation
f.
circumstance, *s.* circonstance *f.*
circus, *s.* cirque *m.*
cistern, *s.* citerne *f.*
citation, *s.* citation *f.*
cite, *v. a.* citer.
citizen, *s.* citoyen, -ne
m. f., habitant *m.*
citizenship, *s.* droit *m.*
de cité.
city, *s.* ville *f.; the City*
Cité *f.*
civil, *adj.* civil; *(polite)*
poli; ~ *servant* fonc-
tionnaire *m.*
civilization, *s.* civilisation *f.*
civilize, *v.a.* civiliser.
claim, *s.* demande *f.,*
réclamation *f.;* droit
m.; — *v.a.* revendi-

quer, réclamer.

clamp, s. crampon m.

clang, s. bruit m. métallique; — v.n. retentir.

clap, s. battement m.; applaudissements m. pl.; — v.n. applaudir.

clash, v.a. choquer; v.n. s'entre-choquer.

clasp, s. agrafe f.; fermoir m.; — v.a. agrafer; joindre.

class, s. classe f.

classic(al), adj. classique.

classify, v.a. classifier.

class-room, s. classe f.

clatter, s. bruit m.; fracas m.; — v.n. faire du bruit.

clause, s. clause f., article m.

claw, s. griffe f.; serre f.; ongle m.

clay, s. glaise f.; argile f.

clean, adj. propre; blanc; pur; — v.a. nettoyer.

cleanse, v.a. nettoyer.

clear, adj. clair; — v.a. déblayer; éclaircir; v.n. s'éclaircir; ~ away enever; ~ out filer.

clearly, adv. clair, clairement; évidemment.

cleave, v.a. fendre; v.n. se fendre.

clergy, s. clergé m.

clergyman, s. ministre m.

clerk, s. employé m., commis m.

clever, adj. habile, adroit; intelligent.

client, s. client m.

cliff, s. falaise f.

climate, s. climat m.

climb, v.a. & n. grimper.

cling, v.n. ~ to se cramponner à.

clinic, s. clinique f.

clip, s. pince; — v.a. tondre; couper; rogner; (tickets) poinçonner.

cloak, s. manteau m.

cloak-room, s. consigne f.; vestiaire m.

clock, s. horloge f.; pendule f.; it is 10 o'clock il est dix heures.

close, v.a. (shut) fermer; (end) terminer; v.n. (se) fermer; se terminer; — adj. fermé; (narrow) étroit; (relations) proche; intime; — adv. tout près; — s. enclos m.; (end) fin f.

closely, adv. de près; étroitement.

closet, s. cabinet m.; armoire f.

cloth, s. drap m.; (table) nappe f.

clothe, v.a. vêtir.

clothes, s.pl. habits m.pl.

clothing, s. vêtements m. pl.

cloud, s. nuage m.

cloudy, adj. couvert.

clover, s. trèfle m.

club, s. (stick) massue f.; (people) cercle m., club m., société f.; (cards) trèfle m.

clue, s. fil m.; (crossword) définition f.

clumsy, adj. gauche.

cluster, s. grappe f.

clutch, v.a. empoigner; m. pour empoigner; (motor) embrayage m.

coach, s. voiture f.; wagon m.; autocar m.; (sports) entraîneur m.

coal, s. charbon m.

coal-mine, s. mine f. de houille.

coarse, adj. grossier; vulgaire.

coast, s. côte f.

coat, s. (jacket) veston m.; (top) pardessus m., manteau m.

cock, s. coq m., mâle m.; (gun) chien m.; (tap) robinet m.

cocktail, s. cocktail m.

cocoa, s. cacao m.

cod, s. morue f.

code, s. code m.

coffee, s. café m.

coffee-pot, s. cafetière f.

coffin, s. cercueil m.

cog-wheel, s. roue f. dentée.

coil, s. rouleau m.; bobine f.; — v.a. lover; enrouler.

coin, s. pièce f.

coincidence, s. coïncidence f.

coke, s. coke m.

cold, adj. froid; be ~ (pers.) avoir froid; (weather) faire froid; — s. froid m.; (in the head) rhume m.; catch a ~ s'enrhumer.

collaborate, v. n. collaborer.

collaborator, s. collaborateur, -trice m.f.

collapse, v.n. s'effondrer; (pers.) s'affaisser; — s. effondrement m.; (pers.) affaissement m. subit.

collar, s. col m.; collet m.

colleague, s. collègue m. f.

collect, v.a. rassembler; recueillir.

collection, s. collection f.; collecte f.; (mail) levée f.

college, s. collège m.

collide, v.n. se heurter (contre), entrer en collision.

colliery, s. houillère f.; mine f.

collision, s. collision f.

colon, s. deux points m. pl.

colonel, s. colonel m.

colony, s. colonie f.

colour, s. couleur f.

colourful, adj. coloré.

colourless, adj. terne, pâle.

column, s. colonne f.

comb, s. peigne m.; — v.a. peigner.

combat, s. combat m.

combination, s. combinaison f.

combine, v.a. combiner.

come, v.n. venir, arriver; ~ across rencontrer; ~ back revenir; ~ by obtenir; passer; ~ down descendre; ~ in entrer; ~ off avoir lieu; se détacher; ~ out sortir; ~ up monter.

comedian, s. comédien m.

comedy, s. comédie f.

comely, adj. avenant, bienséant.

comfort, s. consolation f.; bien-être m.; — v.a. consoler.

comfortable, adj. confortable; commode; be ~ être à l'aise.

comic, adj. comique.

comma, s. virgule f.

command, s. ordre m.; — v.a. commander.

commander, s. commandant m.

commandment, s. commandement m.

commemorate, v.a. commémorer.

commence, v.a.& n. commencer.

commend, v.a. recommander; louer.

comment, s. commentaire *m.;* — *v.n.* commenter.

commentary, *s.* commentaire *m.*

commerce, *s.* commerce *m.*

commercial, *adj.* commercial; ~ *traveller* voyageur *m.* de commerce.

commission, *s.* commission *f.;* commande *f.*

commissioner, *s.* commissaire *m.*

commit, *v.a.* commettre; confier; ~ *oneself* se compromettre.

commitment, *s.* engagement *m.*

committee, *s.* comité *m.*

commodity, *s.* marchandise *f.,* article *m.*

common, *adj.* commun.

commonwealth, *s.* *the British Commonwealth* commonwealth *m.*

communicate, *v. a. & n.* communiquer.

communication, *s.* communication *f.*

communication-cord, *s.* signal *m.* d'alarme.

communion, *s.* communion *f.*

communiqué, *s.* communiqué *m.*

community, *s.* communauté *f.*

compact, *s.* pacte *m.;* poudrier *m.;* — *adj.* compact; concis.

companion, *s.* compagnon, -agne *m. f.*

company, *s.* compagnie *f.;* société *f.*

comparatively, *adv.* comparativement.

compare, *v.a.* comparer

(*to* à, *with* avec).

comparison, *s.* comparaison *f.*

compartment, *s.* compartiment *m.*

compass, *s. (mariner's)* boussole *f.; (pair of)* ~*es* compas *m.*

compassion, *s.* compassion *f.*

compel, *v.a.* forcer.

compete, *v.n.* faire concurrence (à); concourir.

competence, *s.* compétence *f.;* capacité *f.*

competent, *adj.* capable.

competition, *s.* concurrence *f.;* concours *m.;* compétition *f.*

competitor, *s.* concurrent *m.*

compilation, *s.* compilation *f.*

compile, *v.a.* compiler.

complain, *v.n.* se plaindre

complaint, *s.* plainte *f.;* maladie *f.;* réclamation *f.*

complement, *s.* complément *m.*

complete, *v.a.* compléter, achever; — *adj.* complet.

complicated, *adj.* compliqué.

complication, *s.* complication *f.*

compliment, *s.* compliment *m.*

comply, *v.n.* ~ *with* se conformer à.

component, *adj. & s.* composant *(m.).*

compose, *v.a.* composer; *be* ~*d of* se composer de.

composer, *s.* compositeur *m.*

composition, *s.* composition *f.;* dissertation *f.*

compound, *s. & adj.* composé *(m.);* — *v.a.* composer.

comprehend, *v.a.* comprendre.

comprehension, *s.* compréhension *f.*

compress, *v.a.* comprimer.

compromise, *s.* compromis *m.; — v.a.* compromettre.

compulsory, *adj.* obligatoire.

compute, *v.a.* calculer, computer.

computer, *s.* calculateur *m.* (électronique).

comrade, *s.* camarade *m.*

conceal, *v. a.* cacher.

conceit, *s.* vanité *f.*

conceive, *v.a.* concevoir.

concept, *s.* concept *m.*

concern, *v.a.* concerner; regarder; *be ~ed (in, with)* s'intéresser (à); *(about)* s'inquiéter (de); *— s.* affaire *f.;* entreprise *f.;* anxiété *f.*

concerning, *prep.* concernant.

concert, *a.* concert *m.*

concession, *s.* concession *f.*

conciliation, *s.* réconciliation *f.*

concise, *adj.* concis.

conclude, *v.a. &n.* conclure.

conclusion, *s.* conclusion *f.; in ~* pour conclure.

concrete, *s.* béton *m.; — adj.* concret.

condemn, *v.a.* condamner.

condense, *v.a.* condenser.

condition, *s.* condition *f.;* état *m.; on ~ that* à condition que.

conduct, *s.* conduite *f.; — v. a.* conduire; diriger.

conductor, *s.* receveur *m.;* chef *m.* d'orchestre.

cone, *s.* cône *m.*

confederacy, *s.* confédération *f.*

confer, *v.a. & n.* conférer.

conference, *s.* conférence *f.*

confess, *v.a.* avouer; confesser.

confession, *s.* confession *f.*

confidence, *s.* confiance *f.*

confident, *adj.* confiant.

confidential, *adj.* confidentiel.

confine, *v.a.* confiner, enfermer; *be ~d to bed* être alité.

confirm, *v. a.* confirmer.

confirmation, *s.* confirmation *f.*

conflict, *s.* conflit *m.*

confound, *v. a.* confondre.

confront, *v.a.* être en face; confronter.

confuse, *v.a.* brouiller, mettre en désordre.

confusion, *s.* confusion *f.*

congratulate, *v.a.* féliciter (de).

congratulation, *s.* félicitations *f. pl.*

congregation, *s.* assemblée *f.,* congrégation *f.*

congress, *s.* congrès *m.*

conjunction, *s.* conjonction *f.*

connect, *v.a.* joindre, lier; associer.

connection, *s.* connexion *f.;* rapport *m.; (railw.)* correspondance *f.*

conquer, *v.a.* vaincre; conquérir.

conqueror, *s.* vainqueur *m.;* conquérant *m.*

conscience, *s.* conscience *f.*

conscious *adj.* *be ~* (*= not fainting*) avoir connaissance; *be ~ of* avoir la conscience de.

consciousness, *s.* connaissance *f.;* conscience *f.*

conscript, *adj. & s.* conscrit *(m.).*

consent, *s.* consentement; *— v.n.* consentir.

consequence, *s.* conséquence *f.*

consequent, *adj.* conséquent.

consequently, *adv.* par conséquent.

conservation, *s.* conservation *f.*

consider, *v.a.* considérer.

considerable, *adj.* considérable.

considerate, *adj.* attentif; réfléchi.

consideration, *s.* considération *f.; (money)* rémunération *f.*

consign, *v.a.* livrer; consigner, expédier.

consignment, *s.* expédition *f.;* envoi *m.*

consist, *v. n.* ~ *of* se composer de, consister en.

consistent, *adj.* conséquent.

consolation, *s.* consolation *f.*

consonant, *s.* consonne *f.*

conspicuous, *adj.* en vue; frappant.

conspiracy, *s.* conspiration *f.*

conspire, *v. a. & n.* conspirer.

constable, *s.* agent *m.* (de. police).

constant, *adj.* continuel; constant.

constipation, *s.* constipation *f.*

constitute, *v.a.* constituer.

constitution, *s.* constitution *f.*

constrain, *v.a.* contraindre (à).

constraint, *s.* contrainte *f.*

construct, *v. a.* construire.

construction, *s.* construction *f.*

consul, *s.* consul *m.*

consulate, *s.* consulat *m.*

consult, *v.a. & n.* consulter.

consultation, *s.* consultation *f.;* ~ *room* cabinet *m.* (de consultation).

consume, *v.a. (destroy)* consumer; *(use up)* consommer.

consumer, *s.* consommateur, -trice *m.f.;* ~ *goods* articles *m.* de grande consommation.

consumption, *s.* consommation *f.; (disease)* phtisie *f.,* tuberculose *f.*

contact, *s.* contact *m.;* − *v.a.* entrer en relations avec.

contain, *v.a.* contenir.

container, *s.* récipient *m.*

contemplate, *v.a.* contempler; projeter.

contemplation, *s.* contemplation *f.*

contemporary, *adj. & s.* contemporain *(m.).*

contempt, *s.* mépris *m.*

contemptuous, *adj.* méprisant.

contend, *v.n.* lutter contre (pour).

content, *s.* contentement *m.;* ~*s* contenu *m.; table of* ~*s* table *f.* des matières; − *adj.* content.

contest, *s.* lutte *f.; (sport)* rencontre *f.,* match *m.; (dispute)* contestation *f.;* − *v. a.* contester.

continent, *s.* continent *m.*

continental, *adj.* continental.

continual, *adj.* continuel.

continuation, *s.* continuation *f.;* suite *f.*

continue, *v.a. & n.* continuer.

continuous, *adj.* continu.

contract, *s.* contrat *m.;* − *v.a.* contracter.

contractor, *s.* entrepreneur *m.*

contradiction, *s.* contradiction *f.*

contrary, *adj.* contraire; — *adv.* contrairement.

contrast, *s.* contraste *m.*; — *v.a.* mettre en contraste.

contribute, *v. a. & n.* contribuer.

contribution, *s.* contribution *f.*; article *m.*

contributor, *s.* contribuant *m.*; collaborateur *m.*

contrive, *v.a.* inventer.

control, *s.* autorité *f.*; maîtrise *f.*; direction *f.*, commande *f.*; — *v.a.* gouverner, commander, maîtriser, diriger; contrôler.

controversy, *s.* polémique *f.*, controverse *f.*

convenience, *s.* commodité *f.*, convenance *f.*; public ~ cabinets *m. pl.* d'aisances.

convenient, *adj.* commode; be ~ to *s.o.* convenir à qn.

conversation, *s.* conversation *f.*

converse, *v.n.* converser; causer.

convert, *v.a.* convertir.

convey, *v.a.* transporter; transmettre; présenter.

conveyance, *s.* transport *m.*; voiture *f.*, véhicule *m.*

conveyer, *s.* porteur *m.*; ~ belt bande *f.* transporteuse.

convict, *s.* forçat *m.*; — *v.a.* convaincre (de), condamner.

convince, *v. a.* convaincre (de).

convoy, *s.* convoi *m.*

cook, *s.* cuisinier, -ière *m. f.*; head ~ chef *m.*;

— *v.a.* faire cuire; *v.n.* cuire.

cooking, *s.* cuisine *f.*

cool, *adj.* frais (*f.* fraîche); (*fig.*) calme; — *v.a.* rafraîchir.

co-operate, *v.n.* coopérer.

co-operation, *s.* coopération *f.*

copper, *s.* cuivre *m.*

copy, *s.* copie *f.*; exemplaire *m.*; numéro *m.* — *v. a.* copier.

copy-book, *s.* cahier *m.*

copyright, *s.* droit *m.* d'auteur.

coral, *s.* corail *m.*

cord, *s.* corde *f.*

cordial, *adj.* cordial.

cork, *s.* bouchon *m.*

corkscrew, *s.* tire-bouchon *m.*

corn, *s.* grain *m.*; grains *m. pl.*; (*wheat*) blé *m*; (*maize*) maïs *m.*

corner, *s.* coin *m.*

corporal, *adj.* corporel; — *s.* caporal *m.*

corporation, *s.* corporation *f.*

corps, *s.* corps *m.*

corpse, *s.* cadavre *m.*

correct, *adj.* correct; exact; — *v.a.* corriger, rectifier.

correction, *s.* correction *f.*; rectification *f.*

correspond, *v.n.* correspondre; être conforme (à).

correspondence, *s.* correspondance *f.*

correspondent, *s.* correspondant *m.*

corresponding, *adj.* correspondant.

corridor, *s.* corridor *m.*; couloir *m.*

corridor-train, *s.* train *m.* à couloir.

corrupt, *adj.* corrompu

cosmetics, s. pl. cosmétiques m. pl., produits m.pl. de beauté.

cosmonaut, s. cosmonaute m.

cost, s. coût m., frais m. pl.; prix m.; ~ of living coût de la vie; at the ~ of au prix de; — v.n. coûter.

costly, adj. coûteux.

costume, s. costume m.

cosy, adj. confortable.

cottage, s. chaumière f.

cotton, s. coton m.

couch, s. canapé m., divan m.

cough, s. toux f.; — v.n. tousser.

council, s. conseil m.

councillor, s. conseiller m.

counsel, s. conseil m.; avocat m.

count¹, s. compte m.; (title) comte m.

count², v.a. & n. compter.

countenance, s. visage m.; air· m.

counter, s. comptoir m., guichet m.; jeton m.

counterfoil, s. souche f.

countersign, v.a. contresigner.

countess, s. comtesse f.

countless, adj. innombrable.

country, s. pays m.; (not town) campagne f.

countryman, s. campagnard m.

countryside, s. (les) campagnes f.pl.

countrywoman, s. paysanne f.

county, s. comté m.

couple, s. couple f.

courage, s. courage m.

courageous, adj. courageux.

course, s. cours m.: route f.; (meal) service m., plat m.; of ~ bien entendu.

court, s. cour f.; tribunal m.; court m. (de tennis); — v.a. faire la cour à.

courteous, adj. courtois.

courtesy, s. courtoisie f.

courtship, s. cour f.

courtyard, s. cour f.

cousin, s. cousin, -e·m. f.

cover, s. couverture f.; couvercle m.; (meal) couvert m.; (post) enveloppe f.; — v.a. couvrir.

cow, s. vache f.

coward, s. & adj. lâche m.

crab, s. crabe m.

crack, s. craquement m.; — v.a. faire craquer; v.n. craquer; se fêler.

cradle, s. berceau m.

craft, s. habileté f.; embarcation f.; métier m.; profession f.

craftsman, s. artisan m.

cram, v.a. fourrer; bourrer.

crane, s. grue f.

crash, s. fracas m.; débâcle; atterrissage brutal, collision; v.n, tomber avec fracas; s'écraser sur le sol.

crash-helmet, s. serretête m.

crave, v.n. ~ for désirer ardemment.

crawl, v.n. ramper; (pers.) se traîner.

crayon, s. crayon m.

craze, s. manie f.

crazy, adj. fou, toqué.

creak, s. cri m., grincement m.; — v. n. crier, grincer.

cream, s. crème f.

crease, s. (faux) pli m.

create, v.a. créer.

creation, *s.* création *f.*

creature, *s.* créature *f.*

credit, *s.* crédit *m.;* mérite *m.;* honneur *m.;* on ~ à terme: *give* ~ *to* ajouter foi à; — *v.a.* ajouter foi à, créditer.

creditor, *s.* créancier *m.*

creek, *s.* crique *f.*

creep, *v.n.* ramper; se glisser.

crew, *s.* équipage *m.;* équipe *f.*

crib, *s.* mangeoire *f.;* lit *m.* d'enfant; berceau *m.*

cricket, *s.* *(game)* cricket *m.*

crime, *s.* crime *m.*

criminal, *adj. & s.* criminel, -elle.

cripple, *s.* estropié *m.*

crisis, *s.* crise *f.*

crisp, *adj.* croquant, croustillant; *(air)* vif.

critic, *s.* critique *m.*

critical, *adj.* critique.

criticize, *v.a.* critiquer.

critique, *s.* critique *f.*

croak, *v.n.* croasser.

crochet, *s.* crochet *m.*

crop, *s.* récolte *f.;* cueillette *f.*

cross, *s.* croix *f.;* — *v.a.* croiser, traverser.

crossing, *s.* passage *m.;* *(sea)* traversée *f.;* *level* ~ passage à niveau.

cross-question, *s.* contre-interrogatoire *m.;* — *v.a.* contre-interroger.

cross-reference, *s.* renvoi *m.*

crossroad, *s.* chemin *m.* de traverse; ~s carrefour *m.*

cross-section, *s.* coupe *f.* en travers.

cross-word (puzzle) *s.*

mots *m.pl.* croisés.

crouch, *v. n.* se blottir.

crow, *s.* corneille *f.*

crowd, *s.* foule *f.;* tas *m.*

crowded, *adj.* encombré, comble.

crown, *s.* couronne *f ;* — *v.a.* couronner.

crucial, *adj.* décisif.

crude, *adj* brut; cru; grossier.

cruel, *adj.* cruel.

cruelty, *s.* cruauté *f.*

cruet, *s.* burette *f.*

cruise, *v.n.* croiser; — *s.* voyage *m.*

cruising, *adj.* ~ *speed* vitesse *f.* de croisière.

crumb, *s.* mie *f.;* miette *f.*

crumble, *v.a.* émietter; *v.n.* s'émietter.

crusade, *s.* croisade *f.*

crush, *s.* écrasement *m.;* cohue *f.;* — *v.a.* écraser.

crust, *s.* croûte *f.*

crutch, *s.* béquille *f.*

cry, *s.* cri *m.;* — *v.a.* crier; ~ *down* décrier; *v.n.* crier; *(weep)* pleurer.

crystal, *s.* cristal *m.*

cub, *s.* petit *m.;* *(boy scout)* louveteau *m.*

cube, *s.* cube *m.*

cuckoo, *s.* coucou *m.*

cucumber, *s.* concombre *m.*

cue, *s.* réplique *f.*

cuff, *s.* poignet *m.,* manchette *f.*

cuff-links, *s. pl.* boutons *m.pl.* de manchette.

culminate, *v.n.* se terminer.

culprit, *s.* accusé, -e *m. f.*

cultivate, *v.a.* cultiver.

cultural, *adj.* cultural.

culture, *s.* culture *f.*

cunning, *s.* ruse *f.,* finesse *f.;* — *adj.* rusé.

cup, *s.* tasse *f.;* gobelet *m.*

cupboard, s. armoire f.; placard m.

curate, s. vicaire m.

curb, s. gourmetté f.

curd, s. (lait) caillé m.

curdle, v.a. cailler; v.n. se cailler.

cure, s. guérison f.; cure f.; remède m.; — v.a. guérir.

curiosity, s. curiosité f.

curious, adj. curieux.

curl, s. boucle f.; — v.a. & n. boucler, friser; ~ up s'enrouler.

curly, adj. bouclé, frisé.

currant, s. black ~ cassis m.; red ~ groseille f. rouge.

currency, s. circulation f., cours m.; terme m. d'échéance; unité f. monétaire, monnaie f.; foreign ~ monnaie étrangère.

current, adj. courant, en cours; in ~ use d'usage courant; ~ events actualités f.; ~ account compte m. courant; — s. courant m.; cours m.

curse, s. malédiction f.; — v.a. maudire; v.n. blasphémer.

curtain, s. rideau m.

curve, s. courbe f.

cushion, s. coussin m.

custom, s. coutume f.; ~s douane f.; ~s duties droits m. de douane; ~s declaration déclaration f. de douane; ~s formalities la visite de la douane.

customary, adj. coutumier; accoutumé.

customer, s. client m., acheteur m.

custom-house, s. douane f.; ~ officer douanier m.

cut, v.a. couper; trancher; tailler; hacher; ~ down abattre, couper; réduire; ~ off couper; ~ out tailler; ~ up couper, débiter; — s. (knife) coup m.; (wound) coupure f.; (clothes) coupe f.; (meat) morceau m.; (in wages) réduction f.

cutlery, s. coutellerie f.

cutlet, s. côtelette f.

cutter, s. tailleur m.; coupeur m.

cycle, s. cycle m.; bicyclette f.; — v.n. pédaler.

cycling, s. cyclisme m.

cylinder, s. cylindre m.

cynic, adj. & s. cynique m.

Czech, adj. tchèque; — s. Tchèque m.

D

dad, daddy, s. papa m.

dagger, s. poignard m.

daily, adj. journalier, quotidien; — s. (journal) quotidien m.

dainty, adj. friand, délicat; gentil; — s. friandise f.

dairy, s. laiterie f.

daisy, s. marguerite f.

dam, s. barrage m.; digue f.

damage, s. dommage m.; préjudice m.; ~s dommages-intérêts m.

damn, v.a. condamner; — s. juron m.

damp, adj. humide; — s. humidité f.; — v.a mouiller, humecter.

dance, s. danse f.; bal m.; v.n. & a. danser.

dancer, s. danseur, -euse m. f.

dancing-hall, s. salle f. de danse; dancing m.

dancing-shoes, s.pl. souliers m. de bal, escarpins m.

Dane, s. Danois, -e m. f.

danger, s. danger m.

dangerous, adj. dangereux.

Danish, adj. danois; — s. (language) danois m.

dare, v. aux. & a. oser.

daring, adj. audacieux.

dark, adj. obscur, sombre; (colour) foncé; (fig.) triste; be ~ faire sombre; — s. obscurité f.; in the ~ dans l'obscurité.

darken, v.a. obscurcir.

darkness, s. obscurité f.

darling, adj. & s. chéri, -e.

darn, v.a. repriser.

darning, s. reprise f.

dart, s. dard m.; ~s (game) fléchettes f.pl.

dash, v.a. lancer; flanquer (par terre); ~ to pieces briser en morceaux; v.n. ~ against se heurter contre; ~ at se précipiter sur — s. (with pen) trait m., tiret m.; (vigour) élan m., fougue f.; attaque f. soudaine.

dash-board, s. tablier m; tableau m. de bord.

data, s. pl. données f.

date¹, s. date f.; millésime m.; be up to ~ être à la page; — v.a. & n. dater.

date², s. datte f.

daughter, s. fille f.

daughter-in-law, s. belle-fille f.

dawn, s. point m. du jour; aube f.

day, s. jour m.; (whole day) journée f.

daylight, s. jour m.

daytime, s. jour m., journée. f.

daze, v.a. étourdir; éblouir.

dazzle, v.c. éblouir.

deacon, s. diacre m.

dead, adj. mort; the ~ les morts m.pl.

deadly, adj. mortel.

deaf, adj. sourd; ~ and dumb sourd-muet.

deal, v.a. ~ out distribuer; donner; v.n. ~ with traiter qn; commercer, traiter avec qn; traiter (d'un sujet); ~ in commercer de; — s. (cards) donne f.; (commerce) affaire f.; a good ~, a great ~ beaucoup (de).

dealer, s. marchand m. (in de).

dean, s. doyen m.

dear, s. & adj. cher m., chère f.

death, s. mort f.

debate, s. débat m., discussion f.; — v.a. discuter, mettre en discussion.

debt, s. dette f.

debtor, s. débiteur, -trice m. f.

decay, s. décadence f.; — v.n. tomber en décadence; pourrir.

decease, s. décès m.; — v.n. décéder.

deceit, s. déception f.; tromperie f.

deceive, v.a. tromper; décevoir.

December, s. décembre m.

decent, adj. décent; assez bon.

deception, s. déception f.

decide, v.a. décider.

decision, s. décision f.

decisive, *adj.* décisif.

deck, *s.* pont *m.*

deck-chair, *s.* transat-
lantique *f.*

declaration, *s.* déclaration
f.

declare, *v.a.* déclarer.

decline, *s.* décadence *f.;*
— *v.a.* décliner; *v.n.*
baisser.

decorate, *v.a.* décorer (de).

decoration, *s.* décoration
f.

decrease, *v.a. & n.* diminuer; — *s.* diminution *f.*

decree, *s.* décret *m.*

dedicate, *v.a.* dédier.

deed, *s.* action *f.;* acte *m.*

deem, *v.a.* juger.

deep, *adj.* profond; *ten
feet* ~ dix pieds de
profondeur.

deer, *s.* cerf *m.*

deface, *v.a.* défigurer.

defeat, *s.* défaite *f.;* —
v.a. vaincre.

defect, *s.* défaut *m.*

defence, *s.* défense *f.*

defend, *v.a.* défendre.

defender, *s.* défenseur *m.*

defer, *v.a.* retarder, ajourner; ~ *to* déférer à.

defiance, *s.* défi *m.; set
at* ~ défier.

deficiency, *s.* manque *m.*

deficient, *adj.* insuffisant.

defile, *s.* défilé *m.;* —
v.n. défiler; *v.a.* souiller.

define, *v.a.* définir.

definite, *adj.* déterminé,
défini.

definition, *s.* définition *f.*

defy, *v.a.* défier; braver.

degrade, *v.a.* dégrader.

degree, *s.* degré *m.; (university)* grade *m.;* di-
plôme *m.*

delay, *s.* retard *m.,* délai
m.; — *v.a.* retarder;
différer; *v.n.* tarder.

delegate, *s.* délégué *m.*

delegation, *s.* délegation *f.*

deliberate, *adj.* délibéré;
— *v.a. & n.* délibérer.

delicacy, *s.* délicatesse *f.*

delicate, *adj.* délicat.

delicious, *adj* délicieux.

delight, *v.a. be* ~*ed at*
être enchanté de.

delightful, *adj.* déliceux.

delinquent, *s.* délinquant
m.

deliver, *v.a.* *(letters)*
distribuer; *(goods etc.)*
livrer, *(message)* re-
mettre; *(speech)* fai-
re, prononcer; *(free)*
délivrer; *be* ~*ed of*
accoucher de.

delivery, *s.* *(letters)* distribution *f.,* *(message)*
remise *f.,* *(goods)* livraison *f.; (speech)* prononciation *f.,* débit *m.*

delusion, *s.* illusion *f.*

demand, *s.* demande, *f.*
réclamation *f.;* — *v. a.*
demander, réclamer.

democracy, *s.* démocratie
f.

democrat, *s.* démocrate *m.*

democratic, *adj.* démocratique.

demolish, *v.a.* démolir.

demonstrate, *v.a.* dé-
montrer.

demonstration, *s.* dé-
monstration *f.*

den, *s.* antre *m.;* repaire
m.

denial, *s.* dénégation *f.*

denomination, *s.* déno-
mination *f.; secte f.*

denote, *v.a.* dénoter.

denounce, *v.a.* dénoncer.

dense, *adj.* dense, épais.

density, *s.* densité *f.*

dentist, *s.* dentiste *m.*

denture, *s.* *(artificial)*
dentier *m.*

deny, *v.a.* nier.

depart, *v.n.* partir.

department, *s.* départe-
ment *m.*

departure, *s.* départ *m.*

depend, *v.n.* dépendre
(de), compter (sur).

dependence, *s.* dépendance *f.*

dependent, *adj.* dépen-
dant.

deplore, *v.a.* déplorer.

deposit, *s.* dépôt *m.;* —
v.a. déposer.

depot, *s.* dépôt *m.*

depression *s.* abattement
m.

deprive, *v.a.* priver (de).

depth, *s.* profondeur *f.*

deputy, *s.* délégué *m.;*
vice-, sous-.

derive, *v.a.* retirer (de);
be ~d *from* dériver de.

descend, *v.n.* descendre.

descendant, *s.* descen-
dant, -e *m. f.*

descent, *s.* descente *f.*

describe, *v.a.* décrire.

description, *s.* description *f.;* sorte *f.*

desert, *s.* désert *m.;* —
v.a. déserter.

deserve, *v.a.* mériter.

design, *s.* dessein *m.;*
projet *m.;* dessin *m.;*
— *v.a.* dessiner.

desirable, *adj.* désirable.

desire, *s.* désir *m.;* — *v.a.*
désirer.

desk, *s.* bureau *m.*

desolation, *s.* désolation *f.*

despair, *s.* désespoir *m.;*
— *v.n.* désespérer.

despatch *see* dispatch.

desperate, *adj.* désespéré.

despise, *v.a.* mépriser.

despite, *prep.* ~ *(of)* en
dépit de.

dessert, *s.* dessert *m.*

destination, *s.* destination *f.*

destine, *v.a.* destiner.

destiny, *s.* destin *m.*
destinée *f.*

destroy, *v.a.* détruire.

destruction, *s.* destruction
f.

detach, *v.a.* détacher.

detachment, *s.* détache-
ment *m.*

detail, *s.* détail *m.*

detain, *v.a.* retenir;
détenir.

detect, *v.a.* découvrir.

detective, *s.* détective *m.*

detention, *s.* détention *f.*

detergent, *s.* détergent *m.*

deteriorate, *v.n.* se dé-
tériorer.

determination, *s.* détermination *f.*

determine, *v.a. & n.* déterminer, décider.

detrimental, *adj.* pré-
judiciable.

develop, *v.a.* développer;
v.n. se développer.

development, *s.* développe-
pement *m.*

deviation, *s.* déviation *f.*

device, *s* expédient *m.;*
invention *f.*

devil, *s.* diable *m.*

devilish, *adj.* diabolique.

devise, *v.a.* combiner;
tramer.

devote, *v.a.* consacrer.

devoted, *adj.* dévoué.

devotion, *s.* dévotion *f.;*
dévouement *m.*

devour, *v.a.* dévorer.

dew, *s.* rosée *f.*

diagnosis, *s.* diagnostic *m.*

diagram, *s.* diagramme *m.*

dial, *s.* cadran *m.;* —
v.a. composer un
numéro.

dialogue, *s.* dialogue *m.*

diameter, *s.* diamètre *m.*

diamond, *s.* diamant *m.;*
(cards) carreau *m.*

diaper, *s.* couche *f.*

diarrhoea, *s.* diarrhée *f.*

diary, *s.* journal *m.; agen-da *m.*

dictate, *v.a.* dicter; *v.n.* ~ *to* donner des or-dres à.

dictation, *s.* dictée *f.*

dictator, *s.* dictateur *m.*

dictionary, *s.* dictionnaire *m.*

die[1], *s.* dé *m.*

die[2], *v.n.* mourir.

Diesel engine, *s.* moteur *m.* Diesel; diesel *m.*

diet, *s.* alimentation *f.;* régime *m.*

differ, *v.n.* différer.

difference, *s.* différence *f.*

different, *adj.* différent.

difficult, *adj.* difficile.

difficulty, *s.* difficulté *f.*

diffuse, *adj.* diffus.

dig, *v.a.* bêcher.

digest, *v.a.* digérer.

digestion, *s.* digestion *f.*

dignity, *s.* dignité *f.*

diligent, *adj.* diligent.

dim, *adj.* faible, pâle, obscur.

dimension, *s.* dimension *f.*

diminish, *v. a. & n.* dimi-nuer.

dimple, *s.* fossette *f.*

dine, *v.n.* dîner.

dining-car, *s.* wagon-restaurant *m.*

dining-hall, *s.* salle *f.* à manger; réfectoire *m.*

dining-room, *s.* salle *f.* à manger.

dinner, *s.* dîner *m.*

dinner-jacket, *s.* smoking *m.*

dip, *v.a. & n.* plonger.

diploma, *s.* diplôme *m.*

diplomacy, *s.* diplomatie *f.*

diplomat, *s.* diplomate *m.*

diplomatic, *adj.* diploma-tique.

direct, *adj.* direct; — *v. a.* diriger; commander; adresser.

direction, *s.* direction *f.;* instructions *f. pl.*

directly, *adv.* directement; tout de suite.

director, *s.* directeur *m.*

directory, *s.* annuaire *m.;* Bottin *m.*

dirt, *s.* saleté *f.;* boue *f.,* crotte *f.;* crasse *f.*

dirty, *adj.* sale; crotté; crasseux.

disadvantage, *s.* désavan-tage *m.*

disagree, *v.n.* différer; se brouiller; ne pas convenir (à).

disagreeable, *adj.* désagré-able.

disappear, *v. n.* disparaître

disappearance, *s.* dispari-tion *f.*

disappoint, *v.a.* désap-pointer; tromper.

disappointment, *s.* désap-pointement *m.*

disapprove, *v.n.* ~ *of* dé-sapprouver qch.

disaster, *s.* désastre *m.*

disastrous, *adj.* désas-treux.

disc *see* disk.

discern, *v.a.* discerner.

discharge, *v. a.* décharger; *(employee)* congédier; renvoyer; *(prisoner)* élargir; *(gas)* dégager; *(debt f* liquider; *(duty)* s'acquitter de; — *s.* dé-charge *f.; (employee)* congé *m.; (prison)* élargissement *m.*

discipline, *s.* discipline *f.*

disclose, *v.a.* découvrir.

discontented, *adj.* mécon-tent (de).

discourage, *v. a.* découra-ger.

discouragement, *s.* décou-

ragement *m.*
discourse, *s.* discours *m.*
discover, *v.a.* découvrir.
discovery, *s.* découverte *f.*
discredit, *s.* discrédit *m.;*
— *v.a.* discréditer.
discreet, *adj.* discret.
discretion, *s.* discrétion
f.; prudence *f.*
discuss, *v.a.* discuter.
discussion, *s.* discussion *f.*
disdain, *v.a.* dédaigner;
— *s.* dédain *m.*
disease, *s.* maladie *f.*
disembark *v.a. & n.* débarquer.
disgrace, *s.* disgrâce *f.;*
— *v.a.* disgracier.
disgraceful, *adj.* honteux.
disguise, *s.* déguisement;
— *v.a.* déguiser.
disgust, *s.* dégoût *m.;*
— *v.a.* dégoûter.
disgusting, *adj.* dégoûtant
dish, *s.* plat *m.;* mets *m.;*
wash up the ~es laver la
vaisselle.
dishonest, *adj.* malhonnête.
dishonour, *s.* déshonneur
m.; — *v.a.* déshonorer
(bill) ne pas honorer.
disinfect, *v.a.* désinfecter.
disk, *s.* disque *m.*
dislike, *s.* aversion *f.,*
dégoût *m.;* — *v.a.* ne
pas aimer.
dismal, *adj.* lugubre, sombre.
dismay, *s.* consternation
f.
dismiss, *v.a.* congédier;
bannir, écarter.
disobedience, *s.* désobéissance *f.*
disobedient, *adj.* désobéissant.
disobey, *v. a.* désobéir (à).
disorder, *s.* désordre *m.*
dispatch, *s.* expédition
f.; dépêche *f.*

dispensary, *s.* pharmacie
f.
dispense, *v.a.* dispenser;
préparer; *v.n. ~ with*
se disposer de.
disperse, *v.a.* disperser.
displaced, *adj. ~ person*
personne *f.* déplacée.
displacement, *s.* déplacement *m.*
display, *v.a.* exposer;
étaler; déployer, faire
preuve de; — *s.* exposition *f.;* étalage *m.;*
parade *f.*
displease, *v.a.* déplaire à
disposal, *s. at s.o.'s ~*
à la disposition de qn.
dispose, *v.n. ~ of* disposer de; vendre.
disposition, *s.* disposition
f.
dispute, *s.* dispute *f.* discuission *f.;* — *v.a* discuter; *v. n.* se disputer.
disqualify, *v.a.* disqualifier.
dissatisfy, *v.a.* mécontenter.
dissolve, *v.a.* dissoudre;
v.n. se dissoudre.
distance, *s.* distance *f.*
distant, *adj.* lointain; éloigné.
distil, *v. a. & n.* distiller.
distinct, *adj.* distinct (de);
marqué.
distinction, *s.* distinction
f.
distinguish, *v.a.* distinguer.
distract, *v.a.* distraire.
distraction, *s.* distraction
f.; confusion *f.*
distress, *s.* détresse *f.;*
— *v.a.* affliger.
distribute, *v. a.* distribuer.
distribution, *s.* distribution *f.*
district, *s.* région *f.,*
contrée *f.;* district *m.*

disturb, *v.a.* troubler; déranger.

disturbance, *s.* trouble *m.*, dérangement *m.*

ditch, *s.* fossé *m.*

dive, *v.n.* plonger *(into dans).*

diver, *s.* plongeur *m.*, scaphandrier *m.*

divergent, *adj.* divergent.

diversion, *s.* déviation *f.*

divide, *v.a.* divider.

dividend, *s.* dividende *m.*

divine, *adj.* divin.

divinity, *s.* théologie *f.*

division, *s.* division *f.*

divorce, *s.* divorce *m.;* — *v. a.* divorcer (d'avec).

dizzy, *adj.* *feel* ~ avoir le vertige.

do, *v. a.* faire; finir; ~ *away with* supprimer; ~ *up* envelopper; ~ *with* se contenter de.

dock, *s.* bassin *m.*

doctor, *s.* docteur *m.;* médecin *m.*

doctrine, *s.* doctrine *f.*

document, *s.* document *m.*

dog, *s.* chien *m.*

dogma, *s.* dogme *m.*

doll, *s.* poupée *f.*

dollar, *s.* dollar *m.*

domestic, *adj. & s.* domestique *(m. f.).*

domicile, *s.* domicile *m.*

dominate, *v.a. &. n.* dominer.

dominion, *s.* domination *f.;* ~*s* colonies *f.*

donkey, *s.* âne *m.*

doom, *s.* sentence *f.;* — *v.a.* condamner; ~*ed to* voué à.

door, *s.* porte *f.; (vehicle)* portière *f.*

dormitory, *s.* dortoir *m.*

dose, *s.* dose *f.*

dot, *s.* point *m.*

double, *adj. & s.* double *(m.).*

doubt, *s.* doute *m.; no* ~ sans doute; — *v.a. &* n. douter.

doubtful, *adj.* douteux.

doubtless, *adj.* sans doute.

dough, *s.* pâte *f.*

dove, *s.* colombe *f.*

down, *adv.* à bas, en bas, par en bas; *be* ~ *with (illness)* être au lit avec; *fall* ~ tomber à terre; *go* ~ aller en bas; — *prep.* le long de; ~ *the river* en aval; ~ *the street* plus bas dans la rue.

downhill, *s.* pente *f.;* — *adv.* en pente, en descendant.

downstairs, *adv.* en bas.

downwards, *adv.* en bas.

dozen, *s.* douzaine *f.*

draft, *s.* projet *m.; (letter)* minute *f.; (troops)* détachement *m.; (drawing)* esquisse *f.*

drag, *v.a.* traîner; tirer.

drain, *s.* égout *m.*, canal *m.;* — *v.a.* drainer; vider.

drama, *s.* drame *m.;* théâtre *m.*

dramatic, *adj.* dramatique.

draper, *s.* marchand *m.* d'étoffes, (marchand) drapier *m.;* ~*'s* magasin *m.* de nouveautés.

draught, *s.* tirage *m.; (drink)* trait *m.; (air)* courant *m.* d'air.

draw, *v.a. (pull)* tirer, traîner; *(tooth)* arracher; *(sketch)* dessiner; ~ *down* baisser; ~ *on* tirer; ~ *out* prolonger; — *v. n.* tirer; ~ *near* s'approcher.

drawer, *s.* tiroir *m.*

drawing, *s.* dessin *m.*

drawing-pin, *s.* punaise *f.*

drawing-room, *s.* salon *m.*

dread, *v.a.* redouter.

dreadful, *adj.* redoutable.

dream, *s.* rêve *m.;* — *v.a. & n.* rêver.

dress, *s.* habits *m.pl.;* robe *f.;* — *v. a.* habiller; *v.n.* s'habiller; ~ *a wound* panser.

dress-circle, *s.* (premier) balcon *m.*

dressing-gown, *s.* *(woman)* peignoir *m.,* *(man)* robe *f.* de chambre.

dressmaker, *s.* couturière *f.*

drift, *v.n.* flotter; dériver; — *s.* dérive *f.;* amoncellement *m.*

drill, *s.* foret *m.;* *(soldiers)* exercice *m.*

drink, *s.* boisson *f.;* — *v.a.* boire.

drip, *v.n.* dégoutter.

drive, *v.a.* conduire; ~ *in* *(nail)* enfoncer; *v.n.* conduire; aller en voiture.

driver, *s.* *(engine)* mécanicien *m.;* *(bus)* conducteur *m.;* *(car)* chauffeur *m.*

driving, *s.* conduite *f.;* ~ *licence* permis *m.* de conduire.

drop, *s.* goutte *f.;* — *v.a.* laisser tomber; abandonner; *v.n.* (dé)goutter; ~ *in* entrer en passant.

drown, *v.a.* noyer; *v.n.* se noyer.

drug, *s.* drogue *f.*

druggist, *s.* droguiste *m.*

drum, *s.* tambour *m.*

drunk, *adj.* ivre.

dry, *adj.* sec, sèche; aride; tari; — *v.a.* sécher.

dry-clean, *v.a.* nettoyer à sec.

dual, *adj.* double.

dub, *v.a.* doubler.

duchess, *s.* duchesse *f.*

duck, *s.* cane *f.;* canard *m.*

due, *adj.* *(proper)* dû; *(owing)* exigible; échéant, payable; *in* ~ *form* en bonne et due forme; *in* ~ *time* en temps voulu; ~ *to* causé par, par suite de; *the train is* ~ *at* le train arrive à; — *s.* dû *m.;* droit *m.*

duke, *s.* duc *m.*

dull, *adj.* borné; ennuyeux; *(colour)* terne; *(weather, sad)* triste.

dumb, *adj.* muet.

dummy, *s.* mannequin *m.;* *(cards)* mort *m.*

dung, *s.* fumier *m.*

dupe, *s.* dupe *f.;* — *v.a.* duper.

duplicate, *s.* duplicata *m.;* — *adj.* en double; — *v.a.* faire en double.

during, *adv.* pendant, au cours de.

dusk, *s.* crépuscule *m.*

dust, *s.* poussière *f.*

dustbin, *s.* poubelle *f.*

dusty, *adj.* poussiéreux, poudreux.

Dutch, *adj.* hollandais.

Dutchman, *s.* Hollandais *m.*

duty, *s.* devoir *m.;* *(customs)* droit *m.;* *(task)* tâche *f.,* fonction(s) *f.(pl.);* *be on* ~ être de service.

duty-free, *adj.* exempt de droits, en franchise.

dwarf, *s.* nain, -e *m. f.*

dwell, *v.n.* habiter; ~ *(up)on* s'appesantir sur.

dwelling, *s.* habitation *f.*

dwelling-house · s. maison
f. d'habitation.

dwindle, v.n. diminuer.

dye, s. teinte f., teinture
f.; — v.a. teindre.

dynasty, s. dynastie f.

E

each, pron. chacun, -e;
~ other l'un l'autre; —
adj. chaque.

eager, adj. ardent.

eagle, s. aigle m.

ear, s. oreille f.

earl, s. comte m.

early, adv. de bonne heure
— adj. précoce; pre-
mier.

earn, v. a. gagner; mériter

earnest, adj. sérieux.

earnings, s.pl. salaire m.

earth, s. terre f.

earthenware, s. poterie
f.

earthquake, s. tremble-
ment m. de terre.

ease, s. aise f.; repos m.;
at one's ~ à son aise;
with ~ avec facilité.

east, s. est m.; — adj.
d'est, de l'est; — adv.
à l'est (de).

Easter, s. Pâques m. pl.

eastern, adj. (de l')est,
oriental.

eastwards, adv. vers l'est.

easy, adj. facile.

easy-chair, s. fauteuil m.

easy-going, adj. non-
chalant.

eat, v.a. manger; ~ up
finir; dévorer.

ebb, s. reflux m.

ecclesiastic, adj. & s.
ecclésiastique (m.).

economic, adj. écono-
mique.

economical, adj. éco-
nome

economics, s. économie f.
politique.

economize, v.n. faire des
économes.

economy, s. économie f.

ecstasy, s. extase f.

edge, s. tranchant m.,
fil m.; bord m.

edition, s. édition f.

editor, s. rédacteur m.

editorial, s. article m. de
fond.

educate, v.a. élever.

education, s. éducation
f.

effect, s. effet m.

effective, adj. efficace;
effectif.

efficiency, s. efficacité f

efficient, adj. capable.

effort, s. effort m.

egg, s. œuf m.; boiled ~
œuf à la coque; fried ~
œuf sur le plat.

Egyptian, adj. égyptien;
— s. Egyptien, -enne
m. f.

eight, adj. & s. huit.

eighteen, adj. & s. dix-
huit.

eighteenth, adj. dix-hui-
tième.

eighth, adj. huitième.

eighty, adj.&s. quatre-
vingt(s).

either, pron. & adj. l'un
ou l'autre; chacun;
chaque; ~ ... or ou
... ou.

elaborate, v.a. élaborer;
— adj. minutieux.

elastic, adj. élastique.

elbow, s. coude m.

elderly, adj. d'un certain
âge.

elect, v.a. choisir; élire.

election, s. élection f.

electric(al), adj. électrique; ~al engineer
(ingénieur) électricien
m.

electricity, *s.* électricité *f.*
electron, *s.* électron *m.*
electronic, *adj.* électronique.
elegance, *s.* élégance *f.*
elegant, *adj.* élégant.
element, *s.* élément *m.*
elementary, *adj.* élémentaire.
elephant, *s.* éléphant *m.*
elevate, *v.a.* élever.
eleven, *adj. & s.* onze.
eleventh, *adj.* onzième.
elm, *s.* orme *m.*
else, *adj.* autre; *anything ~, madam?* encore quelque chose, Madame?; — *adv. or ~* ou bien, autrement.
elsewhere, *adv.* ailleurs.
embankment, *s.* remblai *m.*
embark, *v.a.* embarquer; *v.n.* s'embarquer.
embarrass, *v.a.* embarrasser.
embassy, *s.* ambassade *f.*
embrace, *v.a.* embrasser.
embroidery, broderie *f.*
emerge, *v.n.* émerger; apparaitre.
emergency, *s.* circonstance *f.* critique; *in case of ~* en cas d'accident *or* d'urgence; *~ exit* sortie *f.* de secours.
emigrant, *s.* émigrant, -e *m. f.*
emigrate, *v.n.* émigrer.
emigration, *s.* émigration *f.*
eminent, *adj.* éminent.
emit, *v.a.* émettre.
emotion, *s.* émotion *f.*
emphasis, *s.* accent *m.*, force *f.*; *lay ~ on* appuyer sur.
emphasize, *v. a.* appuyer sur.
empire, *s.* empire *m.*
employ, *v.a.* employer.

employee, *s.* employé *m.*
employer, *s.* employeur *m.*
employment, *s.* emploi *m.*
empty, *adj.* vide.
enable, *v. a.* rendre capable.
enclose, *v.a.* entourer (de); joindre (à une lettre).
encounter, *v.a.* affronter; rencontrer.
encourage, *v.a.* encourager.
encouragement, *s.* encouragement *m.*
encyclopaedia, *s.* encyclopédie *f.*
end, *s.* bout *m.;* fin *f.;* — *v.a.&n.* finir; *~ in* finir en.
endeavour, *s.* effort *m.;* — *v. n.* s'efforcer (à *or* de).
ending, *s.* terminaison *f.;* fin *f.*
endless, *adj.* sans fin.
endorse, *v.a.* endosser.
endorsement, *s.* endossement *m.*
endow, *v.a.* doter (de).
endure, *v.a.* supporter, endurer.
enemy, *s.* ennemi. -e *m. f.*
energetic, *adj.* énergique.
energy, *s.* énergie *f.*
enforce, *v.a.* imposer; *(law)* faire exécuter.
engage, *v.a.* engager; fiancer; *be ~d* être occupé; être fiancé(e).
engagement, *s.* engagement *m.;* fiançailles *f. pl.*
engine, *s.* machine *f.*
engine-driver, *s.* mécanicien *m.*
engineer, *s.* ingénieur *m.*
English, *adj.* anglais.
Englishman, *s.* Anglais *m.*

Englishwomen, s. Anglaise f.

enjoy, v. a. jouir de; trouver bon; ~ oneself s'amuser.

enjoyment, s. jouissance f.

enlarge, v.a. agrandir.

enlist, v.a. enrôler.

enormous, adj. énorme.

enough, adj. & adv. assez (de).

enquire see **inquire.**

enrage, v.a. exaspérer.

enrol(l), v.a. enrôler.

ensign, s. (flag) drapeau m., pavillon m.; (pers.) porte-drapeau m.

ensue, v.n. s'ensuivre.

enter, v.a. entrer (dans); (in list) inscrire.

enterprise, s. entreprise f.

entertain, v.a. amuser; recevoir; avoir (une opinion).

entertainment, s. divertissement m.; amusement m.; hospitalité f.

enthusiasm, s. enthousiasme. m.

enthusiastic, adj. enthousiaste.

entire, adj. entier.

entirely, adv. entièrement.

entitle, v.a. be ~d to avoir droit à.

entrance, s. entrée f.; ~ examination examen d'entrée. m.

entreat, v.a. supplier.

entry, s. entrée f.; inscription f.

enumerate, v.a. énumérer.

envelope, s. enveloppe f.

envious, adj. envieux (de).

enviromment, s. milieu m.

envy, s. envie f.; − v.a. envier.

epidemic, s. épidémie f.

equal, adj. égal.

equality, s. égalité f.

equation, s. équation f.

equip, v.a. équiper.

equipment, s. équipement m.

erase v.a. effacer.

erect, adj. droit ; − v.a. dresser; ériger.

err, v.n. errer.

error, s. erreur f.

escalator, s. escalator m., escalier m. roulant.

escape, v. n. (s')échapper; − s. fuite f.

escort, s. escorte f.; − v.a. escorter.

essay, s. essai m., composition f.

essential, adj. essentiel.

establish, v.a. établir.

establishment, s. établissement m.

estate, s. propriété f.; biens m. pl.

esteem, s. estime f.; − v.a. estimer.

estimate, s. estimation f.; évaulation f.; − v.a. estimer.

eternal, adj. éternel.

eucharist, s. eucharistie f.

European, adj. européen.

evacuate, v.a. évacuer.

even, adj. uni; égal; pair; − adv. même; ~ if même si.

evening, s. soir m.; (party) soirée f.

event, s. événement m.

eventual, adj. éventuel.

ever, adv. toujours; (any time) jamais.

evermore, adv. toujours.

every, adj. (all) tous; (each) chaque; ~ day tous les jours.

everybody, pron. tout le monde.

everyday, adj. de tous les jours.

everyone see **everybody.**

everything, pron. tout m.

everywhere, *adv*. partout.

evidence, *s*. évidence *f*.

evident, *adj*. évident.

evil, *s*. mal *m*.; — *adj*. mauvais.

evolution, *s*. évolution *f*.

ewe, brebis *f*.

exact, *adj*. exact.

exactly, *adv*. exactement.

exaggerate, *v.a*. exagérer.

exaggeration, *s*. exagération *f*.

examination, *s*. examen *m*.

examine, *v.a*. examiner; vérifier; *(customs)* visiter.

example, *s*. example *m*.; for ~ par exemple.

excavation, *s*. fouille *f*.

exceedingly, *adv*. excessivement.

excel, *v. a*. surpasser; *v. n*. exceller à.

excellent, *adj*. excellent.

except, *v.a*. excepter; — *prep*. excepté; sauf; ~ *for* exception faite pour.

exception, *s*. exception *f*.

exceptional, *adj*. exceptionnel.

excess, *s*. excès *m*.; ~ *luggage* excédent *m*. de bagages.

excessive, *adj*. excessif.

exchange, *s*. échange *m*.; *(telephone)* bureau central *m*.; *foreign* ~ *change m*.; — *v.a*. échanger.

excite, *v.a*. exciter.

excitement, *s*. excitation *f*.

exclaim, *v.n*. s'écrier.

exclamation, *s*. exclamation *f*.

exclude, *v.a*. exclure.

exclusive, *adj*. exclusif.

excursion, *s*. excursion *f*.

excuse, *s*. excuse *f*.; — *v.a*. excuser.

execute, *v.a*. exécuter.

execution, *s*. exécution *f*.

executive, *adj*. & *s*. exécutif *m*.; agent *m*. d'exécution

exempt, *adj*. exempt (de); *v.a*. exempter (de).

exercise, *s*. exercice *m*.; — *v.a*. exercer.

exertion, *s*. effort *m*.

exhaust, *v.a*. épuiser.

exhaust-pipe, *s*. tuyau *m*. d'échappement.

exhibit, *v. a*. présenter, exhiber; exposer.

exhibition, *s*. exhibition *f*.; exposition *f*.

exist, *v.n*. exister.

existence, *s*. existence *f*.

exit, *s*. sortie *f*.

expand, *v.a*. étendre; dilater.

expansion, *s*. expansion *f*.

expect, *v.a*. attendre, s'attendre à; *(think)* croire.

expedient, *s*. expédient *m*.

expedition, *s*. expédition *f*.

expel, *v.a*. expulser.

expense, *s*. dépense *f*.

expensive, *adj*. coûteux, cher.

experience, *s*. expérience *f*.; — *v.a*. éprouver.

experiment, *s*. expérience *f*.; — *v.n*. faire des expériences, expérimenter.

experimental, *adj*. expérimental.

expert, *s*. expert *m*.

expire, *v.n*. expirer.

explain, *v.a*. expliquer.

explanation, *s*. explication *f*.

exploration, *s*. exploration.

explore, *v.a*. explorer.

explosion, *s*. explosion *f*.

export, *s*. exportation *f*.; ~*s* articles *m.pl*. d'exportation; — *v.a.* exporter.

exporter, *s.* exportateur *m.*

expose, *v.a.* exposer.

exposure, *s.* exposition *f.;* révélation *f.*

express, *adj.* exprès; formel; exact; ~ *letter* lettre *f.* par exprès; — *s. (train)* express *m.;* — *v.a.* exprimer.

expression, *s.* expression *f.*

exquisite, *adj.* exquis.

extend, *v.a.* étendre; prolonger.

extension, *s.* extension *f.;* prolongation *f.*

extensive, *adj.* étendu, vaste.

extent, *s.* étendue *f.*

extinguish, *v.a.* éteindre.

extra, *adj.* supplémentaire.

extract, *s.* extrait *m.;* — *v.a.* extraire.

extraordinary, *adj.* extraordinaire.

extravagant, *adj.* extravagant.

extreme, *adj. & s.* extrême *(m.).*

extremely, *adv.* extrêmement.

extremity, *s.* extrémité *f.*

eye, *s.* œil *m.*

eyebrow, *s.* sourcil *m.*

eyelid, *s.* paupière *f.*

eyepiece, *s.* oculaire *m.*

F

fable, *s.* fable *f.*

fabric, *s.* tissu *m.;* textile *m.*

face, *s.* visage *m.;* face *f.;* figure *f.; in* ~ *of* devant; — *v.a.* affronter, faire face à, braver.

facility, *s.* facilité *f.*

fact, *s.* fait *m.; in* ~ de fait; en effet.

factor, *s.* facteur *m.;* élément *m.*

factory, *s.* fabrique *f.;* usine *f.*

faculty, *s.* faculté *f.*

fade, *v.n.* se faner; ~ *away* s'évanouir.

fail, *v.n.* manquer (de); *(not succeed)* échouer, *(in an exam)* être refusé.

failure, *s.* insuccès *m.*

faint, *v.n.* s'évanouir.

fair, *adj.* beau; bel, belle; *(hair)* blond; *(just)* juste; *(weather)* clair; ~ *play* jeu loyal *m.*

fairly, *adv.* assez bien.

faith, *s.* foi *f.*

faithful, *adj.* fidèle.

falcon, *s.* faucon *m.*

fall, *v.n.* tomber; baisser; ~ *back on* avoir recours à; ~ *in* s'effondrer; ~ *off* se déprécier; ~ *under* être compris dans; — *s.* chute *f.;* baisse *f.*

false, *adj.* faux; artificiel.

falter, *v.n.* hésiter.

fame, *s.* réputation *f.;* renommée *f.*

familiar, *adj.* familier, intime (avec).

family, *s.* famille *f.*

famous, *adj.* célèbre, fameux.

fan¹, *s.* éventail *m.;* ventilateur *m.*

fan², *s.* passionné, -e *m. f.,* fervent *m.*

fancy, *s.* fantaisie *f.,* imagination *f.*

fantastic, *adj.* fantastique; fantasque.

far, *adv.* loin; ~ *off* au loin; *as* ~ *as* autant que; *by* ~ de beaucoup; *how* ~ *is it?* à

quelle distance est-ce?;
— *adj.* lointain.
fare, *s.* prix de (la) place
m.; (taxi) prix de la
course *m.; (food)* chère *f.*
farewell, *s.* adieu *m.; bid*
~ *to* dire adieu à.
farm, *s.* ferme *f.*
farmer, *s.* fermier *m.*
farming, *s.* agriculture *f.*
farmyard, *s.* cour *f.* de
ferme.
farther, *adv.* plus loin
(que).
fashion, *s.* mode *f.;*
manière *f.*
fashionable, *adj.* élégant.
fast, *adj.* vite, rapide;
be ~ *(clock)* avancer;
— *adv.* vite.

fasten, *v.a.* attacher.
fastener, *s.* attache *f.;*
agrafe *f.; zip* ~ ferme-
ture éclair *f.*
fat, *adj.* gros, gras; — *s.*
gras *m.;* graisse *f.*
fatal, *adj.* fatal.
fate, *s.* destin *m.,* sort *m.*
father, *s.* père *m.*
father-in-law, *s.* beau-
père *m.*
fatigue, *s.* fatigue *f.*
fault, *s.* défaut *m.;* faute
f.
faultless, *adj.* sans faute.
faulty, *adj.* défectueux.
favour, *s.* faveur *f.; in* ~
of en faveur de; *do a* ~
rendre un service (à).
favourable, *adj.* favorable.
favourite, *adj.* favori.
fear, *s.* crainte *f.;* —
v.a.& n. craindre.
fearful, *adj.* affreux,
effrayant.
feast, *s.* fête *f.;* festin *m.*
feat, *s.* exploit *m.*
feather, *s.* plume *f.*
feature, *s.* trait *m.;* caractéristique *f.;* ~ *film* le

grand film.
February, *s.* février *m.*
federal, *adj.* fédéral.
federation, *s.* fédération *f.*
fee, *s.* honoraires *m. pl.;*
(school) ~*s* frais *m. pl.*
feeble, *adj.* faible.
feed, *v. a.* nourrir; paître.
feel, *v.n.&a.* (se) sentir;
éprouver, ressentir,
(with hand) toucher;
tâter; ~ *cold* avoir
froid.
feeling, *s.* sentiment *m.*
fellow, *s.* camarade *m.;*
compagnon *m.;* gar-
çon *m.; (of a society)*
membre *m., (univer-
sity)* agrégé *m.* ·
fellowship, *s.* camaraderie
f.; communauté *f.*
female, *adj.* féminin;
(animal) femelle; — *s.*
femme *f.;* femelle *f.*
feminine, *adj.* féminin.
fence, *s.* clôture *f.;* pa-
lissade *f.;* — *v.a.*
enclore; *v. n.* faire de
l'escrime.
fencing, *s.* escrime *f.*
fender, *s.* pare-choc(s) *m.*
ferry, *s.* (passage *m.* en)
bac *m.*
ferry-boat, *s.* bac *m.*
fertile, *adj.* fertile.
fertilize, *v.a.* fertiliser.
festival, *s.* festival *m.*
fetch, *v.a.* aller chercher;
apporter.
feudal, *adj.* féodal.
fever, *s.* fièvre *f.*
few, *pron. & adj.* peu
(de); *a* ~ quelques-
(-uns).
fiancé, -e, *s.* fiancé, -e
m. f.
fibre, *s.* fibre *f.*
fiction, *s.* fiction *f.;*
(novels) romans *m. pl.*
field, *s.* champ *m.;*
(sport) terrain *m.*
fierce, *adj.* cruel, violent,

féroce.

fiery, *adj.* de feu; ardent.

fifteen, *adj. & s.* quinze *(m.).*

fifteenth, *adj.* quinzième.

fifth, *adj.* cinquième; cinq.

fiftieth, *adj.* cinquantième.

fifty, *adj. & s.* cinquante *(m.).*

fig, *s.* figue *f.*

fight, *s.* combat *m.; lutte f.*

fighter, *s.* combattant *m.;* avion *m.* de chasse.

figure, *s.* figure *f.; (arithm.)* chiffre *m.*

file[1], *s. (tool)* lime *f.; — .a.* limer.

file[2], *s.* classeur *m.,* dossier *m.;* liasse *f.; (people)* file *f.; — v.a.* classer; enregistrer.

filing-cabinet, *s.* cartonnier *m.,* fichier *m.*

fill, *v.a.* remplir; occuper; ~ *in,* up remplir.

film, *s. (photo)* pellicule *f.; (cinema)* film *m.*

filter, *s.* filtre *m.; — v.a.* filtrer.

filthy, *adj.* sale; *(fig.)* obscène.

fin, *s.* nageoire *f.*

final, *adj.* final.

finally, *adv.* enfin.

finance, *s.* finance *f.*

financial, *adj.* financier.

find, *v.a.* trouver; ~ *out* inventer, découvrir.

fine[1], *s. (penalty)* amende *f.; — v.a.* mettre à l'amende.

fine[2], *adj.* fin; beau.

finger, *s.* doigt *m.; first ~* index *m.*

finger-print, *s.* empreinte *f.* digitale.

finish, *v. a.* finir; terminer.

Finnish, *adj.* finlandais.

fir, *s.* sapin *m.*

fire, *s.* feu *m.; on ~* en feu; — *v.a.* mettre feu à; *(gun)* tirer; *v.n.* tirer.

fire-arm, *s.* arme *f.* à feu.

fire-brigade, *s.* les pompiers *m. pl.*

fire-engine, *s.* pompe *f.* à incendie.

fire-escape, *s.* escalier *m.* de sauvetage.

fireplace, *s.* cheminée *f.*

fire-station, *s.* poste *m.* d'incendie.

fireworks, *s.pl.* feu *m.* d'artifice.

firm[1], *s.* maison *f.* (de commerce).

firm[2], *adj.* ferme.

firmament, *s.* firmament *m.*

firmness, *s.* fermeté *f.*

first, *adj.* premier; — *adv.* premièrement; d'abord; *(railway)* en première; *at ~* d'abord.

firstly, *adv.* premièrement.

first-rate, *adj.* de premier ordre.

fish, *s.* poisson *m.; — v. a. & n.* pêcher.

fisher(man), *s.* pêcheur *m.*

fishmonger, *s.* poissonnier *m.*

fist, *s.* poing *m.*

fit[1], *s.* attaque *f.;* accès *m.*

fit[2], *adj.* convenable, bon, propre; en état (de), capable (de).

five, *adj. & s.* cinq *(m.).*

fix, *v.a.* fixer; ~ *up* arranger.

flag, *s.* drapeau *m.; (navy)* pavillon *m.*

flagrant, *adj.* flagrant.

flake, *s.* flocon *m.*

flame, *s.* flamme *f.*
flannel, *s.* flanelle *f.*
flap, *s.* coup *m.*, tape *f.*
flare, *v.n.* flamboyer.
flash, *s.* éclair *m.;* —
v.n. jeter des éclairs, étinceler.
flashlight, *s.* flash (électronique) *m.*
flat[1], *adj.* plat; insipide; *(postitive)* formel, net; — *s.* plat *m.; (music)* bémol *m.*
flat[2], *s.* appartement *m.;* étage *m.*
flatter, *v.a.* flatter.
flattery, *s.* flatterie *f.*
flavour, *s.* saveur *f.*, goût *m.*, arome *m.*
flax, *s.* lin *m.*
flea, *s.* puce *f.*
flee, *v.a.* & *n.* fuir, se sauver.
fleece, *s.* toison *f.*
fleet, *s.* flotte *f.*
flesh, *s.* chair *f.;* viande *f.*
flexible, *adj.* flexible.
flight, *s.* vol *m. (birds, stairs)* volée *f.; (fleeing)* fuite *f.*
flimsy, *adj.* ténu; fragile; frivole.
fling, *v.a.* jeter.
flirt, *s.* coquette *f.;* — *v.n.* flirter.
float, *v.n.* flotter; *v.a.* faire flotter.
flock, *s.* troupeau *m.*, troupe *f.*
flood, *s.* inondation *f.; (tide)* flux *m.;* — *v.a.* inonder.
flood-light, *v.a.* illuminer par projecteurs.
floor, *s.* plancher *m.*, parquet *m.; (storey)* étage *m.*
flour, *s.* farine *f.*
flourish, *v.n.* fleurir; prospérer.
flow, *v.n.* couler, s'écouler; — *s.* flux *m.;* cours *m.*
flower, *s.* fleur *f.*
flower-bed, *s.* plate-bande *f.*
flu, *s.* grippe *f.*
flue, *s.* tuyau *m.*
fluent, *adj.* facile, coulant.
fluid, *adj.* & *s.* fluide *(m.).*
fluorescent, *adj.* ~ *lamp tube m.* fluorescent.
flush, *v.a.* inonder; nettoyer avec une chasse d'eau; *v. n.* rougir.
flute, *s.* flûte *f.*
flutter, *s.* voltigement *m.;* — *v. a.* agiter; *v. n.* voltiger.
fly[1], *s.* mouche *f.*
fly[2], *v.n.* voler; prendre l'avion (pour).
foam, *s.* écume *f.; (beer)* mousse *f.*
focus, *s.* foyer *m.*
fodder, *s.* fourrage *m.*
fog, *s.* brouillard *m.*
foil[1], *s.* feuille *f.;* tain *m.*
foil[2], *s. (fencing)* fleuret *m.*
fold, *s.* pli *m.;* — *v.a.* plier; envelopper; *(arms)* croiser; ~ *up* replier.
folding, *adj.* pliant.
foliage, *s.* feuillage *m.*
folk, *s.* gens *m. pl.*
follow, *v.a.* suivre; accompagner; *v.n.* suivre; s'ensuivre; *as* ~*s* comme suit.
follower, *s.* suivant *m.*, compagnon *m.*, partisan *m.*
following, *adj.* suivant; *the* ~ ce qui suit.
folly, *s.* sottise *f.*
fond, *adj. be* ~ *of* aimer.
food, *s.* nourriture *f.*, aliments *m. pl.*
fool, *s.* sot *m.*
foolish, *adj.* sot; fou.

foot, *s.* pied *m.; on* ~ à pied.

football, *s.* football *m.;* ballon *m.*

foot-brake, *s.* frein *m.* à pied

foot-note, *s.* note *f.* (au bas de la page).

footstep, *s.* pas *m.*

for¹, *prep.* pour; *(in exchange for)* contre; *(because of)* à cause de; *(time)* pendant; *(in spite of)* malgré.

for², *conj.* car.

forbid, *v.a.* défendre; interdire.

force, *s.* force *f.;* violence *f.;* — *v.a.* forcer.

forearm, *s.* avant-bras *m.*

forecast, *s.* prévision *f.;* — *v.a.* prévoir.

forefinger, *s.* index *m.*

foreground, *s.* premier plan *m.*

forehead, *s.* front *m.*

foreign, *adj.* étranger.

foreigner, *s.* étranger, -ère *m. f.*

foremost, *adj.* premier; — *adv. first and* ~ tout d'abord.

foresee, *v.a.* prévoir.

forest, *s.* forêt *f.*

foretell, *v.a.* prédire.

foreword, *s.* avant-propos *m.*

orge, *v.a.* forger.

forgery, *s.* contrefaçon *f.;* faux *m.*

forget, *v.a.* oublier.

forgetful, *adj.* oublieux.

forgive, *v.a.* pardonner.

fork, *s.* fourchette *f.;* *(hay)* fourche *f.*

form, *s.* forme *f.;* *(bench)* banc *m.;* *(class)* classe *f.;* *(paper)* formule *f.;* ~ *of government* régime *m.;* — *v.a.* former.

formal, *adj.* formel.

formality, *s.* formalité *f.*

former, *pron.* le premier, la première; celui-là, celle-là; — *adj.* premier, -ère; précédent.

formerly, *adv.* autrefois.

formula, *s.* formule *f.*

forsake, *v. a.* abandonner.

fortieth, *adj.* quarantième.

fortification, *s.* fortification *f.*

fortify, *v.a.* fortifier.

fortnight, *s.* quinze jours *m. pl.*

fortress, *s.* forte sse *f.*

fortunate, *adj.* ureux.

fortunately *ad* heureusement

fortune, *s.* fortune *f*

forty, *adj. & s.* quarante *(m.).*

forward, *adv.* en avant; *go* ~ (s')avancer; — *adj.* avancé; — *v.a.* faire suivre; expédier.

forwarding, *s.* expédition *f.;* ~ *agency* entreprise *f.* de transport.

forwards, *adv.* en avant.

foul, *adj.* sale; impure; *(language)* ordurier.

found, *v. a.* fonder.

foundation, *s.* fondation *f.*

founder, *s.* fondateur *m.*

fountain, *s.* fontaine *f.*

fountain-pen, *s.* stylo- (graphe) *m.*

four, *adj. & s.* quatre *(m.).*

fourteen, *adj. & s.* quatorze *(m.).*

fourth, *adj.* quatrième; quatre.

fowl, *s.* poule *f.*

fox, *s.* renard *m.*

fraction, *s.* fraction *f.*

fracture, *s.* fracture *f.*

fragile, *adj.* fragile.

fragment, *s.* fragment *m.*

fragrant, *adj.* parfumé.

frame, s. (picture) cadre m.; (structure) charpente f.; (window) châssis m.

framework, s. charpente f.

frank, adj. franc.

frankness, s. franchise f.

fraud, s. fraude f.

free, adj. libre; ~ of, from exempt de.

freedom, s. liberté f.

freely, adv. librement; gratis.

freeze, v.a. geler.

freight, s. fret m.

French, adj. français; — s. (language) le français; the ~ les Français m. pl.

French-bean(s), s. (pl.) haricots m.pl. verts.

Frenchman, s. Français m.

Frenchwoman, s. Française f.

frequent, adj. fréquent; — v. a. fréquenter.

frequently, adv. fréquemment.

fresh, adj. frais, fraîche; nouveau, nouvel, -elle.

friar, s. moine m.

fricassee, s. fricassée f.

friction, s. friction f.

Friday, s. vendredi m.

fridge, s. frigo m.

friend, s. ami, -e m. f.

friendly, adj. aimable; ami; amical.

friendship, s. amitié f.

fright, s. peur f.; take ~ prendre peur.

frighten, v.a. effrayer.

frightful, adj. affreux; effrayant.

frock, s. robe f.

frog, s. grenouille f.

frolic, s. ébats m. pl.; — v.n. folâtrer, gambader.

from, prep. (place) de; (time) depuis; (separation) de, à; (change) de.

front, s. front m.; devant m.; façade f.; in ~ of en face de, en avant de; — adj. de devant.

front-door, s. porte f. d'entrée.

frontier, s. frontière f.

frost, s. gelée f.

frosty, adj. de gelée; fig. froid.

frown, v.a. & n. froncer les sourcils.

frozen, adj. gelé.

fruit, s. fruit m.

fruitful, adj. fructueux.

fruit-tree, s. arbre fruitier m.

frustrate, v.a. déjouer; décevoir; contrecarres.

fry, v. a. & n. (faire) frire.

frying-pan, s. poêle (à frire) f.

fuel, s. combustible m.

fulfil, v.a. accomplir.

full, adj. plein; complet; ~ name les nom et prénoms m. pl.; ~ stop point m.

full-time, adj. de toute la journée.

fully, adv. pleinement.

fume, s. fumée f.

fun, s. amusement m.; for ~ pour rire.

function, s. fonction f.

fund, s. fonds m.

fundamental, adj. fondamental.

funeral, s. funérailles f. pl.

funnel, s. entonnoir m.; (steamer) cheminée f.

funny, adj. drôle.

fur, s. fourrure f.

fur-coat, s. manteau m. de fourrure.

furious, adj. furieux.

furnace, s. fourneau m.

furnish, v. a. pourvoir (de), fournir; meubler (de).

furniture, s. meubles m. pl., ameublement m.;

piece of ~ meuble m.
furrier, s. fourreur m.
furrow, s. sillon m.
further, adv. plus loin;
(any longer) davanta-
ge; — adj. ultérieur;
autre; plus lointain;
supplémentaire, nou-
veau.
furthermore, adv. en
outre, de plus.
fury, s. fureur f.; (pers.)
furie f.
fuss, s. embarras m.;
bruit m.; make a ~
faire des embarras; —
v. n. faire des embarras;
~ about faire l'affairé.
future, s. avenir m.;
(gramm.) futur m.; in
the ~ à l'avenir; — adj.
futur.

G

gain, s. gain m.; — v.a.
gagner.
gait, s. allure f,
gala, s. gala m.
gale, s. grand vent m.
gall, s. bile f.; fiel m;
amertume f.
gallant, adj. brave;galant.
gallery, s. galerie f.
gallon, s. gallon m.
gallop, s. galop m.; —
v.n. galoper.
gamble, v. n. jouer; — s.
jeu m.
game, s. jeu m.; partie f.;
(animal) gibier m.
gamekeeper, s. garde-
chasse m.
gang, s. bande f.;équipe f.
gangway, s. passage m.
gaol see jail.
gap, s. trou m.; brèche f.;
vide m.
gape, v.n. bâiller; stand
gaping gober des mou-
ches; ~ at regarder
bouche bée.
garage, s. garage m.

garden, s. jardin m.
gardener, s. jardinier m.
garlic, s. ail m.
garment, s. vêtement m.
garnish, s. garniture f.; —
v.a. garnir.
garter, s. jarretière f.
gas, s. gaz m.
gasp, s. soupir m.
gas-works, s. pl. usine f.
à gaz.
gate, s. porte f.
gateway, s. portail m.
gather, v.a. réunir; amasser; cueillir; (under-
stand) conclure; v.n.
s'assembler.
gathering, s. rassemble-
ment m.; abcès m.
gauge, s. jauge f.; calibre
m.; indicateur m.; —
v.a. jauger; calibrer.
gauze, s. gaze f.
gay, adj. gai.
gear, s. attirail m., appareil m.; (motorcar)
vitesse f.
gear-box, s. boîte f. des
vitesses.
gear-lever, s. levier m. des
vitesses.
general, adj. général; — s.
général m. (pl. géné-
raux).
generation, s. génération f.
generator, s. générateur
m.
generosity, s. générosité f.
generous, adj. généreux.
genial, adj. doux, douce;
bienfaisant.
genius s. génie m.
gentle, adj. doux, douce.
gentleman, s. gentleman
m.
genuine, adj. authentique; vrai.
geographical, adj. géographique.
geography, s. géographie f
geology, s. géologie f.
geometric(al), adj. géomé-

trique.

geometry, s. géométrie *f.*

germ, s. germe *m.*

German, *adj.* allemand; — —s. Allemand, -e *m.f.*

gesticulate, *v.n.* gesticuler.

gesture, s. geste *m.*

get, *v.a.* obtenir, procurer, trouver, recevoir; — *v.n.* arriver; *(become)* devenir; ~ *at* parvenir (à); ~ *in* entrer; ~ *off* partir; ~ *on* prospérer; *(agree)* s'accorder (avec); ~ *out of* sortir (de); ~ *over* surmonter; *(illness)* se remettre; ~ *up* se lever.

geyser, s. chauffe-bain *m.*

ghost, s. esprit *m.*; revenant *m.*, fantôme *m.*

giant, s. géant *m.*

gift, s. don *m.*

gifted, *adj.* bien doué.

gills, s. *pl.* ouïes *f.*

gin, s. genièvre *m.*; gin *m.*

giraffe, s. girafe *f.*

girdle, s. ceinture *f.*; — *v.a.* ceinturer.

girl, s. jeune fille *f.*

give, *v. a.* donner; ~ *up* renoncer à; livrer; *v.n.* ~ *in* céder (à).

glacier, s. glacier *m.*

glad, *adj.* heureux; content; joyeux.

gladness, s. joie *f.*

glance, s. coup *m.* d'œil,; — *v. n.* ~ *at* jeter un regard sur.

glare, s. lumière *f.* éblouissante; clinquant *m.*; — *v.n.* briller d'un éclat éblouissant.

glass, s. verre *m.*; *(pane)* vitre *f.*; ~es lunettes *f. pl.*

glazier, s. vitrier *m.*

gleam, s. lueur *f.*; — *v. n.* luire.

glide, *v. n.* glisser; planer.

glider, s. planeur *m.*

glimmer, s. lueur *f.*; — *v.n.* jeter une lueur faible.

glimpse, s. coup *m.* d'œil (rapide).

glitter, *v.n.* étinceler.

globe, s. globe *m.*

gloomy, *adj.* sombre.

glorious, *adj.* glorieux.

glory, s. gloire *f.*

glove, s. gant *m.*

glow, *v.n.* luire rouge; *(joy)* rayonner; *(coal)* être rouge; — s. chaleur *f.*; lumière *f.*; *fig.* ardeur *f.*

glue, s. colle (forte) *f.*; — *v.a.* coller.

gnat, s. cousin *m.*; moustique *f.*

gnaw, *v.a.* & *n.* ronger.

go, *v. n.* aller; ~ *away* s'en aller; ~ *back* retourner; ~ *back on one's word* reprendre sa parole; ~ *down* descendre; baisser; ~ *in for* s'occuper de, s'adonner à, faire (de); ~ *into* entrer dans; ~ *off* s'en aller; ~ *on* continuer; *(happen)* se passer; ~ *out* sortir; ~ *over, through* traverser; *(read)* parcourir; ~*up* monter; ~ *with* accompagner; ~ *without* se passer de; *let* ~ lâcher prise.

goal, s. but *m.*

goalkeeper, s. gardien (de but) *m.*

goat, s. bouc *f.*, chèvre *f.*

God, s. Dieu *m.*

god-child, s. filleul, -e *m. f.*

godfather, s. parrain *m.*

godmother, s. marraine *f.*

goggles, s. *pl.* bésicles *f.*

gold, *s.* or *m.*

golden, *adj.* d'or, en or.

golf, *s.* golf *m.*

good, *adj.* bon; ~ *evening!* bonsoir!; ~ *morning!* bonjour!; *be so ~ as to* avoir la bonté de; *make ~* remplir; indemniser de; — *s.* bien *m.;* ~*s* marchandise *f.;* ~*s station* gare *f.* de marchandises; ~*s train* train *m.* de marchandises.

good-bye, *int.* & *s.* adieu *(m.).*

good-looking, *adj.* de belle mine, beau.

goodness, *s.* bonté *f.*

good-tempered, *adj.* de caractère facile, de bonne humeur.

goodwill, *s.* bonne volonté *f.*

goose, *s.* oie *f.*

gooseberry, *s.* groseille *f.* à maquereau.

gospel, *s.* évàngile *m.*

gossip, *s.* bavardage *m.;* racontar *m.,* cancan *m.;* (*pers.*) compère *m.;* commère *f.;* — *v.n.* bavarder.

Gothic, *adj.* gothique.

govern, *v.a.* & *n.* gouverner.

governess, *s.* gouvernante *f.*

government, *s.* gouvernement *m.*

governor, *s.* gouverneur *m.*

gown, *s.* robe *f.*

grace, *s.* grâce *f.*

graceful, *adj.* gracieux.

gracious, *adj.* gracieux.

grade, *s.* grade *m.;* classe *f.*

gradual, *adj.* graduel.

graduate, *s.* gradué, -e *m. f.;* — *v.a.* graduer;

v.n. prendre ses diplômes.

grain, *s.* grain *m.*

grammar, *s.* grammaire *f.*

grammar-school, *s.* lycée *m.,* collège *m.*

grammatical, *adj.* grammatical.

gram(me), *s.* gramme *m.*

gramophone, *s.* gramophone *m.,* phonographe *m.*

gramophone-record, *s.* disque *m.*

grand, *adj.* grand; magnifique; ~ *stand* tribune *f.*

grandchild, *s.* petit-fils *m.,* petite-fille *f.* (*pl.* petits-enfants *m.*)

granddaughter, *s.* petite-fille *f.*

grandfather, *s.* grand-père *m.*

grandmother, *s.* grand' mère *f.*

grandson, *s.* petit-fils *m.*

granite, *s.* granit *m.*

granny, *s.* grand'maman *f.*

grant, *v.a.* accorder, concéder; accéder; ~ *that* admettre que; — *s.* don *m.,* concession *f.;* subside *m.*

grape, *s.* grain *m.* de raisin; *bunch of ~s* grappe *f.* de raisin.

grape-fruit, *s.* pamplemousse *f.*

graph, *s.* graphique *m.,* courbe *f.*

graphic, *adj.* graphique.

grasp, *v.a.* saisir; comprendre; — *s.* prise *f.,* étreinte *f.*

grass, *s.* herbe *f.;* gazon *m.*

grasshopper, *s.* sauterelle *f.*

grate, *s.* grille *f.;* — *v.a.*

râper; faire grincer; v.n. grincer.

grateful, adj. reconnaissant (à).

gratitude, s. reconnaissance f.

grave[1], s. tombe f., tombeau m.

grave[2], adj. grave.

gravel, s. gravier m.

gravy, s. jus m.

gray, adj. gris.

graze, v.n. paître.

grease, s. graisse f.; — v.a. graisser.

great, adj. grand; a ~ many beaucoup (de).

greatly, adj. très; beaucoup.

greatness, s. grandeur f.

greed, s. avidité f.

greedy, adj. avide.

Greek, adj. grec, grecque; —s. Grec m., Grecque f.

green, adj. vert.

greengrocer, s. fruitier, -ère m. f.

greenhouse, s. serre f.

greet, v.a. saluer.

greeting, s. salutation f.

grey, adj. gris.

grief, s. chagrin m.

grieve, v.a. affliger; v.n. s'affliger.

grill, s. gril m.; — v.a. griller.

grim, adj. sévère, menaçant. sinistre.

grin, v.n. grimacer; ~ at faire des grimaces à; — s. rire m.; grimace f.

grind, v.a. moudre.

grinder, s. (tooth) molaire f.

grindstone, s. meule f.

grip, s. étreinte f.; prise f.; — v.a. saisir, étreindre.

groan, v. n. gémir; — s. gémissement m.

grocer, s. épicier, -ère m.

f.; ~'s (shop) épicerie f.

grocery, s. épicerie f.

groove, s. rainure f.

gross, adj. gros; grossier; (weight) brut.

ground, s. terre f.; terrain m.; (reason) raison f.; ~s jardins m. pl.; — v.a. fonder.

group, s. groupe m.

grow, v.a. cultiver; v.n. (pers.) grandir; (plant) croître; (become) devenir.

growl, s. grondement m.; — v.n. gronder.

grown-up, s. grande personne f.

growth, s. croissance f.; culture f.; récolte f.

grudge, s. rancune f.; — v.a. donner à contre-cœur à.

grumble, v.n. grommeler; — s. grognement m.

grunt, s. grognement m.; — v.n. grogner.

guarantee, s. garantie f.; (pers.) garant, -e m. f.; — v.a. garantir.

guard, s. garde f.; (train) conducteur m.; — v.a. garder; v.n. ~ against se garder.

guardian, s. gardien, -enne m. f.

guess, v.a. & n. deviner; conjecturer; — s. conjecture f.

guest, s. invité m., convive m.; hôte, -esse m. f.

guide, s. guide m.; — v. a. guider.

guide-book, s. guide m.

guilt, s. culpabilité f.

guilty, adj. coupable (de).

guitar, s. guitare f.

gulf, s. golfe m.

gull, s. mouette f.

gullet, s. gosier m.

gum¹, *s.* gomme *f.*; — *v.a.* gommer.

gum², *s.* *(teeth)* gencive *f.*

gun, *s.* fusil *m.*; canon *m.*

gush, *v.i.* jaillir; — *s.* jaillissement *m.*

gutter, *s.* *(street)* ruisseau *m.*

gymnasium, *s.* gymnase *m.*

gymnastics, *s.* gymnastique *f.*

H

haberdashery, *s.* mercerie *f.*

habit, *s.* habitude *f.*

hail, *s.* grêle *f.*; — *v.n.* grêler.

hair, *s.* *(single)* cheveu *m.*; *(whole)* cheveux *m. pl.*; *(animal)* poil *m.*

hairdresser, *s.* coiffeur, -euse *m. f.*

half, *s.* moitié *f.*; demi *m.*; — *adj.* demi; ~ an hour une demi-heure *f.*

half-time, *s.* mi-temps *m.*

half-way, *adv.* à mi-chemin; à moitié chemin; à mi-distance.

hall, *s.* *(grande)* salle *f.*; *(college)* réfectoire *m.*; *(house)* vestibule *m.*; *(hotel)* hall *m.*

halt, *s.* halte *f.*; *v.a.* faire arrêter; *v.n.* faire halte; boiter.

ham, *s.* jambon *m.*

hammer, *s.* marteau *m.*

hand, *s.* main *f.*; *(pers.)* ouvrier *m.*; *(clock)* aiguille *f.*; on the one ~ ...on the other d'une part ... d'autre part.

handbag, *s.* sac (à main) *m.*

handbook, *s.* manuel *m.*

handkerchief, *s.* mouchoir *m.*

handle, *s.* manche *m.*, anse *f.*; poignée *f.*; bras *m.*; — *v.a.* manier; traiter.

hand-made, *adj.* fait à la main.

handsome, *adj.* joli.

handwriting, *s.* écriture *f.*

handy, *adj.* *(pers.)* adroit; *(thing)* commode.

hang, *v.a.* pendre; *(with tapestry)* tendre; ~ up accrocher; *v. n.* pendre; dépendre (de).

hanger, *s.* crochet *m.*; cintre *m.*

happen, *v.n.* arriver; se trouver; I ~ed to be present je me trouvais là par hasard.

happiness, *s.* bonheur *m.*

happy, *adj.* heureux.

harbour, *s.* port *m.*

hard, *adj.* dur; difficile; sévère; ~ up gêné; — *adv.* durement; work ~ travailler dur.

hardly, *adv.* à peine.

hardware, *s.* quincaillerie *f.*

hare, *s.* lièvre *m.*

harm, *s.* mal *m.*; tort *m.*; do ~ to nuire à.

harmful, *adj.* nuisible.

harmless, *adj.* inoffensif.

harmony, *s.* harmonie *f.*

harness, *s.* harnais *m.*

harp, *s.* harpe *f.*

harsh, *adj.* revêche; âpre; rigoureux.

hart, *s.* cerf *m.*

harvest, *s.* moisson *f.*; *(crop)* récolte *f.*

haste, *s.* hâte *f.*; make ~ se dépêcher.

hasten, *v.a.* hâter; *v. n.* se dépêcher.

hasty, *adj.* précipité.

hat, *s.* chapeau *m.*

hate, *v. a.* haïr; — *s.* haine *f.*

hateful, *adj.* odieux.

hatred, *s.* haine *f.*

haul, *v.a.* traîner; haler; — *s.* traction *f.*

haulage, *s.* roulage *m.*; frais *m.pl.* de roulage.

haunch, *s.* hanche *f.*

haunt, *v.a.* fréquenter; hanter.

have, *v.a.* avoir; *(food)* prendre; ~ *to* il faut que, il faut (+ *inf.*); *had rather* préférer (+ *inf.*); ~ *on (clothes)* porter.

haversack, *s.* havresac *m.*

hawk, *s.* faucon *m.*

hay, *s.* foin *m.*

hazard, *s.* hasard *m.*

hazy, *adj.* brumeux; *(fig.)* vegue.

he, *pron.* il, *(alone)* lui; ~ *who* celui qui

head, *s.* tête *f.; chief)* chef *m.; (river)* source *f.;* — *v.a.* être en tête de; — *adj.* principal.

headache, *s.* mal *m.* de tête.

heading, *s.* en-tête *m.*

headlight, *s.* phare *m.*, projecteur *m.*

headline, *s.* manchette *f.*

headmaster, *s.* directeur *m.*

headquarters, *s. pl.* quartier *m.* général.

heal, *v.a.* guérir; *v.n.* se guérir.

health, *s.* santé *f.*

healthy, *adj.* bien portant; sain.

heap, *s.* amas *m.*, tas *m.;* — *v.a.* ~ *up* entasser.

hear, *v.a.* entendre; *(listen to)* écouter; *v. n.* entendre; ~ *from* recevoir une lettre de; ~ *of* avoir des nouvelles de; entendre parler de.

heart, *s.* cœur *m.; by* ~ par cœur.

hearth, *s.* foyer *m.*

hearty, *adj.* cordial.

heat, *s.* chaleur *f.; (anger)* colère *f.;* — *v.a.&n.* chauffer.

heating, *s.* chauffage *m.*

heave, *v.a.* lever; pousser; jeter; *v.n.* se soulever.

heaven, *s.* ciel *m.*

heavy, *adj.* pesant; lourd.

hedge, *s.* haie *f.*

hedgehog, *s.* hérisson *m.*

heed, *s.* attention *f.; take* ~ *to* faire attention à.

heedless, *adj.* insouciant; inattentif.

heel, *s.* talon *m.*

height, *s.* hauteur *f.*

heir, *s.* héritier *m.*

heiress, *s.* héritière *f.*

helicopter, *s.* hélicoptère *m.*

hell, *s.* enfer *m.*

hello, *int.* allô!

helm, *s.* barre (du gouvernail) *f.*

helmet, *s.* casque *m.*

help, *v.a.* aider; secourir; ~ *oneself* se servir; — *s.* aide *f.*

helpful, *adj. (pers.)* serviable; *(thing)* utile.

helping, *s.* portion *f.*

helpless, *adj.* sans secours.

hem, *s.* ourlet *m.;* bord *m.*

hen, *s.* poule *f.*

hence, *adv. (place, time)* d'ici; *(reason)* de là.

her, *pron. (acc.)* la; *(dat.)* lui; *(alone)* elle.

herb, *s.* herbe *f.*

herd, *s.* troupeau *m.*

here, *adv.* ici; *from* ~ d'ici; *look* ~! dites donc!; ~ *he is!* le voici!

heritage, *s.* héritage *m.*

hermit, *s.* ermite *m.*

hero, *s.* héros *m.*

heroic, *adj.* héroïque.

heroine, *s.* héroïne *f.*

herring, *s.* hareng *m.*

hers, *pron.* à elle; le sien, la sienne, les siens, les siennes.

herself, *pron.* elle-même; *(reflex.)* se.

hesitate, *v.n.* hésiter.

hew, *v.a.* couper.

hiccough, hiccup, *s.* hoquet *m.*

hide, *v.a.* cacher; *v.n.* se cacher.

hideous, *adj.* hideux; horrible.

high, *adj.* haut; *(speed)* grand; *(price)* élevé; — *adv.* haut.

highness, *s.* altesse *f.*

highroad, highway, *s.* grande route *f.*

hike, *v.n.* faire du tourisme à pied.

hiker, *s.* touriste *f.*, randonneur, -euse (à pied) *m. f.*

hill, *s.* colline *f.*

hilly, *adj.* montueux.

him, *pron.* *(acc.)* le; *(dat.)* lui; *(alone)* lui.

himself, *pron.* lui-même; *(reflex.)* se; *by* ~ tout seul.

hinder, *v.a.* empêcher.

hindrance, *s.* empêchement *m.*

hinge, *s.* gond *m.*; charnière *f.*; — *v.n.* tourner (sur).

hint, *s.* allusion *f.*; avis *m.*; — *v.n.* ~ at faire allusion à.

hip, *s.* hanche *f.*

hire, *s.* louage *m.*; *for* ~ à louer; — *v.a. & n.* louer.

his, *pron.* son, sa; ses.

hiss, *s.* sifflement *m.*; — *v. a. & n.* siffler.

historic(al), *adj.* historique.

history, *s.* histoire *f.*

hit, *v.a.* frapper; at-

teindre; trouver; — *s.* coup *m.*; succès *m.*

hitch-hike, *v.n.* faire de l'auto-stop.

hive, *s.* ruche *f.*

hoard, *s.* magot *m.*, amas *m.*; — *v. a.* thésauriser; entasser.

hoarse, *adj.* raque.

hobby, *s.* dada *m.*

hockey, *s.* hockey *m.*

hoe, *s.* houe *f.*

hog, *s.* porc *m.*

hoist, *v.a.* hisser; —*s.* monte-charge *m.*

hold, *v.a.* tenir; retenir; maintenir; contenir; *(consider)* tenir (pour); ~ *back* retenir; ~ *out* tendre; offrir ; ~ *that* soutenir que; — *v.n.* tenir; *(be true)* être vrai; ~ *on* ne pas lâcher prise; ~ *out* durer.

holder, *s.* possesseur *m.*

hole, *s.* trou *m.*

holiday, *s.* fête *f.*, jour *m.* férié; *(holidays)* vacances *f. pl.*, congé *m.*; *be on* être en congé, en vacance(s).

hollow, *adj.* reux, -euse; *fig.* faux, fausse.

holy, *adj.* saint; bénit.

home, *s.* foyer *m.*, demeure *f.*; *at* ~ chez soi, à la maison; — *adv.* chez soi; *come, go* ~ rentrer; — *adj.* domestque; de l'intérieur.

homeless, *adj.* sans asile.

homely, *adj.* simple; modeste.

homesickness, *s.* mal du pays *m.*

homeward, *adv.* vers la maison; ~ *bound* en retour.

honest, *adj.* honnête.

honesty, *s.* honnêteté *f.*

honey, *s.* miel *m.*

honeymoon, *s.* lune *f.* de miel.

honour, *s.* honneur *m.;* — *v.a.* honorer.

hood, *s.* capuchon *m.;* capeline *f.; (motor)* capote *f.*

hoof, *s.* sabot *m.*

hook, *s.* crochet *m.,* croc *m.; (fishing)* hameçon *m.*

hoop, *s.* cercle *m.*

hoot, *v.a.* huer; *v.n.* corner; — *s.* huée *f.*

hooter, *s.* sirène *f.;* corne *f.,* trompe *f.*

hop, *v.n.* sautiller.

hope, *s.* espérance *f.;* espoir *m.;* — *v.n.* espérer.

hopeful, *adj.* plein d'espoir.

hopeless, *adj.* sans espoir

horizon, *s.* horizon *m.*

horizontal, *adj.* horizontal.

horn, *s.* corne *f.;* trompe *f.*

horrible, *adj.* affreux, -euse.

horse, *s.* cheval *m.* (*pl.* chevaux).

horseback: on ∼ à cheval.

horseman, *s.* cavalier *m.*

horse-race, *s.* course *f.* de chevaux.

horseshoe, *s.* fer *m.* à cheval.

hose, *s.* bas *m. pl.*

hospitable, *adj.* hospitalier.

hospital, *s.* hôpital *m.*

hospitality, *s.* hospitalité *f.*

host, *s.* hôte *m.*

hostel, *s.* pension *f.* pour étudiants, hôtellerie *f.*

hostess, *s.* hôtesse *f.*

hostile, *adj.* hostile (à).

hostility, *s.* hostilité *f.*

hot, *adj.* chaud.

hotel, *s.* hôtel *m.*

hour, *s.* heure *f.*

house, *s.* maison *f.; (theatre)* salle *f.*

household, *s.* ménage *m.*

housekeeper, *s.* gouvernante *f.*

housekeeping, *s.* ménage *m.*

housewife, *s.* ménagère *f.*

housework, *s.* travaux (*m. pl.*) domestiques; *do the* ∼ faire le ménage.

how, *adv.* comment; ∼ many, much? combien de?; ∼ long? combien de temps?; ∼ are you? comment allez-vous?

however, *adv.* de quelque manière que...; toutefois, cependant.

howl, *v. a. & n.* hurler; — *s.* hurlement *m.*

hue, *s.* couleur *f.;* cri *m.*

hug, *v.a.* serrer dans les bras.

huge, *adj.* énorme.

hullo, *int.* holà!; allô!

hum, *v. n.* bourdonner; — *s.* bourdonnement *m.*

human, *adj.* humain.

humanity, *s.* humanité *f.*

humble, *adj.* humble.

humorous, *adj.* amusant; humoristique; drôle.

humour, *s.* humour *m.; be in a* ∼ *to* être d'humeur à.

hundred, *s.* cent *m.*

hundredth, *adj.* centième.

hundredweight, *s.* quintal *m.*

Hungarian, *adj.* hongrois; — *s.* Hongrois, -e *m. f.*

hunger, *s.* faim *f.;* — *v.n.* avoir faim.

hungry, *adj.* affamé; *be* ∼ avoir faim.

hunt, *v.a. & n.* chasser; *(with hounds)* chasser à courre; — *s.* chasse (à courre) *f.*

hunter, *s.* chasseur *m.*

hurl, *v.a.* jeter; lancer.

hurry, *s.* hâte; *be in a ~ to* être pressé de; — *v.n.* se presser; *~ up!* pressez-vous!; *v.a.* presser, hâter.

hurt, *v.a.* faire mal à; blesser; *(feelings)* froisser.

husband, *s.* mari *m.*

hush, *int.* chut!; — *s.* calme *m.;* — *v.a.* calmer.

husk, *s.* cosse *f.;* glume *f.;* — *v.a.* écosser, monder.

hut, *s.* cabane *f.*

hydrogen, *s.* hydrogène *m.*

hygiene, *s.* hygiène *f.*

hymn, *s.* hymne *m.*

hyphen, *s.* trait d'union *m.*

hypnotize, *v.a.* hypnotiser.

hypocrisy, *s.* hypocrisie *f.*

hysterical, *adj.* hystérique.

I

I, *pron.* je; moi.

ice, *s.* glace *f.*

ice-cream, *s.* glace *f.*

icy, *adj.* glacial.

idea, *s.* idée *f.*

ideal, *adj. & s.* idéal *(m.).*

identical, *adj.* identique.

identity, *s.* identité *f.;* ~ *card* carte *f.* d'identité.

idle, *adj.* désœuvré; *(lazy)* paresseux; — *v.a.* ~ *away* perdre.

idleness, *s.* oisiveté *f.;* paresse *f.*

if, *conj.* si; *as ~ comme si.*

ignition, *s.* ignition *f.;* *(motor)* allumage *m.*

ignorant, *adj.* ignorant; *be ~ of* ignorer.

ignore, *v.a.* refuser de connaître.

ill, *adj.* malade; *(bad)* mauvais; *be taken ~* tomber malade; *~ luck* malheur *m.;* — *adv.* mal; — *s.* mal *m.*

illegal, *adj.* illégal.

illegitimate, *adj.* illégitime.

illicit, *adj.* illicite.

illness, *s.* maladie *f.*

illusion, *s.* illusion *f.*

illustrate, *v.a.* illustrer.

illustration, *s.* illustration *f.;* exemple *m.*

image, *s.* image *f.*

imagination, *s.* imagination *f.*

imagine, *v.a.* imaginer; se figurer.

imitate, *v.a.* imiter.

immediate, *adj.* immédiat.

immense, *adj.* immense.

immigrant, *adj. & s.* immigrant, -e *(m. f.).*

immigrate, *v.n.* immigrer

immigration, *s.* immigration *f.*

immoral, *adj.* immoral.

immortal, *adj.* immortel.

impatience, *s.* impatience *f.*

impatient, *adj.* impatient.

impediment, *s.* obstacle *m.*

impel, *v.a.* forcer; pousser.

imperfect, *adj. & s.* imparfait *(m.).*

imperial, *adj.* impérial.

impertinent, *adj.* impertinent.

implement, *s.* outil *m.,* ustensile *m.*

implication, *s.* implication *f.*

implore, *v.a.* implorer.

imply, *v.a.* impliquer; donner à entendre.

import, *v.a.* importer; *(mean)* signifier; — *s.* *(usu. pl.)* importation(s) *f.*

importance, *s.* importance *f.*

important, *adj.* important.

importer, *s.* importateur *m.*

impose, *v.a.* imposer (à).

impossibility, *s.* impossibilité *f.*

impossible, *adj.* impossible.

impression, *s.* impression *f.*

imprison, *v.a.* emprisonner.

imprisonment, *s.* emprisonnement.

improbable, *adj.* improbable.

improper, *adj.* impropre; inconvenant.

improve, *v.a.* améliorer; perfectionner; *v.n.* s'améliorer.

improvement, *s.* amélioration *f.;* progrès *m.*

impulse, *s.* impulsion *f.*

in, *prep.* dans; en; à; ~ *the morning* le matin; ~ *the evening* le soir; ~ *time* à temps; ~ *spring* au printemps.

inadequate, *adj.* insuffisant.

incapable, *adj.* incapable (de).

incense, *s.* encens *m.*

inch, *s.* pouce *m.*

incident, *s.* incident *m.*

incidental, *adj.* fortuit; incidental.

incline, *v. a. & n.* incliner.

include, *v.a.* comprendre; renfermer.

inclusive, *adj.* inclusif; ~ *of* y compris.

income, *s.* revenu *m.*

income-tax, *s.* impôt *m.* sur (le) revenu.

incompatible, *adj.* incompatible.

incompetent, *adj.* incom-

pétent.

inconsistent, *adj.* inconséquent.

inconvenient, *adj.* incommode, gênant.

increase, *v.a.&n.* augmenter; — *s.* augmentation *f.*

incredible, *adj.* incroyable.

incur, *v. a.* contracter; encourir; s'attirer.

incurable, *adj.* incurable.

indebted, *adj.* endetté.

indeed, *adv.* de fait; vraiment.

independence, *s.* indépendance *f.*

independent, *adj.* indépendant.

index, *s.* index *m.; (on dial)* aiguille *f.; (math.)* exposant *m.; ~ finger* index *m.*

Indian, *adj.* indien; des Indes; ~ *corn* maïs *m.* — *s.* Indien, -enne *m. f.*

india-rubber, *s.* gomme *f.*

indicate, *v.a.* indiquer.

indicator, *s.* indicateur *m.*

indifference, *s.* indifférence *f.*

indifferent, *adj.* indifférent (à).

indigestion, *s.* indigestion *f.*

indignant, *adj.* indigné.

indirect, *adj.* indirect.

indiscreet, *adj.* indiscret.

indiscretion, *s.* indiscrétion *f.;* imprudence *f.*

indispensable, *adj.* indispensable.

individual, *adj.* individuel; — *s.* individu *m.*

indoor, *adj.* d'intérieur.

indoors, *adv.* à la maison; *stay* ~ ne pas sortir.

induce, *v.a.* persuader; *(cause)* occasionner.

inducement, *s.* ~ encouragement *m.* ~s attraits

m. pl.

indulge, *v. a.* se livrer (à); caresser; *v.n.* ~ *in* s'abandonner à; se laisser aller à.

indulgence, *s.* indulgence *f.;* laisser-aller *m.*

industrial, *adj.* industriel.

industrious, *adj.* travailleur.

industry, *s.* industrie *f.*

inefficient, *adj.* incapable; inefficace.

inestimable, *adj.* inestimable.

inevitable, *adj.* inévitable.

inexpensive, *adj.* peu coûteux, peu cher, bon marché.

inexperienced, *adj.* inexpérimenté.

inexplicable, *adj.* inexplicable.

infallible, *adj.* infaillible.

infamous, *adj.* infâme.

infant, *s.* enfant *m. f.*

infantry, *s.* infanterie *f.*

infant-school, *s.* école *f.* maternelle.

infection, *s.* infection *f.*

infer, *v.a.* conclure, déduire.

inferior, *adj.* inférieur.

infinitive, *s.* infinitif *m.*

infirm, *adj.* infirm.

infirmary, *s.* infirmerie *f.*

inflame, *v.a.* enflammer

inflammable, *adj.* inflammable.

inflate, *v.a.* gonfler.

inflexion, *s.* inflexion *f.*

inflict, *v.a.* infliger; imposer à.

influence, *s.* influence *f.;* — *v.a.* influencer.

influenza, *s.* grippe *f.*

inform, *v.a.* informer.

informal, *adj.* sans cérémonie.

information, *s.* information *f.;* renseignements

m. pl.

ingenious, *adj.* ingénieux.

ingenuity, *s.* ingéniosité *f.*

ingredient, *s.* ingrédient *m.*

inhabit, *v.a.* habiter.

inhabitant, *s.* habitant *m.*

inherit, *v.a. & n.* hériter (de).

inheritance, *s.* héritage *m.*

initial, *s.* initiale *f.*

initiative, *s.* initiative *f.*

injection, *s.* injection *f.*

injure, *v.a.* nuire à; blesser.

injury, *s.* préjudice *m.;* dommage *m.;* blessure *f.*

injustice, *s.* injustice *f.*

ink, *s.* encre *f.*

inland, *s. & adj.* intérieur *(m.).*

inn, *s.* auberge *f.;* taverne *f.*

inner, *adj.* intérieur.

innocence, *s.* innocence *f.*

innocent, *adj.* innocent.

innumerable, *adj.* innombrable.

inoculate, *v.a.* inoculer.

inquire, *v.n.* ~ *about* s'enquérir, se renseigner sur; ~ *after* demander après, demander des nouvelles de.

inquiry, *s.* demande *f.;* recherche *f.; make inquiries about* s'informer de; ~ *office* bureau *m.* des renseignements.

insane, *adj.* fou, fol, folle.

inscription, *s.* inscription *f*

insect, *s.* insecte *m.*

insecure, *adj.* peu sûr, mal assuré.

insensible, *adj.* sans connaissance; insensible.

inseparable, *adj.* inséparable.

insert, *v. a.* insérer (dans).

inside, *s. & adj.* intérieur

(m.); — *adv.* à l'intérieur.

insignificant, *adj.* insignifiant.

insist, *v.n.* insister *(on* sur*).*

insistence, *s.* insistance *f.*

inspect, *v.a.* inspecter.

inspection, *s.* inspection *f.*

inspector, *s.* inspecteur *m.*

inspiration, *s.* inspiration *f.*

inspire, *v.a.* inspirer.

install. *v.a.* installer.

instalment, *s.* fraction *f.,* acompte *m.*

instance, *s.* exemple *m.;* cas *m.; for* ~ par exemple.

instant, *adj.* urgent; — *s.* instant *m.*

instead, *adv.* ~ *of* au lieu de.

instinct, *s.* instinct *m.*

institute, *s.* institut *m.;* — *v.a.* instituer.

institution, *s.* institution *f.*

instruct, *v. a.* instruire.

instruction, *s.* instruction *f.*

instructive, *adj.* instructif.

instrument, *s.* instrument *m.*

instrumental, *adj.* instrumental.

insufficiency, *s.* insuffisance *f.*

insufficient, *adj.* insuffisant.

insult, *s.* insulte *f.;* — *v.a.* insulter.

insurance, *s.* assurance *f.*

insure, *v. a.* (faire) assurer.

integral, *adj.* intégral; — *s.* intégrale *f.*

integrity, *s.* intégrité *f.*

intellectual, *adj.* intéllectuel.

intelligence, *s.* intelligence *f.; (information)* renseignements *m.pl.*

intelligent, *adj.* intelligent.

intend, *v. a.* avoir l'intention de (faire qch.), se proposer de: destiner qn., qch. (à); vouloir dire.

intense, *adj.* intense.

intensity, *s.* intensité *f.*

intent, *s.* intention *f.;* — *adj.* ~ *on* absorbé dans.

intention, *s.* intention *f.*

intercontinental, *adj.* intercontinental.

interest, *s.* intérêt *m.;* — *v.a.* intéresser.

interesting, *adj.* intéressant.

interfere, *v. n.* intervenir; ~ *with* gêner; se mêler de.

interior, *adj. & s.* intérieur *(m.).*

intermediate, *adj.* intermédiaire.

intermission, *s.* interruption *f.,* pause *f.*

internal, *adj.* interne; intérieur.

international, *adj.* international.

interpret, *v.a.* interpréter.

interpretation, *s.* interprétation *f.*

interpreter, *s.* interprète *m.*

interrogation, *s.* interrogation *f.*

interrupt, *v.a.* interrompre.

interruption, *s.* interruption *f.*

interval, *s.* intervalle *m.*

intervention, *s.* intervention *f.*

interview, entrevue *f.;* interview *m. f.*

intimate, *adj.* intime.

into, *prep.* dans; en.

intolerable, *adj.* intolérable.

introduce, *v.a.* introduire; *(pers.)* présenter.

introduct.on, *s.* introduction *f.; (pers.)* présentation *f.*

invade, *v.a.* envahir.

invalid[1], *s.* malade *m. f.*

invalid[2], *adj.* invalide.

invasion, *s.* invasion *f.*

invent, *v.a.* inventer.

invention, *s.* invention *f.*

inverted, *adj.* ~ commas guillemets *m.*

invest, *v.a.* *(money)* placer.

investigate, *v.a.* rechercher.

investigation, *s.* investigation *f.*

investment, *s.* placement *m.*

invisible, *adj.* invisible.

invitation, *s.* invitation *f.*

invite, *v.a.* inviter.

invoice, *s.* facture *f.*

involuntary, *adj.* involontaire.

involve, *v.a.* envelopper (dans); impliquer (dans); entraîner.

inward, *adj.* intérieur; interne.

inwards, *adv.* intérieurement; en dedans.

Irish, *adj.* irlandais

iron, *s.* fer *m.* — *v.a.* repasser.

ironical, *adj.* ironique.

ironware, *s.* quincaillerie *f.*

ironworks, *s.* ferronnerie *f.*

irony, *s.* ironie *f.*

irregular, *adj.* irrégulier.

irrelevant, *adj.* non pertinent; hors de la question; inapplicable (à).

irresolute, *adj.* irrésolu.

irritate, *v.a.* irriter.

island, *s.* île *f.; (street)* refuge *m.*

isle, *s.* île *f.*

isolate, *v.a.* isoler.

isotope, *s.* isotope *m.*

issue, *s. (way out)* sortie *f.; (end)* issue *f.,* fin *f.,* résultat *m.; (publication)* publication *f.,* édition, *(paper)* numéro *m.,* (money) émission *f.;* — *v. a.* émettre; publier.

it, *pron.* il, elle; *(acc.)* le, la; *of it* en; *to* ~ y.

Italien, *adj.* italien; — *s.* Italien, -enne *m.f.*

itch, *s.* démangeaison *f.;* — *v.n.* démanger.

itchy, *adj.* galeux.

item, *s.* article *m.,* détail *m.*

its, *pron.* son, sa, *pl.* ses.

itself, *pron.* lui-même, elle-même; se; *(emphatic)* même.

ivory, *s.* ivoire *m.*

ivy, *s.* lierre *m.*

J

jack, *s. (cards)* valet *m.; (lifting)* cric *m.,* lève-auto *m.*

jackal, *s.* chacal *m.*

jacket, *s.* veston *m.*

jail, *s.* prison *f.*

jam[1], *s.* confiture *f.*

jam[2], *v.a.* serrer; coincer; encombrer; — *s.* encombrement *m.*

January, *s.* janvier *m.*

Japanese, *adj.* japonais.

jar, *s.* jarre *f.;* bocal *m.*

javelin, *s.* javeline *f.*

jaw, *s.* mâchoire *f.*

jealous, *adj.* jaloux.

jealousy, *s.* jalousie *f.*

jelly, *s.* gelée *f.*

jerk, *s.* saccade *f.;* secousse *f*

jersey, *s.* jersey *m.*

jet, *s.* jet *m.; (gas)* bec *m.;* ~ plane avion *m.* à réaction.

Jew, s. Juif m.

jewel, s. bijou m.

jeweller, s. bijoutier m.; ~'s shop bijouterie f.

jewellery, s. bijouterie f.

jib, s. foc m.

job, s. tâche f.; travail m. (pl. -aux); emploi m.; odd ~s petits travaux m.

join, v.a. joindre; unir; se joindre (à); v.n. se joindre; s'unir; ~ in prendre part à.

joiner, s. menuisier m.

joint, s. joint m.; articulation f.; (meat) gros morceau m.; — adj. commun; indivis; co-; ~-stock company société f. par actions.

joke, s. plaisanterie f.

jolly, adj. joyeux; jovial.

journal, s. journal m. (pl. -aux).

journalist, s. journaliste m.

journey, s. voyage m.

joy, s. joie f.

joyful, adj. joyeux.

judge, s. juge m.; — v.a.&n. juger.

judg(e)ment, s. jugement m.

jug, s. cruche f.; pot m.

juggler, s. jongleur m.

Jugoslav, adj. yougoslave.

juice, s. jus m.

July, s. juillet m.

jump, s. saut m.; — v.n. & a. sauter.

junction, s. jonction f.; (gare f. d')embranchement. m.

June, s. juin m.

jungle, jungle f.

junior, adj. jeune.

jury, s. jury m.

juryman, s. juré m.

just, adj. juste; — adv. (exactly) juste; (barely) à peine; ~ now il n'y a qu'un instant; ~ so précisément.

justice, s. justice f.

justification, s. justification f.

justify, v.a. justifier.

jut, v.n. ~ out faire saillie.

juvenile, adj. juvénile; d'enfants.

K

kangaro, s. kangourou m.

keel, s. quille f.

keen, adj. aigu; tranchant; (mind) pénétrant; be ~ on être enthousiaste de, avoir la passion de.

keep, v.a. tenir; garder; maintenir; observer; ~ back retenir; ~ up soutenir; — v. n. rester; ~ on continuer à.

keeper, s. gardien m.

kerb, s. bordure f.

kernel, s. amande f.

kettle, s. bouilloire f.

key, s. clé f.; (piano) touche f.; (music) ton m.

keyboard, s. clavier m.

kick, v.a. donner un coup de pied (à); v.n. ruer; — s. coup m. de pied.

kid, s. chevreau m.; (child) gosse m. f.

kidney, s. rein m.; (food) rognon m.

kill, v.a. & n. tuer; abattre.

kilogram(me), s. kilogramme m.

kilometre, s. kilomètre m.

kind, adj. bon; bienveillant; aimable.

kindle, v.a. allumer; exciter; enflammer; v.n. s'enflammer.

kindly, *adj.* bon; doux.

kindness, *s.* bonté *f.;* bienveillance *f.*

kindred, *s.* parenté *f.;* parents *m.pl.*

king, *s.* roi *m.*

kingdom, *s.* royaume *m.*

kinsman, *s.* parent *m.*

kiss, *s.* baiser *m.; v.a.* embrasser; baiser.

kit, *s.* fourniment *m.*

kitchen, *s.* cuisine *f.*

kite, *s.* cerf-volant *m.*

kitten, *s.* petit chat *m.*

knapsack, *s.* havresac *m.*

knee, *s.* genou *m. (pl. -x).*

kneel, *v.n.* s'agenouiller; ~ *down* se mettre à genoux.

knife, *s.* couteau *m.*

knight, *s.* chevalier *m.; (chess)* cavalier *m.*

knit, *v. a.* tricoter; *(brow)* froncer.

knob, *s.* bosse *f.;* bouton *m.*

knock, *s.* coup *m.; — v.a. & n.* frapper; ~ *down* renverser.

knocker, *s.* marteau *m.*

knot, *s.* nœud *m.; — v.a.* nouer; *v.n.* se nouer.

know, *v.a.* savoir; connaître; reconnaître; ~n *for* connu pour; — *v.n.* savoir; ~ *of* avoir connaissance de; *let* ~ prévenir.

knowledge, *s.* connaissance *f.; (acquired)* savoir *m.*

knuckle, *s.* articulation *f.* de doigt.

L

label, *s.* étiquette *f.; — v.a.* étiqueter.

laboratory, *s.* laboratoire *m.*

labour, *s.* travail *m.;* ~ *(e)exchange* bureau *m.* de placement; — *v.n.* travailler.

labourer, *s.* travailleur *m.*

lace, *s.* dentelle *f.*

lack, *s.* manque; — *v.a. & n.* ~ *(for)* manquer (de).

lad, *s.* jeune. garçon *m.*

ladder, *s.* échelle *f.*

lading, *s.* chargement *m.*

ladle, *s.* louche *f.*

lady, *s.* dame *f.; young* ~ jeune dame *f.;* demoiselle *f.,* jeune fille *f.*

lag, *v.n.* ~ *behind* rester en arrière.

lake, *s.* lac *m.*

lamb, *s.* agneau *m.*

lame, *adj.* boiteux.

lamp, *s.* lampe *f.*

lamp-shade, *s.* abat-jour *m.*

land, *s. (not sea)* terre *f.; (country)* pays *m.; — v.n. & a.* débarquer; *(plane)* atterrir.

landing, *s.* débarquement *m.; (plane)* atterrissage *m.*

landing-strip, *s.* piste *f.* d'atterrissage.

landlady, *s.* propriétaire *f.;* aubergiste *f.*

landlord, *s.* propriétaire *m.;* aubergiste *m.*

landscape, *s.* paysage *m.*

lane, *s.* ruelle *f.;* chemin *m.*

language, *s.* langue *f.; (expression)* langage *m.*

lap¹, *s.* genoux *m. pl.; (coat)* pan *m.; (sports)* tour (de piste) *m.*

lap², *v. a.* envelopper (de); laper.

lapse, *s.* faute *f.;* chute *f.;* lapsus *m.; (time)* laps *m.; — v.n.* retomber (dans); *(time)* s'écouler; *(fail)* faire un faux pas.

lard, *s.* saindoux *m.*

larder, *s.* dépense *f.*

large, *adj.* gros, grand; considérable; *at ~* en liberté, en général.

lark, *s.* alouette *f.*

last, *adj.* dernier; — *adv.* dernièrement, en dernier lieu; — *v.n.* durer.

lasting, *adj.* durable.

latch, *s.* loquet *m.*

latch-key, *s.* clef *f.* de porte.

late, *adj.* tardif; *be ~* être en retard; — *adv.* tard; *~r on* par la suite; plus tard.

lately, *adv.* dernièrement, recemment.

latest, *adj.* récent, le dernier; *at (the) ~* au plus tard.

lathe, *s.* tour *m.*

lather, *s.* mousse *f.*

Latin, *adj.* latin; — *s.* latin *m.*

latter, *adj.* dernier; *the ~* ce dernier; celui-ci, celle-ci, ceux-ci.

laugh, *v.n.* rire *(at* de); — *s.* rire *m.*

laughter, *s.* rire *m.*

launch, *v.a.* lancer.

launching, *adj.* *~ site* rampe *f.* à fusées.

laundry, *s.* buanderie *f.*, blanchisserie *f.*

lavatory, *s.* lavabo *m.* cabinet *m.* de toilette,

lavish, *adj.* prodigue (de). — *v.a.* prodiguer.

law, *s.* loi *f.*; droit *m.*

law-court, *s.* cour *f.* de justice, tribunal *m.*

lawful, *adj.* légal; permis; légitime.

lawn, *s.* pelouse *f.*

lawn-mower, *s.* tondeuse *f.*

lawsuit, *s.* procès *m.*

lawyer, *s.* homme *m.* de loi avoué *m.*; avocat *m.*

lay, *v.a.* coucher, poser, étendre; *~ aside, by* mettre de côté; *(money)* réserver; *~ down* poser; *~ on* appliquer; *be laid up* être alité.

lay-by, *s.* refuge *m.*, garage *m.*

layer, *s.* couche *f.*

lazy, *adj.* paresseux.

lead¹, *s. (metal)* plomb *m.*

lead², *v.a. & n.* mener, conduire; *~ the way* montrer le chemin.

leader, *s.* conducteur *m.*; *(newspaper)* éditorial *m.*

leadership, *s.* conduite *f.*; direction *f.*

leaf, *s.* feuille *f.*; *(book)* feuillet *m.*; page *f.*

leak, *s.* fuite *f.*; voie d'eau *f.*; — *v.n.* fuir.

lean, *adj.* maigre.

leap, *v. n. & a.* sauter; — *s.* saut *m.*

learn, *v.a. & n.* apprendre.

learning, *s.* savoir *m.*, science *f.*

leash, *s.* laisse *f.*

least, *adj.* le plus petit; le moindre; — *adv.* le moins; — *s.* moins *m.*; *at ~* au moins, à tout le moins; *not in the ~* pas le moins du monde.

leatner, *s.* cuir *m.*

leave, *v. a.* laisser; quitter; *be left* rester; — *s.* permission *f.*; congé *m.*; *on ~* en congé.

lecture, *s.* conférence *f.* *(on* sur); — *v.n.* faire des conférences.

lecturer, *s.* conférencier

m.; (univ.) professeur m. (de faculté).

left, adj. & s. gauche (f.).

left-luggage office, s. consigne f.

leg, s. jambe f.; patte f.

legal, adj. légal.

legislature, s. législature f.

legitimate, adj. légitime.

leisure, s. loisir m.; be at ~ être de loisir.

lemon, s. citron m.

lemonade. s. limonade f.

lend, v.a. prêter.

length, s. longueur f.; (time) durée f.

lengthen, v.a. allonger; prolonger.

lens, s. lentille f.

leopard, s. léopard m.

less, adj. moindre; moins de; — adv. moins; ~ than moins de.

lessen, v. a. & n. diminuer.

lesson, s. leçon f.

lest, conj. de peur que.

let, v.a. laisser, permettre à; (house) louer; ~ me go laisse-moi aller; ~ down laisser tomber (à); ~ in laisser entrer.

letter, s. lettre f.; ~s belles-lettres f. pl.

lettuce, s. laitue f.

level, s. niveau m.; — adj. uni; plat; horizontal; — v.a. niveler; pointer.

lever, s. levier m.

levy, s. levée f.; — v.a. lever.

lexicon, s. lexique m.

liability, s. responsabilité f.; liabilities passif m.

liable, adj. responsable (de); sujet (à).

liar, s. menteur, m.

liberal, adj. libéral; généreux.

liberty, s. liberté f.

librarian, s. bibliothécaire m. f.

library, s. bibliothèque f.

licence, s. permission f.; permis m., patente f.; (excess of liberty) licence f.

license, v.a. accorder un permis (à).

lick, v.a. lécher.

lid, s. couvercle m.

lie¹, s. mensonge m.; — v.n. & a. mentir.

lie², v.n. être couché; (dead) reposer; (be situated) se trouver; ~ down se coucher; it ~s with you cela dépend de vous.

lieutenant, s. lieutenant m.

life, s. vie f.

life-insurance, s. assurance f. sur la vie.

lifeless, adj. inanimé.

lift, v.a. lever; fig. élever; ~ up soulever; — s. (apparatus) ascenseur m.; give s. o. a ~ faire monter qn (dans sa voiture).

light¹, s. lumière f.; éclairage f.; jour m.; lampe f.; (fire) feu m.; come to ~ se révéler; — v. a. allumer; éclairer; v.n. s'éclairer; — adj. clair; éclairé.

light², adj. léger; make ~ of faire peu de cas de.

lighten¹, v.a. éclairer; v.n. faire des éclairs.

lighten², v.a. alléger.

lighter, s. briquet m.

lighthouse, s. phare m.

lighting, s. éclairage m.

lightning, s. éclair m.

like¹, adj. semblable, pareil, ressemblant; — prep. comme.

like², v.a. aimer; I should ~ to je voudrais + inf.

likely, *adv.* probable.

likeness, *s.* ressemblance *f.;* portrait *m.*

lily, *s.* lis *m.*

limb, *s.* membre *m.*

limit, *s.* limite *f.;* *v.a.* limiter.

limited, *adj.* ~ *liability company* société anonyme *f.*

line, *s.* ligne *f.;* *(poetry)* vers *m.;* *railw.)* voie *f.;* — *v.a.* *(garment)* doubler; *v.n.* ~ *up* s'aligner; faire la queue.

linen, *s.* toile *f.;* ligne *m.*

lining, *s.* doublure *f.*

link, *s.* chainon *m.*, *fig.* lien *m.;* — *v.a.* lier; unir.

lion, *s* lion *m.*

lip, *s.* lèvre *f.*

lipstick, *s.* rouge *m.* à lèvres.

liquid, *adj..* & *s.* liquide *(m.).*

list, *s.* liste *f.;* — *v.a.* enregistrer.

listen, *v.n.* (also ~ *in*) écouter.

listener, *s.* auditeur, -trice *m. f.*

literary, *adj.* littéraire.

literature, *s.* littérature *f.*

litter, *s.* litière *f.*

little, *adj.* petit; peu de.

live, *v.n.* vivre; *(reside)* habiter, demeurer; ~ *on* vivre de.

lively, *adv.* vivant, gai.

liver, *s.* foie *m.*

living-room, *s.* salle *f.* de séjour.

load, *s.* charge *f.;* fardeau *m.;* — *v.a.* charger.

loaf, *s.* pain *m.*

loan, *s.* prêt *m.;* emprunt *m.*

loathe, *v.a.* détester.

lobby, *s.* couloir *m.*, vestibule *m.*

lobster, *s.* homard *m.*

local, *adj.* local.

location, *s.* emplacement *m.;* situation *f.*

lock[1], *s.* serrure *f.*

lock[2], *s.* *(hair)* boucle *f.*

locksmith, *s.* serrurier *m.*

lodger, *s.* locataire *m. f.*

lodging, *s.* logement *m.* *furnished* ~s garni *m.*

log, *s.* bûche *f.;* bille *f.*

logical, *adj.* logique.

loin, *s.* *(pork)* longe *f.;* *(beef)* aloyau *m.;* rein *m.*

lonely, *adj.* solitaire.

long[1], *adj.* long; *a* ~ *time (since)* depuis longtemps; *be* ~ *in* être long à; — *adv.* longtemps; *how* ~? combien de temps?; ~ *ago* il y a longtemps.

long[2], *v.n.* ~ *for* désirer qch., soupirer après.

long-distance, *adj.* à (longue) distance.

long-play(ing), *adj.* ~ *record* microsillon *m.*

look, *v. n.* & *a.* regarder; ~ *after* soigner; ~ *at* regarder; ~ *back* regarder en arrière; ~ *for* chercher; ~ *into* examiner; ~ *out* être sur ses gardes, *int.* gare!; ~ *over* parcourir; ~ *up* chercher; — *s.* regard *m.;* air *m.;* aspect *m.*

looking-glass, *s.* miroir *m.*

loom, *s.* métier *m.* de tisserand

loop, *s.* boucle .

loose, *adj.* lâche; délié, détaché; vague.

loosen, *v.a.* desserrer.

lord, *s.* maitre *m.;* seigneur *m.*

lorrv, *s.* camion *m.*

lose, *v.a.* & *n.* perdre.

loss, s. perte f.

lot, s. sort m.; *(portion)* partage m.; a ~ of beaucoup de.

lottery, s. loterie f.

loud, adj. fort; bruyant.

loud-speaker, s. haut-parleur m.

lounge, s. (grand) vestibule m.; foyer m., hall m.; — v.n. flâner.

lounge-suit, s. complet veston m.

love, s. amour m.; — v.a. aimer.

lovely, adj. beau, bel, belle; charmant.

lover, s. amoureux m.; amant m.

low, adj. & adv. bas.

lower, adj. inférieur; *(deck)* premier (pont); — v.a. baisser; *(flags, sails)* amener.

loyal, adj. loyal; fidèle.

loyalty, s. loyauté f.

lubricate, v.a. lubrifier.

luck, s. chance f.; bad ~ malchance f.

lucky, adj. heureux.

luggage, s. bagages m. pl.

luggage-van, s. fourgon m. (aux bagages).

lump, s. morceau m.

lunch, s. déjeuner m.; — v.n. déjeuner.

lung, s. poumon m.

lute, s. luth m.

luxurious, adj. luxueux.

luxury, s. luxe m.

lyre, s. lyre f.

lyric, adj. lyrique.

M

machine, s. machine f.

machinery, s. machines f.pl.; *fig.* mécanisme m.

mackintosh, s. imperméable m.

mad, adj. fou, fol, folle.

madam, s. madame f.

magazine, s. revue f.; *(rifle)* magasin m.

magic, adj. magique.

magistrate, s. magistrat m.

magnet, s. aimant m.

magnetic, adj. magnétique.

magnificent, adj. magnifique.

maid, s. (jeune) fille f.; bonne f.

mail, s. courrier m.

mail-boat, s. paquebot-poste m.

mail-van, s. wagon-poste m.

main, adj. principal.

mainland, s. terre f. ferme.

mainly, adv. principalement.

mains, s. secteur (de courant) m.

maintain, v.a. maintenir; soutenir.

maintenance, s. entretien m.

majesty, s. majesté f.

major, s. commandant m.; — adj. majeur.

majority, s. majorité f.; plupart f.

make, v.a. & n. faire; rendre; ~ away with détruire; ~ for se diriger vers; ~ off décamper; ~ out comprendre; prouver; ~ over céder; ~ up *(list)* dresser; *(invent)* inventer; ~ up for compenser; — s. forme f., fabrication f.

male, adj. mâle; masculin; — s. mâle m.

malice, s. méchanceté

f.

man, *s.* homme *m.*

manage, *v. a.* conduire, diriger, gérer, gouverner; *I shall* ~ *it* j'en viendrai à bout.

management, *s.* direction *f.;* gérance *f.*

manager, *s.* directeur *m.;* gérant *m.*

manicure, *s.* manicure *n. f.*

manifest, *adj.* manifeste; — *v.a.* manifester.

manipulate, *v.a.* manipuler.

manner, *s.* manière *f.;* air *m.;* ~s manières *f. pl.;* (*morals*) mœurs *f. pl.*

manœuvre, *s.* manœuvre *f.;* — *v.a.* faire manœuvrer.

manor, *s.* manoir *m.*

manual, *adj. & s.* manuel (*m.*).

manufacture, *s.* manufacture *f.;* — *v.a.* fabriquer.

manufacturer, *s.* manufacturier *m.;* fabricant *m.*

manure, *s.* fumier *m.*

manuscript, *s.* manuscrit *m.*

many, *adj.* beaucoup de.

map, *s.* carte *f.* géographique.

marble, *s.* marbre *m.*

march, *s.* marche *f.;* — *v.n.* marcher.

March, *s.* mars *m.*

mare, *s.* jument *f.*

margarine, *s.* margarine *f.*

marine, *s.* marine *f.;* — *adj.* marin; maritime.

mariner, *s.* marin *m.*

mark, *s.* marque *f.;* (*aim*) but *m.;* (*school*) point *m.;* (*coin*) marc *m.;* — *v.a.* marquer; souligner.

market, *s.* marché *m.*

market-price, *s.* prix *m.* courant.

marmalade, *s.* marmelade *f.* (d'oranges).

marriage, *s.* mariage *m.*

married, *adj.* marié.

marry, *v. a.* épouser; *v. n.* (*get married*) se marier.

marsh, *s.* marais *m.*

marshal, *s.* maréchal *m.;* — *v.a.* ranger; conduire.

martial, *adj.* martial.

martyr, *s.* martyr *m.*

marvel, *s.* merveille *f.;* — *v.n.* s'étonner (de).

marvellous, *adj.* merveilleux.

masculine, *adj.* mâle; masculin.

mask, *s.* masque *m.*

mason, *s.* maçon *m.*

mass[1], *s.* masse *f.;* majorité *f.*

mass[2], *s.* (*eccles.*) messe *f.*

mast, *s.* mât *m.*

master, *s.* maître *m.;* — *v. a.* maîtriser.

mat, *s.* (*door*) paillasson *m.;* (*table*) dessous de plat, *m.*

match[1], *s.* égal, -e *m. f.,* pareil, -le *m. f.,* mariage *m.;* (*pers.*) parti *m.;* (*sport*) match *m.;* — *v.a.* assortir; *v.n.* s'assortir.

match[2], *s.* allumette *f.*

mate, *s.* camarade *m.;* (*birds*) mâle *m.,* femelle *f.;* (*chess*) mat *m.;* (*ship*) second *m.;* — *v.a.* marier (à); *v.n.* s'accoupler.

material, *s.* matière *f.;* — *adj.* matériel.

maternal, *adj.* maternel.

mathematical, *adj.* mathématique.

mathematics, *s.* mathématiques *f. pl.*

matinée, *s.* matinée *f.*

matron, *s.* mère de famille, *f.; (hospital)* infirmière-en-chef *f.;* surveillante *f.*

matter, *s.* matière *f.;* affaire *f.;* sujet *m.;* chose *f.; as a* ~ *of fact* en fait; *what is the* ~? qu'est-ce qu'il y a?; — *v.n.* importer; *it does not* ~ n'importe.

mattress, *s.* matelas *m.; spring* ~ sommier *m.,* matelas *m.* à ressort.

mature, *adj.* mûr; — *v.a. & n.* mûrir.

maturity, *s.* maturité *f.*

May, *s.* mai *m.*

may, *v. aux.* pouvoir; ~ *I?* vous permettez?

maybe, *adv.* peut-être.

mayor, *s.* maire *m.*

me, *pron. (acc.)* me; *(alone, with prep.)* moi.

meadow, *s.* pré *m.*

meal, *s.* repas *m.*

mean¹, *s.* moyen terme, *m.; (math.)* moyenne *f.;* ~*s* moyens *m. pl., (way to do)* moyen *m.; by* ~*s of* au moyen de: *by all* ~*s* mais certainement; *by no* ~*s* en aucune façon; — *adj.* moyen.

mean², *v.a. (signify)* vouloir dire, signifier: *(wish)* vouloir (faire), avoir l'intention (de); destiner; *what does that word* ~? que signifie ce mot?; *what do you* ~ *by that?* qu'entendez-vous par là?

mean³, *adj.* misérable, pauvre; bas, vil; ladre.

meaning, *s.* intention *f.;* sens *m.*

meantime, -while, *adv. (in the* ~) dans l'intervalle, pendant ce temps-là.

measure, *s.* mesure *f.;* — *v.a.* mesurer.

meat, *s.* viande *f.; (food)* nourriture *f.*

mechanic, *s.* artisan *m.,* mécanicien *m.*

mechanical, *adj.* mécanique.

mechanics, *s.* mécanique *f.*

mechanism, *s.* mécanisme *m.*

mechanize, *v.a.* mécaniser.

medal, *s.* médaille *f.*

medical, *adj.* médical; ~ *student* étudiant *m.* en médecine.

medicine, *s.* médecine *f.*

meditate, *v.a. & n.* méditer.

medium, *s.* moyen terme *m.; milieu m.;* — *adj.* moyen.

meet, *v.a.* rencontrer (qn.), se rencontrer avec (qn.); *(face)* affronter; *(expenses)* faire face à; ~ *sy at the station* aller recevoir qn. à la gare; — *v. n.* se rencontrer; ~ *with* rencontrer; éprouver.

meeting, *s.* rencontre *f.;* réunion *f.*

mellow, *adj.* mûr; moelleux.

melody, *s.* mélodie *f.*

melon, *s.* melon *m.*

melt, *v.a.* fondre.

member, *s.* membre *m.*

memorial, *s.* monument *m.; mémorial m.*

memory, *s.* mémoire *f.;* souvenir *m.*

mend, *v. a.* raccommoder; réparer; corriger.

mental, *adj.* mental.

mention, v. a. mentionner; citer; *don't ~ it* il n'y a pas de quoi.

merchandise, s. marchandise f.

merchant, s. négociant m.; commerçant m.

merciful, adj. miséricordieux.

mercy, s. pitié f.; miséricorde f.

mere, adj. seul.

merely, adv. purement; simplement.

merit, mérite m.; — v.a. mériter.

merry, adj. gai.

mess, s. gâchis m.; *make a ~ of* gâcher.

message, s. message m.

messenger, s. messager m.

metal, s. métal m.

meteorology, s. météorologie f.

method, s. méthode f.

metre, s. mètre m.

microphone, s. microphone m.

microscope, s. microscope m.

middle, s. milieu m.; — adj. du milieu; moyen.

midnight, s. minuit m.

might, s. force f.; puissance f.

mighty, adj. fort; puissant

migrate, v.n. émigrer.

mild, adj. doux; bénin.

mile, s. mille m.

mileage, s. parcours m.; *(expense)* prix m. par mille.

military, adj. militaire.

milk, s. lait m.

milkman, s. laitier m.

mill, s. moulin m.; fabrique f.

miller, s. meunier m.

milliner, s. modiste f.

million, s. million m.

mince, s. hachis m.; v.a. hacher.

mind, s. esprit m.; *(remembrance)* souvenir m.; *(opinion)* pensée f., avis m.; *change one's ~* changer d'avis; *make up one's ~ to* se décider à, se résigner à; — v.a. faire attention à, prendre garde à; écouter; *(look after)* garder; *(trouble about)* s'inquiéter de; *do you ~ my smoking?* est-ce que cela vous gêne que je fume?; *I don't ~* cela m'est égal; *never ~* ça ne fait rien.

mine¹, s. mine f.; — v.a. miner.

mine², pron. à moi; le mien.

miner, s. mineur m.

mineral, adj. & s. minéral (m.).

minister, s. ministre m.

ministry, s. ministère m.

minor, adj. mineur.

minority, s. minorité.

mint, s. Hôtel m. de la Monnaie; *(plant)* menthe f.

minus, adj. en moins; — adv. moins.

minute, s. minute f.; petit moment, m.; *~ hand* grande aiguille f.

miracle, s. miracle m.

mirror, s. miroir m.

miscarry, v.n. avorter.

miscellaneous, adv. divers.

mischief, s. mal m.; méchanceté f.

miser, s. avare m.

miserable, adj. misérable; malheureux.

misery, s. misère f.

misfortune, s. malheur m.

miss¹, v.a. manquer; ne pas entendre; ne pas voir; s'apercevoir

de l'absence (de); ~
out omettre; be ~ing
manquer.
miss², s. mademoiselle f.
missile, s. projectile m.
mission, s. mission f.
missionary, s. missionnaire m. f.
mist, s. brouillard m.,
brume f.
mistake, s. erreur f., mé-
prise f.; faute f.; —
v.a. se tromper de;
~ for prendre pour; be
~n se tromper.
mistress, s. maîtresse f.
(de maison).
mistrust, s. méfiance f.
misty, adj. brumeux.
misunderstand, v. a. comprendre mal.
mitten, s. mitaine f.
mix, v.a. mêler; mélanger; be ~ed up in être
mêlé à.
mixture, s. mélange m.;
mixture f.
moan, v.n. gémir; —
s. gémissement m.
mob, s. foule f., populace
f.
mobilization, s. mobilisation f.
mobilize, v.a. mobiliser.
mock, s. moquerie f.; —
adj. faux; — v.a.
railler.
mockery, s. moquerie f.
model, s. modèle m.
moderate, adj. modéré;
— v.a. modérer.
moderation, s. modération f.
modern, adj. moderne.
modest, adj. modeste.
modesty s. modestie f.
modify, v.a. modifier.
moist, adj. moite, humide.
moisten, v.a. humecter.
moisture, s. humidité f.

molecule, s. molécule f.
moment, s. moment m.
momentary, adj. mo-
mentané.
monarch, s. monarque m.
monarchy, s. monarchie f.
Monday, s. lundi m.
money, s. argent m.;
monnaie f.
money-order, s. mandat
m.
monk, s. moine m.
monkey, s. singe m.
monopolize, v.a. mono-
poliser.
monopoly, s. monopole m.
monotonous, adj. monotone.
monstrous, adj. mons-
trueux.
month, s. mois m.
monthly, adj. mensuel;
— adv. mensuellement.
monument, s. monument
m.
monumental, adj. mo-
numental.
mood, s. humeur f.; mode
m.
moon, s. lune f.
moonlight, s. clair m.
de lune
moor, s. bruyère f.
mop, balai m.; — v.a.
(also ~ up) éponger,
essuyer.
moral, s. morale f.; ~s
moeurs f. pl.; — adj.
moral; de morale.
more, adj. & pron. plus
de; davantage de;
~ than plus que; some
~ en ... davantage;
no ~ n'en ... pas
davantage, ne ...
plus; — adv. plus;
davantage; ~ and ~
de plus en plus.
moreover, adv. de plus.
morning, s. matin m.;
in the ~ le matin; —
adj. du matin.

mortal, *adj. & s.* mortel *(m., f.).*

mortality, *s.* mortalité *f.*

mortgage, *s.* hypothèque *f.; — v. a.* hypothéquer.

mosquito, *s.* moustique *f.*

moss, *s.* mousse *f.*

most, *adj. & pron.* le plus (de), la plupart (de); *at the ~* tout au plus; *~ people* la plupart des gens; *make the ~ of* tirer le meilleur parti de; *— adv.* très, fort, bien.

mostly, *adv.* pour la plupart; principalement; la plupart du temps.

motel, *s.* motel *m.*

moth, *s.* mite *f.*

mother, *s.* mère *f.*

mother-in-law, *s.* belle-mère *f.*

mother-tongue, *s.* langue *f.* maternelle.

motion, *s.* mouvement *m.;* signe *m.; (proposal)* motion *f.*

motionless, *adj.* immobile.

motive, *s.* motif *m.*

motor, *s.* moteur *m.*

motor-bus, *s.* autobus *m.*

motor-car, *s.* auto(mobile) *f.*

motor-coach, *s.* autocar *m.*

motor-cycle, *s.* motocyclette *f.*

motor-scooter, *s.* scooter *m.*

motorway,, *s.* autoroute *f.*

mould, *s.* moule *m.; — v.a.* mouler.

mount, *s.* mont *m.; — v.a. & n.* monter.

mountain, *s.* montagne *f.*

mountaineering. *s.* alpinisme *m.*

mountainous, *adj.* montagneux.

mourn, *v. n. & a.* pleurer, (se) lamenter.

mouse, *s.* souris *f.*

moustache, *s.* moustache *f.*

mouth, *s.* bouche *f.; (beast)* gueule *f.*

move, *s.* mouvement *m.; (chess)* coup *m.; — v.a.* remuer; déplacer; *(goods)* transporter; *(affect)* émouvoir; *(motion)* proposer *~ house (also: ~)* déménager; *— v.n.* se mouvoir, se déplacer; s'avancer; *(chess)* jouer; *~ forward* s'avancer; *~ in* emménager; *~ out* déménager; *~ on* avancer; *int.* circulez!

movement, *s.* mouvement *m.*

mow, *v.a.* faucher; tondre.

mower, *s.* faucheur *m.;* faucheuse (à moteur) *f.*

much, *adj. & pron.* beaucoup; *— adv.* beaucoup; très; *too ~* trop.

mud, *s.* boue *f.*

muddle, *s.* fouillis *m.; — v.a.* embrouiller.

muddy, *adj.* boueux.

mug, *s.* timbale *f.*

mule, *s.* mulet *m.*, mule *f.*

multiple, *adj.* multiple.

multiplication, *s.* multiplication *f.*

multiply, *v.a.* multiplier.

multitude, *s.* multitude *f.*

municipal, *adj.* municipal.

murder, *s.* meurtre *m.*

murderer, *s.* meurtrier *m.*

murmur, *s.* murmure

m.

muscle, *s.* muscle *m.*

museum, *s.* musée *m.*

mushroom, *s.* champignon *m.*

music, *s.* musique *f.*

musical, *adj.* musical; ~ *instrument* instrument *m.* de musique.

music-hall, *s.* café *m.* concert.

musician, *s.* musicien, -enne *m. f.*

must, *v. aux.* il faut que; devoir.

mustard, *s.* moutarde *f.*

mute, *adj.* muet.

mutter, *s.* murmure *m.;* — *v. n.* murmurer.

mutton, *s.* mouton *m.*

mutual, *adj.* mutuel.

my, *pron.* mon, ma; mes *(pl.).*

myself, *pron.* moi-même; *by* ~ seul.

mysterious, *adj.* mystérieux.

mystery, *s.* mystère *m.*

mystic, *adj.* mystique.

myth, *s.* mythe *m.*

N

nail, *s. (to hammer)* clou *m.; (on fingers)* ongle *m.;* — *v.a.* clouer.

nail-brush, *s.* brosse *f.* à ongles.

naked, *adj.* nu; dénudé.

name, *s.* nom *m.;* — *v.a.* nommer; désigner.

namely, *adv.* savoir.

nap, *s.* somme *m.*

napkin, *s.* serviette *f.; (infant)* couche *f.*

narrate, *v. a.* raconter.

narrow, *adj.* étroit.

nation, *s.* nation *f.*

national, *adj.* national.

nationality, *s.* nationalité *f.*

nationalize, *v.a.* nationaliser.

native, *adj. & s.* natif, -ive *(m. f.).*

natural, *adj.* naturel.

naturalize, *v.a.* naturaliser.

nature, *s.* nature *f.*

naughty, *adj.* méchant.

nava l. *adj.* naval

navigate, *v.n.* naviguer.

navigator, *s.* navigateur *m.*

navy, *s.* marine *f.*

near, *adv.* près, proche; — *prep.* près de, auprès de; — *adj.* proche.

nearly, *adv. (almost)* presque.

neat, *adj.* propre; élégant.

necessary, *adj.* nécessaire.

necessity, *s.* néccesité *f.*

neck, *s.* cou *m.*

necklace, *s.* collier *m.*

necktie, *s.* cravate *f.*

need, *s.* besoin; — *v.a.* avoir besoin (de); demander.

needle, *s.* aiguille *f.*

needless, *adj.* inutile.

needy, *adj.* nécessiteux.

negative, *adj.* négatif; — *s.* négative *f.; (photo)* cliché *m.; in the* ~ négativement.

neglect, *v. a.* négliger (de).

negligence, *s.* négligence *f.*

negotiation, *s.* négociation *f.*

negro, -ess *s.* nègre *m.,* négresse *f.*

neighbour, *s.* voisin, -e *m. f.*

neighbourhood, *s.* voisinage *m.*

neither, *pron. & adj.* ni l'un ni l'autre.

nephew, *s.* neveu *m.*

nerve, *s.* nerf *m.*

nervous, *adj.* nerveux.

nest, *s.* nid *m.*

net¹, *s.* filet *m.*

net², *adj.* net.

network, *s.* réseau *m.*

neutral, *adj.* neutre.

never, *adj.* (ne . . .) jamais..

nevertheless, *adv.* néanmoins.

new, *adj.* neuf, neuve; nouveau, -el, -elle; *New Year* Nouvel An.

news, *s.* nouvelle *f.*

newspaper, *s.* journal *m.*

next, *adj.* le plus proche; prochain, suivant; ∼ *door to* à côté de; *adv.* ensuite, après; — *prep.* ∼ *to* à côté de.

nice, *adj.* agréable, bon; gentil.

niece, *s.* nièce *f.*

night, *s.* nuit *f.;* soir *m.; by* ∼ de nuit; *good* ∼*l* bonne nuit!

nightingale, *s.* rossignol *m.*

nine, *adj. & s.* neuf *(m.).*

nineteen, *adj. & s.* dix-neuf *(m.).*

ninety, *adj. & s.* quatre-vingt-dix *(m.).*

ninth, *adj.* neuvième; neuf.

nip, *v.a.* pincer.

nitrogen, *s.* azote *m.*

no, *adj.* ne . . . pas (de), ne . . . aucun.

noble, *adj.* noble.

nobleman, *s.* gentilhomme *m.*

nobody, no one, *pron.* personne ne (+ *verb*).

noise, *s.* bruit *m.*

noisy, *adj.* bruyant.

none, *pron.* ne . . . aucun; personne ne (+ *verb.*)

nonsense, *s.* bêtise; *m. no* ∼ pas de bêtises

non-smoker, *s.* compartiment *m.* pour non-fumeurs.

non-stop, *adj. & adv.* sans arrêt; sans escale.

noon, *s.* midi *m.*

nor, *conj.* ni; *(and . . . not)* et ne . . . pas, non plus.

normal, *adj.* normal.

north, *s.* nord *m.;* — *adj.* du nord.

north-east, *adj. & s.* nord-est *m.*

northern, *adj.* du nord.

north-west, *adj. & s.* nord-ouest *m.*

nose, *s.* nez *m.*

nostril, *s.* narine *f.*

not, *adv.* ne . . . pas, ne . . . point.

notable, *adj.* notable.

note, *s.* note *f.; (letter and money)* billet *m.; (tone)* ton *m.;* — *v.a.* noter; remarquer.

note-book, *s.* carnet *m.*

noted, *adj.* distingué.

nothing, *pron.* rien; ne . . . rien.

notice, *s.* avis *m.;* attention *f.;* connaissance *f.; take* ∼ *of* faire attention à.

notify, *v.a.* avertir, notifier.

notion, *s.* idée *f.*

noun, *s.* nom *m.*

nourish, *v.a.* nourrir.

novel, *s.* roman *m.*

novelist, *s.* romancier *m.*

novelty, *s.* nouveauté *f.*

November, *s.* novembre *m.*

now, *adv.* maintenant.

nowadays, *adv.* de nos jours.

nowhere, *adv.* ne . . . nulle part.

nuclear, *adj.* nucléaire; ∼ *energy* énergie *f.* nucléaire; ∼ *physics* physique *f.* nucléaire; ∼ *power station* centrale *f.* nucléaire.

nuisance, *s. (pers.)* peste

f.; (thing) ennui *m.*

number, *s.* nombre *m.,* numéro *m.*

number-plate, *s.* plaque *f.* matricule.

numerous, *adj.* nombreux.

nun, *s.* religieuse *f.*

nurse, *s.* nourrice *f.,* bonne (d'enfant) *f.; (hospital)* infirmier, -ère *m. f.; — v.a. (suckle)* allaiter; *(the sick)* soigner.

nursery, *s.* chambre *f.* des enfants.

nut, *s.* noix *f.,* noisette *f.*

nylon, *s.* nylon *m.; ~ stockings (or ~s)* bas nylons *m. pl.*

O

oak, *s.* chêne *m.*

oar, *s.* rame *f.*

oat(s) *s. (pl).* avoine *f.*

oath, *s.* serment *m.*

obedience, *s.* obéissance *f.*

obedient, *adj.* obéissant.

obey, *v.a. & n.* obéir (à)·

object, *s.* objet *m.;* but *m.; (gramm.)* régime *m.; — v.a.* objecter; *v.n.* s'opposer (à).

objection, *s.* objection *f.*

objective, *adj. & s.* objectif *(m.).*

obligation, *s.* obligation *f.*

oblige, *v.a.* obliger.

obscure, *adj.* obscur.

observation, *s.* observation *f.*

observe, *v.a.& n.* observer.

obstacle, *s.* obstacle *m.*

obstinate, *adj.* obstiné.

obtain, *v.a.* obtenir.

obvious, *adj.* évident.

occasion, *s.* occasion *f.*

occasional *adj.* occasionnel.

occasionally, *adv.* de temps en temps.

occupation, *s.* occupation *f.*

occupy, *v.a.* occuper; *~ oneself with* s'occuper de.

occur, *v.n.* arriver; se trouver; *it ~red to me* il m'est venu à l'idée que.

occurrence, *s.* événement *m.*

ocean, *s.* océan *m.*

October, *s.* octobre *m.*

odd, *adj.* impair; dépareillé, déparié; *(strange)* non usuel, bizarre.

odds, *s. pl.* avantage *m.;* chances *f. pl.*

of, *prep.* de.

off, *adv.* à ... de distance; *be ~* s'en aller; *be well ~* être à l'aise; — *prep:* de.

offence, *s* offense *f.*

offend, *v. a. & n.* offenser.

offensive, *s.* offensive *f.*

offer, *s.* offre *f.; — v.a.* offrir.

office, *s.* bureau *m.; (of pers.)* charge *f.;* fonction *f.*

officer, *s.* officer *m.; (police)* agent *m.*

official, *adj.* officiel; — *s.* fonctionnaire *m. f.*

often, *adv.* souvent.

oil, *s.* huile *f.;* pétrole *m.*

ointment, *s.* onguent *m.*

old, *adj.* vieux, -eil, -eille; âgé; ancien; *how ~ are you?* quel âge avez-vous?; *~ age* vieillesse *f.; grow ~* vieillir.

old-fashioned, *adj.* à l'ancienne mode.

omission, *s.* omission *f.*

omit, *v.a.* omettre (de).

on, *prep.* sur; *(prep. omitted with days etc.); ~ Monday* lundi; *~*

time à la minute.

once, *adv*. une fois; autrefois; *at* ~ tout de suite.

one, *adj. & s*. un, une; — *pron*. (~, ~s *omitted if preceded by adj*.); (*people, they*) on; *this* ~ celui-ci; *that* ~ celui-là; ~'s son, sa, ses; *which* ~? lequel ...?

oneself, *pron*. soi-même; *by* ~ tout seul.

onion, *s*. oignon *m*.

onlooker, *s*. spectateur, -trice *m. f*.

open, *adj*. ouvert; découvert; public; franc; — *v.a*. ouvrir; *v.n*. s'ouvrir.

opening, *s*. ouverture *f*.

opera, *s*. opéra *m*.

operate, *v.a. & n*. opérer; ~ *on* opérer (qn).

operating-theatre, *s*. salle *f*. d'opération.

operation, *s*. opération *f*.

operative, *adj*. actif.

opinion, *s*. opinion *f.; in my* ~ à mon avis.

opponent, *s*. adversaire *m*.

opportunity, *s*. occasion *f*.

oppose, *v.a*. s'opposer à; ~*d to* opposé à.

opposition, *s*. opposition *f*.

optional, *adj*. facultatif.

or, *conj*. ou; *whether* ... ~ ou ... ou.

oral, *adj*. oral.

orange, *s*. orange *f*.

orchard, *s*. verger *m*.

orchestra, *s*. orchestre *m*.

order, *s*. ordre *m.; (commerce)* commande *f.; (ruling)* règlement *m.;* — *v.a*. ordonner; *(goods)* commander.

order-form, *s*. bon *m*. commande.

ordinary, *adj*. ordinaire *m*.

ore, *s*. minerai *m*.

organ, *s*. organe *m.; (music)* orgue *m*.

organic, *adj*. organique.

organization, *s*. organisation. *f*

organize, *v.a*. organiser.

oriental, *adj*. oriental.

origin, *s*. origine *f*.

original, *adj*. original.

ornament, *s*. ornement *m.;* — *v.a*. orner.

ornamental, *adj*. ornemental.

orphan, *adj. & s*. orphelin, -e (*m. f.*).

other, *adj. & pron*. autre.

otherwise, *adv*. autrement.

ought, *v. aux*. devoir.

ounce, *s*. once *f*.

our, *adj*. notre, (*pl*.) nos.

ours, *pron*. le, la nôtre; les nôtres.

ourself, *pron*. nous(-mêmes); *ourselves* nous(-mêmes); *by ourselves* seul, -s.

out, *adv*. dehors; — *prep*. ~ *of* hors de.

outdoors, *adv*. dehors, en plein air.

outfit, *s*. trousseau *m*.

outing, *s*. excursion *f*.

outline, *s*. contour *m.;* aperçu *m.;* — *v.a*. esquisser.

outlive, *v.a*. survivre à.

outlook, *s*. perspective *f*.

output, *s*. production *f*.

outrageous, *adj*. outrageant; atroce.

outset, *s*. début *m.; at the* ~ dès le commencement.

outside, *adv*. au dehors; — *prep*. en dehors de; — *adj*. du dehors; — *s*. extérieur.

outskirts, *s. pl*. banlieue

f.; lisière f.

outstanding, *adj.* non réglé, à payer; saillant; éminent.

outward, *adj.* extérieur.

outwards, *adv.* à l'extérieur, en dehors.

oven, *s.* four *m.*

over, *prep.* au-dessus de; *(motion)* par dessus; *(superior)* sur; *(more than)* plus de; *(across)* par; — *adv.* *(more)* davantage; *(finished)* fini, passé; *(too)* trop.

overcoat, *s.* pardessus *m.*

overcome, *v.a.* surmonter; vaincre.

overcrowded, *adj.* surpeuplé.

overdo, *v.a.* faire trop cuire; exagérer.

overexpose, *v.a.* surexposer.

overflow, *s.* débordement *m.;* — *v.a.* inonder; *v.n.* déborder.

overlook, *v.a.* *(look on to)* avoir vue sur; *(neglect)* négliger; *(superintend)* surveiller.

overpower, *v.a.* accabler; subjuguer.

oversea, *adj.* d'outre-mer; ~s *(adv.)* outre-mer.

oversight, *s.* inadvertence *f.*

overtake, *v.a.* rattraper; surprendre (par).

overthrow, *s.* renversement *m.;* — *v.a.* renverser.

overtime, *s.* heures *f. pl.* supplémentaires.

overwhelming, *adj.* accablant.

owe, *v.a.* devoir (à); être redevable (à).

owing, *adj.* ~ *to* à cause de.

owl, *s.* hibou *m.*

own, *adj.* propre; *of my* ~ à moi; — *v.a.* posséder.

owner, *s.* propriétaire *m. f.*

ox, *s.* bœuf *m.*

oxygen, *s.* oxygène *m.*

oyster, *s.* huitre *f.*

P

pace, *s.* pas *m.;* *v.a.* arpenter; *v.n.* aller au pas.

pack, *s.* paquet; *(cards)* jeu *m.;* *(wool)* balle; *(hounds)* meute *f.;* — *v.a.* emballer; faire: ~ *off* expédier.

package, *s.* colis *m.;* paquet *m.*

packet, *s.* paquet *m.*

pact, *s.* pacte *m.*

pad, *s.* bourrelet *m.;* tampon *m.;* bloc *m.;* *blotting* ~ buvard *m.*

paddle, *v.n.* pagayer.

page, *s.* page *f.*

pail, *s.* seau *m.*

pain, *s.* douleur *f.;* *take* ~s se donner de la peine.

painful, *adj.* douloureux.

paint, *s.* peinture *f.;* — *v. a.* peindre.

painter, *s.* peintre *m.*

painting, *s.* peinture *f.*

pair, *s.* paire *f.;* couple *m.*

palace, *s.* palais *m.*

palate, *s.* palais *m.*

pale, *adj.* pâle; *grow* ~ pâlir.

palm, *s.* palme *f.*

pan, *s.* poêle *f.*

pane, *s.* vitre *f.*

panel, *s.* panneau *m.*

panorama, *s.* panorama *m.*

pansy, *s.* pensée *f.*

pantry, *s.* office *f.*

pants, *s.pl.* caleçon *m.;* pantalon *m.*

paper, *s.* papier *m.;*

(newspaper) journal *m.; (essay)* étude *f.; (exam)* composition *f.*

parade, *s.* parade *f.;* — *v.n.* parader.

paraffin, *s.* pétrole *m.*

paragraph, *s.* paragraphe *m.*

parallel, *s. (line)* parallèle *f.; (comparison)* parallèle *m.;* — *adj.* parallèle.

paralysis, *s.* paralysie *f.*

parcel, *s.* paquet *m.*

pardon, *s.* pardon *m.; I beg your* ~ je vous demande pardon; *(I beg your)* ~? comment (dites-vous)?, pardon?; — *v.a.* pardonner.

parents, *s. pl.* père *m.* et mère *f.,* parents.

parish, *s.* paroisse *f.*

Parisian, *adj.* parisien; — *s.* Parisien, -enne *m.f.*

park, *s.* parc *m.; (car)* (parc de) stationnement *m.;* — *v.a.* garer; stationner; *no* ~*ing* stationnement interdit.

parliament, *s.* parlement *m.*

parliamentary, *adj.* parlementaire.

parlour, *s.* petit salon *m.*

parrot, *s.* perroquet *m.*

part, *s.* part *f.;* partie *f.; (theatre)* rôle *m.; (region)* région *f.; on my* ~ de ma part; *take* ~ *in* prendre part à; — *v.a.* diviser; séparer; *v.n.* se diviser; *(pers.)* se séparer (de).

partial, *adj. (unfair)* partial; *(incomplete)* partiel.

participant, *s.* participant *m.*

participate, *v.n.* ~ *in* prendre part à.

participation, *s.* participation *f.*

participle, *s.* participe *m.*

particular, *adj.* particulier; — *s.* détail *m.*

partly, *adv.* en partie.

partner, *s.* associé, -e *m. f.;* partenaire *m. f.*

partridge, *s.* perdrix *f.*

party, *s.* parti *m.;* partie *f.;* groupe *m.;* réception *f.,* soirée *f.*

pass, *v.a.* passer; dépasser; surpasser; *(law)* voter; *(resolution)* prendre; *(exam)* être reçu (à); — *v. n.* passer; — *s.* défilé *m.;* laisser-passer *m.*

passage, *s.* passage *m.;* couloir *m.*

passenger, *s.* voyageur, -euse *m. f.;* passager, -ère *m. f.*

passer-by, *s.* passant *m.*

passion, *s.* passion *f.*

passionate, *adj.* passionné.

passive, *adj. & s.* passif *(m.).*

passport, *s.* passeport *m.*

past, *adj.* passé; dernier; — *s.* passé *m.*

paste, *s.* pâte *f.*

pastime, *s.* passe-temps *m*

pastry, *s.* pâtisserie *f.*

patch, *s.* pièce *f.*

patent, *s.* brevet *m.* d'invention.

path, -way, *s.* sentier *m.*

patience, *s.* patience *f.*

patient, *s.* malade *m. f.;* — *adj.* patient.

patriot, *s.* patriote *m. f.*

patrol, *s.* patrouille; — *v.n.* aller en patrouille.

patron, *s.* patron *m.;* client *m.*

pattern, *s.* modèle *m.*

pause, *s.* pause *f.;* — *v.n* faire une pause.

pave, *v.a.* paver.

pavement, *s.* trottoir *m.*

pavilion, *s*. pavillon *m*.

paw, *s*. pâtte *f*.

pay, *v.a.* payer; *(visit)* faire; ~ *off* acquitter; *v.n.* payer; — *s.* paye *f.*, salaire *m*.

payable, *adj*. payable (à).

payment, *s*. payement *m*.

pea, *s*. pois *m*.

peace, *s*. paix *f*.

peaceful, *adj*. paisible.

peach, *s*. pêche *f*.

peacock, *s*. paon *m*.

peak, *s*. pic *m*., cime *f*.

pear, *s*. poire *f*.

pearl, *s*. perle *f*.

peasant, *s*. paysan, -anne *m. f.*

pebble, *s*. caillou *m*.

peck, *s*. coup *m*. de bec.

peculiar, *adj*. particulier.

pedestrian, *s*. piéton *m*.

peel, *s*. pelure *f.;* — *v.a.* peler.

peer, *s*. pair *m*.

peg, *s*. pince *f.;* piquet *m*.

pen, *s*. stylo *m*.

penalty, *s*. peine *f*.

pencil, *s*. crayon *m*.

penicillin, *s*. pénicilline *f*.

penknife, *s*. canif *m*.

penny, *s*. penny *m*.

pension, *s*. pension *f*.

people, *s*. peuple *m.;* gens *m. pl.* [*f.* with *adj.* before it]; famille *f*.

pepper, *s*. poivre *m*.

per, *prep*. par; ~ *cent* pour cent.

perceive, *v.a.* percevoir.

perch, *s*. perchoir *m.;* — *v.n.* se percher.

perfect, *adj*. parfait; — *v.a.* rendre parfait; achever.

perform, *v.a.* accomplir, exécuter.

performance, *s*. représentation *f*.

perfume, *s*. parfum *m*.

perhaps, *adv*. peut-être.

peril, *s*. péril *m*.

period, *s*. période *f*.

periodical, *s*. périodique *m*.

perish, *v.n.* périr.

perishable, *adj*. périssable.

permanent, *adj*. permanent.

permission, *s*. permission *f*.

permit, *s*. permis *m.;* — *v.a.* permettre.

persecution, *s*. persécution *f*.

Persian, *adj*. persan.

persist, *v.n.* persister.

person, *s*. personne *f*.

personal, *adj*. personnel.

personality, *s*. personnalité *f*.

perspiration, *s*. transpiration *f*.

persuade, *v.a.* convaincre (de), persuader.

pertain, *v.n.* appartenir (à).

pet, *s*. enfant *m.f.* gâté, -e; — *adj*. favori; ~ *dog* chien *m*. familier.

petrol, *s*. essence *f*.

petroleum, *s*. pétrole *m*.

petticoat, *s*. jupon *m*.

phase, *s*. phase *f*.

pheasant, *s*. faisan, -e *m. f.*

phenomenon, *s*. phénomène *m*.

philosopher, *s*. philosophe *m*.

philosophy, *s*. philosophie *f*.

phone, *s*. téléphone *m.;* — *v.a.* & *n.* téléphoner.

photo(graph), *s*. photographie *f*. — *v.a.* photographier.

phrase, *s*. phrase *f*.

physical, *adj*. physique.

physician, *s*. médecin *m*.

physicist, *s*. physicien *m*.

physics, s. physique f.
pianist, s. pianiste m. f
piano, s. piano m.
pick, v. a. cueillir; picoter; (teeth) curer; (bone) ronger; (choose) choisir; ~ out choisir; ~ up ramasser; prendre.
pickle, s. marinade f. ~s pickles m.
picnic, s. pique-nique m.
picture, s. tableau m.; portrait m.; film m.; ~s cinéma m.
pie, s. pâté m.
piece, s. morceau m.; partie f.; pièce f.; ~ of news nouvelle f.; ~ of work ouvrage m.
pier, s. jetée f.
pierce, v.a. percer.
pig, s. cochon m.
pigeon, s. pigeon m.
pile[1], s. tas m.; — v.a. (also ~ up) entasser, amasser.
pile[2], s. pieu m., pilot m.
pill, s. pillule f.
pillar, s. pilier m.
pillar-box, s. boîte f. aux lettres.
pillow, s. oreiller m.
pilot, s. pilote m.
pin, s. épingle f.
pinch, v.a. pincer.
pine, s. pin m.
pineapple, s. ananas m.
pink, adj. & s. rose (m.).
pint, s. pinte f.
pious, adj. pieux.
pipe, s. tuyau m.; (smoking) pipe f.
pistol, s. pistolet.m.
pit, s. fosse f.; creux m.; (theatre) parterre m.
pitch, s. degré m.; ton m.; v.a. (tent) dresser; (camp) asseoir.
pity, s. pitié f.; dommage m.

place, s. lieu m., endroit m.; place f.; emploi m.; — v.a. mettre.
plain, adj. uni; simple; évident; ordinaire.
plait, s. tresse f.
plan, s. plan m.; projet m.; — v.a. faire le plan (de).
plane, s. plan m.; (tool) rabot m.; (aero-) avion m.; — v.a. raboter.
planet, s. planète f.
plank, s. planche f.
plant, s. plante f.; (works) usine f., fabrique f.; — v.a. planter.
plantation, s. plantation f.
plaster, s. (em)plâtre m.
plastic, adj. plastique; ~s plastiques m. pl.
plate, s. plaque f.; planche f.; (china) assiette f.; (silver) vaisselle f.
platform, s. quai m.
platinum, s. platine m.
platter, s. plat m.
play, s. jeu m.; pièce f. de théâtre; — v.a. & n. jouer.
player, s. joueur, -euse m. f.
playground, s. cour f. de récréation.
plea, s. excuse f.; défense f.
plead, v.a.&n. plaider
pleasant, adj. agréable.
please, v.a. & n. plaire (à); be ~ed with, to être content de; as you ~ comme vous voulez; if you ~ s'il vous plaît.
pleasure, s. plaisir m.
pledge, s. gage m.; — v.a. mettre en gage.
plenty, s. abondance f.; ~ of quantité de,

beaucoup de.

plot, s. *(land)* terrain m.; *(story)* intrigue f.; *(conspiracy)* complot m.; v. n. conspirer.

plough, s. charrue f.; — v.a.&n. labourer.

plug, s. tampon m.; prise f. de courant; — v.a. tamponner.

plum, s. prune f.

plume, s. plume f.; plumet m.

plunder, v.a. piller; — s. pillage m.

plunge, v.a. & n. plonger; — s. plongeon m.

plural, s. & adj. pluriel *(m.)*.

plus, prep. plus.

ply, v.a. manier; s'appliquer (à); v.n. faire le service (entre).

pocket, s. poche f.

pocket-book, s. carnet m.; portefeuille m.

poem, s. poème m.

poet, s. poète m.

poetic(al), adj. poétique.

poetry, s. poésie f.

point, s. point m ; pointe f.; — v.a. & n. ~ out montrer du doigt; faire valoir (un fait); ~ to indiquer.

poison, s. poison m.; v.a. empoisonner.

poisonous, adj. vénéneux.

pole, s. pôle m.

Pole, s. Polonais, -e m. f.

police, s. police f.

policeman, -officer, s. agent (de police) m.

police-station, s. poste (de police) m.

policy, s. politique f.; *(insurance)* police f.

polish, s. poli m.; fig. politesse f.; — v. a. polir.

Polish, adj. polonais.

polite, adj. poli.

political, adj. politique.

politician, s. politique m.; politicien m.

politics, s. politique f.

poll, s. vote m.; liste f. (électorale); scrutin m.

pool[1], s. mare f.

pool[2], s. pool m.

poor, adj. pauvre; *(bad)* mauvais.

pope, s. pape m.

popular, adj. populaire.

popularity, s. popularité f.

population, s. population f.

pork, s. porc m.; ~ butcher charcutier m.

port, s. port m.; *(ship)* bâbord m.

portable, adj. portatif.

porter, s. portier m.; *(railw.)* porteur m.

portfolio, s. serviette f.

portion, s. portion f.; — v.a. partager.

portrait, s. portrait m.

Portuguese, adj. portugais; — s. Portugais, -e m. f.

position, s. position f.

positive, adj. & s. positif *(m.)*.

possess, v.a. posséder.

possession, s. possession f.

possibility, s. possibilité f.

possible, adj. possible.

post[1], s. poteau m.; — v.a. afficher, placarder.

post[2], s. poste f.; courrier m. — v.a. mettre à la poste.

postage, s. port m., affranchissement; ~ paid port payé.

postal, adj. postal; ~ order mandat (de poste) m.

poster, s. affiche f.

post-free, *adj.* franco.

postman, *s.* facteur *m.*

post(-)office, *s.* bureau *m.* de poste.

postpone, *v.a.* remettre.

postscript, *s.* post-scriptum *m.*

pot, *s.* pot *m.*

potato, *s.* pomme *f.* de terre.

pottery, *s.* poterie *f.*

pouch, *s.* blague *f.*

poultry, *s.* volaille *f.*

pound, *s.* livre *f.*

pour, *v.a.* verser.

pouring, *adj.* torrentiel.

poverty, *s.* pauvreté *f.*

powder, *s.* poudre *f.*

power, *s.* pouvoir *m.;* puissance *f.;* force *f.*

powerful, *adj.* puissant.

power-plant, -station, *s.* centrale *f.* électrique.

practical, *adv.* pratique.

practice, *s.* pratique *f.;* exercise *m.*

practise, *v.a.* pratiquer, exercer; étudier.

praise, *s.* louange *f.;* — *v.a.* louer.

pray, *v.a. & n.* prier.

prayer, *s.* prière *f.*

preach, *v.a. & n.* prêcher.

preacher, *s.* prédicateur *m.*

precede, *v.a.* précéder.

preceding, *adj.* précédent.

precious, *adj.* précieux.

precision, *s.* précision *f.*

predecessor, *s.* prédécesseur *m.*

predict, *v.a.* prédire.

prefabricated, *adj.* préfabriqué.

preface, *s.* préface *f.*

prefer, *v.a.* préférer *(to* à), aimer mieux.

preferable, *adj.* préférable (à).

preference, *s.* préférence *f.*

pregnant, *adj.* enceinte.

prejudice, *s.* préjugé *m.*

preliminary, *adj.* préliminaire.

premature, *adj.* prématuré.

premier, *s.* premier ministre *m., (in France)* président *m.* du conseil.

premises, *s. pl.* lieux *m. pl.;* local *m.,* immeuble *m.*

premium, *s.* prime *f.*

preparation, *s.* préparation *f.*

prepare, *v.a.* préparer, apprêter; — *v.n.* se préparer.

preposition, *s.* préposition *f.*

Presbyterian, *adj.* presbytérien.

prescribe, *v.a.* prescrire, ordonner; *v.n.* ~ *for* faire une ordonnance pour.

prescription, *s.* prescription *f.; (medical)* ordonnance *f.*

presence, *s.* présence *f.*

present[1], *adj.* présent; actuel; — *s.* présent *m.; at* ~ à présent.

present[2], *s. (gift)* cadeau *m.,* présent *m.; — v.a.* présenter; donner.

presently, *adv.* tout à l'heure.

preserve, *v.a.* préserver; *(fruits)* conserver; — *s.* confiture *f.;* conserve *f.*

president, *s.* président *m.*

press, *s.* presse *f.; — v.a.* presser; serrer.

pressure, *s.* pression *f.*

presume, *v.a.* présumer.

presumption, *s.* présomption *f.*

pretend, *v. a. & n.* feindre,

faire semblant: pré-
tendre (à).

pretention, s. prétension
f.

pretty, adj. joli.

prevail, v.n. prévaloir;
prédominer.

prevent, v.a. empêcher.

prevention, s. empêche-
ment m.

previous, adj. antérieur
(à).

prey, s. proie f.

price, s. prix m.; cours m.

price-list, s. prix-courant
m., tarif m.

prick, v.a. piquer; —
s. piqûre f.

pride, s. orgueil m.

priest, s. prêtre m.

primary, adj. primaire.

prime, adj. ~ minister
see premier.

primitive, adj. primitif.

prince, s. prince m.

princess, s. princesse f.

principal, adj. principal;
— s. directeur m.,
patron, -ne m.f., princi-
pal m.

principle, s. principe m.

print, s. empreinte f.;
impression f.; out of ~
épuisé; — v.a. im-
primer; faire une em-
preinte (sur); (photo)
tirer; ~ed matter im-
primés m. pl.

printing-office, s. imprimerie f.

prison, s. prison f.

prisoner, s. prisonnier,
-ère m. f.

private, adj. particulier;
personel; privé.

privilege, s. privilège m.

prize, s. prix m.

probability, s. probabi-
lité f.

probable, adj. probable.

probably, adv. proba-
blement.

problem, s. problème m.

procedure, s. procédé m.

proceed, v.n. aller (à);
se mettre (à); avan-
cer; passer (à); pro-
céder; ~ with conti-
nuer.

process, s. développe-
ment m.; méthode f.,
procédé m.; — v.n.
aller en procession.

procession, s. cortège m.;
procession f.

proclaim, v. a. proclamer.

proclamation, s. procla-
mation s.

produce, v.a. produire.

producer, s. producteur,
-trice m. f.

product, s. produit m.

production, s. production
f.

profess, v.a. profes-
ser, déclarer.

profession, s. profession f.

professional, adj. professionnel; de profession.

professor, s. professeur m.

profit, s. profit m.; —
v.n. ~ by profiter de.

profitable, adj. profitable.

profound, adj. profond.

programme, s. program-
me m.

progress, s. progrès m.;
marche f.; — v.n.
s'avancer, faire des
progrès.

prohibit, v.a. défendre.

prohibition, s. prohibi-
tion f., défense f.

project, s. projet m.;
— v.a. projeter; v.n.
saillir.

projector, s. projecteur
m.

prolong, v.a. prolonger.

prominent, adj. (pro)émi-
nent.

promise, s. promesse f.;
— v.a. promettre.

promote, v.a. donner de

l'avancement (à); encourager.

promotion, *s.* promotion *f.*, avancement *m.*

prompt, *adj.* prompt; — *v.a. (rheatre)* souffler; inspirer.

pronoun, *s.* pronom *m.*

pronounce, *v.a.* prononcer.

pronunciation, *s.* prononciation *f.*

proof, *s.* preuve *f.*; épreuve *f.*

propeller, *s.* hélice *f.*

proper, *adj.* propre; convenable.

property, *s.* propriété *f.*

prophet, *s.* prophète *m.*

proportion, *s.* proportion *f.*

propose, *v.a.* proposer.

proposition, proposal, *s.* proposition *f.*

prose, *s.* prose *f.*

prospect, *s.* prospective *f.*

prospectus, *s.* prospectus *m.*

prosper, *v.n.* prospérer.

prosperity, *s.* prospérité *f.*

prosperous, *adj.* prospère.

protest, *s.* protestation *f.*; protêt *m.*; — *v.a.* protester.

Protestant, *adj. & s.* protestant, -e *(m. f.).*

proud, *adj.* fier, -ère.

prove, *v.a.* prouver; éprouver.

proverb, *s.* proverbe *m.*

provide, *v.a.* pourvoi de; fournir de; *v.n.* ~ *for* pourvoir à; ~d *that* pourvu que.

providence, *s.* prévoyance *f.*

province, *s.* province *f.*

provincial, *adj.* provincial.

provision, *s.* provision *f.*

provoke, *v. a.* provoquer (à).

prudent, *adj.* prudent.

psalm, *s.* psaume *m.*

psychological, *adj.* psychologique.

psychology, *s.* psychologie *f.*

public, *adj. & s.* public *m.*

publication, *s.* publication *f.*

publicity, *s.* publicité *f.*

publish, *v.a.* publier.

publisher, *s.* éditeur *m.*

pudding, *s.* pouding *m.*

pull, *v.a.* tirer; ~ *down* démolir; ~ *out* arracher; ~ *up* arrêter; *v. n.* tirer; ~ *through* s'en tirer; — *s.* traction *f.*, tirage *f.*

pulpit, *s.* chaire *f.*

pulse, *s.* pouls *m.*

pump, *s.* pompe *f.*; — *v. a.* pomper.

punch[1], *s.* poinçon *m.*; — *v.a.* poinçonner, percer.

punch[2], *s.* punch *m.*

punctual, *adj.* ponctuel.

puncture, *s.* piaûre *f.*; *(tyre)* crevaison *f.*; — *v.a. & n.* crever.

punish, *v.a.* punir.

punishment,, *s.* punition *f.*

pupil[1], *s.* élève *m. f.*

pupil[2], *s. (eye)* pupille *f.*

puppy, *s.* petit chien *m.*

purchase, *s.* achat *m.*; — *v.a.* acheter.

pure, *adj.* pur.

purge, *v.a.* purger.

purify, *v.a.* purifier.

purity, *s.* pureté *f.*

purpose, *s.* but *m.*

purse, *s.* porte-monnaie *m.*, bourse *f.*

pursue, *v.a.* (pour)suivre.

pursuit, *s.* poursuite *f.*

push, *v.a. & n.* pousser; ~ *back* repousser; ~ *on* faire avancer; pousser (jusqu'à); — *s.* poussée *f.*; allant *m.*

puss, *s.* minet *m.*

put, *v.a.* mettre; *(express)* dire; ~ *back* remettre; ~ *down* déposer; attribuer; inscrire; ~ *off* remettre; ôter; ~ *on* mettre; ~ *out* tendre; éteindre; ~ *up* ouvrir; loger; ~ *up with* s'accommoder.

puzzle, *v.a.* embarrasser.

pyjamas, *s. pl.* pyjama *m.*

pyramid, *s.* pyramide *f.*

Q

quadrangle, *s.* quadrilatère *m.*; cour *f.*

quake, *v.n.* trembler.

qualification, *s.* qualification *f.*; compétence *f.*

qualify, *v.a.* qualifier; *v.n.* ~ *for* passer l'examen de.

quality, *s.* qualité *f.*

quantity, *s.* quantité *f.*

quarrel, *s.* querelle *f.*; brouille *f.*; — *v.n.* se brouiller; ~ *with* se quereller avec.

quarter, *s.* quartier *m.*; quart *m.*; ~*s* quartiers *m.pl.*

quartet(te), *s.* quatuor *m.*

quay, *s.* quai *m.*

queen, *s.* reine *f.*; *(cards)* dame *f.*

queer, *adj.* bizarre.

quench, *v.a.* éteindre.

question, *s.* question *f.*; — *v.a.* interroger.

queue, *s.* queue *f.*; — *v.n.* ~ *up* faire (la) queue.

quick, *adj.* prompt, rapide; vif.

quick(ly), *adv.* vite.

quiet, *adj.* tranquille; calme; *be* ~ se taire.

quilt, *s.* courtepointe *f.*

quit, *v.a.* quitter.

quite, *adv.* tout à fait.

quiver, *v.n.* trembler.

quiz, *s.* mystification *f.*; persifleur *m.*; *v.a.* railler.

quotation, *s.* citation *f.*

quote, *v.a.* citer.

R

rabbi, *s.* rabbin *m.*

rabbit, *s.* lapin, -e *m. f.*

race[1], *s.* course *f.*; — *v.n.* faire la course; courir; lutter de vitesse.

race[2], *s.* race *f.*

rack, *s.* râtelier *m.*

racket, *s.* raquette *f.*

radiate, *v.n.* rayonner, irradier; *v.a.* dégager.

radiator, *s.* radiateur *m.*

radical, *adj.* radical.

radio, *s.* radio *f.*

radioactive, *adj.* radioactif.

radish, *s.* radis *m.*

rag, *s.* chiffon *m.*

rage, *s.* rage *f.*

raid, *s.* razzia *f.*, rafle *f.*; raid *m.*

rail, *s.* barre *f.*, rampe *f.*; rail *m.*; *by* ~ par chemin de fer.

railway, *s.* chemin *m.* de fer.

rain, *s.* pluie *f.*; — *v.n.* pleuvoir.

rainy, *adj.* pluvieux.

raise, *v.a.* lever, élever; soulever; *(plants)* faire pousser, cultiver.

rake, *s.* râteau *m.*

rally, *v.n.* se rallier; — *s.* ralliement *m.*

ramify, *v.n.* ramifier.

random, *s. at* ~ par hasard.

range, *s.* rangée *f.*; *(mountains)* chaîne *f.*; *(extent)* étendue *f.*; *(kitchen)* fourneau *m.*; — *v.a.* ranger.

rank, *s.* rang *m.*; grade *m.*

ransom, *s.* rançon *f.*; — *v.a.* payer rançon pour.

rap, *s.* tape *f.*; coup *m.*; — *v.a.* frapper.

rapid, *adj.* rapide.

rare, *adj.* rare.

rascal, *s.* coquin *m.*

rash, *adj.* téméraire; inconsidéré.

raspberry, *s.* framboise *f.*

rat, *s.* rat *m.*

rate, *s.* taux *m.*, cours *m.*, tarif *m.*; *(speed)* vitesse *f.*, allure *f.*; *(tax)* taxe *f.*; *at the* ~ *of* à la vitesse de; *at any* ~ en tout cas, quoi qu'il en soit; — *v.a.* estimer; taxer.

rather, *adv.* plutôt; un peu.

ratify, *v.a.* ratifier.

ration, *s.* ration *f.*

rational, *adj.* raisonnable.

rattle, *s.* bruit *m.*; — *v.n.* faire du bruit.

raven, *s.* corbeau *m.*

raw, *adj.* cru; ~ *material* matière *f.* première.

ray, *s.* rayon *m.*

razor, *s.* rasoir *m.*; *safety* ~ rasoir de sûreté; *electric* ~ rasoir électrique.

razor-blade, *s.* lame *f.* de rasoir.

reach, *v.a.* arriver (à); atteindre; *v. n.* atteindre; parvenir (à); — *s.* étendue *f.*; portée *f.*; *within* ~ à portée.

react, *v.n.* réagir.

reaction, *s.* réaction *f.*

reactor, *s.* réacteur *m.*

read, *v.a.* lire; *(study)* étudier; ~ *for (exam)* préparer.

reader, *s.* lecteur, -trice *m. f.*

reading, *s.* lecture *f.*

ready, *adj.* prêt (à); prompt (à); près (de); *get* ~ (se) préparer.

real, *adj.* réel; véritable.

reality, *s.* réalité *f.*

realization, *s.* réalisation *f.*

realize, *v.a.* réaliser.

really, *adv.* vraiment.

realm, *s.* royaume *m.*; *fig.* domaine *m.*

reap, *v.a. & n.* moissonner.

reaper, *s.* moissonneur *m.*

rear, *adj.* de derrière; — *s.* arrière *m.*; queue *f.*; — *v.a.* élever; *v. n.* se cabrer.

reason, *s.* raison *f.*; — *v. a. & n.* raisonner.

reasonable, *adj.* raisonnable.

reasoning, *s.* raisonnement *m.*

rebellion, *s.* rébellion *f.*

rebuke, *s.* réprimande *f.*; — *v.a.* réprimander.

recall, *v.a.* rappeler; *(remember)* se rappeler.

receipt, *s.* reçu *m.*, quittance *f.*; recette *f.*

receive, *v.a.* recevoir.

receiver, s. destinataire m. f.; (phone, wireless) écouteur m., récepteur m., poste m.

recent, adj. récent.

recently, adv. récemment.

reception, s. réception f.

receptionist, s. portier m. d'auberge; employé à la réception.

recipe, s. recette f.

recital, s. récit m.; récital m.

recite, v.a. & n. réciter.

reckless, adj. insouciant.

reckon, v.a. compter.

recognize, v.a. reconnaître.

recollect, v. a. se rappeler.

recommend, v.a. recommander.

recommendation, s. recommandation f.

reconcile, v. a. réconcilier.

record, s. rapport m. officiel; souvenir m.; mention f.; archives f. pl.; (gramophone) disque m.; (sport) record m.; — v.a. enrégistrer; rapporter.

recount, v.a. raconter.

recover, v.a. recouvrer: v.n. se remettre.

recreation, s. récréation f.

recruit, s. recrue f.; — v.a. recruter.

rectangle, s. rectangle m.

rector, s. recteur m.; curé m.

recur, v. n. revenir.

red, adj. rouge; roux.

redress, v.n. réparer; redresser.

reduce, v.a. réduire.

reduction, s. réduction f.

reed, s. roseau m.

reef, s. ris m.; récif m.

reel, s. dévidoir m.; bobine f.; — v.n. tourner.

refer, v.a. référer; renvoyer; v.n. ~ to se rapporter à, s'en rapporter à, se référer à.

referee, s. arbitre m.; — v.a. arbitrer.

reference, s. renvoi m., référence f.; rapport m.; allusion f.; with ~ to à propos de; have ~ to se rapporter à.

refill, s. recharge f.

reflect, v.a. réfléchir; v.n. méditer (sur).

reflection, s. réflexion f.; image f.

reform, s. réforme f.; — v.a. réformer.

Reformation, s. Réforme f.

refrain, v.n. ~ from se retenir de.

refresh, v.a. rafraîchir.

refreshment, s. rafraîchissement m.; ~ room buffet m.

refrigerator, s. réfrigérateur m.

refuge, s. refuge m.; take ~ se réfugier.

refugee, s. réfugié, -e m. f.

refusal, refus m.

refuse, v.a. refuser.

refute, v.a. réfuter.

regain, v.a. reconquérir; regagner; reprendre.

regard, s. égard m.; with ~ to à l'égard de; kind(est) ~s meilleurs amitiés f. pl.; — v.a. regarder; tenir compte (de); considérer.

regent, s. régent m.

regime, s. régime m.

regiment, s. régiment m.

region, s. région f.

register, v. a. enregistrer.

regret, *v.a.* regretter;
— *s.* regret *m.*

regular, *adj.* régulier.

regulate, *v.a.* régler.

regulation, *s.* ordonnance *f.*; réglementation *f.*

rehearsal, *s.* répétition *f.*

rehearse, *v.a.* répéter.

reign, *s.* règne *m.*; — *v. a.* régner

rein, *s.* rêne *f.*

reject, *v.a.* rejeter; refuser.

relate, *v.a.* raconter; be ~ed to être apparenté à; *v.n.* ~ to se rapporter à; *relating to* relatif à.

relation, *s.* relation *f.*, rapport *m.* (à); *(relative)* parent, -e *m. f.*

relative, *s.* parent, -e *m. f.*; — *adj.* relatif; ~ to au sujet de.

relax, *v.n.* se relâcher; *v. a.* relâcher.

relay, *s.* relais *m.*

release, *s.* délivrance *f.*; — *v.a.* libérer; décharger (de).

reliable, *adj.* digne de confiance.

relic, *s.* relique *f.*

relief[1], *s.* délivrance *f.*; soulagement *m.*; secours *m.*

relief[2], *s.* relief *m.*

relieve, *v.a.* soulager; secourir; délivrer.

religion, *s.* religion *f.*

religious, *adj.* religieux.

rely, *v.n.* ~ upon compter sur.

remain, *v.n.* rester.

remark, *s.* remarque *f.*; — *v.a.* remarquer; *v.n.* faire une remarque.

remarkable, *adj.* remarquable.

remedy, *s.* remède *m.*

remember, *v.a.* se souve-nir (de), se rappeler.

remembrance, *s.* souvenir *m.*

remind, *v. a.* ~ of rappeler (à), faire souvenir (de).

remit, *v.a.* remettre.

remittance, *s.* remise *f.*

remorse, *s.* remords *m.*

remote, *adj.* reculé.

removal, *s.* déménagement *m.*; enlèvement; *(dismissal)* renvoi *m.*

remove, *v.a.* déménager; enlever; *(dismiss)* renvoyer, *(from school)* retirer; *v.n.* déménager; s'en aller.

Renaissance, *s.* Renaissance *f.*

render, *v.a.* rendre.

renew, *v.a.* renouveler.

renounce, *v.a.* renoncer (à); dénoncer; répudier.

rent, *s.* *(house)* loyer *m.*; — *v.a.* louer.

repair, *s.* réparation *f.*; — *v.a.* réparer.

repay, *v.a.* rembourser.

repeat, *v.a.* répéter.

repentance, *s.* repentir *m.*

repetition, *s.* répétition *f.*

replace, *v.a.* replacer.

reply, *s.* réponse *f.*; — *v.a. & n.* répondre.

report, *s.* rapport *m.*, compte *m.* rendu; bruit *m.*; bulletin *m.*; — *v.a.* rapporter; rendre compte (de).

reporter, *s.* reporter *m.*

represent, *v.a.* représenter.

representation, *s.* représentation *f.*

representative, *s.* représentant *m.*

reproach, *s.* reproche *m.*

reproduce, *v.a.* reproduire.

reproduction, *s.* reproduction *f.*

reprove, *v.a.* répriman-

der.
republic, *s.* république *f.*
repulsion *s.* répulsion *f.*
repulsive, *adj.* repoussant.
reputation, repute, *s.* rạputation *f.*
request, *s.* requète *f.;* — *v.a.* demander.
require, *v. a.* demander; exiger.
requirement, *s.* besoin *m.;* exigence *f.*
rescue, *s.* délivrance *f.;* secours *m.;* — *v.a.* délivrer; secourir.
research, *s.* recherche *f.*
resemble, *v.a.* ressembler (à).
resent, *v.a.* ètre froissé (de); ressentir.
reserve, *s.* réserve *f.;* — *v.a.* réserver.
reside, *v.n.* résider.
residence, *s.* résidence *f.*
resident, *s.* habitant *m.;* — *adj.* résidant.
resign, *v.a.* résigner, se démettre (de); *v.n.* donner sa démission.
resignation, *s.* résignation *f.;* démission *f.*
resist, *v. a.* résister (à).
resistance, *s.* résistance *f.*
resolution, *s.* résolution *f.*
resolve, *v.a.* résoudre; *v.n.* se résoudre (à), se décider (à faire).
resort, *s.* recours *m.;* ressource *f.;* — *v.n.* ~ *to* avoir recours à.
resource, *s.* ressource *f.*
respect, *s.* respect *m.;* rapport *m.;* *in this* ~ sous ce rapport; *with* ~ *to* concernant ... — *v.a.* respecter.
respectful, *adj.* respectueux.
respective, *adj.* respectif.
respond, *v.n.* répondre.
response, *s.* réponse *f.*

responsibility, *s.* responsabilité *f.*
responsible, *adj.* responsable (de).
rest[1], *s.* reste *m.; the* ~ les autres.
rest[2], *s.* repos *m.;* pause *f.;* — *v.n.* se reposer.
restaurant, *s.* restaurant *m.*
restless, *adj.* sans repos; inquiet; agité.
restoration, *s.* restauration *f.*
restore, *v.a.* restaurer.
restrain, *v. a.* retenir; ~ *from* empêcher de.
restraint, *s.* contrainte *f.;* retenue *f.*
restrict, *v.a.* restreindre.
restriction, *s.* restriction *f.*
result, *s.* résultat *m.;* — *v.n.* ~ *from* résulter de; ~ *in* avoir pour résultat.
resume, *v. a.* reprendre.
retain, *v.a.* retenir.
retire, *v. n.* se retirer.
retreat, *s.* retraite *f.*
return, *v.n.* revenir, retourner; *v.a.* rendre; renvoyer; *(answer)* faire; — *s.* retour *m ;* renvoi *m.;* ~ *ticket* billet *m.* d'aller et retour.
reveal, *v.a.* révéler.
revenge, *s.* vengeance *f.;* — *v.a.* venger.
revenue, *s.* revenu *m.*
reverend, *adj.* révérend.
reverse, *adj.* inverse; — *s.* revers *m.*
review, *s.* revue *f.;* *(of book)* compte *m.* rendu, critique *f.;* — *v.a.* revoir; *(book)* faire la critique (d'un livre).
revision, *s.* révision *f.*
revolt, *s.* révolte *f.*
revolution, *s.* révolution

f.; (motor) tour m.

reward, s. récompense f.; — v.a. récompenser.

rheumatism, s. rhumatisme m.

rhyme, s. rime f.

rhythm, s. rythme m.

rib, s. côte f.

rice, s. riz m.

rich, adj. riche.

rid, v.a. get ~ of se débarrasser de.

riddle, s. énigme f.

ride, v.n. monter; aller à cheval or à bicyclette; (bus) voyager; aller (en autobus); v. a. monter; — s. promenade f.

ridge, s. crête f.

ridiculous, adj. ridicule.

rifle, s. fusil m.

right, adj. droit; correct, exact; juste, bon; bien; ~ side endroit m.; be ~ avoir raison; that's ~ c'est ça; — s. droit m.; (opposed to left) droite f.; — adv. droit; bien; (very) très.

rim, s. bord m.

ring[1], s. anneau m.; cercle m.; (sport) ring m.

ring[2], v.n. & a. sonner; ~ up appeler (au téléphone); — s. son m.; coup m. de sonnette; there is a ~ at the door on sonne (à la porte).

rinse, v.a. rinser.

riot, s. émeute f.

rip, v.a. déchirer; ~ up arracher; v.n. aller à toute vitesse.

ripe, adj. mûr.

rise, v. n. se lever; (revolt) se soulever; (prices) hausser; (originate) naître (de); — s. montée f.; (salary) augmentation f.; give ~ to donner lieu à.

risk, s. risque m.; — v.a. risquer.

rival, adj. & s. rival, -e (m. f.); — v.a. rivaliser (avec).

rivalry, s. rivalité f.

river, s. fleuve m., rivière f.

road, s. route f., chemin m.

road-map, s. carte f. routière. f.

roar, s. rugissement m.; — v.n. rugir; hurler.

roast, v.a. & n. rôtir; — s. rôti m.

rob, v.a. voler.

robber, s. voleur m.

robbery, s. vol m.

robe, s. robe f.

robin, s. rouge-gorge m.

rock, s. rocher m., roc m.

rocket, s. fusée f.

rocky, adj. rocheux.

rod, s. baguette f.

rogue, s. coquin, -e m. f.

roll, s. rouleau m.; liste f.; — v. a. rouler.

roller-towel, s. essuie-mains m. à rouleau.

Roman, adj. romain; — s. Romain, -e m. f.

romantic, adj. romanesque; romantique.

roof, s. toit m.

room, s. chambre f.; salle f.; (space) place f.

root, s. racine f.; source f.

rope, s. corde f.

rose, s. rose f.

rotten, adj. pourri, carié.

rough, adj. rude; grossier; brut; (sea) gros.

roughly, adv. approximativement.

round, adj. rond; — adv. de tour, en rond, autour; hand ~ faire circuler; go ~ tourner;

turn ~ tourner, se retourner; — *prep.* autour de; — *s.* rond *m.*, cercle *m.*; tournée *f.; tour *m.*

rouse, *v.a.* réveiller.

route, *s.* route *f.*

routine, *s.* routine *f.*

row[1], *s.* rang *m.*, rangée *f.;* ligne *f.*

row[2], *v.n.* ramer; *v.a.* faire aller (à la rame); — *s.* promenade *f.* en canot.

row[3], *s.* chahut *m.*, vacarme *m.*, querelle *f.;* réprimande *f.*

royal, *adj.* royal.

rub, *v.a.* frotter.

rubber, *s.* caoutchouc *m.*

rubbish, *s.* décombres *m. pl.*; ordure(s) *f. (pl)*, immondices *f. pl.*

ruby, *s.* rubis *m.*

rudder, *s.* gouvernail *m.*

rude, *adj.* rude.

ruffian, *s.* bandit *m.*

ruffle, *s.* ride *f.;* — *v.a.* rider; ébouriffer.

rug, *s.* couverture *f.;* tapis *m.*

ruin, *s.* ruine *f.;* — *v. a.* ruiner.

rule, *s.* autorité *f.;* règle *f.; (of the road)* code *m.; as a* ~ généralement; — *v.a.* gouverner; régler; guider; ~ *out* exclure.

ruler, *s.* gouverneur *m.*, souverain *m.; (for lines)* règle *f.*

rum, *s.* rhum *m.*

Rumanian, *adj.* roumain; — *s.* Roumain, -e *m. f.*

rumour, *s.* rumeur *f.*

run, *v.n.* courir; fuir, se sauver; *(flow)* couler; *(veh.)* marcher, faire le service; *(engine)* fonctionner; *(play in*

theatre) se jouer; *v.a.* faire fonctionner; mettre en service; faire marcher, faire aller; ~ *after* courir après; ~ *away* s'enfuir; ~ *down* descendre en courant; *(health)* s'affaiblir; ~ *in (motor)* roder; ~ *into* heurter, rencontrer; ~ *off* s'enfuir; s'écouler; ~ *out* se terminer; ~ *over* passer dessus; ~ *up (debts)* entasser; — *s.* course *f.;* voyage *m.*

runner, *s.* coureur, -euse *m. f.*

runway, *s.* piste (d envol) *f.*

rupture, *s.* rupture *f.*

rural, *adj.* rural.

rush, *v.n.* se précipiter, se jeter; *v.a.* entraîner à toute vitesse; — *s.* ruée *f.*, hâte *f.;* ~ *hours* heures *f.pl.* d'affluence, coup *m.* de feu.

Russian, *adj.* russe; — *s.* Russe *m. f.*

rust, *s.* rouille *f.*

rustic, *adj.* rustique.

rustle, *s.* bruissement *m.*

rye, *s.* seigle *m.*

S

sabre, *s.* sabre *m.*

sack, *s.* sac *m.*

sacrament, *s.* sacrement *m.*

sacrifice, *s.* sacrifice *m.*

sad, *adj.* triste.

saddle, *s.* selle *f.*

sadness, *s.* tristesse *f.*

safe, *adj.* sûr, en sûreté. sans danger; — *s.* coffre-fort *m.*

safely, *adv.* sain et sauf;

en sûreté.

safety, s. sûreté f.

sail, s. voile f.; — v.n. faire voile, naviguer.

sailor, s. marin m., matelot m.

saint, s. saint, -e m. f.

sake: *for the* ∼ *of* pour l'amour de.

salad, s. salade f.

salary, s. traitement m., appointements m. pl.

sale, s. vente f.; *(auction)* vente f. aux enchères.

salesman, s. vendeur m.

saleswoman, s. vendeuse f.

salmon, s. saumon m.

saloon, s. salon m.; ∼ *bar* bar m.

salt, s. sel m.

salt-cellar, s. salière f.

salvation, s. salut m.

same, adj. & pron. même.

sanatorium, s. sanatorium m.

sanction, s. sanction f.; — v.a. sanctionner.

sand, s. sable m.; *the* ∼s la plage.

sandal, s. sandale f.

sandwich, s. sandwich m.

sanitary, adj. sanitaire.

sarcastic, adj. sarcastique.

sardine, s. sardine f.

Satan, s. Satan m.

satellite, s. satellite m.

satire, s. satire f.

satisfaction, s. satisfaction f.

satisfactory, adj. satisfaisant.

satisfy, v.a. satisfaire.

Saturday, s. samedi m.

sauce, s. sauce f.

sausage, s. saucisse f.

save, v. a. sauver; *(spare)* épargner, gagner; v.n. économiser.

savings-bank, s. caisse f. d'épargne.

Saviour, s. Sauveur m.

saw, s. scie f.; — v.a. & n. scier.

say, v. a. dire; *that is to* ∼ c'est-à-dire.

scale[1], s. plateau (de balance) m.; *(pair of)* ∼s balance f.; — v. a. peser.

scale[2], s. échelle f.; *(music)* gamme f.

scale[3], s. *(fish)* écaille f.

scanty, adj. maigre.

scar, s. cicatrice f.

scarce, adj. rare.

scarcely, adv. à peine.

scare, s. panique f.; — v.a. effrayer.

scarf, s. écharpe f., foulard m.

scarlet, adj. écarlate.

scatter, v.a. disperser; éparpiller; dissiper.

scene, s. scène f.; *behind the* ∼s dans les coulisses.

scenery, s. paysage m.; *(theatre)* décor m.

scent, s. odeur f.; *(perfume)* parfum m.; *(dog)* flair m.

schedule, s. liste f.; cédule f.

scheme, s. plan m.; projet m.

scholar, s. *(child)* écolier, -ère m. f.; *(learned)* savant m.

scholarship, s. bourse f.

school, s. école f.; classe f.

schoolboy, -**girl**, s. écolier, -ère m. f.

schoolmaster, s. instituteur m., maître m. d'école.; *(secondary)* professeur m.

schoolmistress, s. maîtresse f. d'école; *(secondary)* professeur m.

schoolroom, s. (salle de) classe f.

science, s. science f.

scientific, *adj.* scientifique.

scientist, *s.* savant *m.*

scissors, *s. pl.* ciseaux *m. pl.*

scold, *v.a.* gronder.

scoop, *s.* écope *f.*

scooter, *s.* scooter *m.*

scope, *s.* portée *f.;* envergure *f.;* carrière *f.*

scorch, *v.a.* roussir, brûler.

score, *s.* entaille *f.; (sum)* compte *m.; (games)* points *m. pl.,* marque *f.,* score *m.; (twenty)* vingtaine *f.; (music)* partition *f.; — v.a.* marquer; ~ *out* rayer.

scorn, *s.* mépris *m.*

Scotch, Scottish, Scots, *adj.* écossais.

Scotsman, *s.* Écossais *m.*

scout, *s.* éclaireur *m.*

scrambled: ~ *eggs* œufs *m. pl.* brouillés.

scrap, *s.* morceau *m.;* bout *m.*

scrape, *v.a.* gratter; râcler; ~ *off* décrotter.

scratch, *v.a.* gratter; égratigner; *v. n.* griffer gratter; — *s.* égratignure *f.; m.* coup d'ongle.

scream, *v.n. & a.* crier; — *s.* cri *m.*

screen, *s.* écran *m.*

screw, *s.* vis *f.*

scrub, *v.a.* frotter; nettoyer à la brosse.

scrupulous, *adj.* scrupuleux.

sculptor, *s.* sculpteur *m.*

sculpture, *s.* sculpture *f.; — v.a.* sculpter.

scythe, *s.* faux *f.*

sea, *s.* mer *f.; by* ~ par (voie de) mer.

seal[1], *s. (animal)* phoque *m.*

seal[2], *s.* sceau *m.; — v.a.* sceller; cacheter.

seam, *s.* couture *f.*

seaport, *s.* port *m.* de mer.

search, *v.a.* chercher; — *s.* recherche *f.*

search-light, *s.* projecteur *m.*

seasickness, *s.* mal *m.* de mer.

seaside, *s.* bord *m.* de la mer.

season, *s.* saison *f.*

seat, *s.* siège *m.; — v.a.* asseoir; placer.

second, *adj.* second; deux; deuxième; — *s.* seconde *f.*

secondary, *adj.* secondaire; ~ *school* école *f.* secondaire.

second-hand, *adj.* de seconde main, d'occasion.

secret, *adj. & s.* secret *(m.).*

secretary, -*s.* secrétaire *m. f.*

section, *s.* section *f.*

secular, *adj.* séculier.

secure, *adj.* en sûreté, sûr; — *v.a.* mettre en sûreté; obtenir; fixer.

security, *s.* sécurité *f.;* caution *f.;* sûreté *f.; securities* valeurs *f. pl.; social* ~ sécurité *f.* sociale.

sediment, *s.* sédiment *m.*

see, *v.a.* voir; *(understand)* comprendre; *(make sure)* s'assurer; *(accompany)* accompagner; ~ *about* s'occuper de; ~ *out* accompagner jusqu'à la porte; ~ *through* voir à travers, pénétrer; mener à bonne fin; ~ *to* veiller à, s'occuper de.

seed, s. semence f.; graine f.

seek, v.a. chercher.

seem, v.n. sembler, paraître.

seize, v.a. saisir; prendre.

seldom, adv. rarement.

select, v.a. choisir.

selection, s. choix m.

self, s. moi m.

self-conscious, adj. gêné.

self-control, s. maîtrise f. de soi-même.

selfish, adj. égoïste.

selfishness, s. égoïsme m.

self-respect, s. respect m. de soi.

self-service, adj. ~ restaurant restaurant à libre service.

sell, v.a. vendre; ~ out vendre tout son stock; v. n. se vendre.

seller, s. vendeur, -euse m. f.

semaphore, s. sémaphore m.

semicolon, s. point (et) virgule m.

senate, s. sénat m.

senator, s. sénateur m.

send, v.a. envoyer; (money) remettre; ~ back renvoyer; ~ for envoyer chercher; ~ forth exha er; ~ off expédier; ~ on faire suivre; ~ out lancer.

sender, s. expéditeur, -trice m. f.

sense, s. sens m.

senseless, adj. insensé; sans connaissance.

sensibility, s. sensibilité f.

sensible, adj. sensible; sensé, raisonnable.

sensitive, adj. sensible.

sensual, adj. sensuel.

sentence, s. jugement m.; sentence f.; phrase f.;

— v. a. condamner.

sentiment, s. sentiment m.

sentry, s. sentinelle f.

separate, adj. séparé; à part; — v.a. séparer; v.n. se séparer.

separation, s. séparation f.

September, s. septembre m.

serenade, s. sérénade f.

sergeant, s. sergent m.

series, s. série f.

serious, adj. sérieux.

sermon, s. sermon m.

servant, s. serviteur, -vante m. f.; domestique m. f.

serve, v. a. & n. servir.

service, s. service m.; utilité f.

service-station, s. station-service f.

session, s. séance f., session f.

set, v.a. mettre, placer; (limb) remettre; (fashion) donner; (jewels) monter; (watch) régler; (problem) donner; (appoint) fixer; (trap) tendre; — v.n. (sun) se coucher; — ~ about se mettre à; ~ aside mettre de côté; ~ down déposer; noter; ~ forth exposer; ~ in commencer; ~ off, out partir; ~ on pousser (à); ~ up dresser; établir; ~ up for se donner pour. — s ensemble m., assortiment m., collection f.; (tea) service m.; (radio) poste m.; (ornaments) garniture f.; (tennis) set m.; (gang) bande f.; ~ of furniture ameublement m.; ~ of false teeth dentier m.

setting, s. mise f., pose f.; montage m.; installation f.; coucher m.

settle, *v. a.* fixer; arranger; régler, payer; décider, résoudre; *v.n.* s'établir; se poser (sur); se décider à; ~ *down* s'établir.

settlement, *s.* colonie *f.*

seven, *adj. & s.* sept.

seventeen, *adj.* dix-sept.

seventh, *adj.* septième.

seventy, *adj. & s.* soixante-dix.

several, *adj.* plusieurs; différent.

severe, *adj.* sévère.

sew, *v.a.* coudre.

sewing-machine, *s.* machine *f.* à coudre.

sex, *s.* sexe *m.*

sexual, *adj.* sexuel.

shabby, *adj.* usé, râpé.

shade, *s.* ombre *f.;* ombrage *m.;* — *v.a.* ombrager.

shadow, *s.* ombre *f.*

shady, *adj.* ombreux.

shaft, *s.* bois *m.;* trait *m.;* flèche *f.;* arbre *m.*

shake, *v.a.* secouer; ébranler; *(hands)* serrer; *v.n.* trembler; s'ébranler; — *s.* secousse *f.*

shaky, *adj.* tremblant, branlant; cassé; faible.

shall, *(future* see *Grammar); (command)* vouloir; *(duty)* devoir.

shallow, *adj.* peu profond.

shame, *s.* honte *f.*

shameless, *adj.* éhonté; honteux.

shampoo, *s.* shampooing *m.*

shank, *s.* jambe *f.*

shape, *s.* forme *f.;* — *v. a.* façonner; former; diriger; *v.n.* se développer; promettre.

shapeless, *adj.* sans forme.

share, *s.* part *f.;* action *f.; have a* ~ *in* contribuer (à); *go* ~*s (in)* partager; — *v. a. & n.* partager.

shareholder, *s.* actionnaire *m. f.*

sharp, *adj.* tranchant; aigu; aigre; piquant; perçant; — *s. (music)* dièse *m.;* — *adv.* net; 9.0 ~ 9 heures précises.

sharpen, *v.a.* aiguiser; tailler.

shatter, *v.a.* fracasser; déranger.

shave, *v.a.* raser; *v.n.* se raser.

shawl, *s.* châle *m.*

she, *pron.* elle.

shear, *v.a.* tondre; couper; — *s. (pair of)* ~*s* cisailles *f. pl.*

sheath, *s.* étui; fourreau *m.*

shed, *v.a.* verser; *(light)* répandre.

sheep, *s.* mouton *m.*

sheer, *adj.* pur; perpendiculaire.

sheet, *s.* drap *m.; (paper)* feuille *f.;* ~ *iron* tôle *f.*

shelf, *s.* rayon *m.*

shell, *s. (egg, nut)* coque *f.; (peas)* cosse *f.*

shelter, *s.* abri *m.; take* ~ s'abriter; — *v.a.* abriter (de); *v. n.* se mettre à l'abri (de).

shepherd, *s.* berger.

shield, *s.* bouclier *m.;* écu *m.*

shift, *s.* changement *m.; (work)* équipe *f.; make* ~ *to* s'arranger (de); — *v. n. & a.* changer de place.

shine, *v. n.* briller; rayonner (de); *the sun is shining* il fait du soleil.

ship, *s.* vaisseau *m.,* navire *m.;* — *v. a.* embarquer.

shipping, s. embarque-
ment m.; navires m. pl.;
~ company compagnie
f. de navigation.

shipping-agent, s. agent
maritime, m.; (goods)
expéditeur m.

shipwreck, s. naufrage
m.; — v.a. be ~ed
faire naufrage.

shipyard, s. chantier m. de
construction.

shirt, s. chemise f.

shiver, v.n. frissonner;
(cold) grelotter;

shock, s. choc m.; coup
m.; — v.a. choquer;
frapper d'horreur.

shocking, adj. affreux;
choquant.

shoe, s. soulier m.

shoeblack, s. décrotteur
m., cireur m.

shoe-lace, s. lacet m.

shoemaker, s. cordon-
nier m.

shoot, v.a. tirer, fusiller;
lancer; décharger;
(game) chasser; (plant)
pousser; (rays) darder;
(film) tourner; v.n.
tirer; se précipiter, se
lancer; (plant) pousser;
(pain) élancer.

shooting, s. tir m., fusillade f.; (game) chasse
f.; — adj. (pain) lan-
cinant.

shop, s. boutique f.,
magasin m.; — v.n. go
~ping faire des achats
or emplettes.

shop-assistant, s. commis
m.; demoiselle f., ven-
deur, -euse m. f.

shopkeeper, s. marchand,
-e m. f.; commerçant,
-e m. f.

shore, s. rivage m.; rive f.

short, adj. court; petit;
bref, brève; (lacking)

de manque; — adv.
be ~ of manquer de.

shorten, v. a. & n. raccourcir; abréger.

shorthand, s. sténogra-
phie f.

shortly, adv. sous peu;
bientôt; brièvement.

shot, s. coup m.; trait m.;
(bullet) balle f., (can-
non) boulet m.

shoulder, s. épaule f.

shout, s. cri m.; — v. a. &
n. crier.

shove, v.a. pousser.

shovel, s. pelle f.

show, v.a. montrer; in-
diquer; manifester; ex-
poser; expliquer; v.n.
se montrer; ~ in faire
entrer; ~ off étaler;
faire ressortir; se don-
ner des airs; ~ out
reconduire; ~ up res-
sortir; — s. blant m.;
spectacle m.; parade f.;
exposition f.

shower, s. averse f.; —
v.a. faire pleuvoir.

shower-bath, s. douche f.

shrill, adj. aigre; aigu, -ë.

shrine, s. châsse f.; lieu
saint m.

shrink, v. a. & n. rétrécir;
reculer.

shroud, s. linceul m.

shrub, s. arbrisseau m., ar-
buste m.

shrug, s. haussement
m. d'épaules; — v.a.
hausser.

shudder, s. frisson m.; —
v. n. frissonner (de).

shut, v.a. fermer; (also ~
in) enfermer; ~ off
couper; ~ up fermer;
se taire.

shutter, s. volet m.

shy, adj. timide.

sick, adj. malade; be ~
vomir; be ~ of être
dégoûté de; fall ~

tomber malade.

sickle, s. faucille f.

sickly, adj. maladif; mal-sain.

sickness, s. maladie f.

side, s. côte m.; bord m.; (team) équipe f.

siege, s. siège m.

sieve, s. crible m.

sift, v.a. cribler.

sigh, s. soupir m.; — v. n. soupirer.

sight, s. vue f.; spectacle m.; ~s curiosités f. pl.

sightseeing: go ~ visiter les curiosités.

sign, s. signe m.; enseigne f.; — v. a. & n. signer; ~ on engager.

signal, s signal m.; — v.a. signaler; v.n.faire des signaux.

signature, s. signature f.

significant, adj. significatif.

signify, v.a. signifier; v.n. importer.

signpost, s. poteau m. indicateur.

silence, s. silence m.

silent, adj. silencieux; muet.

silk, s. soie f.

silly, adj. sot.

silver, s. argent m.; — adj. d'argent; argenté.

similar, adj. semblable.

simple, adj. simple.

simultaneous, adj. simultané.

sin, s. péché m.; — v.n. pécher.

since, adv. & prep. depuis; — conj. depuis que; (because) puisque.

sincere, adj. sincère.

sinew, s. tendon m.

sinful, adj. pécheur.

sing, v. a. & n. chanter.

singer, s. chanteur, -euse m. f.; cantatrice f.

single, adj. simple; seul; célibataire; particulier; ~ ticket billet m. d'aller.

singular, s. singulier m.; — adj. remarquable; singulier.

sink, v. n. tomber au fond, sombrer; s'enfoncer; baisser; v. a. enfoncer; faire baisser; foncer; couler; — s. évier m.

sinner, s. pécheur, -eresse m. f.

sir, s. monsieur m.; Sir m.

sister, s. sœur f.; (nurse) infirmière f.

sister-in-law, s. belle-sœur f.

sit, v.n. s'asseoir; être assis; rester; ~ down s'asseoir; se mettre (à); ~ for (exam) se présenter à; ~ up se dresser; (at night) veiller.

site, s. emplacement m.; terrain m.; site m.

sitting-room, s. petit salon m.

situation, s. situation f.; (employment) position f.; emploi m.

six, adj. & s. six (m.).

sixteen, adj. & s. seize (m.).

sixth, adj. sixième; six.

sixty, adj. & s. soixante.

size, s. grandeur f., mesure f.; (shoes etc.) pointure f.; numéro m., taille f.; (pers.) taille f.

skate, v.n. patiner.

skating, s. patinage m.

sketch, s. croquis m.; esquisse f.; — v.a. esquisser.

ski, s. ski m.

skid, v.n. déraper.

skier, s. skieur m.

skiff, s. esquif m.

skilful, adj. adroit.

skill, s. adresse f.

skim, v.a. écrémer.

skin, s. peau f.; — v.a. écorcher; peler.

skip, v. a. & n. sauter.

skirt, s. jupe f.

skull, s. crâne m.

sky, s. ciel m. (pl. cieux).

slack, adj. lâche; négligent.

slacken, v.a. ralentir; relâcher; v.n. se relâcher; diminuer.

slacks, s. pl. pantalon m.

slander, s. calomnie f.; — v.a. calomnier.

slant, s. biais m.; — v. a. faire pencher; v. n. être en pente.

slap, s. claque f.; soufflet m.; — v. a. claquer; souffleter.

slate, s. ardoise f.

slaughter, s. massacre m.

slave, s. esclave m. f.

sledge, s. traîneau.

sleep, s. sommeil m.; go to ~ s'endormir; — v. a. & n. dormir.

sleeping-car, s. wagon-lit m.

sleepy, adj. somnolent; be ~ avoir sommeil.

sleeve, s. manche f.

slender, adj. mince, faible.

slice, s. tranche f.

slide, s. glissade f.; (photo) diapositive f.

slight, adj. mince; léger.

slim, adj. mince, svelte.

sling, s. fronde f.

slip, v.n. glisser; se glisser (dans); v.a. filer; pousser, glisser; ~ off ôter; ~ on mettre; ~ out s'esquiver; — s.

glissade f.; (mistake) faux pas m.; (paper) fiche f.; (underwear) combinaison f.

slipper, s. pantoufle f.

slope, s. biais m.; pente f.; — v. n. incliner.

slot, s. fente f.

slow, adj. lent; (clock) en retard; (dull) peu intelligent; ~ to lent à; — v.n. & a. ~ down ralentir.

slumber, s. sommeil m.; — v.n. sommeiller.

slump, s. débâcle f.; (in trade) mévente f.; dépression f.

sly, adj. rusé.

small, adj. petit; faible; peu important; menu.

smart, adj. (clever) habile, débrouillard; (witty) spirituel; (dress, pers.) élégant, chic; pimpant; (society) élégant.

smash, v. a. briser; fig. écraser; — s. fracas m.; collision f.

smear, v.a. enduire; — s. tache f.

smell, s. odorat m.; odeur f.; — v. a. & n. sentir; ~ out flairer.

smile, s. sourire m.; v.n. sourire (at à).

smoke, s. fumée f.; — v.a. & n. fumer.

smooth, adj. lisse; uni; doux, -ce; (sea) calme; — v.a. aplanir; lisser.

smuggle, v.a. ~ in faire passer en contrebande; v.n. faire la contrebande.

smuggler, s. contrebandier m.

snack, s. morceau (sur le pouce) m.; have a ~ casser la croûte.

snail, s. colimaçon m.

snake, s. serpent m.

snap, s. fermoir m.; coup m. de dents; claquement m.; (photo) instantané m.; — v. a. faire claquer; fermer;

~ *at* happer; ~ *off* casser.

snapshot, *s.* instantané *m.*

snatch, *s.* action de saisir, *f.;* accès *m.;* fragment *m.; — v. a.* saisir; ~ *at* saisir au vol.

sneeze, *v. n.* éternuer; — *s.* éternuement *m.*

sniff, *v.a.&n.* renifler.

snore, *v. n.* ronfler.

snow, *s.* neige *f.; — v.n.* neiger.

snug, *adj.* commode.

so, *adv.* ainsi; si; donc; ~ *that* de sorte que; afin que.

soak, *v.n.* tremper.

soap, *s.* savon *m.*

soar, *v.n.* prendre son essor; *fig.* s'élancer.

sob, *v.n.* sangloter; — *s.* sanglot.

sober, *adj.* sobre; sensé;

social, *adj.* social.

socialism, *s.* socialisme *m.*

society, *s.* société *f.*

sock, *s.* chaussette *f.*

socket, *s.* cavité *f.; (electric)* prise *f.* de contact.

soda-water, *s.* eau *f.* de Seltz.

sofa, *s.* canapé *m.*

soft, *adj.* mou, mol molle; doux, -ce.

soil, *s.* terroir; *(stain)* tache; — *v. a.* souiller.

soldier, *s.* soldat *m.*

sole[1], *s.* plante *f.;* semelle *f.; (fish)* sole *f.*

sole[2], *adj.* seul.

solicit, *v. a.* solliciter.

solicitor, *s.* avoué *m.* solicitor *m.*

solidarity, *s.* solidarité *f.*

solitude, *s.* solitude *f.*

solution, *s.* solution *f.*

solve, *v.a.* résoudre.

some, *adj.* quelque; de; — *pron.* quelques-uns; les uns; en *(+ verb)*

— *adv.* environ.

somebody, -one, *pron.* quelqu'un.

somehow, *adv.* d'une façon quelconque; ~ *or other* d'une façon ou d'une autre.

something, *s. & pron.* quelque chose *m.*

sometime, *adv.* quelque jour, autrefois.

sometimes, *adv.* quelquefois, parfois.

somewhere, *adv.* quelque part.

son, *s.* fils *m.*

song, *s.* chanson *f.*

son-in-law, *s.* gendre *m.*

soon, *adv.* bientôt.

sore, *adj.* douloureux; *have a* ~ ... avoir mal à ...; — *s.* plaie *f.*

sorrow, *s.* douleur *f.*

sorry, *adj. be* ~ *for* regretter; ~*!* pardon!

sort, *s.* sorte *f.;* genre *m.;* type *m.;* ~ *of* une espèce de.

soul, *s.* âme *f.*

sound[1], *s.* son *m.;* bruit *m.; — v. n.* sonner; — *v.a.* sonner; sonder; *(physician)* ausculter.

sound[2], *adj.* sain; solide; droit; profond; en bon état.

soup, *s.* potage *m.; (clear)* consommé *m.; (thick)* soupe *f.*

sour, *adj.* aigre; acide; *(milk)* tourné.

source, *s.* source *f.*

south, *s.* sud *m.,* midi *m.;* — *adj.* sud; du sud; — *adv.* vers le sud.

southeast, *adj. & s.* sudest *(m.); — adv.* vers le sud-est.

southern, *adj.* du sud.

southwest, *adj. & s.* sudouest *(m.); — adv.* vers

le sud-ouest.

sovereign, *s.* souverain, -e *m. f.*

sow¹, *v. a. & n.* semer (de).

sow², *s.* truie *f.*

space, *s.* espace *m.*

space-craft, -ship, -ve-hicle, *s.* astronef *m.*

space-flight, *s.* navigation *f.* astronautique.

spaceman, *s.* cosmonaute *m.*, astronaute *m.*

spade, *s.* bêche *f.; (cards)* pique *m.*

span, *s.* empan *m.; ouver-ture; — v.a.* traverser; couvrir.

Spaniard, *s.* Espagnol, -e.

Spanish, *adj. & s.* espagnol *(m.).*

spanner, *s.* clef *f.*

spare, *adj.* maigre; dispo-nible; de réserve; ~ *parts* pièces de rechange *f. pl.; ~ time* loisir *m.; — v.a.* épargner; éco-nomiser; *(evade)* éviter.

spark, *s.* étincelle *f.*

sparrow, *s.* moineau *m.*

speak, *v.n.* parler; *v.a.* dire; ~ *out* parler har-diment; ~ *up* parler plus haut; ... ~*ing* ici ...

spear, *s.* lance *f.*

special, *adj.* spécial.

specialist, *s.* spécialiste *m. f.*

specific, *adj.* spécifique.

specify, *v.a.* spécifier.

speck, *s.* grain *m.; tache f.*

spectacles, *s. pl.* lunettes *f.*

spectacular, *adj.* impres-sionnant.

spectator, *s.* spectateur, -trice *m. f.*

speech, *s.* parole *f.; lan-gage m.; (address)* discours *m.*

speed, *s.* vitesse *f.*

speedy, *adj.* rapide;

prompt.

spell¹, *v.a. & n.* épeler; orthographier, écrire; *how is it spelt?* com-ment cela s'écrit-il?

spell², *s.* période *f.; tour m.*

spelling, *s.* ortographe *f.*

spend, *v.a.* dépenser; *(time)* passer; *v.n.* dépenser.

sphere, *s.* sphère *f.*

spice, *s.* épice *f.*

spider, *s.* araignée *f.*

spill, *v.a.* repandre; ren-verser.

spin, *v.a. & n.* filer; faire tourner.

spinach, *s.* épinards *m. pl.*

spine, *s.* épine (dorsale) *f.*

spinster, *s.* vieille fille *f.; célibataire f.*

spiral, *adj.* en spirale.

spire, *s.* flèche *f.*

spirit, *s.* esprit *m.; âme f.; spectre m.; carac-tère m., cœur m.; ~s* spiritueux *m. pl.*

spiritual, *adj.* spirituel.

spit, *s.* crachat *m.; — v. a. & n.* cracher.

spite, *s.* dépit *m.; in ~ of* malgré.

splash, *s.* éclaboussement *m.; — v. a. & n.* écla-bousser (de).

spleen, *s.* rate *f.*

splendid, *adj.* splendide.

splinter, *s.* éclat *m.; (bone)* esquille *f.*

split, *v. a.* fendre; (also ~ *up)* partager; *v.n.* se fendre; se diviser.

spoil, *v.a.* gâter; dépouil-ler (de); endommager; *v.n.* se gâter.

sponge, *s.* éponge *f.*

spontaneous, *adj.* spon-tané.

spoon, *s.* cuiller *f.*

spoonful, *s.* cuillerée *f.*

sport, *s.* sport *m.;* amusements *m. pl.*

sportsman, *s.* sportsman *m.*

spot, *s.* tache *f.;* *(place)* endroit *m.;* — *v.a.* tacher; reconnaître.

spout, *s.* gouttière *f.;* bec *m.;* — *v.a.* lancer.

sprain, *v.a.* donner une entorse (à).

spray, *s.* embrun *m.,* vaporisateur *m.;* atomiseur *m.;* — *v.a.* vaporiser, atomiser; arroser.

spread, *v.a.* étendre; répandre; *(cloth)* mettre; *(cover)* couvrir; *(news)* faire circuler; *v.n.* s'étendre; — *s.* propagation *f.;* étendue *f.*

spring¹, *s.* printemps *m.*

spring², *v.n.* sauter; pousser; jaillir; provenir (de), descendre (de), naître (de); ~ *up* se lever vite; jaillir — *s.* saut *m.;* *(watch etc.)* ressort *m.*

sprinkle, *v.a.* répandre; asperger (de), arroser.

sprout, *v. a. & n.* germer; pousser; — *s.* pousse *f.;* *Brussels* ~s choux *m. pl.* de Bruxelles

spur, *s.* éperon *m.,* aiguillon *m.;* — *v. a.* éperonner; ~ *on* pousser à.

spy, *s.* espion, -onne *m. f.;* — *v.n.* espionner.

squander, *v. a.* gaspiller.

square, *s.* carré *m.;* *(town)* place *f.;* — *adj.* carré; honnête.

squeeze, *v.a.* serrer; presser.

squint, *v.n.* loucher; — *s.* strabisme *m.*

squire, *s.* écuyer *m.;* châtelain *m.*

squirrel, *s.* écureuil *m.*

stability, *s.* stabilité *f.*

stable, *s.* écurie *f.;* — *adj.* stable.

stack, *s.* pile *f.;* meule *f.*

stadium, *s.* stade *m.*

staff, *s.* état-major *m.;* bâton *m.;* hampe *f.;* *(institution)* personnel *m.;* ~ *officer* officier d'état-major *m.*

stag, *s.* cerf *m.*

stage, *s.* scène *f.;* *(drama)* théâtre *m.;* *(period)* période *f.;* *(platform)* estrade *f.;* — *v.a.* mettre en scène.

stagger, *v.n.* chanceler; *v.a.* bouleverser.

stain, *s.* tache *f.;* — *v.a.* tacher; salir.

stair, *s.* marche; ~s escalier *m.*

staircase, *s.* escalier *m.*

stake, *s.* pieu *m.;* *at* ~ en jeu; — *v.a.* garnir de pieux; mettre au jeu; jouer.

stale, *adj.* rassis.

stall, *s.* stalle *f.;* fauteuil *m.;* *(books)* kiosque *m.* à journaux.

stammer, *v. n.* bégayer.

stamp, *s.* timbre-poste *m.;* estampe *f.;* contrôle *m.;* empreinte *f.;* — *v.a.* timbrer; estamper; contrôler.

stand, *v.n.* être debout, se tenir debout, se soutenir; *(be situated)* se trouver; *(remain)* rester; ~ *out* ressortir; ~ *up* se lever; — *s.* position *f.;* *(vehicles)* station *f.;* *(stall)* étalage *m.;* stand *m.*

standard, *s.* étendard *m.;* étalon *m.;* niveau *m.;* — *adj.* régulateur; au titre; *(authors)* classique.

star, *s.* étoile *f.*

stare, v.n. (also ~ at) regarder fixement.

start, v.n. partir; commencer; v. a. faire partir; faire lever; commencer; lancer; — s. commencement m.; départ m.

starve, v.n. mourir de faim; v. a. faire mourir de faim.

state, s. état m.; — v. a. affirmer; porter; déclarer.

statement, s. déclaration f.

statesman, s. homme m. d'état.

station, s. poste m.; endroit m.; (railway) gare f.; (police) poste m. de police.

stationer, s. papetier m.; ~'s shop papeterie f.

statistic(al), adj. statistique.

statistics, s. statistique f.

statue, s. statue f.

statute, s. statut m.; ordonnance f.

stay, v.n. rester; être installé; ~ away rester absent; ~ up veiller.

steady, adj. ferme; soutenu; (pers.) rangé; — int. attention!

steak, s. tranche f.; bifteck m.

steal, v.a. voler.

steam, s. vapeur f.

steamboat, s. bateau m. à vapeur

steam-engine, s. locomotive f.

steel, s. acier m.

steep, adj. raide, escarpé.

steeple, s. clocher m.

steer, v.a. gouverner; diriger.

steering-gear, s. appareil m. de direction.

steering-wheel, s. volant m.

stem, s. tige f.; queue f.

step, s. pas m.; (stair) marche f.; (ladder) échelon m.; take ~s faire des démarches; — v.n. faire un pas; marcher; aller, venir; ~ in entrer.

stepmother, s. belle-mère f.

stereotype, s. cliché m.

sterile, adj. stérile.

stern, s. arrière m. — adj. sévère.

stew, s. ragoût m.; (fruit) compote f.; — v.a. (meat) faire un ragout de; (fruit) faire une compote de.

steward, s. régisseur m.; steward m.

stewardess, s. hôtesse f. de l'air.

stick, s. bâton m., canne f., petite branche f.; — v.a. coller; v.n. se coller; ~ on attacher; ~ to rester fidèle à.

sticky, adj. gluant.

stiff, adj. raide; dur.

still, adj. calme — adv. toujours; encore; cependant.

sting, s. aiguillon m.; — v.a. & n. piquer.

stink, v.n. puer; — s. puanteur f.

stipulate, v.a. stipuler.

stir, v.a. remuer; exciter; v. n. remuer; bouger; — s. remuement m.

stirrup, s. étrier m.

stitch, s. point m.; — v.a. & n. coudre.

stock, s. marchandises f. pl.; provision f.; (tree) tronc m.; (cattle) bestiaux *m. pl.; (finance)* valeurs *f. pl.;* Stock Exchange Bourse *f.*

stockholder, *s.* actionnaire *m. f.*

stocking, *s.* bas *m.*

stomach, *s.* estomac *m.*

stone, *s.* pierre; *(fruit)* noyau *m.;* — *v.a.* lapider.

stony, *adj.* pierreux.

stool, *s.* tabouret *m.*, escabeau *m.*

stop, *v.a.* arrêter; empêcher (de); *(teeth)* plomber; retenir suspendre, *v.n.* s'arrêter; cesser; — *s.* halte *f.;* arrêt *m.; (organ)* jeu *m.; (sign)* signe de ponctuation, *m.*

store, *s.* provision *f.;* ~s grand magasin *m.;* — *v.a.* emmagasiner.

stork, *s.* cigogne *f.*

storm, *s.* orage *m.*

story[1], *s.* histoire *f.*

story[2], *s.* étage *m.*

stout, *adj.* fort; intrépide.

stove, *s.* poêle *m.;* fourneau *m.*

straight, *adj.* droit; honnête; d'aplomb; — *adv.* juste; droit.

straighten, *v.a.* (re)dresser; *v.n.* se redresser.

strain, *s.* effort *m.;* tension *f.;* — *v. a.* tendre; *(filter)* passer; *(muscle)* forcer.

strange, *adj.* étrange(r).

stranger, *s.* étranger -ère *m. f.*

strap, *s.* courroie *f.*

straw, *s.* paille *f.*

strawberry, *s.* fraise *f.*

stray, *adj.* égaré; — *v. n.* errer.

streak, *s.* raie *f.;* bande *f.*

stream, *s.* courant *m.;* — *v.n.* couler, ruisseler.

street, *s.* rue *f.*

strength, *s.* force *f.*

strengthen, *v.a.* fortifier.

stress, *s.* force *f.; (grammar)* accent *m.*

stretch, *s.* effort *m.;* étendue *f.;* — *v.a.* étendre; élargir.

stretcher, *s.* brancard *m.*

strew, *v.a.* semer.

strict, *adj.* strict.

stride, *s.* enjambée *f.;* grand pas *m.;* — *v. n.* enjamber.

strike, *v.a.* frapper; *(blow)* asséner; *(work)* cesser; *v.n.* frapper; *(clock)* sonner; *(workers)* se mettre en grève — *s.* grève *f.;* be on ~ être en grève.

striking, *adj.* frappant.

string, *s.* ficelle *f.;* corde *f.*

strip, *s.* bande *f.;* bout *m.;* — *v. a.* déshabiller; *v.n.* se déshabiller.

stripe, *s.* bande *f.*

strip-lighting, *s.* éclairage *m.* par luminescent.

strive, *v. n.* s'efforcer (de).

stroke, *s.* coup *m.; (swimming)* brasse *f.; (pen)* trait *m.*

strong, *adj.* fort; vigoureux; puissant; solide.

structure, *s.* structure *f.*

struggle, *v.n.* lutter (avec); faire de grands efforts (pour); — *s.* lutte *f.;* mêlée *f.*

stub, *s.* souche *f.;* bout *m.*

stubborn, *adj.* obstiné.

stud, *s.* bouton *m.*

student, *s.* étudiant, -e *m. f.*

studio, *s.* atelier *m.*

study, *s.* étude *f.;* cabinet *m.* de travail —

v. a. & n. étudier.

stuff, *s.* étoffe *f.;* matériaux *m.pl.;* — *v.a.* remplir; fourrer.

stumble, *v.n.* trébucher; ∼ *(up)on* tomber sur; — *s.* faux pas *m.*

stump, *s.* souche *f.;* — *v.a.* estomper.

stupid, *adj.* stupide.

style, *s.* style *m.*

subject, *s.* sujet, -te *m. f.;* — *adj.* ∼ *to* sujet à; —*v.a.* assujettir (à).

submarine, *s.* sous-marin *m.*

submission, *s.* soumission *f.*

submit, *v.a.* soumettre.

subordinate, *adj. & s.* subordonné; — *v.a.* subordonner.

subscribe, *v.a. & n.* (∼ *to*) souscrire (à); s'abonner (à).

subscriber, *s.* souscripteur *m.;* abonné; -e souscripteur *m.;* abonné, -e *m. f.*

subscription, *s.* souscription *f.;* abonnement *m.*

subsequent, *adj.* subséquent.

subsequently, *adv.* par la suite.

subsidy, *s.* subside *m.*

subsist, *v. n.* exister; subsister (de).

subsistence, *s.* subsistance *f.*

substance, *s.* substance *f.*

substantial, *adj.* substantiel.

substantive, *s.* substantif *m.*

substitute, *v.a.* substituer *(for* à).

substitution, *s.* substitution *f.*

subtle, *adj.* subtil.

subtract, *v.a.* soustraire.

subtraction, *s.* soustraction *f.*

suburb, *s.* faubourg *m.;* ∼*s* banlieue *f.*

subway, *s.* souterrain *m.;* métro *m.*

succeed, *v.a.* succéder (à); *v.n. (be successful)* réussir (à); faire ses affaires; ∼ *to* succéder à.

success, *s.* succès *m.*

successful, *adj.* heureux, *(exam)* reçu.

succession, *s.* succession *f.*

successive, *adj.* successif.

such, *adj.* tel, -le; ∼ *and* ∼ tel(le) ou tel(le); — *pron.* ∼ *as* ceux, celles.

suck, *v.a. & n.* sucer; — *s. give* ∼ *to* allaiter.

sudden, *adj.* soudain.

suddenly, *adv.* soudain.

suet, *s.* graisse *f.* de rognon.

suffer, *v. a. & n.* souffrir.

sufficient, *adj.* suffisant.

sufficiently, *adv.* suffisamment.

sugar, *s.* sucre *m.*

suggest, *v.a.* suggérer; proposer.

suggestion, *s.* suggestion *f.*

suicide, *s.* suicide *m.*

suit, *s. (clothes)* complet *m.; (cards)* couleur *f.; (law)* procès *m.; (request)* requête *f.;* — *v.a.* convenir (à); adapter (à); *v.n.* convenir (à); aller (avec).

suitable, *adj.* convenable; ∼ *for* adapté à.

suitcase, *s.* mallette *f.,* valise *f.*

sum, *s.* somme *f.;* ∼ *total* somme totale, *f.;*

— v.a. ~ up résumer
summary, s. résumé m.
summer, s. été m.
summon, v.a. convoquer; appeler.
sun, s. soleil m.
Sunday, s. dimanche m.
sunny, adj. ensoleillé; exposé au soleil.
sunrise, s. lever m. du soleil.
sunset, s. coucher m. du soleil.
sunshine, s. soleil m.
sunstroke, s. coup m. de soleil.
superannuate, v. a. mettre à la retraite.
superficial, adj. superficiel.
superfluous, adj. superflu.
superior, s. & adj. supérieur (m.).
supermarket, s. supermarché m.
supersonic, adj. supersonique.
superstition, s. superstition f.
superstitious, adj. superstitieux.
supervise, v.a. surveiller.
supervision, s. superveillance f.
supper, s. souper m.
supplement, s. supplément m.; — v.a. suppléer (à).
supplementary, adj. supplémentaire.
supply, s. provision f.; approvisionnement m.; ~ and demand l'offre et la demande; — v.a. fourner (de); suppléer.
support, s. appui m.; support m.; — v.a. supporter; soutenir; appuyer.
suppose, v.a. supposer.

supposition, s. supposition f.
suppress, v.a. supprimer.
suppression, s. suppression f.; répression f.
supreme, adj. suprême.
sure, adj. sûr; be ~ to ne pas manquer de; make ~ that s'assurer que.
surely, adv. sûrement.
surface, s. surface f.
surgeon, s. chirurgien m.
surgery, s. chirurgie f.
surname, s. nom m. de famille.
surpass, v.a. surpasser.
surprise, s. surprise f.; — v.a. surprendre.
surprising, adj. surprenant.
surrender, s. abandon m.; reddition f.; — v.a. rendre; renoncer; v.n. se rendre.
surround, v.a. entourer (de).
surroundings, s. pl. environs m. pl.; entourage m.
survey, s. vue f.; examen m.; — v.a. contempler, regarder; examiner; expertiser.
survive, v. n. & a. survivre (à).
suspect, adj. & s. suspect, -e (m. f.); — v. a. & n. soupçonner.
suspenders, s. pl. jarretelles f. pl.
suspicion, s. soupçon m.
suspicious, adj. soupçonneux; suspect.
swallow[1], s. hirondelle f.
swallow[2], v. a. avaler; gober.
swan, s. cygne m.
swarm, s. essaim m.; foule f.; — v.n. essaimer; s'assembler en

foule.

swear, *v.a.* jurer; prêter; *v.n.* jurer.

sweat, *s.* sueur *f.;* — *v.a.* exploiter; *v.n.* suer.

Swede, *s.* Suédois, -e *m. f.*

Swedish, *adj. & s.* suédois *(m.).*

sweep, *v.a.* balayer; *(chimney)* ramoner; — *s.* coup *m.* de balai; courbe *f.;* grand geste *m.; (pers.)* ramoneur *m.*

sweet, *adj.* doux; *(pers.)* gentil; — *s.* bonbon *m.;* entremets *m.*

sweetheart, *s.* bien-aimé, -ée *m. f.;* ~*! mon amour!, ma chérie!

swell, *v.n.* (s')enfler; se gonfler; grossir; *v.a.* gonfler; bouffir; — *s.* houle *f.;* élévation *f.*

swim, *v. n.* nager; aller à la nage; flotter; *v.a* nager; — *s. have a* ~ aller nager.

swimmer, *s.* nageur, -euse *m. f.*

swimming-pool, *s.* piscine *f.*

swine, *s.* cochon *m.*

swing, *s.* va-et-vient *m.;* rythme *m.; (for children)* escarpolette *f.* balançoire *f.;* — *v.a.* balancer; *v. n.* osciller; se balancer.

Swiss, *adj.* suisse; — *s.* Suisse *m. f.*

switch, *s.* badine *f.;* aiguille *f.;* interrupteur *m.;* commutateur *m.;* — *v.a.* cingler; aiguiller; couper; ~ *off* couper (le courant); ~ *on* donner (le courant), tourner (le bouton).

sword, *s.* épée *f.;* sa-

bre *m.*

syllable, *s.* syllabe *f.*

symbol, *s.* symbole *m.*

symmetrical, *adj* symétrique.

symmetry, *s.* symétrie *f.*

sympathy, *s.* sympathie *f.*

symphony, *s.* symphonie *f.*

synagogue, *s.* synagogue *f.*

synthetic, *adj.* synthétique.

syringe, *s.* seringue *f.*

syrup, *s.* sirop *m.*

system, *s.* système *m.*

systematic(al), *adj.* systématique.

T

table, *s.* table *f.;* clear *the* ~ desservir; *lay the* ~ mettre le couvert.

table-cloth, *s.* nappe *f.*

table-spoon, *s.* cuiller *f.* à • soupe.

tablet, *s.* tablette *f.*

tack, *s.* broquette *f.,* petit clou *m.*

tackle, *s.* attirail *m.;* apparaux *m. pl.;* — *v.a.* saisir à bras le corps; *(problem)* essayer de résoudre.

tact, *s.* tact *m.*

tag, *s.* ferret *m.;* étiquette (volante) *f.;* bout *m.*

tail, *s.* queue *f.*

tailor, *s.* tailleur *m.*

take, *v.a.* prendre; *(carry)* porter; *(walk)* faire; ~ *after* ressembler à; ~ *away* enlever; ~ *down* descendre, *(write)* prendre (par écrit); ~ *in (paper)* s'abonner à; ~ *off* ôter; *(v.n.)* prendre son élan; ~ *on* se charger

de; ~ *to* se mettre
à; ~ *up* ramasser,
relever.

tale, *s.* conte *m.*, histoire *f*

talent, *s.* talent *m.*

talk, *v.a. & n.* parler
(*about, of* de); ~*ing of*
à propos de; — *s.*
conversation *f.;* cau-
serie *f.*

tall, *adj.* grand; *how* ~ *is
he?* quelle est sa taille?

tame, *adj.* apprivoisé.

tan, *s.* tan *m.*

tank, *s.* réservoir *m.;* char
m. d'assaut.

t ankard, *s.* chope *f.*

tap, *s.* robinet *m.; (blow)*
tape *f.;* petit coup *m.;*
— *v.a.* mettre en
perce; *(strike)* frap-
per légèrement, taper.

tape, *s.* ruban *m.* (de coton).

tape-recorder, *s.* magnétophone *m.*

tapestry, *s.* tapisserie *f.*

target, *s.* cible *f.*

tariff, *s.* tarif *m.*

tart, *s.* tart *f.*

task, *s.* tâche *f.; (school)*
devoir *m.*

taste, *s.* goût *m.*

tasteless, *adj.* sans saveur.

tasty, *adj.* savoureux,
de bon goût.

tatter, *s.* lambeau *m.*

tavern, *s.* taverne *f.*

tax, *s.* impôt *m.;* ~ *free*
exempt d'impôts.

taxi, *s.* taxi *m.*

tea, *s.* thé *m.*

teach, *v.a.* enseigner,
instruire; *(how to)* ap-
prendre (à).

teacher, *s.* instituteur,
-trice *m. f.;* professeur
m. f.

teaching, *s.* enseignement
m.

team, *s.* équipe *f.*

tea-pot, *s.* théière *f.*

tear¹, *s. (eye)* larme *f.*

tear², *v.a.* déchirer; ~
away, down, out ar-
racher; ~ *up* déchirer;
— *s.* déchirure *f.*

tease, *v.a.* taquiner.

tea-spoon, *s.* cuiller *f.* à
thé.

technical, *adj.* technique.

technique, *s.* technique *f.*

technology, *s.* technologie *f.*

tedious, *adj.* ennuyeux.

teenager, *s.* adolescent,
-e *m. f.*

telecast, *v.a.* téléviser.

telegram, *s.* télégramme
m.

telegraph, *s.* télégraphe
m.

telephone, *s.* téléphone
m.; — *v.a. & n.* télé-
phoner (*to* à).

telescope, *s.* téléscope *m.;*
réfracteur *m.;* — *v.a.*
télescoper.

televise, *v.a.* téléviser.

television, *s.* télévision *f.*

television-set, *s.* appareil *m.* de TV, télé-
viseur *m.*

telex, *s.* télex *m.*

tell, *v.a.* dire; raconter; distinguer; ~ *s.o.*
to do sth. enjoindre,
dire à qn de faire qch.

temper, *s.* colère *f.;*
tempérament *m.*

temperature, *s.* température *f.*

temporary, *adj.* tempo-
raire.

tempt, *v.a.* tenter.

ten, *adj. & s.* dix *(m.).*

tenant, *s.* locataire *m. f.*

tend, *v.n.* tendre (à).

tendency, *s.* tendence *f.*

tender¹, *v.a.* offrir; ~

for soumissionner; — *s.* soumission *f.*

tender[2], *adj.* tendre.

tennis, *s.* tennis *m.*

tension, *s.* tension *f.*

tent, *s.* tente *f.*

tenth, *adj.* dixième; dix.

term, *s.* terme *m.; (school)* trimestre *m.; be on good ~s* être bien (avec); — *v.a.* appeler.

terminate, *v.a.* terminer; *vn.* se terminer.

terminus, *s.* (gare *f.*) terminus *m.*

terrace, *s.* terrasse *f.*

terrible, *adj.* terrible.

territory, *s.* territoire *m.*

test, *s.* épreuve *f.;* examen *m.; (school)* composition *f., (oral)* épreuve *f.;* orale — *v.a.* mettre à l'épreuve.

testify, *v.a.* affirmer.

testimony, *s.* témoignage *m.*

text, *s.* texte *m.*

text-book, *s.* manuel *m.*

textile, *s.* textile *m.*

than, *conj.* que; *(with numbers)* de.

thank, *v.a.* remercier; *~ you* merci; — *s. ~s* remerciements *m. pl.;* merci.

thankful, *adj.* reconnaissant.

that[1], *adj.* ce, cet, cette' ces; — *pron.* celui, celle, ceux; cela; *~'s it* c'est cela.

that[2], *conj.* que.

the, *art.* le, la, les; ce, cet, cette; ces.

theatre, *s.* théâtre *m.*

their, *pron.* leur, leurs.

theirs, *pron.* le leur, la leur, les leurs; à eux, à elles.

them, *pron.* les; leur; eux, elles.

theme, *s.* thème *m.;* sujet *m.*

themselves, *pron.* se; eux-mêmes, elles-mêmes.

then, *adv.* alors; *(after that)* puis; *(consequently)* donc.

theology, *s.* théologie *f.*

theoretical, *adj.* théorique.

theory, *s.* théorie *f.*

there, *adv.* là; *(with verb)* y; *~ is, are* il y a.

therefore *adv.* donc.

thermometer, *s.* thermomètre *m.*

thermos, *s.* thermos *f.*

they, *pron.* ils, elles; *~ say* on dit

thick, *adj.* épais.

thief, *s.* voleur, -euse *m. f.*

thigh, *s.* cuisse *f.*

thimble, *s.* dé *m.*

thin, *adj.* mince; maigre; *fig.* pauvre.

thing, *s.* chose *f.; ~s* effets *m. pl.*

think, *v.a.* croire; concevoir; *v.n.* croire; penser *(about, of* à); *~ out* élaborer; *~ over* réfléchir à, penser.

third, *adj.* troisième; trois; — *s.* tiers *m.*

thirsty, *adj.* altéré; *be ~* avoir soif.

thirteen, *adj. & s.* treize *(m.).*

thirty, *adj. & s.* trente *(m.).*

this, *pl.* **these,** *pron.* cela, — *adj.* ceci; ce, cet, cette; ces.

thorn, *s.* épine *f.*

thorough, *adj.* profond, complet; consommé.

thoroughfare, *s.* artère *f.* principal, grande rue *f.; no ~* rue barrée, passage interdit.

thoroughly, *adv.* tout à fait, à fond.

though, *conj.* quoique, bien que; — *adv.* tout de même.

thought, *s.* pensée *f.*; idée *f.*; *(care)* souci *m.*

thoughtful, *adj.* pensif; attentif.

thoughtless, *adj.* étourdi; insouciant.

thousand, *s.* & *adj.* mille *(m.)*

thrash, *v.a.* battre.

thread, *s.* fil *m.*; — *v. a.* enfiler.

threat, *s.* menace *f.*

threaten, *v. a.* & *n.* menacer (de).

three, *adj.* & *s.* trois *(m.).*

threshold, *s.* seuil *m.*

thrifty, *adj.* économe.

thrill, *s.* tressaillement *m.*; — *v. a.be ~ed with* frissonner de.

thrive, *v. n.* prospérer.

throat, *s.* gorge *f.*

throne, *s.* tône *m.*

through, *prep.* à travers; au travers de; par; par suite de; pendant; — *adv.* d'un bout à l'autre; *be ~ with* avoir fini qch.; — *adj.* direct.

throughout, *prep.* & *adv.* d'un bout à l'autre.

throw, *v.a.* jeter; *~ away* jeter, dissiper; *~ down* renverser; jeter à terre; *~ off* se débarrasser de; ôter; *~ out* rejecter; *~ over* abandonner; — *s.* jet *m.*

thrust, *v.a.* fourrer, pousser; enforcer; — *s.* poussée *f.*; botte *f.*

thumb, *s.* pouce *m.*

thunder, *s.* tonnerre *m.*; — *v.n.* tonner.

Thursday, *s.* jeudi *m.*

thus, *adv.* ainsi.

ticket, *s.* billet *m.*; étiquette *f.*

ticket-collector, *s.* contrôleur *m.*

tide, *s.* marée *f.*; courant *m.*

tidy, *adj.* propre; bien rangé; *(pers.)* ordonné; — *v.a.* (also *~ up*) mettre en ordre.

tie, *v.a.* attacher; lier; nouer; *~ down* lier; *~ up* attacher; — *s.* lien *m.*; cravate *f.*; *(sport)* partie *f.* égale.

tiger, *s.* tigre, -esse *m. f.*

tight, *adj.* serré; tendu.

tighten, *v.a.* serrer.

tile, *s.* tuile *f.*

till, *prep.* jusqu'à; — *conj.* jusqu'à ce que.

tilt, *s.* inclinaison *f.*; — *v. n.* s'incliner, pencher; *v.a.* pencher.

time, *s.* temps *m.*; moment *m.*; *(clock)* heure *f.*; *(occasions)* fois; *at ~s* de temps en temps; *by the ~ that* avant que; *for the ~ being* actuellement; *what ~ is it?* quelle heure est-il?; *have a good ~* s'amuser bien; *keep good ~* marcher bien.

timely, *adj.* opportun.

timetable, *s.* horaire *m.*; indicateur *m.*; *(school)* emploi *m.* du temps.

tin, *s.* étain *m.*; *(conserve)* boîte *f.* (en fer blanc).

tinned, *adj.* en boîte; conservé.

tint, *s.* teinte *f.*

tiny, *adj.* tout petit.

tip¹, *s.* bout *m.*; — *v.a.*

renverser; *v.n.* (also ~ *over*) se renverser.

tip², *s.* (*money*) pourboire *m.*; — *v.a.* donner un pourboire (à).

tire¹, tyre, *s.* pneu(matique) *m.*

tire², *v.a.* fatiguer; *v.n.* se fatiguer.

tired, *adj.* be ~ of être las de.

tissue, *s.* tissu *m.*

tissue-paper, *s.* papier *m.* de soie.

title, *s.* titre *m.*

to, *prep.* à; vers; en,

toast, *s.* rôtie *f.*; (*bread, drink*) toast *m.*; — *v.a.* rôtir.

tobacco, *s.* tabac *m.*

tobacconist, *s.* marchand *m.* de tabac; ~'s débit *m.* de tabac.

today, *adv.* aujourd'hui.

toe, *s.* orteil *m.*, doigt *m.* du pied.

together, *adv.* ensemble; en même temps.

toil, *s.* travail *m.*; — *v.n.* travailler.

toilet, *s.* toilette *f.*

toilet-paper, *s.* papier *m.* hygiénique.

tomato, *s.* tomate *f.*

tomb, *s.* tombeau *m.*

tomorrow, *adv.* demain.

ton, *s.* tonne *f.*

tone, *s.* ton *m.*

tongs, *s. pl.* pincettes *f. pl.*; pince *f.*

tongue, *s.* langue *f.*

tonight, *adv.* cette nuit; ce soir.

tonsil, *s.* amygdale *f.*

too, *adv.* trop; (*also*) aussi.

tool, *s.* outil *m.*; instrument *m.*

tooth, *s.* dent *f.*

toothache, *s.* mal *m.* de dents.

toothbrush, *s.* brosse *f.* à dents.

toothpaste, *s.* pâte *f.* dentifrice.

top, *s.* sommet *m.*, faîte *m.*; dessus *m.*; couvercle *m.*; tête *f.*; premier, -ère *m. f.*; — *v.a.* couronner; dépasser.

topic, *s.* sujet *m.*; ~s of the day actualités *f. pl.*

torch, *s.* torche *f.*

tortoise, *s.* tortue *f.*

toss, *s.* mouvement *m.*; — *v.a.* jeter; lancer en l'air; ballotter; ~ up lancer en l'air.

total, *adj. & s.* total (*m.*).

totter, *v.n.* chanceler.

touch, *s.* toucher *m.*; attouchement *m.*; touche *f.*; légère *f.* attaque,; — *v.a.* toucher.

tough, *adj.* dur; robuste; rude.

tour, *s.* voyage *m.*; tour *m.*; tournée *f.*; — *v.n.* voyager.

tourism, *s.* tourisme *m.*

tourist, *s.* touriste *m.*

tournament, *s.* tournoi *m.*

tow, *s.* étoupe *f.*; remorque *f.*; — *v.a.* remorquer.

toward(s), *prep.* vers; envers; pour.

towel, *s.* essuie-main(s) *m.*, serviette *f.*

tower, *s.* tour *f.*

town, *s.* ville *f.*

town-hall, *s.* hôtel *m.* de ville.

toy, *s.* jouet *m.*; — *v.n.* jouer (avec).

trace, *s.* trace *f.*; trait *m.*; — *v.a.* tracer; ~ back remonter à.

track, *s.* traces *f. pl.*; sentier *m.*; (*railw.*) voie *f.*; (*running*) piste

f.

tractor, *s.* tracteur *m.*

trade, *s.* commerce *m.;* *(occupation)* métier *m.;* *v.n.* commercer; ~ *in* faire le commerce de.

trade-mark, *s.* marque *f.* de fabrique.

tradesman, *s.* commerçant *m.*

trade(s)-union, *s.* syndicat *m.*

tradition, *s.* tradition *f.*

traditional, *adj.* traditionnel.

traffic, *s.* trafic *m.;* circulation *f.;* ~ *lights* feux *m.pl.* de signalisation.

tragedy, *s.* tragédie

tragic(al), *adj.* tragique.

trail, *s.* trace *f.;* — *v.a.* & *n.* traîner.

train, *s.* train *m.; (series)* suite *f.;* — *v.a.* entraîner; former.

trainer, *s.* entraîneur *m.*

traitor, *s.* traître *m.*

tram, *s.* tramway *m.*

tramp, *v.n.* aller à pied; — *s.* bruit *m.* de pas; *(pers.)* chemineau *m.*

transaction, *s.* transaction *f.*

transfer, *s.* transport *m.;* — *v.a.* transférer.

transform, *v.a.* transformer (en).

transfusion, *s.* transfusion *f.*

transgress, *v.a.* transgresser; *v.n.* pécher.

transistor, *s.* transistor *m.*

transit, *s.* transit *m; in* ~ en cours de route.

translate, *v.a.* traduire.

translation, *s.* traduction *f.*

translator, *s.* traducteur,

-trice *m. f.*

transmission, *s.* transmission *f.*

transmit, *v.a.* transmettre, émettre.

transmitter, *s.* (poste) émetteur *m.*

transparency, *s.* diapositive *f.*

transport, *s.* transport *m.;* — *v.a.* transporter.

trap, *s.* piège *m.*

trash, *s.* rebut *m.;* niaiseries *f. pl.*

travel, *v.n.* voyager; — *s.* voyage *m.*

traveller, *s.* voyageur, -euse *m. f.*

tray, *s.* plateau *m.*

treachery, *s.* trahison *f.*

tread, *s.* pas *m.;* — *v.n.* & *a.* marcher (sur).

treasure, *s.* trésor *m.*

treasury, *s.* trésor *m.;* trésorerie *f.*

treat, *v.a.* traiter.

treatment, *s.* traitement *m.*

treaty, *s.* traité *m.*

tree, *s.* arbre *m.*

tremble, *v.n.* trembler.

tremendous, *adj.* terrible; immense.

trench, *s.* tranchée *f.*

trend, *s.* tendance *f.*

trespass, *v.n.* envahir sans autorisation; ~ *against* offenser; ~ *on* abuser de; — *s.* offense *f.*

trial, *s.* essai *m.;* épreuve *f.; (law)* procès *m.*

tribe, *s.* tribu *f.*

tribute, *s.* tribut *m.*

trick, *s.* ruse *f.;* tour *m.;* truc *m.;* — *v.a.* duper.

trifle, *s.* bagatelle *f.;* *a* ~ un peu; — *v.n.* ~ *with* traiter légèrement.

trim, s. état m.; tenue f.;
— adj. bien tenu; —
v.a. arranger; garnir,
orner; dresser.

trip, s. excursion f.;
voyage m.; — v.a. ~ up
faire trébucher.

triumph, s. triomphe m.;
— v.n. triompher.

triumphant, adj. triomphant.

trolley, s. fardier m.,
diable m.; trolley m.

trolley-bus, s. trolleybus
m.

troop, s. troupe f.

trophy, s. trophée m.

tropic(al), adj. tropique.

tropics, s. pl. tropiques
m. pl.

trot, s. trot m.; — v.n.
trotter.

trouble, s. affliction f.;
malheur m.; dérangement m.; difficulté f.;
— v.a. inquiéter; déranger; affliger.

troublesome, adj. ennuyeux.

trousers, s. pl. pantalon m.

trout, s truite f.

truck, s. wagon m.

true, aaj. vrai; exact;
fidèle; come ~ se réaliser.

truly, adv. vraiment.

trumpet, s. trompette
f.; — v. a. proclamer.

trunk, s. melle f. (tree)
tronc m.

trunk-call, s. appel m. interurbain.

trust, s. confiance f.;
espoir m.; dépôt m.;
trust m.; — v.a.
se confier (à); faire
crédit (à); v.n. espérer;
compter sur.

truth, s. vérité f.

try, v.a. essayer, éprouver; (law) mettre en
jugement; ~ on essayer; — s. essai m.

tub, s. bac m.; (bath)
tub m.

tube, s. tube m.; tuyau
m.; métro m.

Tuesday, s. mardi m.

tug, s. effort m.; — v.a.
tirer; remorquer.

tug-boat, s. (bateau) remorqueur m.

tuition, s. enseignement
m.

tumble, v. n. tomber.

tumour, s. tumeur f.

tune, s. air m.; accord m.;
harmonie f.; in ~ d'accord; out of ~ faux; —
v.a.&n. accorder; ~
in to mettre sur; ~
up régler; s'accorder.

tunnel, s. tunnel m.

turbine, s. turbine f.

turbo-jet: ~ engine turboréacteur m.

turbo-prop, s. turbopropulseur m.

turkey, s. dindon, dinde m. f.

Turkish, adj. turc, -que:
— s. Turc, -que m. f.;
(lang.) turc m.

turn, v.a. tourner, détourner; diriger; v.n.
tourner; se diriger; devenir; avoir recours (à);
~ about (se) tourner;
~ back retourner; ~
down plier, baisser;
repousser; ~ upside
down renverser; ~ in
se coucher; ~ off fermer, serrer; éteindre;
~ on ouvrir; allumer;
~ over (se) renverser;
~ up arriver, apparaître — s. tour m.; détour m.; (mind, style)
tournure f.; (tide)
changement m.

turning, s. tournant m.

turnip, s. navet m.

turnover, s. chiffre m. d'affaires.

turret, s. tourelle f.

turtle, s. tortue f.

tutor, s. précepteur m.; — v.a. instruire.

twelfth, adj. douzième; douze.

twelve, adj. & s. douze (m.).

twentieth, adj. vingtième.

twenty, adj. & s. vingt (m.).

twice, adv. deux fois.

twig, s. brindille f.

twin, adj. & s. jumeau (m.), jumelle (f.).

twist, s. (road) coude f.; torsion f.; — v. a. tordre; dénaturer; v. n. s'entortiller.

twitter, v.n. gazouiller.

two, adj. & s. deux (m.).

type, s. type m.; caractère m.; — v.a. taper (à la machine).

type-script, s. manuscrit m. dactylographié.

typewriter, s. machine à écrire, f.

typical, adj. typique.

typist, s. dactilo(graphe) m. f.

tyre see tire.

U

udder, s. mamelle f.

ugly, adj. laid.

ulcer, s. ulcère m.

ultimate, adj. final, dernier.

umbrella, s. parapluie m.

umpire, s. arbitre m. f.

unable, adj. incapable; ~ to impuissant à faire qch.; dans l'impossibilité de.

unaccustomed, adj. inaccoutumé, peu habitué (à).

unaided, adj. sans aide.

unanimous, adj. unanime.

unassisted, adj. sans aide.

unaware: be ~ of ignorer.

unbearable, adj. insupportable.

uncertain, adj. incertain.

uncertainty, s. incertitude f.

unchangeable, adj. immuable.

uncle, s. oncle m.

uncomfortable, adj. peu çonfortable.

uncommon, adj. rare; extraordinaire.

unconditional, adj. sans conditions.

unconscious, adj. sans connaissance; ~ of sans conscience de.

uncover, v. a. découvrir.

undamaged, adj. non endommagé.

undefined, adj. non défini.

undeniable, adj. incontestable.

under, prep sous; au-dessous de; dans.

undercarriage, s. châssis m., train (d'atterrissage) m.

underclothes, s. pl. vêtements m. pl. de dessous.

underdeveloped, adj. sous-développe.

underdone, adj. pas assez cuit, saignant.

undergo, v.a. subir.

undergraduate, s. étudiant, -e (non diplomé) m. f.

underground, s. métro-(politain) m.

underline, v.a. souligner.

undermine, *v.a.* miner.

underneath, *prep. & adv.* au-dessous (de).

undersigned, *adj. & s.* soussigné, -e *(m. f.).*

understand, *v.a.&n.* comprendre; *it is understood that* il est convenu que.

understanding, *s.* entendement *m.;* intelligence *f.*

undertake, *v.a.* entreprendre; ~ *to* se charger de, s'engager à.

undertaking, *s.* entreprise *f.*

underwear, *s.* vêtements *m.pl.* de dessous.

undesirable, *adj.* peu désirable.

undo, *v.a.* défaire.

undress, *v. n.* se déshabiller.

undue, *adj.* indu.

uneasy, *adj.* inquiet; mal à l'aise; incommode.

uneducated, *adj.* sans instruction.

unemployed, *adj. & s.* sans travail; *the* ~ les chômeurs *m.*

unemployment, *s.* chômage *m.*

unequal, *adj.* inégal.

uneven, *adj.* inégal; impair.

unexpected, *adj.* inattendu; soudain.

unfair, *adj.* injuste; déloyal.

unfavorable, *adj.* défavorable.

unfortunate, *adj.* malheureux.

unfortunately, *adv.* malheureusement.

unhappy, *adj.* malheureux.

unhealthy, *adj.* maladif;

. *(place)* insalubre.

uninhabited, *adj.* inhabité.

uninteresting, *adj.* peu intéressant,sans intérêt.

union, *s.* union *f.*

unique, *adj.* unique.

unit, *s.* unité *f.; (motor)* bloc *m.*

unite, *v.a.* unir; *v.n.* s'unir.

unity, *s.* unité *f.;* harmonie *f.*

universal, *adj.* universel.

university, *s.* université *f.*

unjust, *adj.* injuste.

unkind, *adj.* dur; peu aimable.

unknown, *adj.* inconnu.

unless, *conj.* à moins que... ne; à moins de.

unlike, *adj.* dissemblable.

unload, *v.a.* décharger.

unlock, *v.a.* ouvrir.

unmarried, *adj.* célibataire.

unnatural, *adj.* non naturel, dénaturé.

unnecessary, *adj.* inutile.

unnoticed, *adj.* inaperçu.

unoccupied, *adj.* inoccupé; libre; non occupé.

unpack, *v.a.* déballer.

unpaid, *adj.* impayé.

unparalleled, *adj.* incomparable.

unpleasant, *adj.* désagréable.

unprecedented, *adj.* sans exemple. *or.* précédent.

unprejudiced, *adj.* sans préjugés, impartial.

unprepared, *adj.* non préparé; *be* ~ *for* ne pas s'attendre à qch.

unprofitable, *adj.* peu profitable.

unpromising, *adj.* qui s'annonce mal; peu prometteur.

unqualified, *adj.* non qua-

lifié; sans restriction.
unreal, *adj.* irréel.
unreasonable, *adj.* déraisonnable.
unsatisfactory, *adj.* peu satisfaisant.
unseen, *adj.* invisible; inaperçu.
unsettled, *adj.* non réglé; *(in mind)* indécis; incertain.
unskilled, *adj.* non spécialisé.
unsolved, *adj.* non résolu.
unspeakable, *adj.* inexprimable.
unsteady, *adj.* tremblant; peu fixe; chancelant; inconstant.
unsuccessful, *adj.* malheureux; infructueux.
unsuitable, *adj.* inconvenant; peu propre (à).
untidy, *adj.* sans ordre, malpropre; en désordre.
until, *prep.* jusqu'à; — *conj.* jusqu'à ce que; avant que.
unto, *prep.* jusqu'à.
unusual, *adj.* rare, peu commun.
unwell, *adj.* indisposé; souffrant.
unwilling, *adj.* peu disposé (à).
unworthy, *adj.* indigne.
unyielding, *adj.* inflexible.
up, *adv.* en montant, vers le haut; (en) haut; *go* ~ monter; *be* ~ *in* être fort en; *what's* ~? qu'est-ce qu'il y a?; — *prep.* vers le haut de; en haut; — *adj.* montant.
uphill, *adj.* montant; — *adv. go* ~ monter.

uphold, *v.a.* soutenir; appuyer.

upholsterer, *s.* tapissier *m.*
upon, *prep* sur.
upper, *adj.* supérieur; *(deck)* deuxième; *the* ~ *classes* les hautes classes.
upright, *adj.* droit; honnête.
upset, *v.a.* renverser; *fig.* troubler, bouleverser; — *adj.* renversé; *fig.* dérangé; *be* ~ être indisposé.
upside do∖n, *adv.* sens dessus dessous.
upstairs, *adv.* en haut; *go* ~ monter (l'escalier).
up-to-date, *adj* moderne, à la mode.
upwards, *adv.* en haut, vers le haut, en montant.
urge, *v.a.* prier instamment (de); recommander instamment; pousser en avant.
urgent, *adj.* urgent; pressant.
us, *pron.* nous.
usage, *s.* usage *m.*
use, *v.a.* se servir de; traiter; faire usage (de); consommer; ~ *up* user; consommer; ~*d to* habitué à; *get* ~*d to* s'habituer à; — *s.* usage *m.*; emploi *m.*; utilité *f.*; *be of* ~ être utile (à); *(of) no* ~ inutile; *out of* ~ hors d'usage *or* de service.
useful, *adj.* utile (à).
useless, *adj.* inutile.
usher, *s. (court)* (huissier) audiencier *m.*
usherette, *s. (theatre)* ouvreuse *f.*
usual, *adj.* usuel.
usually, *adv.* ordinaire-

ment.
utensil, s. ustensile m.
utility, s. utilité f.
utilize, v.a. utiliser.
utmost, adj. extrême; le plus grand; — s. le plus; tout son possible.
utter[1], adj. le plus grand; absolu.
utter[2], v.a. dire, prononcer; pousser.
utterance, s. prononciation. f.; expression f.; parole f.

V

vacancy, s. vacance f.
vacant, adj. vacant; vide; sans expression.
vacation, s. vacances f. pl.
vaccinate, v.a. vacciner.
vaccination, s. vaccination.
vacuum-cleaner, s. aspirateur m.
vague, adj. vague.
vain, adj. vain; vaniteux; in ~ en vain.
valid, adj. valide.
validity, s. validité f.
valley, s. vallée f.
valuable, adj. de valeur.
value, s. valeur f.; — v.a. évaluer; priser.
valve, s. soupape f.; lampe f., tube m.
van, s. fourgon m.; camion m. de livraison; wagon m.
vanish, v.n. disparaître; (also ~ away) s'évanouir.
vanity, s. vanité f.
variety, s. variété f.
various, adj. divers.
varnish, s. vernis m.
vary, v.a. & n. varier.

vase, s. vase m.
vast, adj. vaste.
vault, s. voûte f.; cave f., caveau m.
veal, s. veau m.
vegetable, s. légume m.
vehicle, s. véhicule m.
veil, s. voile m.
vein, s. veine f.
velvet, s. velours m.
venison, s. venaison f.
vent, s. ouverture f.; give ~ to donner libre cours à.
ventilation, s. ventilation f.
ventilator, s. ventilateur m.
venture, s. risque m.; hasard m.; — v.a. risquer; hasarder; v.n. ~ (up-) on se hasarder à, se risquer à.
verb, s. verbe m.
verdict, s. décision f., verdict m.
verge, s. bord m.
verify, v.a. vérifier.
verse, s. vers m.; strophe f.
version, s. version f.
vertical, adj. vertical.
very, adv. très; ~ good très bien; — adj. vrai; même.
vessel, s. vaisseau m.
vest, s. gilet m.; chemise f. américaine.
vestry, s. sacristie f.; assemblée f.
veterinary, adj. ~ surgeon vétérinaire m.
veto, s. véto m.; — v.a. mettre son véto (à).
vex, v.a. vexer.
vibrate, v.n. vibrer, osciller.
vibration, s. vibration f.
vicar, s. curé m.
vice-, prefix vice-.

vicinity, *s.* voisinage *m.*

victim, *s.* victime *f.*

victorious, *adj.* victorieux.

victory, *s.* victoire *f.*

victuals, *s. pl.* victuailles *f. pl.*

view, *s.* vue *f.; avis m.; on ~ exposé; have in ~* se proposer (de); *with a ~ to* en vue de; *point of ~ ~* point *m.* de vue; — *v.a.* voir; regarder; envisager.

viewer, *s.* spectateur, -trice *m. f.*

vigorous, *adj.* vigoureux.

vigour, *s.* vigueur *f.*

village, *s.* village *m.*

villain, *s.* scélérat *m.*

vine, *s.* vigne *f.*

vinegar, *s.* vinaigre *m.*

vineyard, *s.* vignoble *m.*

vintage, *s.* vendange *f.*

violate, *v.a.* violer.

violation, *s.* violation *f.*

violence, *s.* violence *f.*

violent, *adj.* violent.

violet, *s.* violette *f.; (colour)* violet *m.; — adj.* violet.

violin, *s.* violon *m.*

violinist, *s.* violoniste *m. f.*

violoncellist, *s.* violoncelliste *m.*

violoncello, *s.* violoncelle *m.*

virgin, *s.* vierge *f.*

virtue, *s.* vertu *f.*

visa, visé, *s.* visa *m.*

visibility, *s.* visibilité *f.*

visible, *adj.* visible.

vision, *s.* vision *f.*, vue *f.*

visit, *s.* visite *f.; séjour m.; be on a ~ to* être en visite chez; — *v.a.* visiter.

visitor, *s.* visiteur, -euse *m. f.*

vital, *adj.* vital.

vitamin, *s.* vitamine *f.*

vocabulary, *s.* vocabu-

laire *m.*

vocation, *s.* vocation *f.*

voice, *s.* voix *f.; — v.a.* exprimer.

voltage, *s.* voltage *m.*

volume, *s.* volume *m.*

voluntary, *adj.* volontaire.

volunteer, *s.* volontaire *m.; — v.n.* s'engager (pour).

vomit, *v.a. & n.* vomir.

vote, *s.* voix; — *v.a. & n.* voter (sur).

voucher, *s.* pièce *f.* de dépense ; pièce *f.* de recette; bon *m.*

vo v, *s.* vœu *m.; — v. a.* vouer; jurer; *v. n.* faire un v cu; jurer.

vowel, *s.* voyelle *f.*

voyage, *s.* voyage *m.; — v. n.* voyager (par mer).

vulgar, *adj.* vulgaire.

W

wade, *v.a.* passer à gué.

wafer, *s.* gaufrette *f.;* hostie *f.*

wag, *v.a.* hocher; *(tail)* agiter; *v.n.* s'agiter.

wage(s), *s. (pl.)* salaire *m.*, gages *m. pl.; — v.a. ~ war* faire la guerre.

wag(g)on, *s.* wagon *m.*

waist, *s.* taille *f.*

waistcoat, *s.* gilet *m.*

wait, *v. a. & n.* attendre *(for* qn, qch).

waiter, *s.* garçon *m.* (de restaurant); *head~* premier garçon *m.*, maître *m.* d'hôtel.

waiting-room, *s.* salle *f.* d'attente.

wake, *v.a.* (also *~ up*) réveiller; *v.n.* (also *~*

up) s'éveiller.

waken, *v.a.* éveiller; *v.n.* s'éveiller .

walk, *s.* marche *f.;* promenade *f.; (path)* allée *f.;* go for a ~ faire une promenade; — *v.n.* aller à pied; marcher; *(pleasure)* se promener; ~ *off* s'en aller; ~ *out* sortir.

wall, *s.* mur *m.*

wallet, *s.* portefeuille *m.*

walnut, *s.* noyer *m.; (fruit)* noix *f.*

waltz, *s.* valse *f.*

wander, *v.n.* errer; s'égarer (de); divaguer.

want, *s.* besoin *m.;* manque *m.; for ~ of* faute de; — *v.a.* avoir besoin (de); manquer (de); vouloir; demander; *v.n.* faire défaut; *be ~ing in* manquer de.

war, *s.* guerre *f.*

ward, *s.* pupille *m. f.; (hospital)* salle *f.*

warden, *s.* gouverneur *m.;* directeur *m.*

warder, *s.* gardien, -enne *m. f.*

wardrobe, *s.* armoire *f.*

ware, *s.* marchandise(s) *f. (pl.);* article *m.*

warehouse, *s.* magasin *m.;* dépôt *m.*

warm, *adj.* chaud; *be ~* avoir chaud; — *v.a.* chauffer; ~ *up* réchauffer; *v.n.* se chauffer.

warmth, *s.* chaleur *f.*

warn, *v.a.* avertir; prévenir; mettre sur ses gardes (contre).

warning, *s.* avertissement *m.;* avis *m.*

warrant, *s.* autorisation *f.;* mandat *m.;* — *v. a.* garantir; justifier.

wash, *v.a.* laver; *v.n.* se laver; ~ *away* effacer; ~ *up the dishes* faire la vaisselle; — *s.* lavage *m.;* lotion *f.;* toilette *f.;* lessive *f.*

wash-basin, *s.* cuvette *f.* (de lavabo).

washing-machine, *s.* machine *f.* à laver.

wasp, *s.* guêpe *f.*

waste, *s.* désert *m., (money)* gaspillage *m.; (energy)* déperdition *f.; (loss)* perte *f.;* déchets *m. pl.;* ~ *of time* perte de temps *f.;* — *adj.* inculte; de rebut; ~ *paper* papier *m.* de rebut; — *v.a.* gaspiller; perdre; ravager.

watch, *s.* garde *f.;* gardien *m.,* garde *m.; (to indicate time)* montre *f.;* — *v. a.* veiller, garder; observer; regarder; *v.n.* veiller; ~ *out!* ouvrez l'œil!

watch-maker, *s.* horloger *m.*

water, *s.* eau *f.*

water-closet, *s.* cabinet *m.*

waterfall, *s.* chute *f.* d'eau

watering-place, *s.* station *f.* balnéaire; ville *f.* d'eaux.

waterproof, *adj.* imperméable; — *s.* caoutchouc *m.*

wave, *s.* vague *f.;* onde *f.;* — *v.a.* agiter; *(hair)* onduler; *v. n.* flotter; onduler.

wave-length, *s.* longueur *f.* d'onde.

waver, *v.n.* vaciller.

wax, *s.* cire *f.*

way, *s.* chemin *m.,* route

f.; distance *f.;* côte *m.;* *(means)* moyen *m.;* façon *f.;* manière *f.;* *which* ~*?* de quel côté?; *it's a long* ~ *to* il y a loin pour aller (à); *on the* ~ chemin faisant; ~ *in* entrée *f.;* ~ *out* sortie *f.;* *out of the* ~ retiré; extraordinaire; *this* ~ de ce côté-ci, par ici; *by* ~ *of* par; *by the* ~ à propos; *in a* ~ à certains égards; *give* ~ *to* céder à.

we, *pron.* nous.

weak, *adj.* faible.

weakness, *s.* faiblesse *f.*

wealth, *s.* richesse *f.;* profusion *f.*

wealthy, *adj.* riche.

weapon, *s.* arme *f.*

wear, *v.a.* porter; ~ *away, down, out* (s')user; ~ *off* (s')effacer; — *s.* usage *m.;* usure *f.*

weary, *adj.* las, fatigué.

weather, *s.* temps *m.*

weather-forecast, *s.* prévisions *f. pl.* du temps; bulletin *m.* météorologique.

weave, *v. a.* tisser.

web, *s.* tissu *m.;* *(spider)* toile *f.*

wedding, *s.* mariage *m.*

wedding-ring, *s.* alliance *f.*, anneau *m.* de mariage.

wedge, *s.* coin *m.;* — *v.a.* coincer; caler.

Wednesday, *s.* mercredi *m.*

weed, *s.* mauvaise herbe *f.;* — *v.a.* sarcler.

week, *s.* semaine *f.*

week-day, *s.* jour *m.* de semaine; *on* ~*s* en semaine.

week-end, *s.* fin *f.* de semaine, week-end *m.*

weekly, *adj.* de la semaine; hebdomadaire; — *s.* (journal) hebdomadaire *m.*

weep, *v.n.* pleurer.

weigh, *v.a. & n.* peser; ~ *down* faire pencher, surcharger, accabler.

weight, *s.* poids *m.;* *put on* ~ prændre du corps.

welcome, *adj.* bienvenu; ~*!* soyez le bienvenu!; — *s.* accueil *m.;* — *v.a.* souhaiter la bienvenue (à); accueillir (avec plaisir).

well[1], *adv.* bien; ~, ~*!* allons, allons!; — *adj.* bien (portant).

well[2], *s.* puits *m.*

well-being, bien-être *m.*

well-informed, *adj.* bien informé, renseigné.

well-to-do, *adj.* aisé; *be* ~ être dans l'aisance

west, *s.* ouest *m.*

western, *adj.* de l'ouest.

westward, *adv.* vers l'ouest.

wet, *adj.* mouillé, humide; pluvieux; ~ *through* trempé jusqu'aux os; — *v.a.* mouiller; tremper.

whale, *s.* baleine *f.*

what, *rel. pron.* ce qui, ce que; — *interrog. pron.* qu'est-ce qui, que; — *int.* quoi!

wheat, *s.* blé *m.*, froment *m.*

wheel, *s.* roue *f.;* *(steering)* volant *m.*

when, *adv. & conj.* quand.

whenever, *adv.* toutes les fois que.

where, *adv.* où.

whereas, *conj.* tandis que;

vu que. _

wherever, *adv.* partout où.

whether, *conj.* soit que; *(if)* si; ~ *or not* . . . qu'-il en soit ainsi ou non . . .

which, *(interrogative) adj.* quel, quelle; *pron.* lequel; *(relative) adj.* lequel, laquelle; *pron.* qui, que, lequel.

while, *conj.* pendant que; *(whereas)* tandis que; *(as long as)* tant que; — *s.* temps *m.; be worth* ~ *to* cela vaut la peine de; — *v.a.* ~ *away* faire passer.

whip, *s.* fouet.

whisk, *v.a.* fouetter; — *s.* époussette *f.; (eggs)* fouet à œufs, *m.*

whisper, *s.* chuchotement *m.;* murmure *m.; v.a.* dire à l'oreille; *v.n.* chuchoter; murmurer.

whistle, *s.* sifflet *m.;* — *v.a. & n.* siffler.

white, *adj.* blanc, blanche; pâle.

Whit Sunday, dimanche *m.* de la Pentecôte.

who, *pron.* qui.

whole, *s.* tout *m.;* totalité *f.; on the* ~ à tout prendre; — *adj.* tout le, toute la; entier, -ère.

wholesale, *adj. & adv.* en gros.

wholesome, *adj.* sain.

wholly, *adv.* entièrement.

whom, *pron.* que; lequel; *interrog.* qui?, qui est-ce que?

whose, *pron.* dont; *interrog.* de qui?

why, *adv.* pourquoi.

wicked, *adj.* méchant.

wide, *adj.* large; étendue; *6 feet* ~ 6 pieds de largeur.

widow, *s.* veuve *f.*

widower, *s.* veuf *m.*

width, *s.* largeur *f.*

wife, *s.* femme *f.*

wild, *adj.* sauvage; déréglé; impétueux; frénétique.

wilful, *adj.* volontaire.

will, *s.* volonté *f.;* intention *f.;* testament *m.; at* ~ à volonté; *of one's own free* ~ de plein gré; — *v.n. & aux.* vouloir; *(future tense unexpressed,* see grammar*).*

willing *adj.* bien disposé; *be* ~ vouloir bien.

willingly, *adv.* volontiers.

win, *v. a. & n.* gagner.

winch, *s.* manivelle *f.*

wind^1**,** *s.* vent *m.;* souffle *m.*

wind^2**,** *v. a.* enrouler; dévider; ~ *up (clock)* remonter; *fig.* liquider; *v.n.* tourner, serpenter; s'enrouler.

window, *s.* fenêtre *f.; (car)* glace *f.*

windscreen, *s.* pare-brise *m.*

windy, *adj.* venteux.

wine, *s.* vin *m.*

wing, *s.* aile *f.;* vol *m.; take* ~ s'envoler.

wink, *s.* clin d'œil, *m.;* — *v.a.* clignoter.

winner, *s.* gagnant *m.*

winter, *s.* hiver *m.*

wipe, *v.a.* essuyer; ~ *out* effacer; — *s.* coup *m.* de torchon.

wire, *s.* fil *m.* (de fer); télégramme *m.; live* ~ fil *m.* en charge; — *v.a. & n.* télégraphier.

wireless, *s.* T.S.F.; télégraphie sans fil; ~ *set* poste *m.* (de T.S.F.).

wise, *adj.* sage; prudent.

wish, *s.* désir *m.;* ~es vœux *m. pl.;* — *v.a.* désirer (de); souhaiter; *(should like)* vouloir *(in conditional).*

wit, *s.* esprit *m.; (pers.)* bel esprit *m.*

witch, *s.* sorcière *f.*

with, *prep.* avec; *(at)* chez.

withdraw, *v.n.* se retirer; *v.a.* retirer.

within, *adv.* dedans; — *prep.* *(time)* en; *(place)* dans; à.

without, *prep.* sans; *(place)* en dehors de.

witness, *s.* témoignage *m.; (pers.)* témoin *m.;* — *v.a.* être témoin de; *(attest)* témoigner; *(document)* signer (à).

witty, *adj.* spirituel.

wizard, *s.* sorcier *m.*

wolf, *s.* loup, louve *m. f.*

woman, *s.* femme *f.*

womb, *s.* matrice *f.; fig.* sein *m.*

wonder, *s.* étonnement *m.; (a thing)* merveille *f.;* — *v.n.* ~ at être étonné de; *(curious)* se demander; *I* ~ je me le demande.

wonderful, *adj.* étonnant.

wood, *s.* bois *m.*

wooden, *adj.* de bois.

woodman, *s.* bûcheron *m.*

wool, *s.* laine *f.*

woollen, *adj.* de laine.

word, *s.* mot *m.; (utterance)* parole *f.; (term)* terme *m.; (information)* avis *m.; upon my* ~! ma parole!; *have a* ~ *with* avoir deux mots avec.

work, *s.* travail *m.; (achievement)* ouvrage *m.;* ~ *(of art)* œuvre *f.* d'art; ~s *(of s.o.)* œuvres *f.pl., (factory)* usine *f.; set to* ~ se mettre à l'œuvre; — *v.a.* faire travailler; *(wood)* ouvrager; *v.n.* travailler; *(operate)* fonctionner, marcher.

worker, *s.* travailleur, -euse *m. f.,* ouvrier, -ère *m. f.*

workman, *s.* ouvrier *m.*

workshop, *s.* atelier *m.*

world, *s.* monde *m.*

world-war, *s.* guerre *f.* mondiale.

world-wide, *adj.* universel; mondial.

worm, *s.* ver *m.*

worry, *s.* ennui *m.,* tracas *m.;* — *v.a.* tracasser; importuner; *v.n.* se tracasser (de), se tourmenter; *don't* ~! soyez tranquille!

worse, *adj.* pire, plus mauvais; *grow* ~ empirer; — *adv.* pis.

worship, *s.* culte *m.;* — *v.a. & n.* adorer.

worst, *adj.* le, la pire; le, la plus malade; — *adv.* le plus mal; — *s.* pis *m.*

worth, *s.* valeur *f.;* — *adj. be* ~ valoir; *is it* ~ *while?* cela (en) vaut-il la peine?; *it is not* ~ *the trouble* cela ne vaut pas la peine.

worthless, *adj.* sans valeur, indigne.

worthy, *adj.* digne.

wound, *s.* blessure *f.*

wounded, *adj.* blessé; *the* ~ les blessés.

wrap, *s. (garment)* peignoir *m.; v.a.* ~ *up* envelopper; *fig.* être absorbé *(in* dans).

wrapper, *s.* toile d'emballage *f.; (book)* bande *f.*

wreck, *s.* naufrage *m.;* navire *m.* naufragé; *fig.* ruine *f.; v.a.* ruiner: *be ~ed* faire naufrage; être naufragé.

wrench, *s.* torsion *f.; (tool)* clef (à écrous) *f.; — v.a.* tordre; *(ankle)* fouler.

wrestle, *v.n.* lutter (avec).

wrestler, *s.* lutteur *m.*

wrestling, *s.* lutte *f.*

wring, *v.a.* tordre.

wrinkle, *s.* ride *f.; (crease)* faux pli *m.; — v.a.* rider.

wrist, *s.* poignet *m.*

writ, *s.* exploit *m.*

write, *v.a. & n.* écrire; *~ down* noter; *~ off* amortir; *~ out* transcrire.

writer, *s.* écrivain *m.*

writing, *s.* écriture *f.;* écrit *m.; in ~* par écrit.

writing-desk, *s.* bureau *m.*

wrong, *adj.* incorrect, faux; *be ~* avoir tort; se tromper (de); *take the ~ train* se tromper de train; *it is the ~ book* ce n'est pas le livre qu'il faut.

X

Xmas, *s.* Noël *m.*

x-ray, *adj. ~ treatment* radiothérapie *f.; ~ photograph* radiograph e *f.*

Y

yacht, *s.* yacht *m.*

yard, *s.* yard *m.;* cour *f.*

yarn, *s.* fil *m;* histoire *f.*

yawn, *s.* bâillement *m.; — v.n.* bâiller.

year, *s.* an *m.;* année *f.*

yearly, *adv.* annuellement.

yearn, *v.n. ~ for* soupirer après.

yeast, *s.* levure *f.*

yell, *v. n.* hurler.

yellow, *adj.* jaune.

yes, *adv.* oui; *(after negation)* si.

yesterday, *adv.* hier.

yet, *adv.* encore; *not ~* pas encore; *as ~* jusqu'à présent; *— conj.* néanmoins.

yield, *v.a.* produire; accorder; rendre; *v.n.* céder (à); fléchir.

yoke, *s.* joug *m.*

yolk, *s.* jaune *m.*

you, *pron.* tu; vous.

young, *adj.* jeune; *(animal)* petit; *~er* plus jeune. cadet.

your, *adj.* votre, *(pl.)* vos.

yours, *pron.* à vous; le, la vôtre, les vôtres.

yourself, *pron.* vous-même, *-s.*

youth, *s.* jeunesse *f.; (pers.)* jeune homme *m.*

youth-hostel, *s.* auberge *f.* de la jeunesse.

Z

zeal, *s.* zèle *m.*

zealous, *adj.* zélé.

zero, *s.* zéro *m.*

zest, *s.* enthousiasme *m.;* goût *m.*

zigzag, *s.* zigzag *m.; — adv.* en zigzag.

zinc, *s.* zinc *m.*
zipper, *s.* fermeture éclair.
   f.

zone, *s.* zone *f.*
zoo, *s.* zoo *m.*
zoology, *s.* zoologie *f.*

FRENCH-ENGLISH

DICTIONARY

A

à, au, *prep.* to; at.

abaisser, *v. a.* lower, let down; s'~ stoop.

abandonner, *v. a.* forsake, abandon.

abat-jour, *s. m.* lampshade.

abbaye, *s. m.* abbey.

abbé, *s. m.* abbot.

abdication, *s. f.* abdication.

abdiquer, *v. n.* abdicate; *v. a.* renounce.

abeille, *s. f.* bee.

abject, *adj.* abject, low.

abjurer, *v.a.* abjure; give up.

abolir, *v. a.* abolish.

abondance, *s. f.* plenty, abundance.

abondant, *adj.* abundant.

abonder, *v. n.* abound.

abonner: s'~ subscribe to, take in.

abord, *adv.* d'~ (at) first.

aboutir, *v. n.* end in, come to.

aboyer, *v. n.* bark.

abricot, *s. m.* apricot.

abrupt, *adj.* steep.

absence, *s. f.* absence; ~ d'esprit absence of mind.

absent, *adj.* absent.

absenter: s'~ leave, depart.

absolu, *adj.* absolute.

absorber, *v. a.* absorb;

absoudre*, *v. a.* absolve.

abstraction, *s. f.* abstraction.

abstrait, *adj.* abstract.

absurde, *adj.* absurd.

abus, *s. m.* abuse.

académie, *s. f.* academy.

accélérer, *v. a.* accelerate, hasten.

accent, *s.m.* accent, stress.

accentuer, *v.a.* accent.

accepter, *v. a.* accept; admit.

accès, *s. m.* access; fit.

accessible, *adj.* accessible.

accident, *s. m.* accident; par ~ accidentally.

accidentel, -elle, *adj.* accidental.

acclamer, *v.a.* acclaim.

acclimater, *v.a.* acclimatize; 's'~ become acclimatized.

accommoder, *v. a.* accommodate; fit up; s'~ put up with, come to terms.

accompagner, *v. a.* accompany.

accomplir, *v. a.* accomplish, carry out.

accord, *s. m.* agreement, accord, harmony.

accorder, *v.a.* grant, confer; agree.

accoutumer, *v. a.* accustom; s'~ get accustomed (to).

accréditer, *v. a.* accredit.

accrocher, *v. a.* hang up, hook; run against.

accroître, *v. a.* increase; s'~ increase.

accueil, *s. m.* reception.

accueillir, *v. a.* receive, welcome.

accumuler, *v. a.* accumulate, heap up.

accusation, *s. f.* accusation, charge.

accuser, *v.a.* accuse.

achat, *s. m.* purchase; faire des ~s go shopping.

acheter, *v.a.* purchase, buy.

achèvement, *s. m.* completion.

achever, *v.a.* complete finish; achieve.

acide, *adj.* acid, sour; — *s. m.* acid.

acier, *s. m.* steel.

acoustique, *s. f.* acoustics.

acquérir*, *v.a.* acquire, purchase; get.

âcre, *adj.* acrid, sour.

acte, *s. m.* action, deed, act; transaction, document, certificate; *(theatre)* act.

acteur, *s. m.* actor.

actif, -ive, *adj.* active; — *s.m.* assets *(pl.);*

action, *s. f.* action; act, deed; effect; lawsuit; plot; story.

activité, *s. f.* activity.

actrice, *s. f.* actress.

actualité, *s. f.* topic of the hour; ~s current events; news-reel.

actuel, -elle, present, of present interest; actual.

adapter, *v.a.* adapt; s'~ adapt oneself.

addition, *s. f.* addition; bill.

additionner, *v. a.* add up.

adhérer, *v. a.* adhere, stick.

adieu, *s. m. (pl. -x)* good-bye; *faire ses ~x* take one's leave.

adjoint, *adj. & s. m.* assistant; deputy.

adjuger, *v. a.* adjuge.

administrateur, -trice, *s. m. f.* manager, director.

administratif, -ive- *adj.* administrative.

administration, *s. f.* management, direction; administration.

administrer, *v.a.* administer; manage.

admirable, *adj.* admi-rable.

admiration, *s. f.* admiration.

admirer, *v. a.* admire, wonder at.

admission, *s. f.* admission, admittance.

adolescent, *s. m.* adolescent, youth.

adopter, *v.a.* adopt, pass.

adoption, *s.f.* adoption.

adorer, *v.a.* adore.

adresse, *s. f.* address; skill, dexterity.

adresser, *v. a.* address, direct; s'~ apply (to).

adroit, *adj.* clever, skilful.

adulte, *adj. & s.* adult.

adversaire, *s. m.* adversary.

aérien, -enne, *adj.* aerial.

aérodrome, *s. m.* airport.

aéroport, *s. m.* airport.

affaiblir, *v. a.* weaken.

affaire, *s. f.* business, affair, matter; lawsuit.

affamé, *adj.* hungry.

affecter, *v. a.* affect, feign; move; assume.

affection, *s.f.* affection; disease.

affectueux, -euse, *adj.* affectionate.

affermir, *v. a.* strengthen; s'~ become stronger.

affiche, *s. f.* poster, bill.

afficher, *v. a.* post up, stick up, placard.

affiler, *v.a.* sharpen.

affirmatif, -ive, *adj.* affirmative.

affirmer, *v. a.* affirm.

affliger, *v. a.* afflict.

affluer, *v. n.* flow into.

affranchir, *v. a.* (set) free; stamp.

affreux, -euse, *adj.* dreadful, terrible.

affronter, *v.a.* face.

afin, *conj.* ~ de in order to; ~ que in order

that, so that.

africain (A.), *adj. & s. m. f.* African.

âge, *s. m.* age; period; *quel ~ avez-vous?* how old are you?

agence, *s. f.* agency.

agent, *s. m.* agent; policeman.

aggraver, *v. a.* aggravate.

agile, *adj.* agile, active.

agilité, *s. f.* agility.

agir, *v. n.* act; take effect; behave; *s'~* be in question.

agitation, *s. f.* agitation.

agiter, *v. a.* agitate.

agneau, *s. m.* lamb.

agonie, *s. f.* agony.

agréable, *adj.* agreeable.

agréer, *v. a.* accept, receive favourably.

agrément, *s. m.* consent, approval; pleasure.

agressif, -ive, *adj.* aggressive.

agression, *s. f.* aggression, attack.

agriculture, *s. f.* agriculture.

aide, *s. f.* help.

aider, *v. a.* help.

aïeux, *s. m. pl.* ancestors.

aigle, *s. m.* eagle.

aigre, *adj.* sour, acid.

aigrir: *s'~* turn sour.

aigu, *adj.* pointed, sharp; keen; *accent ~* acute accent.

aiguille, *s. f.* needle; hand, index; point, switch; *grande ~* minute hand.

aiguiser, *v. a.* sharpen.

ail, *s. m.* garlic.

aile, *s. f.* wing; flank; aisle; mudguard.

ailleurs, *adv.* somewhere else, elsewhere; *d'~* in addition, besides.

aimable, *adj.* amiable, pleasant, kindly.

aimer, *v. a. & n.* like, love, be fond of, care to.

aîné, *adj. & s. m. f.* elder, eldest; senior.

ainsi, *adv. & conj.* so, thus; likewise; *~ de suite* and so on; *~ que* as well as.

air, *s. m.* air; look(s), appearance, manner; *(music)* air.

aisance, *s. f.* ease; comfort; facility; *être dans l'~* be well off.

aise, *s. f.* ease, comfort.

aisé, *adj.* easy; well-off.

ajourner, *v. a.* adjourn.

alcool, *s. m.* alcohol.

alcoolique, *adj.* alcoholic.

algèbre, *s. f.* algebra.

aliment, *s. m.* aliment, food.

alimentation, *s. f.* alimentation; feeding.

alimenter, *v. a.* feed.

aliter, *v. a. être alité* be confined to bed, be laid up.

allaiter, *v. a.* give suck to; nurse.

allée, *s. f.* (garden) path, lane, walk, alley.

alléger, *v. a.* lighten; alleviate, soothe.

allégresse, *s. f.* gaiety, delight.

allemand (A.), *adj. & s. m. f.* German.

aller*, *v. n.* go, proceed; get on; grow, get; *~ à pied* walk; *~ en auto* drive; *~ en avion* fly; *~ bien* be well; *comment allez-vous?* how are you?; *allons!* come on!; *allez!* indeed; *s'en ~* go away, be off.

alliance, *s. f.* alliance, union; wedding-ring.

allié, -e, *s. m. f.* ally; — *adj.* allied.

allier, *v. a.* alloy; match;

unite; s'~ join with, unite.

allonger, v.a. lengthen, stretch out, prolong; ~ le pas step out; s'~ get longer.

allumer, v.a. light (up), set on fire; excite.

allumette, s.f. match.

allure, s.f. gait, pace; manner, behaviour; direction.

allusion, s.f. allusion, hint; reference.

alors, adv. then.

alpinisme, s.m. mountaineering.

altérer, v.a. alter, change; s'~ alter, degenerate.

alternance, s.f. alternation.

alternatif, -ive, adj. alternate, alternative.

alterner, v.n. & a. alternate.

altitude, s.f. altitude.

aluminium, s.f. aluminium.

amaigrir, v.a. make thin; s'~ grow thin.

amant, -e, s.m.f. lover.

amas, s.m. heap, mass, pile.

amateur, s.m. amateur, lover, fancier.

ambassade, s.f. embassy.

ambassadeur, s.m. ambassador.

ambassadrice, s.f. ambassadress.

ambitieux, -euse, adj. ambitious.

ambition, s.f. ambition.

ambulance, s.f. ambulance; ~ (automobile) ambulance(-car).

âme, s.f. soul; mind.

améliorer, v.a. ameliorate, improve; s'~ improve.

aménager, v.a. fit up, out.

amender, v.a. amend, improve.

amener, v.a. bring, draw; bring before, in, out; introduce; induce.

amer, -ère, adj. bitter.

américain, -e (A.), adj. & s.m.f. American.

ami, -e, s.m.f. friend; sweetheart; bon ~, bonne ~e sweetheart.

amical, adj. friendly, kind.

amiral, s.m. admiral.

amitié, s.f. friendship; affection; meilleures ~s kindest regards.

amortir, v.a. lessen, soften; pay (off), write off.

amortisseur, s.m. shockabsorber.

amour, s.m. love; faire l'~ court, make love to; mon ~ my darling.

amoureux, -euse, adj. in love (de with), enamoured (de of).

amplificateur, s.m. amplifier.

amplifier, v.a. amplify.

ampoule, s.f. blister; bulb.

amulette, s.f. amulet.

amusant, adj. amusing.

amusement, s.m. amusement, pastime, fun.

amuser, v.a. amuse, entertain; s'~ enjoy oneself.

an, s.m. year; il y a un ~ a year ago.

analogie, s.f. analogy.

analogue, adj. analogous.

analyse, s.f. analysis.

analyser, v.a. analyse.

ananas, s.m. pineapple.

anatomie, s.f. anatomy.

ancêtre, s.m.f. ancestor.

ancien, -enne, adj. ancient, old, antique.

ancre, s.f. anchor; lever l'~ weigh anchor.

âne, s.m. ass.

anéantir, v.a. annihilate.

anecdote, s.f. anecdote.

ange, *s. m.* angel.

anglais, -e (A.), *adj.* English; — *s. m. f.* Englishman, Englishwoman.

angle, *s. m.* angle, corner; bend.

angoisse, *s.f.* anguish.

animal, *s.m.* animal; beast.

anneau, *s. m.* circle, ring.

année, *s. f.* year; ~ *scolaire* school-year; *bonne* ~ a happy New Year!

annexer, *v. a.* annex.

anniversaire, *s. m.* anniversary, b rthday.

annonce, *s. f.* announcement, advertisement.

annoncer, *v. a.* announce, give notice of; advertise.

annuaire, *s. m.* year-book, annual, directory.

annuel, -elle, *adj.* annual.

annuler, *v. a.* annul.

anonyme, *adj.* anonymous; *société* ~ joint-stock company.

anormal, *adj.* abnormal.

anse, *s. f.* handle; creek.

antécédent, -e, *adj. & s. m.* antecedent.

antenne, *s. f.* aerial.

antérieur, *adj.* anterior, previous.

antibiotique, *s. m.* antibiotic.

antichambre, *s. f.* entrance hall.

anticiper, *v. a. & n.* anticipate; encroach.

antipathie, *s. f.* antipathy.

antiquaire, *s. m.* antiquarian.

antique, *adj.* antique, ancient.

antiquité, *s. f.* antiquity.

antiseptique, *adj. & s. m.* antiseptic.

anxiété, *s. f.* anxiety.

anxieux, -euse, *adj.* anxious.

août, *s.m.* August.

apaiser, *v. a.* appease, pacify, quiet.

apercevoir, *v. a.* perceive, catch sight of; remark, notice.

aplanir, *v.a.* smooth, level, even off; s'~ become level.

aplatir, *v.a.* fl atten.

apologie, *s. m.* apology, defence.

apoplexie, *s. f.* apoplexy.

apostolique, *adj.* apostolic(al).

apostrophe, *s. f.* apostrophe.

apôtre, *s. m.* apostle.

apparaître, *v. n.* appear.

appareil, *s. m.* apparatus, device, appliance, gear; camera; ~ *de TV* TV-set; ~ *de direction* steering-gear.

apparence, *s. f.* appearance, look(s); likelihood; *en* ~ apparenty.

apparent, *adj.* apparent.

apparition, *s. f.* appearance; apparition.

appartement, *s.m.* flat; apartment.

appartenir, *v.n.* belong, appertain *(à to)*.

appel, *s. m.* call; appeal; *faire l'*~ call the roll.

appeler, *v. a.* call in, out, up, down; ring up; name, term; *en* ~ appeal; *faire* ~ send for; s'~ be called, call oneself.

appendice, *s. m.* appendix.

appendicite, *s.f.* appedicitis.

appesantir, *v.a.* make heavy, weigh down.

appétit, *s. m.* appetite.

applaudir, *v. n.* applaud, clap.

application, *s. f.* application; diligence.

appliquer, *v. a.* apply; lay on.

apporter, *v.a.* bring.

appréciation, *s.f.* appreciation; estimation.

apprécier, *v. a.* value.

appréhension, *s. f.* apprehension, fear.

apprendre, *v. a.* learn, acquire; hear of; teach.

apprentissage, *s. m.* apprenticeship.

apprêter, *v. a.* prepare; season; dress; s'~ prepare oneself, get ready.

approbation, *s.f.* approbation, approval.

approche, *s. f.* approach, advance.

approcher, *v.a.* bring toward, forward.

approprié, *adj.* appropriate.

approprier: s'~ appropriate, take; accommodate, adapt oneself.

approuver, *v. a.* sanction; approve.

approximatif, -ive, *adj.* approximate.

approximation, *s.f.* approximation.

appui, *s. m.* support.

appuyer, *v. a.* support; lean; *v. n.* ~ *sur* lay stress (up)on; s'~ lean, rest, rely (upon).

après, *adv.* after; behind; next (to); ~ *coup* too late; ~ *tout* after all; d'~ after, according to; by.

après-demain, *adv.* & *s. m.* (the) day after tomorrow.

après-midi, *s. m.* afternoon.

à-propos, *adv.* in good time; — *s. m.* timely word; fitness.

apte, *adj.* apt, suitable.

aptitude, *s. f.* aptitude, ability, talent.

aquarelle, *s.f.* water-color.

arabe (A.), *adj.* & *s. m. f.* Arab, Arabian; Arabic.

araignée, *s. f.* spider.

arbitre, *s. f.* arbiter, judge; umpire, referee.

arbre, *s. m.* tree; shaft; ~ *fruitier* fruit-tree; ~ *coudé* crank shaft.

arc, *s. m.* bow; arc(h).

arcade, *s. f.* arcade.

arche, *s. f.* arch, vault.

archet, *s.m.* bow.

archevêque, *s.m.* archbishop.

architecture, *s.f.* architecture.

archives *s. f. pl.* archives.

ardemment, *adv.* ardently.

ardent, *adj.* burning, fiery, ardent, eager.

ardeur, *s. f.* keenness; ardour, zeal.

arête, *s. f.* fish-bone; edge; ridge.

argent, *s. m.* silver; money; ~ *en caisse* cash in hand ~ *comptant* ready money; ~ *de la poche* pocket-money; *à-court* d'~ pressed for money.

argenterie, *s. f.* plate.

argentin[1], *adj.* silvery.

argentin[2], -e (A.), *adj.* & *s. m. f.* Argentine.

argile, *s.f.* clay.

argot, *s. m.* slang.

argument, *s.m.* argument, proof, evidence.

aristocratie, *s.f.* aristocracy.

aristocratique, *adj.* aristocratic.

arme, *s.f.* arm, weapon; ~s *à feu* fire-arms; *faire des* ~s fence.

armée, *s. f.* army.

armer, *v.a.* arm; fortify; s'~ arm oneself.

armoire, *s. f.* cupboard;

wardrobe.

armure, *s. f.* armour; armature.

arracher, *v.a.* pull (out), tear up; extract, draw; remove from.

arrangement, *s. m.* arrangement; agreement, settlement; ~s terms.

arranger, *v. a.* arrange, settle, fix (up); s'~ come to an agreement, make arrangements (for); make shift (to).

arrestation, *s. f.* arrest.

arrêt, *s. m.* stop (of bus, tram etc.); pause; standstill; sentence; arrest; ~*facultatif* request stop; *sans* ~ non-stop.

arrêter, *v.a.* check, stop; arrest; engage, book; decide, decree; settle; s'~ stop; draw up; leave off.

arrière. *adv.* behind, backward; *en* ~ back(ward); ~ *s. m.* back part, rear.

arriéré, *adj.* overdue; backward; under-developed; — *s.m.* arrears *(pl.).*

arrivée, *s. f.* arrival; *à l'*~ on arrival.

arriver, *v. n.* arrive, come; turn up; happen; occur; ~ *à* attain, arrive at, reach; *le train arrive à* the train is due at.

arrogance, *s. f.* arrogance.

arroser, *v. a.* water, sprinkle; baste.

art, *s. m.* art; *les beaux* ~s the fine arts.

artère, *s.f.* artery; thoroughfare.

article, *s. m.* article; ~s *de grande consommation* consumer(s') goods.

articulation, *s. f.* joint.

articuler, *v.a.* articulate.

artificiel, -elle, *adj.* artificial.

artillerie, *s. f.* artillery.

artisan, *s. m.* craftsman.

artiste, *s. m. & f.* artist; player

ascenseur, *s. m.* lift.

asile, *s. m.* refuge, asylum.

aspect, *s.m.* aspect.

asperge, *s. f.* asparagus.

aspirateur, *s.m.* vacuumcleaner.

aspiration, *s. f.* aspiration.

aspirer, *v.a.* inspire; *v. n.* aspire *(à to).*

assaillir*, *v. a.* assault.

assaisonner, *v.a.* season; dress.

assassin, *s. m.* assassin.

assassiner, *v. a.* assassinate, murder.

assaut, *s.m.* assault.

assemblage, *s. m.* assemblage, gathering, collection.

assemblée, *s.f.* assembly, meeting.

assembler, *v. a.* assemble; put together; gather; s'~ assemble.

asseoir*, *v. a.* seat; place; s'~ take a seat.

assez, *adv.* enough; pretty, fairly.

assiduité, *s.f.* assiduity.

assiéger, *v.a.* attack, besiege.

assiette, *s. f.* posture; seat; position; plate.

assimiler, *v. a.* assimilate *(' to).*

assistance, *s.f.* presence, attendance; audience; assistance, help.

assister, *v. n.* attend, be present *(à at); v. a.* assist, help.

association, *s. f.* association; partnership, company.

associer, *v.a.* associate, link up; share interests with; s'~ associate oneself *(avec* with).

assommant, *adj.* boring, dull.

assortir, *v.a.* match, assort; **s'~** be suitable, go well together.

assoupir, *v. a.* make drowsy, sleepy; **s'~** grow sleepy.

assujettir, *v.a.* subject, subjugate.

assumer, *v. a.* assume.

assurance, *s. f.* assurance; insurance; **~** *sur la vie* life-insurance.

assuré, *adj.* assured, confident, sure; insured.

assurer, *v.a.* assure, secure; insure; **s'~** make sure (of).

astre, *s. m.* star.

astronaute, *s. m.* astronaut, space man.

astronautique, *s. f.* astronautics, space travel.

astronef, *s. m.* spacecraft, space-ship.

atelier, *s.m.* workshop; studio.

athée, *s.m.f.* atheist.

athlète, *s.m.* athlete.

athlétique, *adj.* athletic.

atome, *s.m.* atom.

atomique, *adj.* atomic; *bombe* **~** atom(ic) bomb *énergie* **~** atomic energy.

attache, *s. f.* tie, fastener; bond, strap; *fig.* attachment.

attaché, *s. m.* attaché.

attacher, *v.a.* fasten, tie (up); attach; associate; engage; **s'~** attach (to), become attached (to).

attaque, *s. f.* attack.

attaquer, *v.a.* attack.

attarder, *v.a.* delay; *être attardé* be delayed.

atteindre*, *v. a.* attain, reach; hit, stirke.

atteinte, *s. f.* blow, stroke; fit; injury; *hors d'~* out of reach.

attendre, *v. a. & n.* await, wait for, expect; **s'~** hope for, expect.

attendrir, *v. a.* soften; *fig.* move, touch; **s'~** be moved.

attendrissement, *s.m.* compassino; tenderness.

attente, *s. f.* waiting; hope

attentif, *-ive, adj.* attentive, considerate.

attention, *s.f.* attention, notice, heed, care; *(pl.)* attentions; *faire* **~** be careful, mind, take notice of, take heed (to); **~!** look out!

atténuer, *v. a.* extenuate, attenuate.

atterrir, *v. n.* land.

atterrissage, *s. m.* landing; *piste d'* **~** landing-strip.

attester, *v.a.* attest.

attirail, *s. m.* implements *(pl.),* utensils *(pl.),* gear; tackle.

attirer, *v.a.* attract.

attitude, *s. f.* attitude.

attraction, *s. f.* attraction.

attrape, *s. f.* trap; catch.

attribuer, *v. a.* assign, allot; attribute, ascribe.

attribut, *s. m.* attribute.

au *(pl.* aux), to the, at the.

auberge, *s. f.* inn, tavern; **~** *de la jeunesse* youth hostel.

aucun, *adj. & pron.* no, none, no one, not any.

au-dessous, *adv.* below; **~** *de* under.

au-dessus, *adv.* (**~** *de)* above, over.

audience, *s. f.* audience; public; sitting, session.

audiovisuel, *-elle, adj.* audio-visual.

auditeur, *-trice, s. m. f.* listener; auditor.

auditoire, *s. m.* audience;

congregation.

auge, *s.m.* trough; bucket.

augmentation, *s.f.* augmentation, increase; rise.

augmenter, *v. a.* augment, increase; s'~ increase.

aujourd'hui, *adv.* today.

auparavant, *adv.* previously, earlier; before.

auprès, *adv.* near, by, close by; ~ *de* near.

auquel, *rel.pron.* to whom, to which.

aurore, *s.f.* dawn.

aussi, *adv.* also, too; ~ ... *que* as ... as; — *conj.* and so, therefore; ~ *bien que* as well as; ~ *bien* in fact.

austère, *adj.* austere, severe.

autant, *adv. & conj.* as much, as many, as far; ~ *que* as far as, as much as.

autel, *s. m.* altar.

auteur, *s. m.* author.

authentique, *adj.* authentic, genuine.

auto, *s. f.* car.

autobus, *s.m.* (motor-)bus.

autocar, *s. m.* (motor-) coach.

automatique, *adj.* automatic; — *s.m.* dial-telephone.

automne, *s. m. f.* autumn.

automobile, *s. m. f.* motorcar.

autonomie, *s.f.* autonomy.

autorisation, *s. f.* authorization, permission; licence.

autoriser, *v.a.* authorize.

autorité, *s. f.* authority; rule.

autoroute, *s. f.* motorway.

auto-stop, *s. m.* hitch-hiking.

auto-stoppeur, -euse, *s. m. f.* hitch-hiker.

autour, *adv. & prep.* ~ *de* about, (a)round; *tout* ~ all round.

autre, *adj.* different, other, another, else; *un* ~ another; *d'*~ *part* on the other hand; ~ *part* elsewhere; *de temps* ~ now and then, at times; *l'*~ *jour* the other day; *l'un et l'*~ both; *l'un l'*~ each other.

autrefois, *adv.* formerly, long ago.

autrichien, -enne (A.), *adj. & s.m.f.* Austrian.

autrui, *pron.* others, other people.

avalanche, *s.f.* avalanche.

avaler, *v.a.* swallow; *fig.* endure, pocket.

avance, *s.f.* advance.

avancé, *adj.* advanced.

avancement, *s.m.* advance, progress; promotion.

avancer, *v.a.* advance, bring, put forward; pay in advance; — *v. n.* advance, proceed, move on; s'~ come, move ,go forward.

avant, *prep. & adv.* before, in front (of), in advance; ~ *tout* above all, before everything; *en* ~ forward, to the front; *mettre en* ~ bring forward; *en* ~ *de* in front of; — *s.m.* front (part); bow (of ship); forward.

avantage, *s. m.* advantage, benefit, profit; *(tennis)* vantage.

avantageux, -euse, *adj.* advantageous.

avant-hier, *adv.* day before yesterday.

avant-propos, *s. m.* foreword, preface.

avare, *s. m. f.* miser; — *adj.* avaricious, miserly.

avarice, *s.f.* avarice.

avec, *prep.* with.

avenir, *s. m.* future; *à l'~* in the future.

aventure, *s. f.* adventure; chance, luck.

aventurer, *v.a.* risk; (s'~) venture.

aventurier, -ère, *s. m. f.* adventurer.

avenue, *s. f.* boulevard; avenue.

averse, *s.f.* shower (of rain).

aversion, *v. f.* aversion, dislike.

avertir, *v.a.* inform, let know; warn; *faire ~ de* give notice of.

avertissement, *s. m.* information, notification; advice; warning.

aveu, *s. m.* admission, confession; consent.

aveugle, *adj.* blind.

aveuglement, *s. m.* blindness.

avide, *adj.* greedy, eager.

avidité, *s.f.* avidity.

avilir, *v.a.* debase, disgrace, degrade.

avion, *s.m.* (aero)plane; *~ de ligne* air-liner; *~ à réaction* jet plane; *par ~* by air-mail.

avis, *s. m.* opinion; advice, counsel; information, notice; hint; mind; *changer d'~* change one's mind.

aviser, *v.a.* perceive; inform; let know; advise; *s'~ de* think, find.

avocat, *s. m.* barrister, advocate, counsel.

avoine, *s.f.* oat(s).

avoir*, *v. a.* have, possess; have on, wear; feel; *~ raison* be right; *~ faim* be hungry; *~ de* take after; *~ à* have to; *il y a* there is, there are; ago.

avorter, *v. n.* miscarry, have a miscarriage.

avorton, *s. m.* abortion.

avoué, *s. m.* attorney, solicitor; lawyer.

avouer, *v. a. & n.* admit, confess; acknowledge; approve.

avril, *s.m.* April.

axe, *s.m.* axis; axle.

azote, *s.m.* nitrogen.

B

baccalauréat, *s. m.* baccalaureate, bachelor's degree.

bachelier, *s. m.* bachelor (of arts etc.).

bacille, *s.m.* bacillus.

bagage, *s. m.* luggage; *plier ~* pack up one's kit.

bague, *s.f.* ring.

bai, *adj.* bay.

baie¹, *s. f.* bay.

baie², *s. f.* berry.

baigner: *se ~* bathe.

baignoire, *s.m.* bath, bathtub; pit-box.

bailler, *v. n.* yawn, gape.

bain, *s. m.* bath; *salle de ~* bath-room.

baïonette, *s.f.* bayonet.

baiser, *v.a.* kiss.

baisse, *s.f.* fall; decline.

baisser, *v.a.* lower, let down; bring down; turn down; cast down; *v.n.* decline, fall; sink; *se ~* stoop.

bal, *s. m.* ball; *~ costumé* fancy-dress ball.

balai, *s.m.* broom, mop; (house-)brush; *donner un coup de ~* sweep.

balance, *s. f.* balance, scales *(pl.)*.

balancer, *v.a.&n.* balance; weigh; swing, rock; give the sack; se ~ swing, wave; balance.

balayer, *v.a.* sweep (out), clear away.

balcon, *s. m.* balcony; dress-circle.

baleine, *s.f.* whale.

ballade, *s.f.* ballad.

balle, *s.f.* ball; bullet; bale.

ballon, *s.m.* balloon; (foot-)ball.

balnéaire, *adj.* pertaining to baths; *station* ~ watering place.

bambou, *s.m.* bamboo.

ban, *s. m.* ban; ~s *de mariage* banns.

banal *adj.* banal, common, ordinary.

banane, *s. f.* banana.

banc, *s. m.* bench, form; bank; pew; stand.

bande, *s.f.* band, strip; bandage; troop, gang, set; ~ *de papier* slip of paper; ~ *transporteuse* conveyer belt.

bander, *v. a.* bind up.

bandit, *s. m.* bandit.

banlieue, *s. f.* outskirts, suburbs *(pl.)*.

bannir, *v. a.* banish, exile.

banque, *s. f.* bank; *billet de* ~ banknote; *compte en* ~ bankaccount.

banquet, *s. m.* banquet, feast.

banquier, -ère, *s.m.f.* banker.

baptême, *s. m.* baptism.

baptiser, *v.a.* baptize.

barbare, *adj. & s.m.* barbarian.

barbárie, *s. f.* barbarousness, cruelty.

barbe, *s. f.* beard; *faire la* ~ *à* shave.

barbet, *s. m.* poodle.

barbier, *s. m.* barber.

baron, *s. m.* baron.

baronne, *s.f.* baroness.

barque, *s.f.* boat, barge.

barrage, *s.m.* barrier, barrage, dam.

barre, *s.f.* bar.

barreau, *s. m.* (small) bar; the Bar.

barrer, *v.a.* fasten, bar; cut off, shut out; steer.

barrière, *s. f.* barrier, town-gate, gate; bar; obstacle.

barrique, *s.f.* barrel, cask.

bas[1]**,** *adj.* low; *à* ~ *prix* cheap; *terre* ~se lowland; *en* ~ (down) below, down(-wards), — *s. m.* bottom, lower part

bas[2]**,** *s. m.* stocking; ~ *nylons* nylon stockings.

base, *s. f.* base; basis.

basique, *adj.* basic.

basse, *s.f.* bass; bass-viol.

bassesse, *s.f.* lowness, meanness.

basset, *s. m.* basset (dog).

bassin, *s. m.* basin, pool.

bataille, *s.f.* battle.

bataillon, *s. m.* battalion.

bateau, *s. m.* boat.

batelier, *s.m.* boatman.

bâtiment, *s. m.* building; building trade; ship.

bâtir, *v.a.* build, erect.

bâtisseur, -euse *s. m. f.* builder.

bâton, *s. m.* stick, staff.

batte, *s.f.* bat; beater.

battement, *s.m.* clap(ping); flapping.

batterie, *s.f.* battery; fight, row; percussive instruments *(pl.)*; ~ *de cuisine* kitchen utensils *(pl.)*.

battre*, *v. a. & n.* beat, strike, thrash; **se ~** fight.

battu, *adj.* beaten.

bavard, -e *s.m.f.* gossip.

bavarder, *v.n.* chat(ter), gossip.

bazar, *s.m.* bazaar.

beau, bel; belle; beaux, belles, *adj.* beautiful, handsome, good-looking, fair; considerable; *il y a ~ temps que* it seems an age since; *un ~ jour* one fine day; — *s.m.* beauty.

beaucoup, *adv.* (*~ de*) a good deal, many, much; plenty (of); *à ~ près, de ~* by far.

beau-frère, *s. m.* brother-in-law.

beau-père, *s. m.* father-in-law.

beauté, *s. f.* beauty

beaux-arts, *s. m. pl.* (the) fine arts.

bébé, *s. m.* baby.

bec, *s. m.* beak, bill nib; mouth-piece; jet; *~ de gaz* gas-burner, gas-jet.

bêche, *s. f.* spade.

bégayer, *v. n. &a.* stammer, stutter.

belge (B.), *adj. & s. m. f.* Belgian.

belle-fille, *s. f.* daughter-in-law; step-daughter.

belle-mère, *s. f.* mother-in-law; stepmother.

belle-sœur, *s. f.* sister-in-law.

bémol, *s. m. & adj.* flat *(music)*.

bénédiction, *s.f.* benediction, blessing.

bénéfice, *s. m.* benefit, advantage, profit.

bénir, *v. a.* bless; praise.

berceau, *s. m.* cradle; *fig.* origin.

bercer, *v. a.* rock, lull (to sleep); *fig.* lull (with promises).

béret, *s.m.* beret.

berger, *s. m.* shepherd.

bergère, *s. f.* shepherdess; deep easy chair.

bésicles, *s. f. pl.* spectacles; goggles.

besogne, *s. f.* (piece of) work, job, task.

besoin, *s. m.* need, want; requirement; *avoir ~ de* want, need; *être dans le ~* be poor.

bétail, *s. m.* cattle.

bête, *s. f.* beast; animal; — *adj.* foolish, silly, stupid, dull.

bêtise, *s. f.* foolishness, stupidity; nonsense; ·trifle.

beurre, *s. m.* butter.

biais, *s. m.* bias, slant, slope.

biaiser, *v. n.* slant, slope.

bibelot, *s. m.* trinket, gew-gaw.

biberon, *s. m.* feeding-bottle.

bible, *s.f.* Bible.

bibliothécaire, *s. m. f.* librarian.

bibliothèque, *s. f.* library; bookcase; bookstall.

bicyclette, *s. f.* bicycle, bike.

bicycliste, *s. m. f.* cyclist.

bien, *adv.* well, right, properly, fully; *assez ~* fairly; *faire du ~* benefit; *ou ~* or else; *très ~* very well, all right; *~ avant* long before; *~ que* (al)though; — *s. m.* good, welfare, benefit; property, goods;

aller à ~ prosper, be successful.

bien-être, *s. m.* welfare, well-being.

bienfaisance, *s. f.* beneficence.

bienfaisant, *adj.* charitable, kind; humane.

bienfait, *s.m.* kindness; benefaction.

bientôt, *adv.* soon, shortly; *à ~!* so long!

bienveillance, *s.f.* benevolence, kindness.

bienveillant, *adj.* kind(ly), benevolent, charitable.

bienvenu, *adj.* welcome; *soyez le ~* welcome!

bière, *s.f.* beer.

bifteck, *s. m.* beef-steak.

bijou, *s. m. (pl.* -x) jewel.

bijouterie, *s.f.* jewellery; jeweller's shop.

bijoutier, -ière *s. m. f.* jeweller.

bile, *s. f.* bile; *se faire de la ~* worry, fret.

bille, *s. f.* billiard-ball.

billet, *s. m.* note; ticket; certificate; *~ d'aller et retour* return ticket; *~ d'entrée* admission ticket; *~ de banque* banknote.

billot, *s.m.* block; yoke.

biographe, *s. m. f.* biographer.

biographie, *s. f.* biography.

biologie, *s. f.* biology.

biologiste, biologue, *s. m. f.* biologist.

bis, *int.* encore!

biscuit, *s. m.* biscuit.

bison, *s. m.* bison.

bistro, *s. m.* pub; wine-shop.

bizarre, *adj.* strange, odd.

blague, *s.f.* pouch.

blaireau, *s. m.* badger; shaving-brush.

blâme, *s. m.* blame, reprimand.

blâmer, *v. a.* blame; find fault with.

blanc, blanche, *adj.* white; hoary; blank.

blanchir, *v.a.* whiten, bleach; whitewash; *v.n.* turn white, whiten.

blasphème, *s. m.* blasphemy.

blasphémer, *v.a. & n.* blaspheme.

blé, *s. m.* wheat.

blême, *adj.* pale.

blesser, *v. a.* wound, injure, hurt; offend; *se ~* wound oneself; be offended.

blessure, *s. f.* wound, injury; offence.

bleu, *adj. & s. m.* blue; *~ marine* navy blue.

bloc, *s. m.* block; *en ~* in the lump.

blond, *adj.* fair, blond.

bloquer, *v.a.* blockade; block (up); tighten.

blouse, *s.f.* blouse, smock.

bobine, *s. f.* bobbin, spool.

bœuf, *s. m.* ox, beef.

bohème, *adj.* bohemian.

boire*, *v. a. & n.* drink; swallow; *~ à la santé de X* drink X's health; *— s. m.* drink(ing).

bois, *s. m.* wood; timber; *de, en ~* wood(en).

boisson, *s. f.* drink, beverage.

boîte, *s. f.* box, case; can, tin; *~ aux lettres* letter-box; *~ de vitesse* gear-box; *en ~* tinned.

boiteux, -euse *adj.* lame.

bombardement, *s. m.* bombardment.

bombarder, *v. a.* bombard, shell.

bombe, *s. f.* bomb, shell; *~ H* H-bomb.

bon, bonne, *adj.* good; kind, nice; right; valid; *c'est* ~! (all) right!; ~ *à rien* good for nothing; ~ *ne année!* happy new year!; *de* ~*ne heure* early; — *s. m.* good(ness); bond, order.

bonbon, *s. m.* bonbon, sweet.

bond, *s. m.* bound, leap.

bondé, *adj.* crowded.

bonder, *v. a.* load, cram.

bondir, *v. n.* bound, leap, spring.

bonheur, *s. m.* happiness; good fortune; success.

bonhomme, *s. m.* good-natured man; simple man; fellow.

bonjour, *s. m.* good morning; salutation.

bonne, *s. f.* maid-servant; ~ *(d'enfants)* nursery-maid.

bonnet, *s. m.* cap, hood.

bonsoir, *s. m.* good evening.

bonté, *s. f.* goodness, kindness, benevolence.

bord, *s. m.* edge, border, brink, (b)rim, verge; side, board, bank; *à* ~ on board; *monter à* ~ go on board.

border, *v. a.* border, adjoin.

bordure, *s. f.* border, edging; verge; kerb.

borne, *s. f.* milestone; bound(ary), limit.

borner, *v. a.* bound, limit, restrict.

bosse, *s. f.* bump, protuberance; knob.

botanique, *adj.* botanical; — *s. f.* botany.

botte¹, *s. f.* (high) boot.

botte², *s. f.* bottle; truss.

bottine, *s. f.* boot.

bouche, *s. f.* mouth; orifice, muzzle.

boucher, *s. m.* butcher.

boucherie, *s. f.* butcher's (shop).

bouchon, *s. m.* plug, cork, stopper.

boue, *s. f.* mud, dirt.

bouger, *v. n.* stir, budge.

bougie, *s. f.* candle. (sparking-)plug.

bouillir*, *v. n. & a.* (also *faire* ~) boil.

bouillon, *s. m.* bubble; stock; ~ *de bœuf* beef-tea.

bouillotte, *s. f.* kettle.

boulanger, -ère, *s. m. f.* baker; baker's wife.

boulangerie, *s. f.* bakery, baker's (shop).

boule, *s. f.* ball, bowl.

boulevard, *s. m.* boulevard.

bouleverser, *v. a.* overthrow, upset; turn upside down; distract.

boulon, *s. m.* bolt, pin.

bouquet, *s. m.* cluster, bunch; bouquet.

bourdonnement, *s. m.* buzz(ing), humming.

bourdonner, *v. n.* buzz, hum, drone.

bourg, *s. m.* (small) town; village.

bourgeois, e, *s. m. f.* citizen; townsman.

bourgeoisie, *s. f.* citizens *(pl.)*; middle class.

bourse, *s. f.* purse; exchange; Stock Exchange; scholarship, bursary.

bousculade, *s. f.* hustling.

bousculer, *v. a.* upset, hustle, jostle; *se* ~ hustle each other.

bout, *s. m.* end, extremity, tip, top, button; *un* ~ *de chemin* a short distance.

bouteille, *s. f.* bottle.

boutique, s.f. shop; booth, stall.

bouton, s. m. button; stud; bud; nipple; knob; ~s de manchette cuff-links.

boutonnière, s. f. button-hole.

boxer, v. n. box, fight.

boxeur, s.m. boxer.

bracelet, s. m. bracelet.

braconner, v. n. poach.

braconnier, s. m. poacher.

brancard, s. m. stretcher; shaft.

branche, s.f. branch.

branler, v. a. shake, totter, waver.

bras, s. m. arm; hand; branch.

braser, v.a. braze, solder

brasserie, s. f. brewery; beershop.

brave, adj. brave; honest. worthy, good.

braver, v. a. face, brave.

bravoure, s. f. bravery, courage.

brebis, s. f. ewe, sheep.

brèche, s. f. breach, gap.

bref, brève, adj. brief, short.

bretelles, s. f. pl. braces.

brevet, s. m. patent; certificate.

bride, s. f. bridle, reins.

brièveté, s. f. brevity.

brigade, s. f. brigade.

brigadier, s. m. corporal, overseer.

brigand, s. m. brigand, armed robber.

brillant, adj. brilliant, shiny, glittering.

briller, v.n. shine, glitter, sparkle.

brin, s. m. shoot, sprig, blade (of grass).

brioche, s. f. brioche.

brique, s. f. brick; bar (of soap).

briquet s. m. lighter.

briquette, s. f. briquette.

brise, s. f. breeze.

briser, v. a. break (to pieces), smash; v. n. break; se ~ break to pieces.

britannique, adj. British.

broche, s. f. brooch; knitting-needle; spindle spit.

brochure, s. f. pamphlet.

broder, v. a. embroider.

broderie, s. f. embroidery, braid.

bronchite, s. f. bronchitis.

bronze, s. m. bronze.

brosse, s. f. brush; ~ à barbe shaving-brush; ~ à dents tooth-brush; ~ à cheveux hairbrush; donner un coup de ~ a brush up.

brosser, v.a. brush; se ~ brush oneself.

brouillard, s. m. mist, fog.

brouille, s. f. quarrel.

brouiller, v.a. mingle, mix; confuse, embroil; shuffle (cards).

broyer, v. a. crush, pound.

bruire, v.n. rustle.

bruit, s. m. noise, din; fuss; rumour.

brûlant, adj. burning, hot, scorching; fiery.

brûler, v. a. & n. burn, schorch, roast; ~ de long for.

brume, s. f. mist, fog.

brumeux, -euse adj. foggy.

brun, adj. brown.

brusque, adj. sudden, curt, gruff.

brutal, adj. brutal, rude savage.

brute, s. f. brute.

bruyant, adj. noisy, loud.

budget, s. m. budget.

buffet, s. m. sideboard; buffet; refreshment room.

buisson, s. m. bush, shrub.

bulbe, *s. m.* bulb.
bulle, *s. f.* bubble; bull.
bulletin, *s.m.* bulletin.
bureau, *s. m.* (writing-)
desk; bureau, office;
department; board,
committee; ~ *de loca-*
tion box-office; ~ *de*
poste post-office; ~ *de*
tabac tobacconist's
(shop); ~ *central* ex-
change.
burlesque, *adj.* burlesque,
ridiculous; — *s.m.*
burlesque.
but, *s. m.* butt, target;
goal; aim, object, pur-
pose; scope.
buter, *v.n.* stumble
(*contre* against); **se ~**
grow obstinate.
butin, *s. m.* booty.

butte, *s. f.* hill, mound,
knoll.

C

ça, *pron.* that; *comme ~*
in that way; — *adv.*
here; — *int.* now then!
cabaret, *s. m.* tavern;
wine-shop; night-club,
music-hall.
cabine, *s. f.* cabin, berth;
cage, car; ~ *télé-*
phonique call-box.
cabinet, *s.m.* small room;
study; water-closet; of-
fice; business; cabi-
net (council); cabinet;
~ *de consultation* con-
sulting room; surgery.
câble, *s. m.* rope, cable.
cabriolet, *s. m.* cabriolet,
cacao, *s. m.* cocoa.
cacher, *v.a.* hide, conceal; **se ~** hide oneself.
cadeau, *s. m.* present,
gift.
cadet, *adj. & s.m.* young-
er, junior; cadet.

café, *s. m.* coffee; café,
coffee-house; ~ *au lait*
white coffee; ~ *con-*
cert music-hall.
cafetière, *s. f.* coffee-pot.
cage, *s.f.* cage; coop;
case, crate.
cahier, *s. m.* exercise book.
caillou, *s.m.* pebble,
stone.
caisse, *s.f.* box, case;
cash(-box), till; cash-
ier's office; drum; *en ~*
in hand.
caissier, **-ère,** *s.m.f.*
cashier.

calcul, *s. m.* calculation,
reckoning; arithmetic.
calculateur, *s. m.* calcu-
lator, computer.
calculer, *v.a. & n.*
calculate, reckon, com-
pute.
caleçon, *s. m.* pants *(pl.);*
~ *de bain* bathing-
drawers *(pl.).*
calendrier, *s. m.* calendar.
calme, *adj.* quiet, calm;
fig. cool; — *s. m.* calm.
calmer, *v. a.* quiet, calm.
calomnier, *v. a.* calumni-
ate, slander.
calorie, *s. f.* calorie.
calorifère, *s. m.* heating
apparatus.
calvaire, *s. m.* Calvary.
camarade, *s. m.* comrade,
fellow; ~ *d'école* school-
friend.
cambrioler, *v. a.* burgle,
break into.
cambrioleur, *s.m.* burglar.
caméra, *s. f.* (cine-)cam-
era.
camion, *s. m.* lorry.
camp, *s. m.* camp; side.
campagnard, *s. m.* countryman, peasant.
campagne, *s. f.* country-
(side), fields *(pl.);*
campaign, expedition.
camper, *v. n.* camp.

camping, *s. m.* camping; *(terrain de)* ~ camping site; *matériel de* ~ camping equipment; *faire du* ~ camp.

canal, *s. m.* canal; channel.

canapé, *s. m.* sofa, couch.

canard, *s. m.* duck, drake.

candidature, *s. f.* candidature, candidacy.

canif, *s. m.* penknife.

canne, *s. f.* stick, cane; ~ *á pêche* fishing-rod.

canon, *s. m.* gun, cannon

canot, *s. m.* boat.

cantine, *s. f.* canteen.

canton, *s.m.* canton, district.

cantonade, *s.f.* wings *(pl.); à la* ~ behind the scenes.

caoutchouc, *s.m.* rubber; waterproof, mackintosh.

capable, *adj.* capable, able; efficient; fit.

capacité, *s. f.* capacity, (cap)ability.

capitaine, *s. m.* captain, leader.

capital, *adj.* capital, chief; —*s.m.* main point; capital, fund.

capitale, *s.f.* capital; capital letter.

capitalisme, *s. m.* capitalism.

capituler, *v. n.* capitulate.

caprice, *s. m.* caprice.

capricieux, *adj.* capricious, fickle.

capsule, *s. f.* capsule.

captif, -ive, *adj. & s. m. f.* captive.

captiver, *v. a.* captivate.

capturer, *v. a.* capture.

car, *conj.* for, because.

caractère, *s. m.* character, temper; nature; type, print, letter.

caractériser, *v.a.* characterize, distinguish.

caractéristique, *adj. &. s.f.* characteristic.

cardinal, *s.m.* cardinal; — *adj.* chief, cardinal; *points card naux* cardinal points.

caresser, *v.a.* caress, fondle; foster.

caricature, *s. f.* caricature.

carnaval, *s. m.* carnival.

carnet, *s. m.* note-book, pocket-book; book of tickets; ~ *de chèques* cheque-book.

carotte, *s. f.* carrot.

carreau, *s. m.* square; (paving-)tile; tile flooring; pane; diamond.

carrière, *s.f.* career; race-course; race; quarry.

carrosserie, *s.f.* body.

carte, *s.f.* card; map; ticket; bill (of fare); *partie de* ~s game of cards; ~ *postale* postcard; ~ *routière* road-map; ~ *de visite* visiting-card; ~ *marine* chart; ~ *d'entrée* admission ticket; ~ *grise* driving licence; *à la* ~ à la carte.

carton, *s. m.* pasteboard, cardboard; (paper) box.

cas, *s.m.* case, event; instance, fact; *dans le* ~ *où, en* ~ *de* in case; *en tout* ~ in any case.

caserne, *s.f.* barracks *(pl.).*

casquette, *s. f.* cap.

casser, *v. a. & n.* break; crack, snap; annul; dismiss; *se* ~ break, get broken.

casserole, *s. v.* saucepan

casuel, -elle, *adj.* casual,

accidental.

catalogue, s. m. catalogue.

catastrophe, s. f. catastrophe, disaster.

catégorie, s. f. category, class.

cathédrale, s. f. cathedral.

catholicisme, s. m. catholicism.

catholique, adj. catholic.

cause, s. f. cause, reason, ground; case; à ~ de on account of, owing to.

causer[1], v. a. cause.

causer[2], v.n. talk, converse, chat.

cavalerie, s. f. cavalry.

cavalier, s. m. horseman, cavalier.

cave, s. f. cave; cellar.

caverne, s. f. cave(rn).

ce[1], **c'**, pron. this, it.

ce[2], **cet; cette;** dem. adj. (pl. ces) this (pl. these); that (pl. those).

ceci, pron. this.

céder, v. a. give up, yield, cede, make over; v. n. yield, give in, up.

ceinture, s. f. belt, girdle.

cela, pron. that, it; c'est ~ that's right.

célébration, s. f. celebration.

célèbre, adj. celebrated.

célébrer, v. a. celebrate.

célibataire, adj. unmarried, single.

cellule, s. f. cell.

celtique, adj. Celtic.

celui, celle, dem. pron. (pl. ceux, celles) he, she, they, those.

celui-ci, celui-là, celle-ci, celle-là, dem. pron. (pl. ceux-ci, -là, celles-ci, -là) this one, this person, the latter, these ones.

cément, s. m cement.

cendre, s. f. ash(es).

cendrier, s. m. ash-tray.

cent, adj. & s. m. hundred; pour ~ per cent.

centime, s. m. centime.

centimètre, s. m. centimetre.

central, adj. central.

centrale, s. f. ~ électrique power-plant, -station.

centre, s. m. centre.

cependant, conj. however, yet, still, nevertheless; in the meantime; ~ que while.

céramique, s. f. ceramics; — adj. ceramic.

cercle, s. m. circle, ring; party, club.

cercueil, s. m. coffin.

cérémonie, s. f. ceremony.

cerf, s. m. stag, hart,

cerise, s. f. cherry.

certain, adj. certain, sure.

certainement, adv. certainly, surely.

certificat, s. m. certificate, testimonial.

certifier, v. a. certify.

certitude, s. f. certainty.

cerveau, s. m. brain(s).

ces see **ce**[2]

cesse, s. f. ceasing, pause; sans ~ unceasingly.

cesser, v. a. & n. cease, stop; give up; faire ~ put an end to.

c'est-à-dire, conj. that is to say, viz., i.e.

cet see **ce**[2].

ceux see **celui.**

chacun, pron. each, each one, every one; everybody.

chagrin, s. m. grief, sorrow, vexation; — adj. sad, sorrowful; sorry; gloomy.

chaîne, s. f. chain; range (of mountains); ~ de

montage assembly line.

chair, *s. f.* flesh; pulp (of fruit).

chaire, *s. f.* chair; pulpit; seat, see.

chaise, *s. f.* chair.

châle, *s. m.* shawl.

chaleur, *s. f.* heat; fire.

chambre, *s.f.* room; bedroom; chamber; apartment; hall; ~ *à coucher* bedroom; ~ Haute Upper House; ~ *de commerce* chamber of commerce.

chameau, *s.m.* camel.

champ, *s.m.* field, country; *fig.* space, opportunity, theme.

champagne, *s. m.* champagne.

champignon, *s. m.* mushroom.

champion, -onne, *s.m. f.* champion.

championnat, *s. m.* championship.

chance, *s. f.* chance, fortune, risk; luck.

chancelier, *s. m.* chancellor.

chancellerie, *s.f.* chancery.

chandail, *s. m.* sweater, pullover.

chandelle, *s. f.* candle.

change, *s. m.* change, changing; succession; (foreign) exchange, barter; *agent de* ~ stockbroker; *bureau de* ~ exchange office; *lettre de* ~ bill of exchange.

changer, *v. a.* change, alter; exchange; se ~ betransformed; change one's clothes.

chanson, *s. f.* song.

chant, *s. m.* singing; song, tune; chant(ing).

chanter, *v. a. & n.* warble; chant; praise.

chanteur, -euse, *s.m.f.* singer

chantier, *s.m.* yard, timber-yard, work-yard.

chapeau. *s.m.* hat; bonnet; cap.

chapelain, *s. m.* chaplain.

chapelle, *s. f.* chapel.

chapitre, *s.m.* chapter; subject, head.

chaque, *adj.* each, every.

charbon, *s. m.* coal; embers *(pl.)*; ~ *de bois* charcoal.

charcuterie, *s. f.* pork-butchery.

charcutier, -ière, *s. m. f.* pork-butcher.

charge, *s. f.* load, burden; post, function, charge, office; attack; accusation.

charger, *v. a. & n.* load; burden; charge; entrust.

charité, *s. f.* charity.

charmant, *adj.* charming.

charme, *s. m.* charm.

charpente, *s.f.* timber-work.

charpentier, *s.m.* carpenter.

charrette, *s:f.* cart, wagon.

charrue, *s. f.* plough.

charte, *s. f.* charter.

chasse, *s. f.* chase, hunt(ing), shooting.

chasser, *v. a. & n.* chase, pursue, hunt, shoot, go shooting; drive out.

chasseur, *s.m.* hunter; page-boy.

chaste, *adj.* chaste, pure.

chat, *s. m.* (he-)cat.

châtaigne, *s. f.* chestnut.

château, *s.m.* castle; palace.

chatte, *s. f.* (she-)cat.

chaud, *adj. & adv.* hot, warm; ardent.

chauffage, *s. m.* heating,

warming; ~ central central heating.

chauffe-bain, s. m. geyser.

chauffer, v. a. & n. heat, warm; urge on; coach.

chauffeur, s. m. driver.

chausse, s.f. hose

chausser, v. a. & n. put on (shoes etc.), wear; se ~ put on one's stockings etc.

chaussette, s. f. sock.

chaussure, s. f. footwear, shoes (pl.).

chauve, adj. bald.

chef, s. f. chief; ~ de train guard; ~ d'orchestre conductor.

chemin, s. m. road, way; lane; se mettre en ~ start; ~ de fer railway.

cheminée, s. f. chimney. fireplace, funnel.

chemise, s. f. shirt.

chêne, s. m. oak(-tree).

chèque, s. m. cheque; ~ en blanc blank cheque; ~ de voyage traveller's cheque.

cher, chère, adj. dear.

chercher, v. a. seek, look for, search for.

chéri, -e, adj. dear; — s. m. f. darling.

cheval, s. m. horse; à ~ on horseback; monter à ~ ride.

chevalerie, s. f. chivalry.

chevalier, s. m. knight.

chevelure, s. f. hair.

cheveu, s. m. hair; en ~ bareheaded.

cheville, s.f. wooden pin, peg; ankle.

chèvre, s.f. (she-)goat.

chevreau, s. m. kid-(leather).

chez, prep. at, in, at the house of; ~ X at X's.

chic, adj. smart, spruce, fashionable; — s. m. chic; trick; elegance.

chien, -enne, s. m. f. dog.

chiffon, s. m. rag, scrap; chiffon.

chiffre, s. m. figure, digit; number.

chignon, s.m. knot (of hair), bun.

chimie, s.f. chemistry.

chimique, adj. chemical.

chimiste, s. m. f. chemist.

chinois, -e (Ch.), adj & s.m.f. Chinese.

chirurgie, s. f. surgery.

chirurgien, -enne, s.m.f. surgeon.

choc, s.m. shock, clash, collision.

chocolat, s. m. chocolate.

chœur, s. m. chorus; choir.

choisir, v.a. choose, pick out, select.

choix, s. m. choice.

chômage, s. m. stoppage, cessation of work; unemployment.

choquer, v. a. run into, strike against, collide with; shock, offend; se ~ come into collision; be shocked.

chose, s. f. thing, object, matter; goods; event; quelque ~ something, anything.

chou, s. m. cabbage, cole.

chou-fleur, s. m. cauliflower.

chrétien, -enne, adj. & s.m. f. Christian.

christianisme, s.m. Christianity.

chronique, adj. chronic; — s. f. chronicle.

chuchoter, v.n.&a. whisper.

chute, s. f. fall, downfall, descent; slope.

ci, adv. here.

ci-dessous, adv. below, underneath.

ci-dessus, adv. above; aforesaid.

cidre, *s. m.* cider.

ciel, *s. m. (pl.* cieux) heaven; sky; weather; climate.

cierge, *s. m.* wax candle.

cigare, *s. m.* cigar.

cigarette, *s. f.* cigarette.

cigogne, *s. f.* stork.

cil, *s. m.* eyelash.

cime, *s. f.* top, summit.

ciment, *s. m.* cement.

cimetière, *s. m.* cemetery; churchyard.

cinéma, *s. m.* cinema.

cinérama, *s. m.* cinerama.

cinq, *adj. & s. m.* five; fifth.

cinquante, *adj. & s. m.* fifty; fiftieth.

circonstance, *s.f.* circumstance; occurrence, occasion, event.

circuit, *s. m.* circuit.

circulation, *s. f.* circulation; currency; traffic.

circuler, *v. n.* circulate; *circulez!* move on!

cire, *s. f.* wax.

cirer, *v. a.* wax; polish.

ciseau, *s.m.* chisel.

ciseaux, *s. m. pl.* scissors.

citation, *s.f.* citation.

cité, *s. f.* city, town.

citer, *v.a.* cite; quote.

citoyen, -enne, *s.m.f.* citizen.

citron, *s. m.* lemon.

citronnade, *s.f.* lemon squash.

civil, *adj.* civil; — *s. m.* civilian.

civilisation, *s. f.* civilization, culture.

clair, *adj.* light, clear.

clapet, *s. m.* valve.

claquement, *s. m.* clap-(ping); snap.

claquer, *v.. n. a.* crack, clap; chatter; bang,

clarté, *s. f.* light, brightness; clearness.

classe, *s. f.* class; order, rank; form, class-room.

classer, *v.a.* class, rank.

classifier, *v.a.* classify.

classique, *adj.* classic(al).

clause, *s. f.* clause.

clé, **clef**, *s. f.* key; spanner, wrench; *fig.* clue; ∼ *de contact* ignition key.

clerc, *s. m.* clerk; scholar.

clergé, *s. m.* clergy.

clérical, *adj.* clerical.

client, *s. m.* client, customer, patron.

clientèle, *s.f.* clients *(pl.).*

cligner, *v. a. & n.* wink.

clignotant, *s. m.* indicator.

clignoter, *v.a.&n.* blink, wink.

climat, *s. m.* climate.

clinique, *adj. & s.f.* clinic, clinical.

cloche, *s. f.* bell.

cloître, *s. m.* cloister.

clore*, *v. a.* shut, close.

clos, *adj.* closed.

clôture, *s. f.* enclosure, fence; close.

clou, *s. m.* nail, stud; boil, furuncle.

clouer, *v. a.* nail (down).

club, *s. m.* club.

cocher, *s. m.* coachman, driver.

cochon, *s. m.* pig, swine.

code, *s. m.* code; law, rule.

cœur, *s. m.* heart; *fig.* mind, soul, courage; *par* ∼ by heart.

coffre, *s. m.* chest.

coffre-fort, *s. m.* safe.

cognac, *s. m.* cognac.

cogner, *v. n. & a.* beat, knock, strike; *se* ∼ knock against.

coiffer, *v. a.* put on (hat); dress, do s.o.'s hair.

coiffeur, -euse, *s.m.f.* hairdresser.

coiffure, *s. f.* head-dress, cap; hair-do; *salon de* ~ hairdresser.

coin, *s. m.* corner; angle.

coïncider, *v.n.* coincide.

coke, *s.m.* coke.

col, *s.m.* collar; neck.

colère, *s.f.* anger.

colis, *s.m.* parcel; item (of luggage).

collaborateur, -trice, *s. m. f.* fellow worker; collaborator.

collaborer, *v.n.* work jointly, collaborate.

collectif, -ive, *adj.* collective.

collection, *s. f.* collection.

collège, *s.m.* college; grammar school.

collègue, *s.m.f.* colleague, fellow worker.

coller, *v.a.* stick, paste.

collet, *s.m.* collar; neck.

collier, *s.m.* necklace; collar.

colline, *s.f.* hill.

collision, *s.f.* collision; *entrer en* ~ collide.

colombe, *s. f.* dove.

colonel, *s.m.* colonel.

colonie, *s. f.* colony; dominion.

colonne, *s.f.* column.

coloré, *adj.* coloured; colourful.

colossal, *adj.* colossal.

combat, *s.m.* fight, combat.

combattre, *v.a.&n.* fight (against), combat (with).

combien, *adv.* (~ *de*) how much, how many, how far; ~ *de temps?* how long?

combinaison, *s.f.* combination.

combiner, *v.a.* combine, unite; contrive, devise.

comédie, *s.f.* comedy.

comédien, *s.m.* comedian, actor.

comestible, *adj.* edible.

comique, *adj.* comic; — *s. m.* comic actor.

comité, *s. m.* committee.

commandant, *s. m.* commander.

commande, *s.f.* order.

commandement, *s. m.* command, order; commandment.

commander, *v. a.* command, order; control.

comme, *adv. & conj.* as, like; as . . . as; while; ~ *il faut* decent, proper; *tout* ~ just like; ~ *si* as if, as though.

commémorer, *v.a.* commemorate.

commençant, -e, *s. m. f.* beginner; — *adj.* beginning.

commencement, *s.m.* beginning.

commencer, *v. a. & n.* begin, commence.

comment, *adv.* how, in what manner; why; ~ *allez-vous?* how are you?; ~ *(dites-vous)?* (I beg your) pardon?

commentaire, *s. m.* comment; commentary.

commenter, *v. a.* comment (on); criticize.

commerçant, -e, *s. m. f.* merchant, dealer.

commerce, *s. m.* commerce, trade; *voyageur de* ~ commercial traveller; ~ *de gros* wholesale trade; *faire le* ~ trade.

commercer, *v. n.* trade, deal with, in.

commercial, *adj.* commercial.

commettre, *v. a.* commit; *se* ~ commit oneself.

commis, *s.m.* clerk, employee.

commissaire, *s.m.* commisary; commissioner.

commissariat, *s.m.* police-station.

commission, *s. f.* commission; charge; committee; errand.

commode, *adj.* convenient, handy, comfortable; — *s. f.* chest of drawers.

commun, *adj.* common; joint; usual; vulgar; *peu ~* unusual; — *s.m.* common people.

communauté, *s. f.* community.

commune, *s. f.* district.

communication, *s. f.* communication, message; call.

communier, *v. n.* communicate.

communion, *s.f.* communion.

communiqué, *s. m.* communiqué.

communiquer, *v. a. & n.* communicate.

compact, *adj.* compact.

compagnie, *s.f.* company.

compagnon, *s. m.* companion, fellow.

comparaison, *s. f.* comparison.

comparer, *v. a.* compare.

compartiment, *s. m.* compartment; *~ de fumeurs* smoking compartment; *~ pour non-fumeurs* non-smoker.

compas, *s.m.* compass(es).

compatriote, *s. m. f.* compartiot, (fellow) countryman.

compensation, *s. f.* compensation.

compenser, *v.a.&n.* com-

pensate.

compétent, *adj.* competent.

compétiteur, -trice, *s. m. f.* competitor.

compétition, *s. f.* competition.

compilation, *s.f.* compilation.

compiler, *v. a.* compile.

complainte, *s.f.* complaint.

complaisance, *s. f.* complaisance, kindness.

complaisant, *adj.* complaisant, obliging, kind.

complément, *s. m.* complement; object.

complémentaire, *adj.* complementary.

complet, -ète, *adj.* complete, full.

compléter, *v.a.* complete.

complexe, *adj.* complex, compound.

complication, *s. f.* complication.

compliment, *s. m.* compliment; congratulation.

compliquer, *v.a.* complicate.

comploter, *v.a.* plot.

composant, -e, *adj. & s. f.* component.

composer, *v. a.* compose, *se ~ de* be composed of, consist of.

compositeur, -trice ,*s. m. f.* composer.

composition, *s. f.* composition; paper.

comprendre, *v. a.* comprehend; unterstand.

comprimé, -e, *adj.* pressed; — *s. m.* tablet.

compromettre, *v. a.* compromise, commit; *se ~* commit oneself.

compromis, *s. m.* compromise.

comptabilité, *s. f.* book-keeping, accounts *(pl.)*

compte, *s.m.* account; amount, sum; ~ *courant* current account; *faire le* ~ *de* count; *régler un* ~ settle an account; ~ *rendu* report, account, statement; review; *tenir* ~ *de* take into account.

compter, *v. a. & n.* count, reckon, calculate.

comptoir, *s. m.* counter.

computer, *v. a.* compute.

comte, *s. m.* count.

comtesse, *s. f.* countess.

concéder, *v. a.* grant.

concentration, *s. f.* concentration; reduction.

concentrer, *v. a.* condense, concentrate.

concept, -tion, *s. m. f.* concept(ion), idea.

concernant, *prep.* concerning.

concerner, *v. a.* concern, relate to.

concert, *s. m.* concert.

concevoir*, *v. a. & n.* conceive; think; imagine; apprehend.

concierge, *s. f. m.* porter.

concile, *s. m.* council.

concis, *adj.* concise.

conclure*, *v.a.&n.* conclude, end.

conclusion, *s.f.* conclusion, end.

concombre, *s. m.* cucumber.

concorder, *v.n.* agree.

concourir, *v. n.* contribute, concur; compte.

concours, *s. m.* concourse; help; assistance; competition.

concret, -ète, *adj.* concrete.

concurrence, *s. f.* competition; rivalry.

concurrent, *s. m.* competitor; rival.

condamnation, *s. f.* condemnation; sentence.

condamner, *v.a.* condemn, sentence.

condenser, *v. a.* condense.

condition, *s. f.* condition, state; service; stipulation, condition; *à* ~ *que* on condition that, provided that.

conditionnel, *adj.* conditional.

conditionnement, *s.m.* ~ *de l'air* air-conditioning.

conducteur, -trice, *s. m. f.* conductor; driver.

conduire*, *v. a. & n.* conduct, lead; drive; show (to), take (to); manage; *permis de* ~ driving licence.

conduit, *s. m.* pipe, tube.

conduite, *s. f.* conducting, leading; driving; behaviour, conduct.

cône, *s. m.* cone.

confection, *s. f.* ready-made clothes *(pl.).*

confédération, *s. f.* confederation, confederacy.

conférence, *s. f.* comparison; conference; lecture; *maître de* ~s lecturer; *faire une* ~ deliver a lecture.

conférencier, -ère, *s. m. f.* lecturer.

conférer, *v.a.* grant, confer, bestow; compare.

confesser, *v.a.* confess.

confession, *s. f.* confession.

confiance, *s. f.* confidence, trust, reliance; *avoir* ~ count on, trust.

confiant, *adj.* confident.

confidence, *s. f.* confidence.

confidentiel, -elle *adj.*

confidential.

confier, *v.a.* trust; entrust, give in charge.

confinement, *s. m.* imprisonment.

confiner, *v. n. & a.* confine.

confirmation, *s.f.* confirmation.

confirmer, *v.a.* confirm.

confiserie, *s.f.* confectionery, sweet-shop.

confiture, *s.f.* jam, preserve.

conflit, *s. m.* conflict.

confondre, *v. a.* confound.

conformer, *v. a.* conform, adapt; se ~ à conform oneself (to).

confort, *s.m.* comfort, ease.

confortable, *adj.* comfortable.

confrère, *s.m.* fellow-worker, colleague.

confronter, *v. a.* confront, compare.

confus, *adj.* confused.

confusion, *s. f.* confusion.

congé, *s. m.* leave, holiday; permission; discharge; warning, notice; *donner* ~ give notice (to); dismiss; *prendre* ~ *de* take leave of; *être en* ~ be on holiday.

congédier, *v. a.* dismiss.

congratulation, *s. f.* congratulation.

congrès, *s.m.* congress, assembly.

conjecture, *s.f.* conjecture.

conjecturer, *v.a.&n.* conjecture, guess.

conjonction, *s.f.* conjunction, union.

connaissance, *s. f.* knowledge; acquaintance; *faire* ~ *avec* get acquainted with.

connaître*, *v.a.* know, understand; be acquainted with.

connexion, *s.f.* connection.

conquérir*, *v. a. & n.* conquer; win (over).

conscience, *s. f.* consciousness; conscience; *avoir la* ~ *de* be conscious of, be aware of.

conscient, *adj.* conscious.

conscrit, *s. m.* conscript.

conseil, *s. m.* counsel, advice; adviser; council, board, staff.

conseiller[1], -ère, *s. m. f.* counsellor, councillor.

conseiller[2], *v. a.&n.* advise, counsel.

consentir, *v. n.* consent, agree (à to).

conséquence, *s. f.* consequence, result.

conséquent, *adj.* consistent; *par* ~ consequently.

conservatoire, *s. m.* conservatory.

conserver, *v.a.* keep, preserve; tin.

considérable, *adj.* considerable.

considération, *s. f.* consideration; esteem.

considérer, *v. a.* consider; esteem.

consigne, *s. f.* cloak-room, left-luggage office.

consigner, *v.a.* deposit.

consister, *v.n.* consist (of), be made (of).

consoler, *v.a.* console.

consommateur, -trice, *s. m. f.* consumer, customer.

consommer, *v.a.* consummate; consume.

consomption, *s.f.* consumption.

consonne, *s. f.* consonant.

conspiration, *s.f.* conspiracy.

conspirer, *v. a.* & *n.* conspire, plot.

constant, *adj.* constant, firm.

constipation, *s.f.* constipation.

constituer, *v. a.* constitute, compose.

constitution, *s. f.* constitution.

constitutionnel, -elle, *adj.* constitutional.

constructeur, *s. m.* builder.

construction, *s.f.* construction, building.

construire*, *v.a.* build, construct.

consul, *s. m.* consul.

consulat, *s. m.* consulate.

consulter, *v.a.* consult.

consumer, *v. a.* consume.

contact, *s.m.* contact, touch, switch.

contaminer, *v. a.* contaminate.

conte, *s.m.* story, tale.

contemplation, *s.f.* contemplation.

contempler, *v.a.* & *n.* contemplate.

contemporain, -e, *adj.* & *s. m. f.* contemporary.

contenance, *s. f.* capacity, contents *(pl.)*.

contenir, *v.a.* contain, hold; restrain; **se ~** restrain oneself.

content, *adj.* content.

contentement, *s. m.* content, satisfaction.

contenter, *v.a.* content, satisfy; **se ~** be contented, do with.

contenu, *s.m.* contents *(pl.)*.

conter, *v.a.* & *n.* tell, relate.

continent, *s. m.* continent.

continental, *adj.* continental.

continuation, *s.f.* continuation, continuance.

continuel, -elle, *adj.* continual.

continuer, *v.a.* & *n.* go on (with), keep on; **se ~** be continued.

contour, *s.m.* contour, outline.

contracter, *v. a.* contract, bargain for.

contradiction, *s. f.* contradiction.

contraindre*, *v. a.* compel, force; **se ~** restrain oneself.

contrainte, *s.f.* constraint.

contraire, *adj.* & *s. m.* contrary; *au ~* on the contrary.

contrairement, *adv.* **~** *à* contrary to.

contraste, *s. m.* contrast.

contraster, *v. n.* contrast *(avec* with).

contrat, *s.m.* contract.

contre, *prep.* against.

contrée, *s.f.* country.

contrefaçon, *s. f.* counterfeit(ing); forgery.

contrefaire, *v. a.* counterfeit; pirate; forge.

contre-partie, *s. f.* counterpart.

contresigner, *v. a.* countersign.

contribuant, *s. m.* contributor.

contribuer, *v. n.* contribute *(à* to).

contribution, *s.f.* contribution, tax.

contrôle, *s.m.* control, check; hall-mark.

contrôler, *v.a.* control, check.

contrôleur, *s. m.* ticket-collector.

contusion, *s. f.* bruise.

convaincre, *v.a.* convince.

convenable, *adj.* suitable, appropriate.

convenance, *s.f.* suitability, convenience.

convenir, *v.n.* suit, be convenient (to), fit.

conventionnel, -elle, *adj.* conventional.

conversation, *s.f.* conversation, talk.

converser, *v. n.* converse.

convertir, *v.a.* convert.

conviction, *s. f.* conviction.

convier, *v.a.* invite.

convive, *s.m.* guest.

convoi. *s.m.* convoy; funeral procession.

convoquer *v.a.* convoke.

coopération, *s. f.* co-operation.

coopérer, *v. n.* co-operate.

copie, *s. f.* (fair) copy.

copier, *v.a.* copy.

coq, *s. m.* cock.

coquille, *s. f.* shell.

coquin, *s.m.* rogue.

corail, *s.m.* coral.

corbeau, *s. m.* raven.

corbeille, *s. f.* basket.

corde, *s.f.* cord, rope.

cordial, *adj.* cordial.

cordonnier, *s.m.* shoemaker.

corne, *s. f.* horn; hooter.

corneille, *s. f.* crow, rook.

cornet, *s. m.* horn; cornet.

cornichon, *s. m.* gherkin.

corporation, *s. f.* corporation.

corps, *s. m.* body, corpse; corporation, corps.

correct, *adj.* correct.

correction, *s. f.* correction.

correspondance, *s. f.* correspondence; relation; communication; connection.

correspondant, *adj.* corresponding.

correspondre, *v. n.* correspond; communicate.

corriger, *v.a.* correct.

corrompre, *v.a.* corrupt, spoil; se ~ become corrupted.

corruption, *s. f.* corruption.

corset, *s. m.* stays (pl.).

cortège, *s. m.* escort.

cosmétique, *adj.* cosmetic; — *s. m.* ~s cosmetics.

cosmonaute, *s. m.* cosmonaut, spacemen.

costume, *s. m.* dress, costume; ~ de bain(s) bathing-costume.

côte, *s. f.* rib; slope; shore.

côté, *s. m.* side, part; à ~ by the side; de ~ on one side; d'un ~ on the one hand; de l'autre ~ on the other hand; passer à ~ pass by; à ~ de next (door) to; beside.

côtelette, *s. f.* chop.

coton, *s. m.* cotton.

cottage, *s. m.* cottage.

cou, *s. m.* neck.

couche, *s. f.* bed; napkin, diaper; coat; layer; (pl.) confinement.

coucher, *v. a.* put to bed; lay; *v.n.* lie down; sleep; être couché lie; se ~ go to bed, lie down; — *s. m.* bedtime; setting.

couchette, *s.f.* berth, bunk; napkin.

coude, *s. m.* elbow; angle, bend.

coudre*, *v. a. & n.* sew.

couler, *v.n.* flow, run, stream; leak; sink.

couleur, *s. f.* colour.

coulisse, *s. f.* groove; slip, wings (pl.); dans les ~s behind the scenes.

couloir, *s.m.* passage; corridor; lobby.

coup, *s. m.* blow, stroke, knock; smack; pull;

kick; shot; draught; cast, move; *d'un seul* ~ at once; ~ *de feu* rush hours *(pl.); de froid* chill; ~ *de main* sudden attack; ~ *d'œil* glance, look; ~ *de soleil* sunstroke.

coupe, *s.f.* wine-cup.

couper, *v.a.* cut; cut down, off, up; divide; cross; mix; **se** ~ cut oneself, cut one's (finger etc.).

couple, *s. f.* pair, brace; *m.* couple.

cour, *s. f.* (court)yard; court; courting, courtship; *faire la* ~ *à* court, make love to.

courage, *s. m.* courage.

courageux, -**euse**, *adj.* courageous, brave.

courant, *adj.* current; running; — *s.m.* current; stream; course run; ~ *d'air* draught.

courbe, *s. f.* curve, bend.

courbé, *adj.* curved; bent.

courber, *v. a. & n.* bend, bow; **se** ~ bend, be bent; bow.

courir*, *v. n.* run; hurry; flow; be curent.

couronne, *s.f.* crown.

couronner, *v.a.* crown.

courrier, *s. m.* messenger, courier, post, mail.

cours, *s. m.* course; current, flow; currency.

course, *s. f.* race, run; course; drive.

court, *adj.* short, brief; — *adv.* short; suddenly; — *s. m.* tennis-court.

courtiser, *v. a.* pay court to, court.

courtois, *adj.* courteous, polite.

courtoisie, *s. f.* courtesy.

cousin, -**e** *s. m. f.* cousin.

coussin, *s.m.* cushion.

coût, *s.m.* cost, price.

couteau, *s.m.* knife.

coûter, *v. n. & a.* cost.

coûteux, -**euse**, *adj.* costly, expensive, dear; *peu* ~ inexpensive.

coutume, *s.f.* custom, habit; *de* ~ customary.

couture, *s. f.* sewing, seam; needlework; scar.

couturière, *s.m.* dressmaker.

couvent, *s.m.* convent.

couver, *v.a.* brood (on), sit; hatch, breed.

couvercle, *s. m.* cover, lid, cap.

couvert, *adj.* covered; covert, sheltered; cloudy; secret; — *s.m.* set (of fork and spoon); cover; protection; *mettre le* ~ lay the table.

couverture, *s. f.* cover(ing); blanket; ~*s* bedclothes.

couvrir*, *v.a.* cover; load; protect; be sufficent for.

crabe, *s. m.* crab.

cracher, *v.n. & a.* spit.

craie, *s. f.* chalk.

craindre, *v.a.* fear, be afraid of.

crainte, *s. f.* fear; *de* ~ *de* for fear of; *de* ~ *que* lest.

crampe, *s.f.* cramp.

crampon, *s.m.* cramp.

crâne, *s. m.* skull; — *adj.* bold.

craquer, *v.n.* crack.

cravate, *s. f.* (neck)tie.

crayon, *s. m.* pencil; crayon.

créance, *s. f.* credence, belief, trust.

créancier, -**ère**, *s. m. f.* creditor.

création, *s. f.* creation.

créature, *s. f.* creature.

crèche, *s. f.* crèche.

crédit, *s. m.* credit; *à ~* on credit.

créditer, *v.a.* credit.

crediteur, *s.m.* creditor.

créer, *v.a.* create, make.

crème, *s. f.* cream, custard; *~ à raser* shaving cream.

crémerie, *s. f.* dairy.

crêpe, *s. m.* crape, crêpe.

creuser, *v. a.* dig; deepen.

creux, -euse, *adj.* hollow, empty; — *s. m.* hollow.

crevaison, *s. f.* puncture.

crever, *v. a. & n.* burst; puncture; die.

cri, *s. m.* cry, scream; call, shout.

crible, *s.m.* sieve, screen.

cric, *s. m.* jack.

crier, *v.a. & n.* cry (out).

crime, *s. m.* crime, guilt.

criminel, -elle, *adj. & s. m. f.* criminal.

crise, *s. f.* crisis.

crisper, *v.a.* contract, shrivel.

cristal, *s. m.* crystal.

critique, *adj.* critical; — *s.f.* criticism, critique; *s.m.f.* critic, reviewer.

crochet, *s. m.* hook; crochet(-work); hanger.

croire*, *v. a. & n.* believe, credit, trust; think.

croiser, *v.a.* cross; *v.n.* cruise.

croître*, *v.n.* grow, increase; grow up; *v.a.* increase.

croix, *s. f.* cross.

croquis, *s.m.* sketch.

crouler, *v. n.* fall (to pieces), fall in.

croûte, *s. f.* crust; *casser la ~* have a snack.

croyance, *s.f.* belief, faith; creed.

croyant, -e, *s. m. f.* believer; — *adj.* faithful.

cru, *adj.* raw; crude.

cruauté, *s. f.* cruelty.

crue, *s. f.* rise, growth.

cruel, -elle, *adj.* cruel.

crypte, *s. f.* crypte.

cube, *s. m.* cube.

cueillir*, *v.a.* gather, pick, glean.

cuiller, -ère, *s. f.* spoon; *~ à pot* ladle; *~ à café* teaspoon.

cuir, *s. m.* skin; leather.

cuire*, *v. a. & n.* cook; boil; roast; burn; *faire trop ~* overdo.

cuisine, *s. f.* kitchen; cooking, cookery; *batterie de ~* kitchen utensils; *de ~* culinary; *livre de ~* cookery-book.

cuisinière, *s.f.* cook; kitchen range, cooker.

cuisse, *s. f.* thigh; leg.

cuit, *adj.* cooked, baked.

cuivre, *s. m.* copper.

cul, *s. m.* bottom.

culinaire, *adj.* culinary.

culotte, *s. f.* panties; breeches *(pl.)*.

culte, *s. m.* cult, worship.

cultivateur, -trice, *s. m. f.* farmer.

cultiver, *v.a.* cultivate, till; *fig.* improve.

culture, *s.f.* culture.

culturel, -elle, *adj.* cultural.

cure, *s. f.* care; cure.

curé, *s. m.* priest; vicar.

cure-dent, *s. m.* toothpick.

curieux, -euse, *adj.* curious, strange, inquisitive.

curiosité, *s. f.* curiosity; *~s* sights.

cuve, *s. f.* tub, vat.

cuvette, *s. f.* *~ (de lavabo)* wash-basin.

cycle, *s. m.* cycle.

cygne, *s. m.* swan.

cylindre, *s. m.* cylinder.

D

dactylo(graphe), *s. m. f.* typist.

dame, *s.f.* lady; queen.

danger, *s. m.* danger.

dangereux, -euse, *adj.* dangerous.

danois, -e (D.), *adj.* & *s. m. f.* Dane, Danish.

dans, *prep.* in, into; inside; during; ~ *le temps* formerly.

danse, *s. f.* dance.

danser, *v. n.* dance.

danseur, *s. m.* dancer.

danseuse: *s. f.* ballet-girl, dancer.

date, *s. f.* date; *prendre* ~ fix a day.

dater, *v. a.* & *n.* date.

datte, *s. f.* date.

davantage, *adv.* more, further; *bien* ~ much more; *pas* ~ no more; *en* ~ some more.

de, *prep.* of, from, out of, on account of.

dé, *s. m.* thimble.

déballer, *v. a.* unpack.

débarquer, *v. a.* & *n.* land, disembark, arrive.

débarrasser, *v. a.* clear (up), rid, free; **se** ~ get rid (of).

débat, *s. m.* debate.

débattre, *v. a.* & *n.* debate.

débit, *s. m.* sale; debit; output; utterance; ~ *de tabac* tobbaconist's shop.

déborder, *v. n.* & *a.* overflow, run over.

débouché, *s. m.* outlet, issue.

déboucher, *v. a.* uncork, open; *v. n.* run into.

débourser, *v. a.* disburse.

debout, *adv.* upright, standing; *être* ~ stand.

début, *s.m.* start, outset; first appearance.

débuter, *v. n.* begin, start; make one's first appearance.

décadence, *s.f.* decadence.

décagramme, *s.m.* decagramme.

décéder, *v.n.* die, decease.

décembre, *s. m.* December.

déception, *s. f.* deception, deceit; disappointment.

décharge, *s. f.* discharge; outlet.

décharger, *v.a.* unload, unburden; release; discharge; **se** ~ unburden oneself.

déchausser, *v.a.* take off (shoes).

déchéance, *s.f.* decadence, decay; decline.

déchiffrer, *v.a.* decipher; make out.

déchirer, *v.a.* tear, rend.

dechoir*, *v.n.* fall off, decay.

décider, *v. a.* & *n.* decide, settle; **se** ~ make up one's mind; be settled.

décilitre, *s. m.* decilitre.

décimal, -e, *adj.* & *s. f.* decimal.

décimètre, *s.m.* decimetre.

décisif, -ive, *adj.* decisive, final.

décision, *s.f.* decision.

déclaration, *s.f.* declaration, statement.

déclarer, *v.a.* declare, state; **se** ~ declare itself.

décliner, *v.n.* decline.

décolletage, *s.m.* low neck.

décolleter, *v.a.* cut low

turn; *tour* a ~ turning lathe.

décomposer, *v. a.* decompose; spoil; se ~ decompose.

décomposition, *s. f.* decomposition.

décompte, *s. m.* discount; particulars *(pl.).*

décor, *s. m.* decoration; scene, environment; scenery.

décoratif, -ive, *adj.* decorative.

décorer, *v.a.* decorate; trim.

découper, *v.a.*· cut out, carve.

décourager, *v.a.* discourage

découverte, *s. f.* discovery.

découvrir*, *v. a.* discover, find out; uncover; se ~ uncover oneself, disclose oneself.

décret, *s. m.* decree, order.

décrier, *v.a.* cry down.

décrire, *v.a.* describe.

décrocher, *v.a.* unhook, take down.

décroissance, *s. m.* decrease.

décroître, *v. n.* decrease.

déçu, *adj.* disappointed.

dédain, *s.m.* disdain, scorn.

dedans, *adv.* within, inside; indoors, at home.

dédicace, *s. f.* dedication.

dédier, *v.a.* dedicate.

déduire*, *v.a.* deduct.

défaire, *v. a.* undo; break; unfasten; take off; defeat; se ~ come undone.

défaite, *s. f.* defeat

défaut, *s. m.* defect, deficiency, want; fault; flaw; *à* ~ *de* for want

of; *sans* ~ faultless.

défavorable, *adj.* unfavourable.

défendre, *v.a.* defend; forbid; se ~ defend oneself.

défense, *s.f.* defence, protection; prohibition; tusk; *se mettre en* ~ stand on one's guard.

défiance, *s.f.* distrust, mistrust.

défier, *v. a.* defy.

défigurer, *v. a.* disfigure, deface, spoil.

défiler, *v. n.* defile.

défini, *adj.* definite.

définir, *v. a.* define.

définitif, -ive, *adj.* definitive, final.

définition, *s. f.* definition.

défunt, -e, *adj. & s. m. f.* deceased, defunct.

dégager, *v. a.* redeem, release, disengage; emit.

dégorger, *v.a.* disgorge, discharge; *v.n.* discharge, overflow.

dégoût, *s. m.* disgust.

dégoûtant, *adj.* disgusting.

dégoûter, *v.a.* disgust; se ~ get tired of.

dégradation, *s. f.* degradation.

dégrader, *v.a.* degrade; damage.

degré, *s. m.* degree.

déguisement, *s.m.* disguise.

déguiser, *v.a.* disguise, hide.

dehors, *adv.* out, outside, out of doors; *au* ~ outside, abroad; *en* ~ *de* outside of, apart from.

déjà, *adv.* already; previously.

déjeuner, *s. m.* lunch(eon); *petit* ~ breakfast; — *v.n.* have breakfast; take lunch.

delà, *prep.* beyond; *au ~ de* beyond.

délai, *s. m.* delay; *à bref ~* at short notice.

délégation, *s. f.* delegation.

déléguer, *v. a.* delegate.

délibération, *s. f.* deliberation, resolution; *en ~* under consideration.

délibérer, *v. n.* deliberate, ponder; *v.a.* bring under discussion.

délicat, *adj.* delicate; feeble; fastidious, dainty.

délicatesse, *s. f.* delicacy; delicateness; daintiness.

délice, *s. m.* delight.

délicieux, -euse, *adj.* delicious, delightful.

délier, *v. a.* untie; loosen.

délivrance, *s. f.* deliverance.

délivrer, *v.a.* deliver, (set) free.

déloyal, *adj.* disloyal, unfair.

demain, *adv.* tomorrow.

demande, *s.f.* request, application, inquiry, call, request, demand.

demander, *v.a.* ask, inquire (after); beg, demand; request, require; *se ~* wonder.

démanger, *v.n.* itch.

démarche, *s. f.* walk, gait; proceeding.

démasquer, *v. a.* unmask.

déménagement, *s. m.* removal, moving.

déménager, *v.n.&a.* move (house); remove.

démesuré, *adj.* immoderate, excessive.

demeure, *s.f.* delay; home, dwelling.

demeurer, *v.n.* live; stay.

demi, -e, *adj.* half; *à ~* by half; *une heure et ~e*

half past one; an hour and a half; — *s. f.* half-hour.

demi-cercle, *s. m.* semi-circle.

demi-heure, *s. f.* half an hour.

demi-jour, *s. m.* twilight.

démobiliser, *v.a.* demobilize.

démocratie, *s. f.* democracy.

démocratique, *adj.* democratic.

démodé, *adj.* old-fashioned.

demoiselle, *s.f.* young lady, miss.

démolir, *v. a.* demolish, pull down.

démon, *s. m.* demon.

démonstratif, -ive, *adj.* demonstrative.

démonstration, *s.f.* demonstration.

démontrer, *v. a.* demonstrate.

dénaturé, *adj.* unnatural.

dénombrer, *v. a.* number.

dénomination, *s. f.* denomination.

dénoncer, *v. a.* denounce.

dénoter, *v. a.* denote; indicate.

dense, *adj.* dense, compact.

densité, *s. f.* density.

dent, *s. f.* tooth; *mal de ~s* toothache.

dental, *adj.* dental.

dentelle, *s. f.* lace.

dentier, *s. m.* set of (false) teeth, denture.

dentifrice, *s. m. pâte ~* tooth-paste.

dentiste, *s. m. f.* dentist.

dénué, *adj.* destitute.

dénuement, *s. m.* destitution.

départ, *s. m.* departure.

département, *s. m.* department; territory.

départir, v. a. grant, allot;
se ~ give up

dépasser, v. a. & n. pass,
exceed, go beyond.

dépêche, s. f. despatch,
wire, telegram.

dépêcher, v. a. dispatch;
v. n. & se ~ hurry.

dépendance, s. f. depen-
dance.

dépendant, -e, adj. de-
pendent; — s. m. f. de-
pendant:

dépendre, v. n. depend.

dépense, s. f. expense;
larder.

dépenser, v. a. & n. spend;
waste.

dépit, s. m. spite; en ~ de
in spite of.

déplacement, s. m. dis-
placement; shift.

déplacer, v.a. displace,
move, shift; se ~ move.

déplaire, v.n. displease.

déplier, v.a. unfold, lay
out.

déplorer, v. a. deplore.

déportation, s. f. transpor-
tation, deportation.

déposer, v. a. put down,
set down; deposit; —
se ~ settle.

dépôt, s.m. deposit;
store-room, warehouse;
lock-up.

dépourvu, adj. needy.

dépraver, v. a. deprave.

déprécier, v. a. depreciate.

dépression, s. f. depres-
sion.

déprimer, v. a. depress.

depuis, prep. since, from;
~ longtemps long since.

députation, s. f. deputa-
tion.

député, s.m. deputy;
member of the French
parliament.

dérangé, adj. deranged;

upset.

déranger, v. a. upset, put
out of order.

déraper, v. n. skid.

dérèglement, s. m. irregu-
larity; disorder.

dérivation, s. f. deriva-
tion.

dériver, v.n. drift; be
derived.

dernier, -ère, adj. & s. m.
f. latter, last, latest; le
~ the latter.

dernièrement, adv. lately.

dérober, v. a. rob, steal.
se ~ steal away.

déroger, v.n. derogate
(from).

dérouler, v.a. unroll,
unfold.

déroute, s.f. defeat.

derrière, adv. & prep.
behind, back; — s. m.
back (part); bottom.

dès, prep. from, as early
as, since; ~ que as
soon as.

désagréable, adj. disa-
greeable, unpleasant.

désarmer, v.a. disarm.

désastre, s.m. disaster.

désavantage, s. m. dis-
advantage.

descendance, s.f. de-
scent.

descendant, adj. de-
scending; en ~ down-
ward, downhill.

descendre, v. n. descend,
come down, go down;
alight; ~ terre land;
— v.a. take down.

descente, s.f. descent;
landing.

description, s. f. description.

désert[1], s. m. desert.

désert[2], adj. deserted,
desolate.

déserter, v. n. & a. leave,
desert.

désespérer, v.n. despair,

give up.

désespoir, *s. m.* despair.

déshabiller, *v. a.* undress; take off clothes.

déshonneur, *s.m.* dishonour, disgrace.

déshonorer, *v.a.* dishonour, disgrace.

désigner, *v. a.* designate; denote; appoint.

desinfecter, *v. a.* disinfect.

désir, *s. m.* desire.

désirable: *adj.* desirable.

désirer, *v. a. & n.* desire, long for.

désireux, -euse, *adj.* desirous, anxious.

désobéir, *v.n.* disobey.

désobéissance, *s.f.* disobedience.

désobéissant, *adj.* disobedient.

désœuvré, *adj.* idle, unoccupied.

désolation, *s. f.* devastation; desolation.

désoler, *v.a.* desolate; afflict, distress; se ~ grieve, be sorry.

désordre, *s.m.* disorder.

dessert, *s. m.* dessert.

dessin, *s.m.* drawing, sketch; design; ~ animé cartoon.

dessiner, *v.a.* draw; sketch; design.

dessous, *adv. & prep.* under, underneath, below, beneath; — *s. m.* under-part; undies *pl.*

dessus, *adv. & prep.* on, upon, over, above, on top; — *s. m.* upper part, top.

destin, *s. m.* destiny, fate.

destinataire, *s. m. f.* receiver, addressee.

destination, *s. f.* destination.

destinée, *s.f.* destiny.

destiner, *v.a.* destine;

mean (for); se ~ be destined (á for).

détachement, *s. m.* disengagement; detachment.

détacher, *v.a.* loose(n), unfasten; detach; se ~ get loose, come undone.

détail, *s.m.* detail, particular; retail; *en* ~ in detail.

détention, *s. f.* detention.

détermination, *s.f.* determination.

déterminé, *adj.* definite, determinate; resolute; limited.

déterminer, *v.a.* determine, fix; limit; settle.

détestable, *adj.* hateful.

détester, *v.a.* detest.

détonation, *s.f.* detonation.

détour, *s.m.* turning, winding, turn; roundabout way; evasion.

détourner, *v.a.* turn aside; lead astray.

détroit, *s. m.* strait, pass.

détruire*, *v.a.* destroy, ruin; do away with.

dette, *s. f.* debt.

deuil, *s.m.* mourning.

deux, *adj. & s. m.* two; both.

deuxième, *adj.* second.

devancer, *v. a.* precede; anticipate.

devant, *prep. adv.* before; in front of; opposite to; ~ *que* before; *au-*~ *de* ~ in front of; — *s. m.* front; foreground.

dévaster, *v. a.* devastate, destroy.

développement, *s. m.* development, growth.

développer, *v.a.* (also se ~) develop.

devenir, *v.n.* become, get, turn, grow.

dévier, *v. a. & n.* deviate, turn away.

devise, *s. f.* device.

dévoiler, *v. a.* unveil, reveal.

devoir*, *v.a.* owe, be in debt for; have to, must, be bound to, ought to; — *s. m.* duty; task; work., prep.

dévorer, *v. a.* devour, eat up.

dévouement, *s. m.* devotion.

dévouer, *v. a.* devote, dedicate; se ~ devote oneself.

diable, *s. m.* devil; trolley, truck.

diacre, *s. m.* deacon.

diadème, *s. m.* diadem.

diagnostic, *s. m.* diagnosis.

dialecte, *s. m.* dialect.

dialogue, *s. m.* dialogue.

diamant, *s. m.* diamond.

diapositive, *s. f.* transparency, slide.

diarrhée, *s. f.* diarrhoea.

dictée, *s. f.* dictation.

dicter, *v. a.* dictate.

dictionnaire, *s. m.* dictionary.

diesel, *s. m.* diesel engine.

dieu, *s. m. (pl. -x)* God.

différence, *s. f.* difference.

différent, *adj.* different.

différer, *v.a.* defer, put off; *v.n.* differ, be different, vary.

difficile, *adj.* difficult, hard.

difficulté, *s. f.* difficulty, trouble.

diffusion, *s. f.* diffusion.

digne, *adj.* worthy; ~ *de* ... worthy of ...

dignité, *s.f.* dignity.

diligence, *s.f.* diligence.

diligent, *adj.* diligent.

dimanche, *s. m.* Sunday.

dimension, *s.f.* dimension.

diminuer, *v.a.* & *n.*

diminish, lessen, reduce.

dindon, *s.m.* turkey.

dîner, *s. m.* dinner; — *v. n.* dine.

diplomate, *s. m.* diplomat.

diplomatie, *s. f.* diplomacy.

diplomatique, *adj.* diplomatic.

diplôme, *s.m.* diploma.

dire*, *v.a.* say, tell; speak; ~ *à qn de faire qch.* tell s.o. to do sth.; *c'est à* ~ that is to say; *pour ainsi* ~ as it were; *vouloir* ~ mean; *dites donc!* look here!

direct, *adj.* direct.

directeur, *s.m.* director, manager; head master.

direction, *s.f.* direction; management; guidance; streering-gear.

directrice, *s. f.* directress; head mistress.

diriger, *v.a.* direct; lead, guide; manage; turn; steer.

disciple, *s.m.* disciple, follower.

discipline, *s. f.* discipline.

discorde, *s.f.* discord.

discours, *s.m.* discourse, speech.

discrédit, *s.m.* discredit.

discréditer, *v. a.* discredit.

discret, -ète *adj.* discreet; discrete.

discrètement, *adv.* discreetly.

discrétion, *s. f.* discretion.

discussion, *s. f.* discussion.

discuter, *v.a.* discuss, debate.

disparaître, *v.n.* disappear.

dispenser, *v. a.* dispense; se ~ *de* dispense with.

disposer, *v. a. & n.* dispose, lay out; se ~ prepare (to), be about (to); *bien disposé* willing.

disposition, *s. f.* disposition, arrangement; *la ~ de qn.* at s.o.'s disposal.

dispute, *s. f.* dispute.

disputer, *v. a. & n.* dispute, contest, argue; *se ~* quarrel, dispute.

disqualifier, *v.a.* disqualify.

disque, *s. m.* disc, record; discus; *~ microsillon* or *longue durée* long playing record.

dissimulation, *s. f.* dissimulation, dissembling.

dissimuler, *v.a. & n.* dissemble, conceal; *se ~* conceal oneself.

dissolution, *s. f.* dissolution; undoing, breaking up.

dissoudre*, *v. a.* dissolve, disperse.

distance, *s. f.* distance; *a quelle ~ est-ce?* how far is it?

distant, *adj.* distant, far.

distiller, *v.a. & n.* distil.

distinct, *adj.* distinct, clear.

distinction, *s.f.* distinction.

distinguer, *v.a.* distinguish, discriminate; make out, tell.

distraction, *s. f.* abstraction; recreation; entertainment; distraction.

distraire, *v.a.* subtract; divert, distract; amuse, entertain.

distrait, *adj.* inattentive, absent-minded.

distribuer, *v. a.* distribute; deal out.

district, *s.m.* district.

divan, *s.m.* sofa, divan.

divergence, *s.f.* divergence; difference.

divers, *adj.* diverse, different, miscellaneous.

diversion, *s. f.* diversion.

divertir, *v. a.* divert, entertain; *se ~* enjoy oneself.

divertissement, *s. m.* diversion; entertainment.

divin, *adj.* divine.

diviser, *v.a.* divide, separate.

division, *s.f.* division, department.

divorce, *s. m.* divorce.

divorcer, *v n. & n.* divorce, be divorced.

dix, *adj. s. m.* ten.

dix-huit, *adj. & s.m.* eighteen.

dixième, *adj. & s.f.* tenth.

dix-neuf, *adj. & s-m.* nineteen.

dix-sept, *adj. & s.m.* seventeen.

dizaine, *s. f.* ten.

docteur, *s. m.* doctor.

document, *s.m.* document.

documentaire, *s. m.* documentary (film).

dogme, *s. m.* dogma.

doigt, *s.m.* finger; toe.

dollar, *s.m.* dollar.

domaine, *s.m.* domain; landed property.

dôme, *s. m.* dome.

domestique, *adj. & s. m. f.* domestic, servant.

domicile, *s. m.* domicile, dwelling.

domination, *s. f.* domination, rule.

dominer, *v. a. & n.* dominate, rule.

dommage, *s. m.* damage; pity.

dompter, *v. a.* subdue, master, tame.

don, *s. m.* present, gift.

donateur, *s.m.* giver.

donc, *conj.* therefore, then, so; of course.

donne, *s. f.* deal.

donner, *v. a.* give, grant, present with, afford, hand over; ~ *congé* give notice to; se ~ *pour* claim to be.

dont, *pron.* whose, of whom; of which.

dormir*, *v.n.* sleep.

dortoir, *s. m.* dormitory.

dos, *s. m.* back.

dose, *s. f.* dose.

dossier, *s. m.* back-piece; record, file.

dot, *s. f.* dowry.

doter, *v. a.* endow.

douane, *s.f.* customs; custom-house; duty; *déclaration de* ~ customs declaration; *droits de* ~ customs duties; *la visite de la* ~ customs formalities.

douanier, *s.m.* custom-house officer.

double, *s.m.* double; *en* ~ duplicate; — *adj.* double, dual.

doubler, *v. a.* double (up); line; dub.

doublure, *s.f.* lining; understudy.

douce *see* **doux.**

douceur, *s. f.* sweetness; gentleness.

douche, *s. f.* shower-bath.

douer, *v. a.* endow, gift.

douleur, *s. f.* pain, ache.

douloureux, -euse, *adj.* painful.

doute, *s. m.* doubt; *sans* ~ no doubt, undoubtedly.

douter, *v. n.* doubt; se ~ suspect.

douteux, -euse, *adj.* doubtful, dubious.

doux, douce, *adj.* sweet; mild, soft.

douzaine, *s.f.* dozen.

douze, *adj. & s. m.* twelve; twelfth.

douzième, *adj.* twelfth.

dramatique, *adj.* dramatic; *l'art* ~ drama.

drame, *s.m.* drama.

drap, *s.m.* cloth, sheet.

drapeau, *s.m.* flag.

dresser, *v. a.* set up, erect; prepare; se ~ stand up, get up.

drogue, *s. f.* drug.

droguerie, *s. f.* drugs *pl.*

droit, *s. m.* right; law; duty, due; *avoir* ~ *à* be entitled to; ~ *de cité* citizenship; ~ *d'auteur,* copyright; *exempt de* ~s duty-free; ~(s) *de sortie,* export duty; — *adj.* right, direct, straight.

droite, *s. f.* right hand.

drôle, *adj.* droll, funny, strange; — *s. m.* rogue.

du, *art.* of the, some, any.

dû, *adj. & s. m.* due.

duc, *s. m.* duke.

duchesse, *s.f.* duchess.

duel, *s. m.* duel.

duplicata, *s. m.* duplicate, copy.

dur, *adj.* hard, tough.

durable, *adj.* lasting.

durant, *prep.* during, for.

durcir, *v. a. & n.* harden.

durée, *s.f.* duration, term.

durer, *v.n. & a.* last, endure, hold out.

dureté, *s. f.* hardness.

dynastie, *s.f.* dynasty.

E

eau, *s. f. (pl. -x)* water;

~ *de mer* salt water;
~ *de Seltz* soda-water.

ébaucher, *v.a.* sketch; outline.

ébouriffer, *v.a.* ruffle.

ébullition, *s.f.* boiling.

écaille, *s.f.* scale.

écailler, *v.a.* scale.

écart, *s.m.* deviation; *à l'*~ aside, apart.

écarter, *v.a.* set aside; dispel, take away; *s'*~ turn aside.

ecclésiastique, *adj. & s. m.* ecclesiastic.

échafaud, *s. m.* scaffold-(ing).

échange, *s. m.* exchange.

échanger, *v. a.* exchange.

échapper, *v. n.* escape, get away.

échauder, *v.a.* scald.

échauffer, *v. a.* heat; *s'*~ get hot.

échéance, *s. f.* expiration.

échéant, *adj.* due.

échec, *s. m.* check.

échecs, *s. m. pl.* chess.

échelle, *s.f.* ladder; scale.

échine, *s.f.* backbone.

écho, *s.m.* echo.

échoir*, *v.n.* expire, fall due; happen.

éclabousser, *v. a.* splash, spatter with mud.

éclair, *s.m.* lightning; flash.

éclairage, *s. m.* lighting; ~ *au néon* strip-lighting.

éclaircir, *v. a.* make clear, clear up; clarify; throw light on; *s'*~ become clear, clear up.

éclairer, *v. a.* light, illuminate; enlighten.

éclaireur, *s. m.* boy scout.

éclat, *s.m.* splinter; burst; brightness.

éclatant, *adj.* bright.

éclater, *v. n.* split; burst; break out; flash.

éclipser, *v. a.* eclipse; *s'*~ be eclipsed; take French leave.

école, *s.f.* school; *maître d'*~ schoolmaster; ~ *normale* teachers' training college; ~ *secondaire* grammar-school.

écolier, *s. m.* schoolboy.

écolière, *s. f.* schoolgirl.

économe, *adj.* economical; — *s. m.* bursar.

économie, *s. f.* economy; thrift; ~ *politique* political economy; ~*s* savings; *faire des* ~*s* save up.

économique, *adj.* economic; economical.

économiser, *v. a. & n.* economize, save, spare.

écorce, *s. f.* bark; rind.

écossais, *adj.* Scottish, Scotch.

Écossais, *s. m.* Scotsman.

écouler, *v.a.* sell.

écouter, *v.a.* listen to; hear.

écouteur, *s.m.* head-phone; receiver.

écran, *s.m.* screen; *le petit* ~ television.

écrier: *s'*~ cry out.

écrire*, *v. a.* write (down); *machine à* ~ type-writer.

écrit, *adj.* written; — *s. m.* writing; *par* ~ in writing.

écriture, *s.f.* writing, handwriting; style.

écrivain, *s.m.* writer, author.

écuelle, *s. f.* bowl, basin, dish.

écume, *s.f.* foam.

écureuil, *s.m.* squirrel.

écurie, *s.f.* stable.

édifice, *s.m.* building.

édifier, *v.a.* build, erect; edify.

édit, *s.m.* edict, decree.

éditer, *v. a.* publish; edit.

éditeur, *s. m.* publisher.

édition, *s. f.* publication; edition.

éducation, *s. f.* education; training.

effacer, *v. a.* efface, rub out; wipe out.

effectif, -ive *adj.* actual, real.

effectuer, *v.a.* effect, carry out.

effet, *s. m.* effect, result; impression; bill (of exchange); *(pl.)* clothes, belongings.

efficacité, *s. f.* efficacy.

effondrer: s'~ fall in, collapse.

effort, *s. m.* effort, exertion, endeavour.

effrayant, *adj.* frightful.

effrayé, *adj.* afraid.

effrayer, *v.a.* frighten; s'~ be frightened.

effroi, *s.m.* fright.

effroyable, *adj.* frightful.

effusion, *s.f.* effusion, gush.

égal, *adj.* equal, like, alike; (all the) same; even.

également, *adv.* equally.

égaler, *v.a.* equal.

égalité, *s.f.* equality.

égard, *s. m.* regard; *à cet* ~ on that account; *à l'~ de* with regard to; *en* ~ *à* considering.

égarer, *v. a.* mislead, misguide; s'~ lose one's way.

égayer, *v. a.* cheer (up); s'~ cheer up.

église (É), *s. f.* church.

égoïste, *adj.* egoistic, selfish.

egyptien, -enne (E.), *adj.* & *s.m.f.* Egyptian.

eh, *int.* ah!;~ *bien!* well!

élaborer, *v. a.* work out, think out, elaborate.

élan, *s.m.* dash; run; élan, zest.

élancé, *adj.* slim.

élancer, *v. n.* shoot; s'~ bound, dash, rush; soar.

élargir, *v. a.* make wider, enlarge; set at liberty.

élastique, *adj.* & *s. m.* elastic.

électeur, -trice, *s. m. f.* voter.

élection, *s.f.* election.

électricien, -enne, *s. m. f.* electrician.

électricité, *s.f.* electricity; *usine d'~* power-plant, -station.

électrique, *adj.* electric(al).

électron, *s.m.* electron.

électronique, *adj.* electronic.

élégance, *s.f.* elegance.

élégant, *adj.* elegant.

élément, *s. m.* element.

élémentaire, *adj.* elementary.

éléphant, *s. m.* elephant.

élévation, *s.f.* elevation.

élève, *s.m.f.* pupil.

élevé, *adj.* educated.

élever, *v. a.* raise, lift up; increase; bring up, educate; rear; s'~ rise; exalt oneself.

éliminer, *v. a.* eliminate.

élire, *v. a.* choose; elect.

elle, *pron. (pl.* elles*)* she, it, her; they.

elle-même, *pron.* herself.

éloigné, *adj.* far, distant.

éloigner, *v.a.* remove; take away; set aside.

émail, *s. m.* enamel.

émaner, *v.n.* emanate.

emballer, *v.a.* pack up; pack off.

embarquement, *s. m.* em~

barking; shipment.

embarquer, *v.a.* ship, embark; *v.n.* go on board.

embarrasser, *v. a.* embarrass.

embellir, *v. a.* embellish.

embêter, *v.a.* bore; annoy.

emblème, *s. m.* emblem.

embouchure, *s. f.* mouthpiece; mouth (of river).

embranchement, *s.m.* branchline; junction.

embrasser, *v. a.* embrace; kiss; s'~ kiss.

embrayage, *s. m.* clutch, coupling.

embrouillement, *s.m.* tangle; muddle.

embrouiller, *v. a.* embroil, entangle; muddle; s'~ become confused.

émetteur, *s. m.* transmitter.

émettre *v. a.* emit; transmit, broadcast.

émigration, *s. f.* emigration.

émigré, -e, *s.m.f.* emigrant.

émigrer, *v.n.* emigrate.

éminent, *adj.* eminent.

emmener, *v.a.* take away.

émotion, *s.f.* emotion; feeling.

émouvoir, *v.a.* move, touch; s'~ be moved.

emparer: s'~ *de* get hold of, seize.

empêchement, *s.m.* hindrance.

empêcher, *v.a.* keep from; prevent; hinder.

empire, *s.m.* empire.

emplette, *s. f.* purchase.

emplir, *v.a.* fill (up).

emploi, *s.m.* employment, job; use.

employé, -e, *s.m.f.* employee; clerk; attendant.

employer, *v.a.* employ; use.

empoigner, *v.a.* grasp, grip; lay hands on.

empoisonner, *v. a.* poison.

emporter, *v.a.* carry, take away, carry off, remove; s'~ get angry, lose one's temper.

empreinte, *s. f.* stamp, print, impression.

empresser: s'~ hurry, hasten.

emprisonnement, *s.m.* imprisonment.

emprisonner, *v.a.* imprison.

emprunter, *v. a.* borrow.

en, *prep.* in; to; into; at; like, as; by, through;

— *pron.* of him, of her, of it, of them, their; any, some.

encan, *s.m.* auction.

enceinte, *adj.* pregnant.

enchaîner, *v.a.* chain; link up; detain.

enchantement, *s. m.* spell; delight.

enchanter, *v.a.* charm, delight.

enclore, *v.a.* enclose.

enclose, *s. m.* enclosure; close.

enclume, *s.f.* anvil.

encombrement, *s. m.* stoppage; (traffic) jam.

encombrer, *v. a.* block up, jam.

encore, *adv.* yet, still; again; *pas* ~ not yet; ~ *une fois* once again; ~ *que* although; ~ *du* some more; ~ *quelque chose, Madame?* anything else, madam?

encouragement, *s. m.* encouragement.

encourager, *v. a.* encourage; cheer.

encre, *s.f.* ink.

encyclopédie, s. f. encyclopaedia.

endommager, v.a. damage; injure.

endormir, v.a. put to sleep; s'~ go to sleep, fall asleep.

endosser, v.a. endorse.

énergie, s. f. energy; ~ atomique atomic energy.

énergique, adj. energetic.

enfance, s.f. infancy, childhood.

enfant, s. m. f. infant, child; chambre d'~s nursery; d'~s juvenile.

enfermer, v.a. shut in, up, lock up.

enfin, adv. at last; finally; in short.

enflammer, v. a. set on fire; s'~ take fire.

enfler, v. a. swell (up); s'~ swell.

enflure, s. f. swelling.

engagement, s. m. obligation; commitment; engagement.

engager, v. a. & n. pledge; pawn; engage, sign on.

engloutir, v. a. swallow up, devour.

engraisser, v.a. fatten; v.n. grow fat.

enlèvement, s.m. removal.

enlever, v.a. remove, clear away, take away.

ennemi, s.m. enemy.

ennui, s. m. bore(dom); vexation; nuisance.

ennuyer, v. a. bore, weary; s'~ be bored.

ennuyeux, -euse, adj. boring, tedious.

énoncer, v.a. state.

énorme, adj. enormous.

enquérir: s'~ de inquire about.

enrager, v. n. be enraged.

enregistrer, v. a. register, enter, record.

enrhumer, v.a. être enrhumé have a cold; s'~ catch a cold.

enrôler, v. a. enrol, draft.

enroué, adj. hoarse.

enrouler, v. a. roll (up).

enseignement, s. m. instruction, tuition.

enseigner, v.a. & n. teach, instruct (in).

ensemble, adv. together; — s. m. whole, mass; unity; two-piece suit; set of furniture, suite.

ensuite, adv. then; next.

ensuivre: s'~ follow, ensue.

entasser, v.a. heap up.

entendement, s. m. understanding.

entendre, v. a. & n. hear; understand; ~ parler de hear of; ne pas ~ miss; qu'entendez-vous par là? what do you mean by that?; bien entendu of course; c'est entendu! that's settled!, agreed!

entente, s.f. meaning; understanding; agreement.

enterrement, s. m. burial.

enterrer, v.a. bury.

enthousiasme, s. m. enthusiasm.

enthousiaste, adj. enthusiastic; keen.

entier, -ère, adj. entire.

entièrement, adv. entirely, wholly.

entorse, s.f. sprain; donner une ~ a sprain one's (foot, ankle).

entourage, s. m. circle of friends; surroundings (pl.); attendants (pl.).

entourer, v.a. surround; encircle.

entracte, s. m. interval.

entrailles, s. f. pl. entrails.

entraîner, v.a. draw

along; carry away; involve, entail; coach.

entraîneur, *s. m.* trainer, coach.

entre, *prep*, between, among; into, in.

entrée, *s. f.* entry, entrance, beginning; free access; duty.

entremets, *s. m.* second course.

entreprendre, *v.a.* attempt, undertake, contract for; worry.

entrepreneur, *s.m.* contractor.

entreprise, *s. f.* undertaking, enterprise.

entrer, *v. n.* enter; come in, go in; get in; get into; *faire* ~ show in.

enveloppe, *s. f.* envelope; wrapper, cover.

envelopper, *v. a.* wrap up, do up; envelop.

envers, *prep.* towards, to.

enviable, *adj.* enviable.

envie, *s. f.* envy; desire.

envier, *v. a.* envy; desire.

environ, *adv. & prep.* about.

environner, *v.a.* surround.

environs, *s. m. pl.* surroundings.

envoi, *s. m.* sending; consignment, shipment.

envoler: s'~ fly away, take wing.

envoyer*, *v.a.* send, dispatch, forward.

envoyeur, *s.m.* sender.

épais, **-aisse**, *adj.* thick.

épaisseur, *s. f.* thickness.

épargne, *s.f.* savings *(pl.).*

épargner, *v. a.* save (up).

épaule, *s.f.* shoulder.

épée, *s.f.* sword.

éperon, *s.m.* spur.

épice, *s. f.* spice.

épicerie, *s.f.* grocery, grocer's (shop).

épicier, **-ère**, *s. m. f.* grocer.

épidémie, *s. f.* epidemic.

épinard, *s.m.* spinach,

épine, *s. f.* thorn; spine, backbone; obstacle.

épingle, *s. f.* pin; ~ *de sûreté* safety-pin.

épisode, *s.m.* episode.

éplucher, *v. a.* peel; pick; sift, preen, thin out.

éponge, *s.f.* sponge.

éponger, *v. a.* sponge; mop (up).

époque, *s. f.* period, age, epoch, time.

épouse, *s.f.* wife.

épouser, *v.a.* marry.

épouvante, *s.f.* fright.

époux, *s. m.* husband.

épreuve, *s. f.* test, trial; proof; print.

éprouver, *v. a.* test, prove; feel; experience.

épuisé, *adj.* exhausted; out of print.

épuiser, *v. a.* exhaust; use up; wear out.

équation, *s.f.* equation.

équilibre, *s.m.* balance, equilibrium.

équipage, *s. m.* suite, retinue; carriage; crew.

équipe, *s. f.* gang, shift; crew, team, side; train.

équipement, *s. m.* equipment.

équiper, *v.a.* equip.

équivalent, *adj.* equivalent.

ère, *s.f.* era.

errant, *adj.* wandering.

errer, *v. n.* stray; err.

erreur, *s. f.* error, mistake.

érudit, *adj.* learned.

érudition, *s.f.* learning.

escalateur, *s. m.* escalator.

escale, *s.f.* port; landing; *sans* ~ non-stop.

escalier, *s. m.* stairs *(pl.),* staircase; ~ *de sauve-*

tage fire-escape; ~ *de service* backstairs *(pl.)*; ~ *roulant* escalator.

escargot, *s.m.* snail.

escarpins, *s. m. pl.* puinps.

esclavage, *s.m.* slavery.

esclave, *s. m. f.* slave; — *adj.* slavish.

escrime, *s.f.* fencing; *faire de l'~* fence.

escrimer, *v.n.* fence.

espace, *s. m.* space; room.

espagnol, -e (E.), *adj.* Spanish; — *s. m. f.* Spaniard; Spanish.

espèce, *s. f.* species, kind.

espérance, *s. f.* hope, expectation.

espérer, *v. a.* hope (for).

espion, -onne, *s.m.f.* spy.

espionnage, *s. m.* espionage, spying.

espoir, *s.m.* hope.

esprit, *s. m.* spirit; mind; character; wit; sense.

esquille, *s.f.* splinter.

esquiver, *v.a.* evade.

essai, *s.m.* trial, test; essay; attempt.

essayer, *v. a.* try, attempt; essay; assay.

essence, *s.f.* essence; petrol.

essentiel, -elle, *adj.* essential.

essieu, *s.m.* axle.

essor, *s.m.* flight.

essoreuse, *s. f.* spin-drier.

essuie-glace, *s. m.* wind-screen wiper.

essuie-main(s), *s. m. (pl.)* towel; ~ *à rouleau* roller-towel.

essuyer, *v.a.* dust; wipe; dry; mop up.

est, *s.m.* cast.

esthétique, *adj.* aesthetic.

estime, *s.f.* esteem.

estimer, *v.a. & n.* estimate, value; esteem, regard; consider.

estomac, *s.m.* stomach.

estrade, *s.f.* platform.

estuaire, *s.m.* estuary.

et, *conj.* and; ~ ...~ both ... and.

étable, *s.f.* cow-shed; ~ *à porcs* pigsty.

établi, *s.m.* (joiner's) bench.

établir, *v.a.* establish, found, settle, set up; build; prove; s'~ settle (down).

établissement, *·s. m.* establishment.

étage, *s. m.* floor, stor(e)y.

étagère, *s. f.* shelf.

étaler, *v.a.* display; spread (out); show off; s'~ stretch oneself out.

étang, *s. m.* pond.

étape, *s.f.* stage.

état, *s.m.* state; condition; profession, station office; statement; *homme d'~* statesman; *coup d'~* revolt.

été, *s.m.* summer.

éteindre*, *v. a.* put out, extinguish; turn off; s'~ be extinguished.

étendre, *v. a.* spread out; stretch out; extend; s'~ lie down; stretch one-self out.

étendu, *adj.* wide, vast, extensive.

étendue, *s.f.* expanse, reach, range; extent.

éternel, -elle, *adj.* eternal.

éternuement, *s. m.* sneeze.

éternuer, *v.n.* sneeze.

étincelle, *s.f.* spark.

étiquette, *s.f.* ticket, label; etiquette.

étoffe, *s.f.* cloth, material.

étoile, *s.f.* star.

étonnant, *adj.* astonishing, amazing.

étonnement, *s. m.* astonishment, wonder.

étonner, *v.a.* astonish,

amaze; s'~ be astonished.

étouffer, v.a. choke.

étrange, adj. strange.

étranger, -ère, adj. foreign, strange; —-s.m.f. foreigner; à l'~ abroad.

être*, v.n. be, exist; il est... it is...; ~ bien be good-looking; be well; c'est que the fact is; ~ à belong to; — s.m. being.

étreindre*, v.a. clasp; press; embrace.

étreinte, s.f. embrace.

étrier, s. m. stirrup.

étroit, adj. narrow, strait; close.

étude, s. f. study; chambers (pl.).

étudiant, -e, s.m.f. student, undergraduate.

étudier, v. a. study, read; practise.

étui, s.m. case, box.

étuver, v.a. stew, steam.

eucharistie, s.f. eucharist.

européen, -enne, adj. European.

eux, pron. m. they, them.

évader: s'~ escape; get away.

évaluer, v. a. value, estimate.

évangélique, adj. evangelical.

évangile, s.m. gospel.

évaporer, v. a. evaporate; s'~ evaporate.

éveil, s. m. en ~ on the lookout.

éveiller, v. a. awaken; s'~ wake up.

événement, s.m. event.

éventail, s.m. fan.

éventuel, -elle, adj. eventual.

évêque, s.m. bishop.

évidemment, adv. evidently, obviously.

évidence, s.f. evidence.

évident, adj. evident, obvious.

éviter, v. a. avoid, evade.

évoluer, v.n. evolve.

évolution, s. f. evolution.

exact, adj. exact, accurate.

exactement, adv. exactly.

exactitude, s.f. exactitude, precision.

exagérer, v. a. exaggerate.

examen, s. m. exam(ination); test.

examiner, v. a. examine; investigate, look into.

excédent, s.m. surplus; ~s de bagages excess luggage.

excéder, v. a. exceed, surpass; tire out.

excellence, s. f. excellence; excellency.

excellent, adj. excellent.

excepté, adj. excepted; — prep. except(ing), but.

excepter, v.a. except.

exception, s. f. exception.

exceptionnel, -elle, adj. exceptional.

excès, s. m. excess.

excessif, -ive, adj. excessive.

excitation, s.f. excitement.

exciter, v.a. excite, stir up; urge on.

exclamation, s.f. exclamation.

exclure*, v.a. exclude.

exclusif, -ive, adj. exclusive.

excursion, s. f. excursion.

excursionniste, s.m.f. holiday-maker, tourist.

excuse, s. f. excuse; apology; faire des ~s apologize.

excuser, v.a. excuse; pardon; apologize for; s'~ apologize; ask to be

excused; *excusez-moi*
I beg your pardon;
excuse me.

exécuter, *v.a.* execute,
carry out, perform.

exécutif, -ive, *adj.* executive.

exécution, *s. f.* execution.

exemplaire, *s.m.* copy.

exemple, *s. m.* example;
par ~ for example;
sans ~ unprecedented.

exempt, *adj.* exempt, free
(de from).

exemption, *s.f.* exemp-
tion.

exercer, *v.a.* exercise;
practise; carry on; s'~
practise.

exercice, *s.m.* exercise.

exhibition, *s.f.* exhibition; display.

exigence, *s.f.* demand;
exigency.

exil, *s.m.* exile.

existence, *s. f.* existence.

exister, *v. n.* exist.

expansif, -ive, *adj.* expan-
sive.

expansion, *s.f.* expansion.

expédient, *s.m.* expedi-
ent, device.

expédier, *v.a.* forward,
send off.

expéditeur, -trice, *s. m. f.*
sender, shipping-agent.

expédition, *s. f.* consignment; expedition. for-
warding, dispatch.

expérience, *s. f.* experience; experiment; *faire
des* ~s to experiment.

expérimental, *adj.* experimental.

expert, *adj.* expert.

expirer, *v.n.* expire; die.

explication, *s. f.* explanation.

expliquer, *v.n.* explain,
account for, show.

exploration, *s. f.* exploration.

explorer, *v.a.* explore.

explosion, *s. f.* explosion.

exportateur, *s.m.* exporter.

exportation, *s. f.* export,
exportation.

exporter, *v. a.* export.

exposé, *s.m.* statement.

exposer, *v.a.* expose,
show; state; set forth.

exposition, *s. f.* exhibition, display; state-
ment, exposure; exposi-
tion.

exprès, *adv.* on purpose.

express, *adj.* express; —
s.m. express (train).

expression, *s.f.* expression

exprimer, *v.a.* express.

expulser, *v.a.* expel.

expulsion, *s.f.* expulsion.

extension, *s. f.* extension;
extent.

exténuer, *v.a.* tire out,
exhaust.

extérieur, *s. m.* exterior;
outside; *à l'*~ outwards
— *adj.* outward.

extinction, *s.f.* extinction; quenching.

extraire, *v. a.* extract;
draw, pull out.

extraordinaire, *adj.* extraordinary, unusual.

extravagant, *adj.* extravagant.

extrême, *adj.* extreme.

extrêmement, *adv.* ex-
tremely, very.

extrémité *s. f.* extremity;
last moment.

F

fabricant, *s.m.* manu-
facturer, maker.

fabrication, *s.f.* manu-
facture; fabrication.

fabrique, *s.f.* factory,
works.

fabriquer, *v.a.* manufacture, make.

façade, *s.f.* front.

face, *s.f.* face; look; *en ~ de* opposite, in front of.

facétieux, -euse, *adj.* facetious; humorous.

fâché, *adj.* offended.

fâcher, *v. a.* offend; make angry; se ~ get angry.

facile, *adj.* easy; fluent.

facilité, *s.f.* ease; facility; convenience.

faciliter, *v.a.* facilitate; make easy.

façon, *s. f.* making; fashion, shape; way, manner; *de ~ a* so as to; *de ~ que* so that; *en aucune ~* by no means; *d'une ~ quelconque* somehow.

facteur, *s.m.* factor; postman; porter, carrier; *fig.* circumstance.

faction, *s.f.* faction; sentry, watch.

facture, *s.f.* bill, invoice.

facultatif, -ive, *adj.* optional.

faculté, *s.f.* faculty.

fade, *adj.* flat, insipid.

faible, *adj.* weak; feeble.

faiblesse, *s. f.* weakness.

faiblir, *v. n.* become weak.

faillir, *v. n.* fail, fall short; err; ~ + *inf.* nearly; *j'ai failli manquer le train* I nearly missed the train.

faim, *s.f.* hunger; *avoir ~* be hungry.

faire*, *v.a.* make; do; build; cause; ~ *allusion* refer to; ~ *attention (a)* pay attention (to); ~ *une chambre* do a room; ~ *le commerce* trade; ~ *la cuisine* do the cooking; ~ *ses*

études study; be at school; ~ *la guerre* make war; ~ *un lit* make a bed; ~ *mal a* hurt; ~ *part a* let know; ~ *des progrès* make progress; ~ *une promenade* take a walk; ~ *queue* queue; ~ *savoir* let know, inform (of); ~ *usage (de)* make use (of); ~ *voir* show; *que ~?* what's to be done?; *qu'est-ce que cela fait?* what does it matter?; *n'avoir rien a ~* have nothing to do; *deux et deux font quatre* two and two make four; ~ *70 km. a l'heure* do 70 km. an hour; *il fait du vent* it is windy; *il fait chaud* it is warm; *il fait jour* it is daylight; — se ~ be made, be done; get used (to).

faisan, *s. m.* pheasant.

fait, *s. m.* fact; *en ~* in fact, after all, as a matter of fact.

falloir*, *v. impers.* be necessary, be required; must, have to, should, ought to; *comme il faut* proper, decent; *s'en ~* be wanting.

fameux, -euse, *adj.* famous.

familier, -ière, *adj.* familiar.

famille, *s. f.* family.

faner, *v.n.* fade.

fantaisie, *s.f.* fancy.

fantastique, *adj.* fantastic.

fardeau, *s.m.* burden.

farine, *s.f.* flour, meal.

fatal, *adj.* mortal, fatal.

fatigant, *adj.* fatiguing.

fatigue, *s.f.* fatigue.

fatigué, *adj.* tired, weary.

fatiguer, *v. a.* tire, weary,

fatigue.

faubourg, *s.m.* suburb.

faucher, *v.a.* mow, cut.

faucheuse, *s.f.* ~ *(a moteur)* (lawn-)mower.

faucille, *s. f.* sickle.

faucon, *s.m.* falcon.

faute, *s. f.* mistake, error, fault; lapse; want; *faire* ~ fail.

fauteuil, *s. m.* arm-chair, easy chair; stall, dress-circle seat.

fauve, *s.m.* wild beast.

faux[1], **fausse,** *adj.* false.

faux[2], *s. f.* scythe.

faveur, *s. f.* favour; *en* ~ *de* in favour of, on behalf of.

favorable, *adj.* favourable.

favori, **-ite,** *adj.* favorite.

fécond, *adj.* fertile.

féconder, *v.a.* fertilize.

fédéral, *adj.* federal.

fédération, *s.f.* federation.

fédéré, **-e,** *adj. & s. m. f.* federate.

feindre*, *v. a. & n.* feign.

félicitation, *s.f.* congratulation.

félicité, *s.f.* happiness.

féliciter, *v.a.* congratulate.

féminin, *adj.* feminine.

femme, *s.f.* woman; wife.

fendre, *v. a.* split; rend.

fenêtre, *s. f.* window.

fente, *s. f.* crack, split.

fer, *s. m.* iron; ~ *à cheval* horseshoe.

férié, *adj. jour* ~ holiday.

ferme[1], *adj.* firm; — *adv.* fast; firmly.

ferme[2], *s. f.* farm.

fermé, *adj.* closed.

fermer, *v. a.* close, shut; *se* ~ close, be shut.

fermeté, *s. f.* firmness.

fermeture, *s. f.* shutting; shutter; ~ *éclair* zip fastener, zipper.

fermier, *s. m.* farmer.

féroce, *adj.* wild, cruel.

férocité, *s. f.* ferocity.

ferronnerie, *s.f.* ironworks.

fertile, *adj.* fertile.

fervent, *adj.* fervent.

ferveur, *s. f.* fervour.

fesse, *s.f.* buttock.

festin, *s.m.* feast.

fête, *s. f.* feast, holiday; birthday.

fêter, *v. a.* observe; celebrate.

fêteur, **-euse,** *s. m. f.* holiday-maker.

feu, *s. m.* fire, flame; light; *mettre le* ~ *à* set on fire; *prendre* ~ take fire; ~ *d'artifice* fireworks *(pl.)*; ~*x de circulation* traffic lights; ~*x d'arrière* tail lights.

feuillage, *s.m.* foliage.

feuille, *s.f.* leaf; sheet.

février, *s.m.* February.

fiancé, **-e,** *s. m. f.* fiancè, -e.

fiancer, *v.a.* engage; *se* ~ be engaged.

fibre, *s. f.* fibre.

ficelle, *s. f.* string.

fiche, *s. f.* pin, peg; slip (of paper).

ficher, *v. a.* drive in, fix; do, work; deal (a blow).

fidèle, *adj.* faithful.

fidélité, *s. f.* fidelity.

fier: se ~ trust, count on.

fierté, *s. f.* pride.

fièvre, *s. f.* fever.

figue, *s. f.* fig.

figure, *s. f.* form, shape; face; figure.

figurer, *v.a.* figure, represent; *se* ~ imagine.

fil, *s.m.* thread, yarn; edge; clue; ~ *(de fer)* wire.

file, *s. f.* row, file, line.
filer, *v.a.* & *n.* spin.
filet, *s.m.* net; fillet; rack.
fille, *s. f.* daughter; girl; maid; *jeune* ~ young lady.
fillette, *s.f.* little girl.
filleul, -e, *s. m. f.* god-son, god-daughter.
film, *s. m.* film; *le grand* ~ feature film; ~ *avec* film featuring ...; ~ *annonce* trailer.
fils, *s. m.* son.
fin[1], *s.f.* end; close; *à la* ~ in the end, finally; *mettre* ~ *à* put an end to; *tirer à sa* ~ come to an end; ~ *de semaine* week-end.
fin[2], *adj.* fine; nice.
final, *adj.* final.
finance, *s. f.* finance.
financier, *adj.* financial.
fini, *adj.* finished; ended; over.
finir, *v. a.* & *n.* end, finish, put an end to; eat up.
finlandais, -e (F.), *adj.* Finnish; — *s. m. f.* Finn; Finnish.
fixe, *adj.* fixed, firm.
fixer, *v.a.* fix, fasten; stare at; settle.
flacon, *s. m.* flagon, bottle.
flagrant, *adj.* flagrant.
flairer, *v. a.* smell, scent.
flambeau, *s. m.* torch.
flamboyer, *v.n.* flame, flare.
flamme, *s.f.* flame.
flanelle, *s. f* flannel.
flanquer, *v.a.* fling.
flatter, *v. a.* caress; flatter.
flatterie, *s.f.* flattery.
flèche. *s. f.* arrow.
fléchir, *v. a.* bend, bow; *fig.* move.
fleur, *s. f.* flower, blossom.
fleurir, *v.n.* flower, blossom.

fleuve, *s. m.* river.
flirter, *v. n.* flirt.
flocon, *s. m.* flake *(snow etc.).*
flot, *s. m.* wave; flood; *être à* ~ be floating.
flottant, *adj.* floating.
flotte, *s.f.* fleet; navy.
flotter, *v.n.* & *a.* float.
fluide, *s. m.* & *adj.* fluid.
flute, *s. f.* flute.
foi, *s.f.* faith, belief; credit.
foie, *s. m.* liver.
foin, *s.m.* hay; grass.
foire, *s.f.* fair, market.
fois, *s.f.* time; *une* ~ once; *encore une* ~ again; *deux* ~ twice; *à la* ~ at same time; *chaque* ~ every time.
folie, *s. f.* folly, madness.
folle *see* fou.
foncer, *v. a.* sink; darken, deepen.
fonction, *s.f.* function, duty.
fonctionnaire, *s.m.f.* functionary, official.
fonctionner, *v.n.* function, operate, work.
fond, *s. m.* bottom, ground, foundation; *à* ~ thoroughly.
fondamental, *adj.* fundamental, basic.
forcer, *v. a.* force; break open; compel, impel.
forêt, *s. f.* forest.
forger, *v. a.* forge.
formalité, *s. f.* formality.
forme, *s. f.* form, shape.
formel, -elle, *adj.* formal, express; flat.
former, *v. a.* form, shape.
formidable, *adj.* formidable, terrible.
formule, *s.f.* formula.
formuler, *v. a.* formulate, draw up.
fort, *adj.* strong, robust; fat; stout, stiff; skil-

ful; heavy; *être* ~ *en* be well up in; — *adv.* very (much), highly, hard; ~ *bien* very well; — *s. m.* strong man; stronghold.

forteresse, *s. f.* fortress.

fortification, *s. f.* fortification.

fortifier, *v. a.* strengthen, fortify.

fortune, *s.f.* fortune; chance; luck; wealth, property.

fou, fol, folle, *adj.* mad, foolish; crazy.

foudre, *s.f.* lightning, thunderbolt.

fouille, *s. f.* excavation.

fouiller, *v. a. & n.* dig, excavate.

fouillis, *s.m.* muddle, mess.

foule, *s. f.* crowd, mass.

four, *s. m.* oven, furnace.

fourchette, *s.f.* fork *(table)*.

fourgon, *s. m.* (delivery) van; wagon; ~ *(aux bagages)* luggage-van.

fourmi, *s.f.* ant.

fourneau, *s.m.* stove, range; ~ *à gaz* gas-ring, -stove; ~ *électrique* electric cooker.

fourniment, *s.m.* outfit, kit.

fournir, *v.a.* furnish (with), supply; provide (with).

fourreau, *s.m.* sheath, case, scabbard.

fourreur, *s.m.* furrier.

fourrure, *s.f.* fur.

foyer, *s.m.* fireside, home; foyer, lounge.

fracas, *s.m.* crash; up-roar; fuss; noise.

fracasser, *v.a.* shatter, smash.

fraction, *s.f.* fraction; portion; instalment.

fracture, *s.f.* fracture.

fragile, *adj.* fragile.

frais[1], **fraîche**, *adj.* fresh, cool; chilly.

frais[2], *s. m. pl.* expenses, charges, fees.

fraise, *s.f.* strawberry.

framboise, *s. f.* raspberry.

franc, franche, *adj.* frank, free, open.

français (F.), *adj.* French; — *s. m.* Frenchman; French (language).

Française, *s.f.* French-woman.

franchir, *v.a.* clear, jump over, cross.

franchise, *s. f.* exemption; frankness.

frapper, *v.a.* strike, hit, knock; impress; sur-prise.

frein, *s. m.* bit (of bridle); brake; *fig.* check.

frêle, *adj.* weak, frail.

fréquent, *adj.* frequent.

frère, *s.m.* brother.

fricassée, *s.f.* fricassee.

friction, *s.f.* friction.

frigidaire, *s.m.* refriger-ator.

frigo, *s.m.* fridge.

frileux, -euse, *adj.* chilly.

frire*, *v.n. & a.* fry.

friser, *v.a. & n.* curl.

frissonner, *v. n.* shiver, tremble.

frivole, *adj.* frivolous, flimsy.

froid, *s. m.* cold; *avoir* ~ feel cold; — *adj.* cold, cool; *il fait froid* it is cold.

froisser, *v.a.* rumple, crumple; bruise; *fig.* offend, hurt; se ~ take offence.

frôler, *v.a.* graze.

fromage, *s.m.* cheese.

front, *s.m.* forehead; face; front (part).

frontière, *s.f.* frontier, border.

frotter, *v. a.* rub.

fruit, *s.m.* fruit; produce.

fruitier, *s.m.* fruiterer, greengrocer.

fuir*, *v. n. & a.* run away, flee.

fuite, *s. f.* flight; leakage, leak.

fumée, *s.f.* smoke.

fumer, *v. a. & n.* smoke.

fumeur, -euse *s.m.f.* smoker.

fumier, *s.m.* dung.

funèbre, *adj.* funereal.

funérailles, *s.f.pl.* funeral.

funiculaire, *s.m.* rope railway.

fureur, *s.f.* fury, rage.

furie, *s. f.* fury.

furieux, -euse, *adj.* furious.

furoncle, *s.m.* boil, furuncle.

fusée, *s.f.* fuse; rocket.

fusil, *s.m.* gun.

fusillade, *s.f.* firing, shooting.

futur, *adj. & s. m.* future.

fuyant, *adj.* flying, fleeing; passing.

G

gâchis, *s.m.* mortar; mire; *fig.* muddle, mess.

gaffe, *s. f.* blunder.

gage, *s. m.* pledge; security; ~s wages.

gagner, *v. a.* gain; win.

gai, *adj.* gay, cheerful.

gaieté, *s.f.* gaiety.

gain, *s.m.* gain, profit.

galant, *adj.* courteous.

galerie, *s. f.* gallery.

galop, *s. m.* gallop.

gamin, *s.m.* urchin.

gamme, *s. f.* scale; range.

gant, *s. m.* glove.

garage, *s.m.* garage; siding.

garantie, *s. f.* guarantee.

garantir, *v. a.* guarantee.

garçon, *s. m.* boy; young man; fellow; bachelor; waiter.

garde¹, *s. f.* guard; watch; police; nurse.

garde², *s.m.* warden, guardian; watch.

garde-bébé, *s. m.* babysitter, sitter-in.

garde-boue, *s.f.* mudguard.

garde-chasse, *s. m.* gamekeeper.

garder, *v.a.* keep, take care of; attend (to).

garde-robe, *s.f.* wardrobe.

gardien, -enne, *s.m. f.* guardian, keeper; warden; watch(man); ~ de la paix constable; ~ (de but) goalkeeper.

gare, *s. f.* station; depot; ~ des marchandises goods station; *aller recevoir qn à la* ~ meet sy at the station.

garni, *s.m.* furnished lodgings *(pl.),* digs.

garnir, *v. a.* furnish; fit up, trim.

garnison, *s. f.* garrison.

garniture, *s.f.* fittings *(pl.);* set; garnishing.

gâteau, *s. m.* cake.

gâter, *v. a.* waste, impair; spoil.

gauche, *adj.* left.

gaz, *s. m.* gas; *usine à* ~ gas-works.

gazon, *s. m.* grass; lawn.

géant, *s. m.* giant.

gelée, *s. f.* jelly.

gémir, *v. n.* groan.

gênant, *adj.* inconvenient, annoying.

gendre, *s. m.* son-in-law.

gêne, *s. f.* inconvenience;

trouble; *être dans la* ~ be hard-up.

gêné, *adj.* uneasy; stiff; embarrassed.

gêner, *v.n.* inconvenience; be in the way of; interfere with.

général, *adj. & s. m.* general; *en* ~ in general, generally.

généraliser, *v.a. & n.* generalize.

générateur, *s.m.* generator.

génération, *s.f.* generation.

généreux, -euse, *adj.* generous.

générosité, *s.f.* generosity.

génie, *s. m.* genius; corps of engineers.

genou, *s.m.* (*pl.* -x) knee; (*pl.*) lap; *se mettre à* ~s kneel down.

genre, *s. m.* genus, kind.

gens, *s.m. f.* people; attendants.

gentil, -ille, *adj.* gentle.

géographie, *s.f.* geography.

géographique, *adj.* geographic(al).

géologie, *s. f.* geology.

géométrie, *s. f.* geometry.

géométrique, *adj.* geometric(al).

gérant, -e, *s. m. f.* manager; manageress.

gérer, *v. a.* manage.

germanique, *adj.* Germanic.

germe, *s.m.* germ.

gésir*, *v.n.* lie.

geste, *s.m.* gesture.

gesticuler, *v. n.* gesticulate.

gibier, *s. m.* game.

gifle, *s. f.* slap, box on the ear.

gifler, *v. a.* give s.o. a slap (in the face).

gilet, *s.m.* waistcoat, vest.

girafe, *s. f.* giraffe.

glace, *s. f.* ice; ice-cream; mirror; *mer de* ~ glacier.

glacer, *v. a.* freeze, chill.

glacial, *adj.* icy, glacial.

glacier, *s. m.* glacier.

glissade, *s. f.* slide; slip.

glissant, *adj.* slippery.

glisser, *v.n.* slide; slip; glide over; *se* ~ slip, creep (into).

globe, *s. m.* globe; earth.

gloire, *s. f.* glory, fame.

glorieux, -euse, *adj.* glorious; proud.

gober, *v.a.* swallow.

golfe, *s. m.* gulf.

gomme, *s. f.* gum; india-rubber.

gommer, *v. a.* gum.

gonfler, *v.a.* inflate.

gorge, *s.f.* throat, gullet.

gorgée, *s. f.* gulp.

gosse, *s.m.* kid, brat.

gothique, *adj.* Gothic.

goudron, *s. m.* tar.

gourmand, *adj.* greedy.

goût, *s. m.* taste; savour.

goûter, *v. a.* taste; relish, enjoy; — *s.m.* tea (*meal*).

goutte, *s. f.* drop.

gouvernail, *s. m.* rudder, helm.

gouvernante *s. f.* governess.

gouvernement, *s.m.* government.

gouverner, *v. a.* govern, control, rule; manage; steer.

gouverneur, *s. m.* governor; tutor, preceptor.

grâce, *s. f.* grace; pardon; thanks (*pl.*); favour.

gracieux, -euse, *adj.* graceful; gracious.

grade, *s. m.* rank; grade.

grain, s. m. grain, berry, corn; a touch (of).

graine, s. f. seed, berry.

graissage, s. m. lubrication.

graisse, s. f. fat, grease, lard.

graisser, v.a. grease, lubricate.

grammaire, s. f. grammar.

grammatical, adj. grammatical.

gramme, s. m. gramme.

gramophone, s. m. gramophone.

grand, adj. great; large; big; tall; grand.

grandeur, s.f. size; length; breadth; greatness.

grandir, v.n. grow (up); grow big, tall.

grand'mère, s. f. grandmother.

grand-père, s. m. grandfather.

granit, s. m. granite.

grappe, s. f. bunch; ~ de raisin bunch of grapes.

gras, grasse, adj. fat; thick.

gratitude, s.f. gratitude.

gratter, v. a. & n. scratch, overtake; brush.

gratuit, adj. free (of charge).

grave, adj. grave; heavy.

graver, v.a. engrave.

gravure, s.f. engraving.

grec, grecque (G.), adj. & s. m. f. Greek.

grêle, adj. slender, delicate, slim.

grelotter, v.n. shiver.

grenier, s. m. loft; granary.

grenouille, s. f. frog.

grève, s. f. strike; beach.

grief, s. m. grievance.

griffe, s. f. claw; clutch.

grill, s. m. grill, gridiron.

grille, s. f. iron railing, grating.

griller, v.a. grill, toast.

grimace, s.f. grimace.

grimacer, v.n. grimace.

grimper, v. n. & n. climb.

grincer, v. n. & a. grind, grate; creak.

grippe, s.f. influenza.

gris, adj. gray.

grogner, v.n. groan; grunt, grumble.

gronder, v. n. roar; rumble; v.a. scold.

gros, grosse, adj. large, big; stout; great; thick: — s. m. bulk; wholesale; en ~ roughly; wholesale.

grossier, adj. coarse, gross.

grossir, v. a. make bigger; increase; v. n. grow bigger.

grotesque, adj. grotesque.

groupe, s.m. group.

grouper, v.a. group.

grue, s.f. crane.

gué, s. m. ford (across river).

guêpe, s. f. wasp.

guérir, v.a. cure, heal; v. n. & se ~ be cured, get well again.

guerre, s. f. war.

gueule, s. f. mouth, jaws (pl.); opening.

guichet, s.m. ticket window; counter; booking-office.

guide, s. m. guide; conductor; guide-book.

guider, v. a. guide, lead.

guillemets, s. m. pl. inverted commas.

guise, s. f. way, manner; à votre ~ as you like.

guitare, s. f. guitar.

gymnastique, s. f. gymnastics.

H

habile, *adj.* able, clever.

habileté, *s. f.* skill, cleverness; ability.

habiller, *v. a.* clothe; dress (up); s'~ dress, put on one's clothes.

habit, *s. m.* (dress-)suit; coat; ~s clothes.

habitant, -e, *s.m.f.* inhabitant.

habitation, *s. f.* habitation, dwelling.

habiter, *v. a. & n.* inhabit, live in, dwell in.

habitude, *s. f.* habit, use.

habituel, -elle, *adj.* habitual, usual.

habituer, *v. a.* accustom; s'~ *à* get accustomed to, get used to.

hache, *s. f.* axe.

hacher, *v.a.* chop, cut up, hack, mince.

hachis, *s. m.* hash.

haine, *s. f.* hate, hatred.

haïr*, *v.a.* hate.

haleine, *s. f.* breath.

hall, *s. m.* lounge; ~ *de montage* erecting shop.

halle, *s.f.* market-hall.

hanche, *s.f.* haunch, hip.

hangar, *s. m.* shed, hangar.

happer, *v.a.* snap up.

harasser, *v.a.* harass.

hardi, *adj.* bold, daring.

hareng, *s.m.* herring.

haricot, *s.m.* bean; ~s *verts* French-beans.

harmonie, *s. f.* harmony.

harmonieux, -euse, *adj.* harmonious.

harnais, *s.m.* harness.

harpe, *s.f.* harp:.

hasard, *s. m.* hazard, risk; *par* ~ by chance.

hasarder, *v.a.* hazard, risk, stake.

hasardeux, -euse, *adj.* risky; unsafe.

hâte, *s. f.* haste, hurry, rush; *à la* ~ in a hurry.

hâter, *v. a.* hasten, urge on; se ~ hurry (up).

hausse, *s. f.* rise.

hausser, *v. a. & n.* raise, lift; se ~ rise.

haut, *adj.* high; elevated; upright; loud; upper; *terre* ~e highland; *à voix* ~e aloud: — *adv.* high, highly, up; aloud; *en* ~ at the top; upstairs; — *s. m.* top, height, summit.

hauteur, *s.f.* height, altitude.

haut-parleur, *s. m.* loud-speaker.

havresac, *s.m.* haversack, knapsack.

hebdomadaire, *adj. & s. m.* weekly.

hébreu (H.), *adj. & s. m.* Hebrew.

hectare, *s.m.* hectare.

hélice, *s.f.* air-screw, propeller.

hélicoptère, *s.m.* helicopter.

herbe, *s.f.* herb, grass; pot-herb.

herbeux, -euse, *adj.* grassy.

hérédité, *s.f.* heredity.

hérisser, *v.a.* bristle; ruffle; se ~ bristle up, stand on end.

hérisson, *s. m.* hedgehog.

héritage, *s. m.* inheritance, heritage.

hériter, *v.a. & n.* inherit.

héritier, *s.m.* heir.

héritière, *s.f.* heiress.

héroïne, *s.f.* heroine.

héros, *s. m.* hero.

hésitation, *s.f.* hesitation.

hésiter, *v.n.* hesitate.

heure, *s. f.* hour, time; *quelle ~ est-il?* what time is it?; *il est dix ~s moins le quart* it's a quarter to ten; *dix ~s* ten o'clock; *dix ~s et quart* a quarter past ten; *dix ~s et demie* half past ten; *de bonne ~* early; *~s de pointe* rush hours; *~s d'ouverture* business hours; *~s supplémentaires* overtime.

heureux, -euse, *adj.* happy, fortunate, successful.

heurter, *v. a. & n.* knock against, hit, run into, against; se ~ run, hit, dash against, collide.

hibou, *s. m. (pl. -x)* owl.

hideux, -euse, *adj.* hideous, terrible.

hier, *adv.* yesterday; ~ *soir* last night.

hirondelle, *s. f.* swallow.

histoire, *s. f.* (hi)story,

historique, *adj.* historic.

hiver, *s.m.* winter.

hollandais, -e (H.), *adj. & s. m. f.* Dutch(man), Dutch-woman.

homard, *s.m.* lobster.

homme, *s.m.* màn; ~ *d'affaires* business man; ~ *d'état* statesman.

hongrois, -e, (H.), *adj. & s.m.f.* Hungarian.

honnête, *adj.* honest.

honnêteté, *s. f.* honesty.

honneur, *s.m.* honour; credit.

honorable, *adj.* honourable.

honoraires, *s. m. pl.* fee(s).

honorer, *v.a.* honour.

honte, *s.f.* shame; *avoir ~ de* be ashamed of.

honteux, -euse, *adj.* shameful, disgraceful.

hôpital, *s. m. (pl. -aux)* hospital.

hoquet, *s.m.* hiccup.

horaire, *s.m.* time-table.

horizon, *s.m.* horizon.

horizontal, *adj.* horizontal.

horloge, *s.f.* clock.

horloger, *s.m.* watch-maker.

horreur, *s.f.* horror.

horrible, *adj.* horrible.

hors, *adv.* out, outside; — *prep.* out of, outside.

hospitalité, *s. f.* hospitality.

hostie, *s. f.* wafer *(Church)*.

hostile, *adj.* hostile.

hostilité, *s.f.* hostility.

hôte, *s.m.* host; guest.

hôtel, *s.m.* hotel; large house; ~ *de ville* town-hall.

hôtesse, *s. f.* hostess; ~ *de l'air* air-hostess.

houe, *s. f.* hoe,

houillère, *s.f.* colliery.

hublot, *s.m.* window.

huile, *s. f.* oil.

huissier, *s. m.* usher.

huit, *adj. & s. m.* eight.

huitième, *adj.* eighth.

huître, *s. f.* oyster.

humain, *adj.* human.

humanité, *s. f.* humanity.

humble, *adj.* humble.

humecter, *v.a.* wet.

humer, *v. a.* inhale, suck in.

humide, *adj.* humid, wet.

humidité, *s. f.* humidity.

humiliation, *s. f.* humiliation.

humilier, *v. a.* humiliate.

humilité, *s. f.* humility.

humoristique, *adj.* humorous.

humour, *s. m.* humour.

hurlement, *s. m.* howl(ing), roar(ing).

hurler, *v.n.* howl, roar.

hutte, *s.f.* hut, cabin.

hydrogène, *s. m.* hydrogen.

hygiène, *s. f.* hygiene.

hymne, *s. m.* hymn.

hypocrite, *s. m. f.* hypocrite; — *adj.* hypocritical.

hypothèse, *s. f.* supposition; hypothesis.

hystérique, *adj.* hysterical.

I

ici, *adv.* here; d'~ from here; *par* ~ this way.

idéal, -e, *adj.* ideal.

idéalisme, *s. m.* idealism.

idéaliste, *s. m. f.* idealist.

idée, *s. f.* idea, notion; *il m'est venu à l'*~ it occurred to me.

identique, *adj.* identical.

identité, *s.f.* identity.

idiome, *s. m.* language, dialect.

idiot, *adj.* idiotic; — *s. m.* idiot.

idiotisme, *s. m.* idiom.

ignition, *s. f.* ignition.

ignorance, *s. f.* ignorance.

ignorant, *adj.* ignorant.

ignorer, *v.a.* not know, be ignorant of, be unaware of.

il, elle, *pron.* (pl. ils, elles) he, she, it; they; there.

île, *s. f.* island.

illégal, *adj.* illegal.

illicite, *adj.* illicit, unlawful.

illumination, *s. f.* illumination; ~ *par projecteurs* flood-lighting.

illuminer, *v. a.* illuminate, light up; ~ *par projecteurs* flood-light.

illusion, *s.f.* illusion, delusion.

illustration, *s. f.* illustration.

illustrer, *v.a.* illustrate, explain.

image, *s. f.* image, picture, likeness.

imagé, *adj.* vivid.

imaginaire, *adj.* imaginary, fantastic.

imaginatif, -ive, *adj.* imaginative.

imagination, *s. f.* imagination, fancy.

imaginer, *v.a.* s'~ imagine.

imbécile, *s.m. f.* fool, idiot; — *adj.* foolish.

imitation, *s.f.* imitation, copy.

imiter, *v. a.* imitate, copy.

immédiat, *adj.* immediate.

immense, *adj.* immense.

immeuble, *s. m.* real estate, landed property.

immigrant, -e, *adj. & s. m. f.* immigrant.

immigration, *s.f.* immigration.

immigrer, *v. a.* immigrate.

immobile, *adj.* immobile.

immoral, *adj.* immoral.

immortel, -elle, *adj.* immortal.

• imparfait, *adj. & s. m.* imperfect.

impartial, *adj.* impartial.

impatience, *s. f.* impatience.

impatient, *adj.* impatient.

impayé, *adj.* unpaid.

impératif, -ive, *adj. & s. m.* imperative.

impératrice, *s. f.* empress.

imperfection, *s.f.* imperfection.

impérial, *adj.* imperial.

impérialisme, *s.m.* imperialism.

imperméable, *adj.* impermeable; waterproof.

impertinent, *adj.* impertinent.

impétueux, -euse, *adj.* impetuous, headlong.

impliquer, *v. a.* implicate,

involve, imply.

implorer, *v.a.* implore, beg.

impoli, *adj.* impolite.

impopulaire, *adj.* unpopular.

importance, *s.f.* importance.

important, *adj.* important.

importateur, -trice, *s. m. f.* importer.

importation, *s.f.* importation; ~s imports.

importer, *v.n.* matter, be of moment; *n'importe* it does not matter.

importun, *adj.* troublesome, importunate.

importuner, *v.a.* annoy, molest, worry.

imposer, *v.a.* impose, inflict, lay (on); levy.

impossible, *adj.* impossible.

impôt, *s. m.* tax, duty.

impression, *s. f.* impression; print, edition; *faute d'~* misprint.

impressionner, *v. a.* impress, affect.

imprimé, *s.m.* printed matter.

imprimer, *v. a.* (im)print, impress; publish.

imprimerie, *s. f.* printing; printing office.

impropre, *adj.* unfit, improper.

imprudent, *adj.* imprudent.

impuissant, *adj.* powerless, ineffectual, helpless.

impulsion, *s. f.* spur, impulse.

inaccoutumé, *adj.* unaccustomed.

inachevé, *adj.* unfinished.

inanimé, *adj.* inanimate.

inapplicable, *adj.* inapplicable, irrelevant.

inattendu, *adj.* unexpected.

inattentif, -ive, *adj.* inattentive, heedless.

incapable, *adj.* incapable, unable, inefficient.

incendie, *s. m.* fire.

incendier, *v. a.* set fire to.

incertain, *adj.* uncertain.

incessant, *adj.* incessant.

incident, *s. m.* incident; — *adj.* incidental.

inciter, *v.a.* incite, urge.

inclinaison, *s. f.* inclination, gradient.

inclination, *s. f.* inclination; bent; love.

incliner, *v. a. & n.* incline, bend; slope; slant; *s'~* bow down, bend.

inclusif, -ive *adj.* inclusive.

incommode, *adj.* inconvenient, uncomfortable.

incommoder, *v.a.* inconvenience, annoy.

incomparable, *adj.* incomparable.

incompatible, *adj.* incompatible.

incompétent, *adj.* incompetent.

incomplet, *adj.* incomplete, imperfect.

inconscient, *adj.* unconscious.

inconséquent, *adj.* inconsistent.

inconvenant, *adj.* improper, unsuitable.

inconvénient, *s.m.* inconvenience.

incorrect, *adj.* incorrect.

incroyable, *adj.* incredible.

incurable, *adj.* incurable.

indécis, *adj.* uncertain.

indécision, *s. f.* indecision.

indéfini, *adj.* indefinite,

underïned.

indépendance, *s.f.* independence.

index, *s.m.* forefinger, index.

indicateur, *s. m.* indicator, gauge; time-table.

indication, *s. f.* indication; direction; sign.

indice, *s. m.* sign, token, mark; index.

indien, -enne (I.), *adj. & s.m.f.* Indian.

indifférent, *adj.* indifferent.

indigestion, *s. f.* indigestion.

indignation, *s. f.* indignation.

indiquer, *v.a.* indicate, point out, show.

indirect, *adj.* indirect.

indiscret, -ète, *adj.* indiscreet.

indiscrétion, *s. f.* indiscretion.

indispensable, *adj.* indispensable, essential.

indisposé, *adj.* unwell; upset.

individu, *s. m.* individual, person.

individuel, -elle, *adj.* individual.

indulgence, *s. f.* indulgence.

indulgent, *adj.* indulgent.

industrie, *s. f.* industry.

industriel, -elle, *adj.* industrial; — *s. m.* manufacturer.

inefficace, *adj.* inefficient.

inégal, *adj.* unequal.

inégalité, *s. f.* inequality.

inerte, *adj.* inert; dull.

inévitable, *adj.* inevitable.

inexpérimenté, *adj.* inexperienced.

inexplicable, *adj.* inexplicable.

infâme, *adj.* infamous.

infanterie. *s. f.* infantry.

infection, *s. f.* infection.

inférieur, *adj.* inferior.

infinitif, *s. m.* infinitive.

infirmerie, *s. f.* infirmary.

infirmier, -ère, *s. m. f.* nurse.

influence, *s. f.* influence.

influencer, *v. a.* influence.

information, *s. f.* information.

informer, *v. a.* inform, let know; s'~ *de* inquire about.

infructueux, -euse, *adj.* unsuccessful.

ingénieur, *s. m.* engineer.

ingénieux, -euse, *adj.* ingenious.

ingéniosité, *s. f.* ingenuity.

ingrat, *adj.* ungrateful.

ingrédient, *s. m.* ingredient.

inhabité, *adj.* uninhabited.

inintéressant, *adj.* uninteresting.

initial, -e, *adj. & s. f.* initial.

initiative, *s. f.* initiative; *syndicat* d'~ tourist office.

injection, *s. f.* injection.

injure, *s.f.* injury.

injurier, *v.a.* insult.

injurieux, -euse, *adj.* injurious.

injuste, *adj.* unjust.

injustice, *s. f.* injustice.

innocence, *s. f.* innocence.

innocent, *adj.* innocent.

innombrable, *adj.* innumerable, countless.

inoccupé, *adj.* unoccupied.

inoculer, *v.a.* inoculate.

inondation, *s. f.* flood.

inonder, *v. a.* flood.

inquiet, -ète, *adj.* anxious, restless, uneasy.

inquiéter, *v.a.* worry.

insecte, *s.m.* insect.

insensé, *adj.* insane, mad.

insensible, *adj.* insensible.

inséparable, *ad.j* inseparable.

insigne, *s. m.* badge.

insignifiant, *adj.* insignificant.

insipide, *adj.* dull, flat.

insister, *v. a.* insist, lay stress on.

insolence, *s. f.* insolence.

insolent, *adj.* insolent.

insouciant, *adj.* careless.

inspecter, *v.a.* inspect, survey.

inspiration, *s. f.* inspiration.

inspirer, *v.a.* inspire, suggest; inhale.

installation, *s. f.* installation; fitting up.

installer, *v.a.* install; fit up; *v.n.* **s'~** to settle down.

instant, *adj.* instant, pressing; — *s.m.* instant, moment; *a l'~* instantly, at once.

instantané, *s.m.* snap-(shot).

instinct, *s. m.* instinct.

instituer, *v.a.* institute.

institut, *s.m.* institute.

institution, *s. f.* institution; boarding-school.

instruction, *s. f.* instruction, tuition; knowledge, learning; direction; inquiry.

instruire*, *v.a.* instruct, teach.

instrument, *s. m.* instrument, implement, tool.

instrumental, *adj.* instrumental.

insuffisance, *s. f.* insufficiency.

insuffisant, *adj.* insufficient, deficient.

insulte, *s. f.* insult.

insulter, *v. a. & n.* insult.

insupportable, *adj.* intolerable, unbearable.

intact, *adj.* intact, entire.

intégral, *adj.* integral.

intégrité, *s.f.* integrity.

intellectuel, -elle, *adj. & s.m.* intellectual.

intelligence, *s. f.* intelligence, understanding.

intelligent, *adj.* intelligent, clever.

intendant, *s. m.* manager.

intense, *adj.* intense.

intensité, *s. f.* intensity.

intention, *s. f.* intention, purpose; *avoir l'~* intend, mean.

interdire, *v. a.* forbid.

intéressant, *adj.* interesting; *peu ~* uninteresting.

intéressé, *adj.* interested, concerned.

intéresser, *v. a. & n.* interest; concern; **s'~** take an interest (*à* in); be concerned.

intérêt, *s.m.* interest; concern; share; *avoir ~ à* have an interest in.

intérieur, *s.m.* inside, interior; *à l'~* inside, indoors; *Ministre de l'Intérieur* Home Secretary.

intermédiaire, *adj.* intermediate; — *s. m. f.* intermediary.

international, *adj.* international.

interne, *adj.* internal, inward.

interpellation, *s. f.* interpellation.

interpeller, *v. a.* interpellate, question.

interposer, *v. a.* interpose.

interprétation, *s. f.* interpretation.

interprète, *s. m. f.* interpreter.

interpréter. *v.a.* interpret; render.

interrogation, s. f. interrogation; inquiry.

interrogatoire, s.m. (cross-)examination.

interroger, v.a. interrogate, cross-examine, question.

interrompre, v.a. interrupt.

interrupteur, s. m. interrupter; switch.

interruption, s. f. interruption.

intervalle, s.m. interval; *dans l'~* in the meantime.

intervenir, v.n. intervene, interfere, go between.

intervention, s. f. intervention.

interview, s. f. m. interview.

intime, adj. intimate.

intimité, s.f. intimacy.

intolérable, adj. intolerable.

intrigue, s.f. intrigue.

intriguer, v.n. & n. intrigue.

introduction, s. f. introduction.

introduire, v.a. introduce; show in.

inutile, adj. useless.

invalide, adj. invalid, disabled.

invasion, s. f. invasion.

inventer, v.a. make up.

inventeur, s. m. inventor.

invention, s. f. invention.

investigation, s. f. investigation, inquiry.

invisible, adj. invisible.

invitation, s.f. invitation.

invité, -e, s. m. f. guest.

inviter, v. a. invite.

iris, s. m. iris.

irlandais (I.), adj. Irish;

— s. m. Irishman.

ironie, s. f. irony.

ironique, adj. ironical.

irradier, v. a. (ir)radiate.

irréel, adj. unreal.

irrésistible, adj. irresistible.

irritation, s. f. irritation.

irriter, v.a. irritate.

isolement, s. m. isolation.

isoler, v.a. isolate.

isotope, s.m. isotope.

issue, s. f. issue, outlet, way out.

italien, -enne (I.), adj. & s. m. f. Italian.

itinéraire, adj. itinerary; — s.m. guide-book.

ivre, adj. drunk.

J

j' *see* je.

jadis, adv. once, long ago, formerly.

jalousie, s.f. jealousy; blind.

jaloux, -se, adj. jealous.

jamais, adv. never, ever.

jambe, s. f. leg, shank.

jambon, s. m. ham.

janvier, s. m. January.

japonais, -e (J.), adj. & s. m. f. Japanese.

jardin, s. m. garden.

jardinier, -ère, s. m. f. gardener.

jarre, s. f. jar.

jarretière, s. f. garter.

jauge, s. f. gauge.

jauger, v. a. gauge.

jaune, adj. yellow; — s. m. yolk.

je, j', pron. I.

jersey, s. m. jersey.

jet, s.m. throw(ing).

jeter, v.a. throw, throw away, down; cast,

fling; shoot; discharge;
se ~ rush.

jeton, *s. m.* counter.

jeu, *s.m.* game, play, set.

jeudi, *s. m.* Thursday.

jeune, *adj.* young.

jeûne, *s.m.* fast(ing).

jeûner, *v.n.* fast.

jeunesse, *s. f.* youth.

joie, *s. f.* joy, delight

joindre*, *v. a. & n.* join, unite; se ~ join.

joint, *s. m.* joint, articulation.

jointure, *s. f.* joint.

joli, *adj.* pretty, nice.

jonction, *s. f.* junction.

jongleur, *s. m.* juggler.

joue, *s. f.* cheek *(face)*.

jouer, *v. a. & n.* play; gambol; gamble.

jouet, *s. m.* toy.

joueur, -euse, *s. m. f.* player; gambler.

joug, *s. m.* yoke.

jouir, *v.n.* (~ *de*) enjoy.

jouissance, *s.f.* enjoyment, pleasure, joy.

jour, *s. m.* day; daylight, light; life; ~ *de fête* holiday; ~ *de semaine* week-day; *un* ~ some day; *tous les* ~s every day; *à* ~ up to date.

journal, *s. m.* (news)paper; journal; diary.

journalier, -ère, *adj.* daily; — *s.m.* day-labourer.

journaliste, *s. m. f.* journalist.

journée, *s. f.* day; day's wages *(pl.)*; day's work.

joyau, *s. m.* jewel.

joyeux, -euse, *adj.* joyful, merry.

judiciaire, *adj.* judicial, legal.

judicieux, -euse, *adj.* judicious, sensible, reasonable.

juge, *s. m.* judge.

jugement, *s. m.* judg(e)ment; sentence.

juger, *v. a. & n.* judge.

juif, -ive (J.), *adj.* Jewish; — *s. m. f.* Jew.

juillet, *s. m.* July.

juin, *s. m.* June.

jumeau, -elle *adj. s. m. f.* twin; *f. pl.* binoculars.

jungle, *s. f.* jungle.

jupe, *s. f.* skirt.

juré, *s. m.* juryman.

jurer, *v. a. & n.* swear.

jurisprudence, *s..f* jurisprudence.

juron, *s. m.* oath.

jury, *s. m.* jury.

jus, *s.m.* juice.

jusque, jusqu'à, *prep.* till; as far as.

juste, *adj.* just, right; fair.

justice, *s.f.* justice.

justification, *s.f.* justification.

justifier, *v.a.* justify.

juvénile, *adj.* juvenile.

K

kangourou, *s. m.* kangaroo.

kayak, *s. m.* kayak.

képi, *s. m.* cap.

kilogramme, *s.m.* kilogram(me).

kilomètre, *s.m.* kilometre.

kiosque, *s. n.* kiosk.

L

l' = le or la.

la, *art.* the; —*pron.* her, it.

là, *adv.* there; here.

labeur, *s.m.* labour, work.

laboratoire, *s.m.* laboratory.

laborieux, -euse, *adj.* laborious, hard-working.

labourer, *v.a.* plough.

lac, *s. m.* lake.

lacer, *v. a.* lace.

lacet, *s. m.* lace; braid; bowstring; shoe-lace.

lâche, *adj.* loose; cowardly; — *s. m.* coward.

lâcher, *v.a.* loosen, slacken; let go.

lactation, *s. f.* lactation.

laid, *adj.* ugly; plain.

laideur, *s. f.* ugliness.

lainage, *s.m.* woollen goods *(pl.);* wool.

laine, *s. f.* wool; *pure ~* all wool.

laïque, *adj.* lay.

laisser, *v.a.* leave, quit; give up; let alone; leave behind, off; *~ aller* let go, neglect.

lait, *s. m.* milk.

laiterie, *s. f.* dairy.

laitier, *s. m.* milkman, dairyman.

laitière, *s. f.* dairymaid.

laitue, *s. f.* lettuce.

lambeau, *s. m.* rag, strip.

lame, *s. f.* blade; plate, sheet; *~ de rasoir* razor-blade.

lamentation, *s. f.* lamentation.

lampe, *s. f.* lamp.

lancement, *s.m.* throwing; launching.

lancer, *v. a.* throw, fling; se *~* dart, rush.

langage, *s. m.* language, tongue; speech, way of speaking.

lange *s. m.* baby's nappy.

langue, *s. f.* tongue; language; *~ maternelle* mother-tongue.

laper, *v. a.* lap (up).

lapin, *s. m.* rabbit.

laps, *s. m.* lapse, space (of time).

lapsus, *s. m.* lapse, slip.

laque, *s. f.* lacquer.

lard, *s. m.* bacon.

large, *adj.* broad, wise; generous; liberal; — *s.m.* room, breadth.

largeur, *s. f.* width.

larme, *s. f.* tear.

las, lasse, *adj.* weary.

lasser, *v.a.* tire, wear out; se *~ de* get tired of.

latéral, *adj.* lateral, side.

latin, -e, *adj.* & *s. m. f.* Latin.

latitude, *s.f.* latitude; scope, freedom.

lavable, *adj.* washable.

lavabo, *s. m.* wash-basin; lavatory.

lavage, *s.m.* washing; *~ de vaisselle* washing-up.

lavande, *s. f.* lavender.

laver, *v. a.* wash; se *~* wash (oneself); *machine à ~* washing-machine.

layette, *s. f.* baby-linen.

le, la, l', *art.* the; —*pron.* *(pl.* les) him, her, it; them.

lécher, *v. a.* lick, lap.

leçon, *s. f.* lesson; lecture.

lecteur, -trice, *s. m. f.* reader; lector.

lecture, *s. f.* reading.

légal, *adj.* legal, lawful.

légende, *s. f.* legend.

léger, -ère, *adj.* light, slight; loose.

légèreté, *s. f.* lightness; ease.

légion, *s. f.* legion.

législation, *s.f.* legislation.

législature, *s. f.* legislature.

légitime, *adj.* legitimate, lawful.

légume, *s.m.* vegetable.

lendemain, *s.m.* next day, day after.

lent, *adj.* slow; tardy.

lenteur, *s.f.* slowness.

lentille, *s.f.* lentil; lens.

léopard, *s.m.* leopard

lequel, laquelle, *rel. pron.* *(pl.* lesquels, lesquelles*)* who, whom; which, that.

lettre, *s.f.* letter; type character; ~s literature; arts; *à la* ~ literally, word for word; ~ *de change* bill of exchange; ~ *de crédit* letter of credit; ~ *recommandée* registered letter; *boîte aux* ~s letter-box.

lettré, *adj.* learned; literary.

leur, *poss. adj. (pl. -s)* their; — *pron.* to them, them; *le* or *la* ~, *les* ~s theirs, their own.

levée, *s. f.* raising; removal; levy.

lever, *v. a.* lift (up), raise; hoist; *v. n.* rise; se ~ rise get up.

levier, *s. m.* lever; ~ *des vitesses* gear-lever.

lèvre, *s. f.* lip.

lexique, *s.m.* lexicon.

liaison, *s.f.* joining, junction; union; connection; tie; liaison.

libéral, *adj.* liberal.

libérer, *v.a.* liberate.

liberté, *s.f.* liberty.

libraire, *s.m. f.* bookseller.

librairie, *s. f.* bookshop.

libre, *adj.* free; unoccupied.

licence, *s.f.* licence, degree.

licencié, -e, *s. m. f.* licenciate; licensee.

licencieux, -euse, *adj.* licentious.

lie, *s. f.* dregs, grounds *(pl.).*

liège, *s.m.* cork.

lien, *s.m.* tie, bond; band, strap, cord; link.

lier, *v. a.* bind, tie (up); fasten; link up.

lieu, *s. m.* place; *au* ~ *de* instead of; *avoir* ~ take place.

lieutenant, *s. m.* lieutenant.

lièvre, *s. m.* hare.

ligne, *s. f.* line; ~ *aérienne* air-line.

lilas, *s. m.* lilac.

limace, *s. f.* slug.

limaçon, *s. m.* snail.

lime, *s. f.* file.

limer, *v. a.* file.

limite, *s.f.* bound(s), border, limit.

limiter, *v.a.* limit, restrict.

limon, *s.m.* mud, silt.

limonade, *s. f.* lemonade.

lin, *s. m.* flax.

linge, *s. m.* linen.

linger, -ère, *s.m.f.* linendraper.

lingerie, *s. f.* ladies' underclothing, lingerie.

lion, *s. m.* lion.

liqueur, *s. f.* liqueur.

liquide, *adj.* liquid.

liquider, *v.a.* liquidate.

lire*, *v.a.* read.

liste, *s. f.* list, roll; panel.

lit, *s. m.* bed.

litre, *s. m.* litre.

littéraire, *adj.* literary.

littérature, *s.f.* literature.

livraison, *s.f.* delivery; part (of book).

livre[1], *s. m.* book; work; *teneur de* ~s bookkeeper.

livre[2], *s. f.* pound.

livrer, *v.a.* deliver; give up.

local, *s.m.* spot, premises; — *adj.* local.

localité, *s. f.* place, spot.

locataire, *s. m. f.* tenant, lodger.

location, *s. f.* letting out; hiring, renting; *prendre en* ~ hire; *bureau de* ~ box-office; ~ *des places* seat reservation.

locomotive, *s.f.* (railway) engine.

loge, *s. f.* hut. cabin; box.

logement, *s. m.* lodging.

loger, *v.a.* accommodate, lodge; house; *v. n.* reside, live (in).

logeur, *s. m.* landlord.

logeuse, *s. f.* landlady.

logique, *s. f.* logic; — *adj.* logical.

loi, *s.f.* law, statute; *projet de* ~ bill, draft.

loin, *adv.* far, far off, away; *au* ~ far off.

lointain, *adj.* far, remote.

loisif, *s. m.* spare time, leisure.

long, longue, *adj. & s. m. f.* long; *être* ~ *à* be long in.

longitude, *s. f.* longitude.

longtemps, *adv.* long, a long time; *depuis* ~ for a long time, long since.

longueur, *s. f.* length.

loquet, *s. m.* latch.

lors, *adv.* then; *dès* ~ from that time.

lorsque, *conj.* when.

lot, *s. m.* lot, fate; prize.

loterie, *s. f.* lottery.

lotion, *s. f.* lotion.

louage, *s.m.* hiring; hire.

louche, *s.f.* ladle.

louer[1], *v.a.* hire (out); let; *à* ~ for hire; to let.

louer[2], *v. a.* praise.

loup, *s. m.* wolf.

lourd, *adj.* heavy; clumsy.

louve, *s. f.* she-wolf.

loyal, *adj.* loyal, true.

loyauté, *s.f.* honesty.

loyer, *s. m.* rent; hire.

lubrifier, *v.a.* lubricate.

lucratif, -ive, *adj.* lucrative.

luge, *s. f.* sledge.

lugubre, *adj.* dismal.

lui, *pron.* (to) him, (to) her, (to) it.

lui-même, *pron.* himself.

luire*, *v. n.* shine, gleam.

lumière, *s. f.* light, daylight.

lumineux, -euse, *adj.* luminous, bright.

lundi, *s. m.* Monday.

lune, *s. f.* moon; ~ *de miel* honeymoon.

lunette, *s. f* telescope; *(pl.)* spectacles, specs; ~s *de soleil* sun-glasses.

luthérien, -enne, *adj. & s. m. f.* Lutheran.

lutte, *s. f.* wrestling; fight, struggle.

lutter, *v.n.* wrestle, fight.

lutteur, *s. m.* wrestler.

luxe, *s. m.* luxury.

luxeux, -euse, *adj.* luxurious.

lycée, *s.m.* secondary

school,grammar-school.

M

m' *see* me.

ma *see* mon.

mâcher, *v. a.* chew.

machine, *s. f.* machine, engine, apparatus; ~ *à coudre*, sewing-machine.

mâchoire, *s. f.* jaw.

maçon, *s m.* mason.

madame, *s. f. (pl.* mesdames) madam.

mademoiselle, *s. f. (pl.* mesdemoiselles) miss.

magasin, *s.m.* shop; store; warehouse; *grand* ~ department store.

magique, *adj.* magic.

magnétique, *adj.* magnetic.

magnétophone, *s.m.* tape-recorder.

magnifique, *adj.* magnificent.

mai, *s. m.* May.

maigre, *adj.* lean, thin.

maigrir, *v.n.* grow lean, get thin.

maille, *s. f.* stitch; knot.

maillot, *s.m.* tights (*pl.);* ~ *(de bain)* bathing-costume.

main, *s. f.* hand; lead; *en* ~ in hand; *se donner la* ~ shake hands; *tenir la* ~ *à* see to, see that; *de seconde* ~ second-hand.

maintenant, *adv.* now, at present

maintenir, *v. a.* (up)hold, support, keep (up), maintain.

maintien, *s. m.* maintenance.

maire, *s. m.* mayor.

mais, *conj.* but.

maïs, *s. m.* maize.

maison, *s. f.* house, resi-

dence; home; firm; *à la* ~ at home, indoors; *tenir* ~ keep house.

maître, *s.m.* master; proprietor; teacher; ~ *d'école* schoolmaster; ~ *de maison* host.

maîtresse, *s. f.* mistress; (land)lady; sweetheart; ~ *d'école* schoolmistress.

maîtrise, *s.f.* mastery, control.

maîtriser, *v.a.* master.

majesté, *s. f.* majesty.

majeur, *adj.* major; main; chief; — *s. m.* major.

majorité, *s. f.* majority.

majuscule, *s. f.* capital letter.

mal, *s. m.* ill, evil, wrong; pain, harm; trouble, hardship; *avoir* ~ *à* have a pain in; — *adv.* wrong, badly, ill.

malade, *adj.* sick, ill; *tomber* ~ fall ill, be taken ill; — *s. m. f.* invalid, patient.

maladie, *s.f.* illness; sickness; disease.

maladroit, *adj.* awkward, clumsy.

malaise, *s. m.* uneasiness.

malchance, *s.f.* bad luck.

mâle, *s. m.* male.

malentendu, *s. m.* misunderstandig.

malgré, *prep.* in spite of; ~ *tout* for all that.

malheur, *s.m.* misfortune, ill luck; mischance; accident.

malheureux, -euse, *adj.* unfortunate, unlucky.

malice, *s. f.* malice.

malin, maligne, *adj.* malicious, malignant; evil.

malle, *s. f.* trunk; mail;

faire la ~ pack.

mallette, *s.f.* suit-case.

malpropre, *adj.* dirty, filthy; untidy.

malsain, *adj.* unhealthy.

malveillant, *adj.* male-volent, evil-minded.

maman, *s.f.* mamma.

manche¹, *s.m,* handle. holder.

manche², *s. f.* sleeve.

Manche, *s.f.* English Channel.

manchette, *s. f.* cuff.

mandat, *s. m.* mandate; money-order.

manger, *v.a.* eat; *donner à* ~ feed; *salle à* ~ dining-room; — *s. m.* eating; food.

manicure, *s. m. f.* mani-cure.

manier, *v.a.* handle.

manière, *s. f.* manner, way, fashion; *(pl.)* man-ners.

manifestation, *s.f.* man-ifestation.

manifester, *v.a.* mani-fest, show; *se* ~ man fest oneself.

manipuler, *v. a.* manip-ulate, operate.

manœuvre, *s.f.* action; proceeding; manœu-vre; *s. m.* labourer.

manœuvrer, *v. a. & n.* handle, manœuvre, work.

manoir, *s. m.* manor.

manque, *s.m.* want; de-ficiency.

manquer, *v. a.* miss; *v. n.* fail; be missing, be wanting.

mansarde, *s.f.* garret.

manteau, *s. m.* coat.

manuel, -elle, *adj.* manu-al; — *s. m.* manual, handbook.

manufacture, *s. f.* manu-facture; factory.

manufacturer, *v. a.* manu-facture.

manuscrit, *s. m.* manu-script.

maquillage, *s.m.* make-up.

marbre, *s. m.* marble.

marchand, -e, *s. m. f.* merchant, tradesman; shopkeeper.

marchandise, *s. f.* mer-chandise, goods *(pl.)*.

marche, *s. f.* walk; march; progress; move.

marché, *s. m.* market; bargain; agreement: *bon* ~ cheap.

marcher, *v.n.* walk; travel; march; work; run; proceed.

mardi, *s. m.* Tuesday; ~ *gras* Shrove Tuesday.

mare, *s.f.* pool, pond.

maréchal, *s. m.* marshal.

marée, *s.f.* tide, flood.

margarine, *s. f.* marga-rine.

marge, *s. f.* margin.

mari, *s.m.* husband.

mariage, *s. m.* marriage.

marié, -e, *adj.* married; — *s. m. f.* bridegroom, married man; bride, married woman.

marier, *v. a.* marry; match; — *se* ~ marry, get married.

marin, *adj.* marine; — *s.m.* seaman, sailor, mariner.

marmelade, *s. f.* marma-lade.

marque, *s. f.* mark, im-print; trade-mark.

marquer, *v.a.* mark; stamp; brand.

marron, *s. m.* chestnut.

mars, *s. m.* March.

marteau, *s. m.* hammer.

martyr, -e, *s.m.f.* mar-tyr.

masque, s. m. mask.
masquer, v.a. mask.
massacre, s. m. massacre.
massage, s. m. massage.
masse, s. f. mass; heap.
massif, -ive, adj. massive, bulky, clumsy.
mât, s. m. mast.
match, s. m. match.
matelas, s. m. mattress.
matelot, s.m. sailor, seaman.
matérialisme, s. m. materialism.
matériaux, s.m.pl. material(s).
matériel, -elle, adj. material; — s. m. matter; material; implements (pl.).
maternel, -elle, adj. maternal; motherly; école ~le infant-school.
mathématicien, -enne, s. m. f. mathematician.
mathématique, adj. mathematical; — s. f. mathematics.
matière, s.f. matter; material; substance; ~ première raw material.
matin, s.m. morning; le ~ in the morning; du ~ a.m.
matinal, adj. morning.
matinée, s.f. morning; matinée.
matrice, s. f. womb.
maturité, s. f. maturity.
maudire*, v.a. curse.
mauvais, adj. bad, ill, evil; — s. m. bad.
me, m' pron. (to) me; (to) myself.
mécanicien, s. m. mechanic; engine-driver.
mécanique, adj. mechanic(al); — s.m. mechanics; machine; mechanism.

mécaniser, v. a. mechanize.
mécanisme, s. m. mechanism; machinery.
méchant, adj. evil, bad.
mécontent, adj. displeased, dissatisfied, unhappy.
mécontenter, v. a. dissatisfy.
médaille, s. f. medal.
médecin, s.m. doctor, physician.
médecine, s. f. medicine.
médical, adj. medical.
médicament, s. m. medicament; medicine.
médiéval, adj. medieval.
méditation, s. m. meditation.
méditer, v. a. & n. meditate.
méfiance, s. f. mistrust.
méfier: se ~ be suspicious (de of); mistrust.
meilleur, -e, adj. better; — s. m. f. the best.
mélancolie, s. f. melancholy, gloom.
mélancolique, adj. melancholy, sad.
mélange, s.m. mixture, blend.
mélanger, v.a. mix, blend.
mêler, v.a. mix (up), mingle; se ~ mingle, be mixed; interfere with.
mélodie, s. f. melody.
melon, s.m. melon.
membre, s.m. member, limb.
même, adj. same; self; — adv. even, also, likewise; de ~ in the same way; de ~ que as well as; quand ~ even if.
mémoire, s.f. memory; s.m. memorandum; bill; (pl.) memoirs.

menace, *s.f.* menace.

menacer, *v.a.* threaten.

ménage, *s. m.* housekeeping; household.

ménager, *v. a.* be sparing of; take care of; manage.

ménagère, *s.f.* housewife, housekeeper.

mendiant, -e, *s.m.f.* beggar.

mendier, *v. a. & n.* beg.

mener, *v.a.* guide, conduct, lead.

mensonge, *s.m.* lie.

mensuel, *adj.* monthly.

mental, *adj.* mental.

mention, *s.f.* mention.

mentionner, *v. a.* mention.

mentir*, *v.n.* lie, tell a lie.

menton, *s.m.* chin.

menu, *adj.* slim; small; minute; — *s. m.* bill of fare, menu.

menuisier, *s. m.* joiner, carpenter.

méprendre: se ~ make a mistake, be mistaken.

mépris, *s.m.* contempt.

mer, *s.f.* sea; *par* ~ by sea; *bord de la* ~ seaside.

mercerie, *s. f.* haberdashery.

merci, *s. f.* mercy; — *int.* thanks!, (no) thank you!

mercredi, *s. m.* Wednesday.

mercure, *s.m.* mercury.

mère, *s.f.* mother.

mérite, *s. m.* merit, worth.

mériter, *v.a.* merit, deserve.

merveille, *s.f.* wonder.

merveilleux, -euse, *adj.* wonderful.

message, *s.m.* message.

messe, *s.f.* mass.

mesure, *s.f.* measure, gauge, measurement; size; metre.

mesurer, *v.a.* measure.

métal, *s.m.* metal.

métallique, *adj.* metallic.

météorologie *s. f.* meteorology.

méthode, *s.f.* method.

méthodique, *adj.* methodical, systematic.

métier, *s. m.* trade; business; employment, occupation.

mètre, *s. m.* metre.

métro, *s. m.* tube, underground.

métropolitain, *adj.* metropolitan; underground.

mets, *s.m.* dish, food.

mettre*, *v.a.* put, set, place; put in, on; bring; ~ *de cté* set aside, save; ~ *en ordre* set in order, tidy up; se ~ sit down; *se* ~ *à* set about, take to.

meuble, *s. m.* (piece of) furniture; — *adj.* movable; *biens* ~s personal property.

meubler, *v.a.* furnish, fit up.

meunier, *s.m.* miller.

meurtre, *s.m.* murder.

meurtrier, *s. m.* murderer.

meurtrir, *v.a.* bruise, injure.

mi-, half, mid.

microbe, *s. m.* microbe.

microphone, *s. m.* microphone.

microscope, *s. m.* microscope.

midi, *s. m.* noon, midday; south.

miel, *s. m.* honey.

mien, *pron.* mine, my own.

miette, *s. f.* crumb.

mieux, *adv.* better.

mignon, -onne, *adj.* tiny; — *s.m.f.* darling.

migraine, *s. f.* headache.

milieu, *s.m.* middle, centre; environment.

militaire, *adj.* military; — *s. m.* soldier.

mille[1], *adj. & s.m.* thousand.

mille[2], *s. m.* mile (= 1609 metres).

millier, *s.m.* thousand.

million, *s.m.* million.

millionaire, *s. m. f.* millionaire.

mince, *adj.* thin, slim.

mine[1], *s.f.* mine.

mine[2], *s.f.* look(s); *de bonne* ~ good-looking.

miner, *v. a.* (under)mine.

mineral, *s.m.* ore.

minéral, *adj.* mineral.

mineur[1], *s.m.* miner.

mineur[2], -e, *adj. & s. m. f.* minor.

ministère, *s. m.* ministry.

ministre, *s. m.* minister; *premier* ~ prime minister, premier.

minorité, *s. f.* minority.

minuit, *s.m.* midnight.

minuscule, *s.f.* small letter.

minute, *s.f.* minute; instant.

miracle, *s.m.* miracle.

miraculeux, -euse, *adj.* miraculous, wonderful.

miroir, *s.m.* mirror.

misérable, *adj.* miserable.

misère, *s. f.* misery.

miséricorde, *s. f.* mercy.

mission, *s.f.* mission.

missionnaire, *adj. & s. m. f.* missionary.

mite, *s. f.* moth.

mobile, *adj.* movable, mobile.

mobilier, *s. m.* furniture, suite.

mobilisation, *s. f.* mobilization.

mobiliser, *v.a.&n.* mobilize.

mode[1], *s.f.* fashion, vogue; *à la* ~ in vogue, in fashion.

mode[2], *s. m.* mode, way; mood.

modèle, *s.m.* model.

modération, *s. f.* moderation.

modérer, *v.a.* moderate.

moderne, *adj.* modern.

modeste, *adj.* modest.

modestie, *s.f.* modesty.

modification, *s. f.* modification, change.

modifier, *v.a.* modify.

modiste, *s.f.* milliner.

moelleux, -euse, *adj.* soft, mellow.

mœurs, *s. f. pl.* manners, customs, ways.

moi, *pron.* me, to me.

moi-même, *pron.* myself.

moindre, *adj.* less, lesser, smaller; *le* ~ the least.

moineau, *s. m.* sparrow.

moins, *adv. & s. m.* less (*que, de* than); fewer (*de* than); minus; *le* ~ the least; *à* ~ *que* unless; *au* ~ at least.

mois, *s. m.* month; *par* ~ monthly; a month.

moisson, *s.f.* harvest, crop.

moissonner, *v. a.* harvest, reap.

moitié, *s.f.* half.

molécule, *s. f.* molecule.

mollet, *s. m.* calf (*of leg*).

moment, *s. m.* moment, instant.

mon, ma, *pron.* (*pl.* mes) my.

monarchie, *s. f.* monarchy

monastère, *s. m.* monastery, convent.

mondain, *adj.* worldly.

monde, *s.m.* world; people, company; *mettre au* ~ give birth to; *tout le* ~ everybody.

monnaie, *s.f.* money, coin, change; currency; ~ *légale* legal tender; ~ *étrangère* foreign currency.

monopole, *s.m.* monopoly.

monotone, *adj.* monotonous.

monseigneur, *s.m.* my lord, your lordship.

monsieur, *s. m.* gentleman; M. Mr.

monstrueux, -euse, *adj.* monstrous.

mont, *s. m.* mountain.

montage, *s. m.* carrying up; mounting, setting; wiring.

montagne, *s. f.* mountain.

montagneux, -euse, *adj.* mountainous.

montant, *adj.* ascending, uphill; *en* ~ upwards.

monte-charge, *s. m.* goods lift.

montée, *s. f.* rise, slope.

monter, *v.n.* go up, come up, ascend, climb; mount; ride; amount (*à* to); equip, fit up; ~ *à cheval* ride; *faire* ~ *qn. (dans sa voiture)* give s.o. a lift.

montre¹, *s.f.* watch.

montre², *s.f.* display, show; show-window.

montrer, *v.a.* show, display, point out; *se* ~ show oneself.

montueux, -euse, *adj.* hilly, steep.

monument, *s. m.* monument.

monumental, *adj.* monumental.

moquerie, *s. f.* mockery.

moral, *adj.* moral.

morale, *s. f.* ethics; morality.

moralité, *s. f.* morality, morals (*pl.*).

morceau, *s. m.* piece,

morsel, bit; snack.

mordre, *v. a.* bite; gnaw.

mors, *s. m.* bit; *fig.* check.

mort, *s. f.* death; — *adj.* dead, lifeless.

mortel, -elle, *adj.* mortal; boring, tedious.

mot, *s. m.* word; short note; ~*s croisés* crossword (puzzle).

motel, *s. m.* motel.

moteur, *s. m.* motor, engine.

motif, *s. m.* motive; cause.

motion, *s.f.* motion, movement.

motocyclette, *s. f.* motor-(bi)cycle, motor-bike.

mou, mol, molle, *adj.* soft; loose.

mouche, *s. f.* fly.

moucher: se ~ blow one's nose.

mouchoir, *s. m.* handkerchief.

moudre*, *v.a.* grind.

mouette, *s.f.* gull.

mouiller, *v.a. & n.* soak, wet.

moule, *s. m.* mould, cast.

moulin, *s. m.* mill; ~ *à vent* windmill; ~ *à café* coffee-mill.

mourant, *adj.* dying, expiring.

mourir*, *v. n.* die, expire.

mousse, *s. f.* foam, froth, lather; moss.

moustache, *s. f.* moustache.

moustique, *s.m.* mosquito.

moutarde, *sf.* mustard.

mouton, *s.m.* sheep; mutton.

mouvement, *s. m.* movement, motion, move.

mouvoir*, *v.a.* move; start; se ~ move, stir.

moyen, -enne, *adj.* mean, middle, average; *le ~ âge* the Middle Ages; *— s. m.* means, way, manner; *au ~ de* by means of; *avoir les ~s de* can afford.

moyenne, *s. f.* average, mean; *en ~* on the average.

muet, -ette, *adj.* dumb, mute; speechless.

multiplication, *s. f.* multiplication.

multiplier, *v.a.&n.* multiply.

multitude, *s. f.* multitude, crowd.

municipal, *adj.* municipal, city.

munir, *v.a.* provide *(de* with).

munition, *s. f.* (am)munition.

mur, *s. m.* wall.

mûr, *adj.* ripe; mature.

mûrir, *v. a. & n.* ripen.

murmure, *s.m.* murmur.

murmurer, *v.n.* murmur.

muscle, *s.m.* muscle.

muse, *s. f.* muse.

museau, *s. m.* muzzle. musician; *— adj.* musical.

musical, *adj.* musical.

musicien, -enne, *s. m. f.*

musique, *s.f.* music; *instrument de ~* musical instrument.

mutuel, -elle, *adj.* mutual.

myope, *adj.* short-sighted.

mystère, *s.m.* mystery.

mystérieux, -euse, *adj.* mysterious.

mystification, *s. f.* mystification.

mystique, *adj.* mystic.

N

nacre, *s.f.* mother-of-pearl.

nage, *s.f.* swimming; rowing, paddling.

nager, *v.n.* swim; float; row.

nageur, -euse, *s. m. f.* swimmer.

naïf, -ïve, *adj.* naïve.

nain, -e, *s. m. f.* dwarf.

naissance, *s. f.* birth; *lieu de ~* birth-place.

naître*, *v. n.* be born; arise (from).

nappe, *s.f.* table-cloth.

narine, *s.f.* nostril.

nasal, *adj.* nasal.

natal, *adj.* natal, native, birth.

natif, -ive, *adj. & s. m. f.* native.

nation, *s.f.* nation.

national, *adj.* national.

nationalité, *s.f.* nationality.

naturaliser, *v.a.* naturalize.

nature, *s.f.* nature.

naturel, -elle, *adj.* natural, native.

naturellement, *adv.* naturally, of course.

naufrage, *s. m.* shipwreck; *faire ~* be shipwrecked.

nausée, *s.f.* nausea.

nautique, *adj.* nautical.

naval, *adj.* naval.

navigateur, *s.m.* navigator.

navigation, *s.f.* navigation; sailing; *compagnie de ~* shipping company; *~ spatiale* space-flight.

naviguer, *v. a. & n.* navigate.

navire, *s.m.* ship; *~s*

shipping.

ne, n', *adv.* not; ~... *pas*
not; ~ ... *que* only.

né, -e, *adj.* born; née.

nécessaire, *adj.* neces-
sary.

nécessité, *s. f.* necessity.

nécessiter, *v.a.* necessi-
tate, make necessary.

nef, *s. f.* ship, vessel;
nave; ~ *latérale* aisle.

négatif, -ive, *adj. & s. m.*
negative.

négative, *s. f.* negative.

négligence, *s. f.* neglect,
negligence.

négligent, *adj.* negligent.

négliger, *v.a.* neglect.

négociant, -e, *s. m. f.*
merchant, trader.

négociation, *s. f.* negotiation, transaction.

nègre, *s.m.* negro.

neige, *s.f.* snow.

neiger, *v.n.* snow.

neigeux, -euse, *adj.* snowy

néon, *s. m.* neon.

nerf, *s. m.* nerve; sinew.

nerveux, -euse, *adj.* nervous.

net, nette, *adj.* clean, neat,
clear, tidy; net; — *adv.*
flatly, point-blank.

nettoyage, *s. m.* cleaning,
cleansing.

nettoyer, *v.a.* clean,
cleanse, clear.

neuf[1], *adj. & s. m.* nine.

neuf[2], neuve, *adj.* new.

neutre, *adj.* neutral.

neuvième, *adj.* ninth.

neveu, *s.m.* nephew.

nez, *s.m.* nose.

ni, *conj.* ~ ... ~ (n)ei-
ther ... (n)or; ~
l'un ~ *l'autre* neither
(one).

nid, *s.m.* nest; berth.

nièce, *s.f.* niece.

nier, *v.a.* deny.

niveau, *s. m.* level.

noble, *adj.* noble.

noblesse, *s.f.* nobility.

noce, *s. f. (often pl.)* wedding; *(sing.)* revelry.

Noël, *s. m.* Christmas;
veillée de ~ Christmas
eve.

nœud, *s. m.* knot, bow,
tie.

noir, *adj.* black.

noix, *s. f.* (wal)nut; ~ *de
coco* coconut.

nom, *s. m.* name, sur-
name; fame; noun; ~
de famille surname.

nombre, *s.m.* number.

nombreux, -euse, *adj.*
numerous.

nomination, *s. f.* nomination, appointment.

nommer, *v. a.* name, give
name to; appoint,
nominate.

non, *adv.* no, not.

nonne, *s. f.* nun.

nord, *s. m.* north; *du* ~,
au ~ northern.

nord-est, *s. m.* northeast.

nord-ouest, *s. m.* north-
west.

normal, *adj.* normal.

norvégien, -enne (N.),
adj. & s. m. f. Norwe-
gian.

nos, *poss. adj.* our.

notable, *adj.* notable, remarkable.

notaire, *s. m.* notary
(-public).

note, *s. f.* note, mark;
bill, account; note
(music); ~ *(au bas de
la page)* foot-note.

noter, *v.a.* note, jot
down; notice.

notice, *s. f.* notice.

notion, *s. f.* notion, idea.

notre, *poss. adj.* our.

nôtre, *pron. poss.* ours, our
own.

nourrir, *v.a.* nourish,
feed.

nourriture, *s. f.* nourishment food.

nous, *pron.* we; us.

nous-mêmes, *pron.* ourselves.

nouveau, -el, -elle, *adj.* new; further; *de* ∼ again.

nouvelle, *s.f.* news; short story.

novembre, *s. m.* November.

noyau *s.m.* stone, kernel; nucleus, core.

noyer[1], *v. a.* drown; se ∼ be drowning; drown oneself.

noyer[2], *s. m.* walnut-tree.

nu, *adj.* naked, bare.

nuage, *s. m.* cloud.

nuageux, -euse, *adj.* cloudy, clouded.

nuance, *s. f.* shade, tint, nuance.

nucléaire, *adj.* nuclear.

nuire*, *v. n.* hurt, harm, be harmful.

nuit, *s. f.* night; *il (se) fait* ∼ it is night, it is getting dark; *de* ∼ by night; *la* ∼ at night, *bonne* ∼! good night!

nul, nulle, *adj.* not one, not any; null, nil; — *pron.* no one, nobody.

numéro, *s. m.* number, size; ticket; copy, issue.

nu-pied, *adv.* barefoot.

nylon, *s. m.* nylon.

O

obéir, *v.n.* obey.

obéissance, *s. f.* obedience.

objectif, -ive, *adj.* objective; — *s. m.* object, purpose; lens.

objection, *s. f.* objection.

objet, *s. m.* object, thing, article; purpose; ∼

d'art work of art.

obligation, *s. f.* obligation.

obligatoire, *adj.* compulsory, obligatory.

obliger, *v.a.* oblige, compel.

obscur, *adj.* dark, dim.

obscurité, *s. f.* darkness, dimness; *dans l'*∼ in the dark.

observation, *s. f.* observation; remark.

observer, *v. a. & n.* observe, watch; keep.

obstacle, *s. m.* obstacle; hindrance; bar.

obstine, *adj.* obstinate.

obtenir, *v. a.* obtain, get.

occasion, *s. f.* occasion, chance, event; *a l'*∼ if need be, eventually; *d'*∼ second-hand.

occidental, *adj.* western, occidental.

occupant, -e, *s. m. f.* occupier, occupant.

occupation, *s. f.* occupation; pursuit.

occupé, *adj.* occupied, busy, engaged; *non* ∼ unoccupied.

occuper, *v.a.* occupy, employ; s'∼ occupy oneself *(de* with), be engaged; think *(de* of).

occurrence, *s.f.* occurrence; *en l'*∼ in this case.

océan, *s.m.* ocean.

octobre, *s.m.* October.

odieux, -euse, *adj.* odious.

œil, *s. m. (pl.* yeux) eye, sight; *coup d'*∼ glance; *au premier coup d'*∼ at first sight, at a glance; *ouvrez l'*∼! look out!

œillet, *s.m.* carnation; eyelet.

œuf, *s.m.* egg; ∼ *à la coque* boiled egg; ∼s

brouillés scrambled eggs; ~*s durs* hard-boiled eggs; *blanc d'*~ white of egg; *jaune d'*~ egg-yolk.

œuvre, *s. f.* work; composition; ~ *d'art* work of art.

offense, *s. f.* offence, insult; trespass.

offenser, *v.a.* offend, shock, injure; s'~ take offence, be offended (*de* with), be angry.

office, *s.m.* office; service; post; agency; *exercer un* ~ hold an office.

officiel, -elle, *adj.* official.

officier, *s.m.* officer.

offre, *s. f.* offer, tender.

offrir*, *v. a.* offer, present, hold out; s'~ offer, propose oneself.

oh!, *int.* oh!, O!, indeed!

oie, *s.f.* goose.

oignon, *s. m.* onion; bulb.

oiseau, *s. m.* bird.

olympique, *adj.* Olympic; *les jeux* ~ the Olympic games.

ombre, *s.m.* shade; ghost; obscurity, darkness.

ombreux, -euse, *adj.* shady, shaded.

omelette, *s.f.* omelet.

omettre, *v. a.* omit.

omission, *s. f.* omission, oversight.

omnibus, *s. m.* bus; — *adj.* slow; *train* ~ slow train.

on, *pron.* one, we, people (*pl.*); you; they; somebody; some one; ~ *dit* they say, it is said, people say; *ferme!* closing time!

oncle, *s.m.* uncle.

onde, *s. f.* wave; undulation;

ondulation, *s. f.* undulation; waving.

onduler, *v. a. & n.* undulate, wave; ripple.

ongle, *s. m.* nail (*finger*).

onze, *adj. & s. m.* eleven; eleventh.

opéra, *s. m.* opera; opera-house; ~ *comique* comic opera.

opérateur, *s. m.* operator; cameraman.

opération, *s. f.* operation; *salle d'*~ operating-theatre.

opérer, *v. a. & n.* operate (on); *se faire* ~ undergo an operation.

opérette, *s.f.* operetta.

opinion, *s.f.* opinion.

opportun, *adj.* opportune, timely.

opposer, *v.a.* oppose.

opposition, *s. f.* opposition.

oppression, *s. f.* oppression.

opprimer, *v. a.* oppress.

optimiste, *adj.* optimistic; — *s. m. f.* optimist.

optique, *adj.* optic(al); — *s. f.* optics.

or, *s. m.* gold: *d'*~, *en* ~ golden.

orage, *s.m.* storm.

orange, *s.f.* orange.

orateur, *s.m.* speaker.

orbite, *s. f.* orbit.

orchestre, *s. m.* orchestra.

ordinaire, *adj.* ordinary, usual, common.

ordinairement, *adv.* usually, generally.

ordonnance, *s. f.* order; statute; prescription.

ordonner, *v.a.* order, command.

ordre, *s. m.* order, command; *mettre en* ~ arrange, clear up.

ordure, *s. f.* refuse, rubbish.

oreille, *s. f.* ear; hearing; *prêter l'~ a* listen to, lend an ear to.

oreiller, *s.m.* pillow.

organe, *s.m.* organ.

organique, *adj.* organic.

organisation, *s. f.* organization, arrangement.

organiser, *v. a.* organize.

organisme, *s. m.* organism, system.

orgue, *s.m.* organ.

orgueil, *s.m.* pride.

orient, *s. m.* the East; *de l'~* eastern.

oriental, *adj.* oriental, eastern.

original, *adj.* original.

origine, *s. f.* origin, source; *avoir ~* come from.

ornement, *s. m.* ornament, adornment.

orner, *v. a.* adorn, ornament, trim, decorate.

orphelin, -e, *s. m. f.* orphan.

orthographie, *s. f.* spelling.

os, *s. m.* bone.

osciller, *v.n.* oscillate.

oser, *v. a. & n.* dare, venture.

ôter, *v.a.* take away, take off, remove, pull off; *s'~* remove oneself.

ou, *conj.* or, either, else.

où, *adv.* where; whence; at which, in which; *n'importe ~* anywhere.

ouate, *s.f.* cotton-vool

oublier, *v. a. & n.* forget; overlook.

ouest, *s. m.* west; *à l'~* to, in the west, westward; *de l'~* western.

oui, *adv.* yes.

ouragan, *s. m.* hurricane.

ours, *s.m.* bear.

ourse, *s.f.* she-bear.

outil, *s.m.* tool.

outré, *adj.* exaggerated.

ouvert, *adj.* open; free; open-hearted; *à bras ~s* with open arms.

ouverture, *s. f.* opening; overtures *(pl.)*, proposal; overture.

ouvrage, *s. m.* (piece of) work.

ouvre-boîte, *s. m.* tin-opener.

ouvreuse, *s.f.* box-opener, attendant.

ouvrier, -ère, *s. m. f.* workman, worker; workwoman; hand; *premier ~* foreman.

ouvrir*, *v. a. & n.* open (up); break open; *s'~* be opened, open.

oxygène, *s. m.* oxygen.

P

pacifique, *adj.* pacific, peaceful; *l'Océan ~* the Pacific Ocean.

pacte, *s. m.* pact.

page[1], *s. f.* page; *être à la ~* be up to date.

page[2], *s. m.* page *(boy)*.

paiement *see* payement.

paille, *s. f.* straw, chaff.

pain, *s.m.* bread, loaf; cake, tablet.

pair[1], *adj.* equal, even; *au ~* at par; "au pair".

pair[2], *s. m.* peer.

paire, *s. f.* pair; couple.

paisible, *adj.* peaceful.

paître*, *v. a. & n.* graze, feed.

paix, *s. f.* peace; calm.

palais[1], *s. m.* palace.

palais[2], *s. m.* palate.

pâle, *adj.* pale.

paletot, *s. m.* overcoat.

pâleur, s. f. pallor.
pâlir, v. n. & a. (grow) pale.
palmier, s.m. palm-tree.
palpiter, v.n. palpitate.
pamphlet, s.m. pamphlet.
pamplemousse, s. m. grapefruit.
pan, s. m. flap; coat-tail.
panache, s.m. plume.
panier, s. m. basket.
panique, s. f. panic.
panne, s.f. break-down; power-cut.
panneau, s. m. panel.
panorama, s. m. panorama.
pansement, s. m. dressing, bandage.
pantalon, s. m. trousers *(pl.)*.
pantoufle(s), s. f. *(pl.)* slipper(s).
papa, s. m. dad, daddy.
papauté, s. f. papacy.
pape, s. m. pope.
papeterie, s. f. paper-mill; stationery.
papetier, s. m. stationer.
papier, s.m. paper; ~ *hygiénique* toilet-paper; ~ *peint* wallpaper.
papillon, s. m. butterfly.
pâques, s. m. pl. Easter.
paquet, s.m. packet, parcel.
par, prep. by, by way of, by means of; across; through; per; for.
parade, s. f. parade, show.
paragraphe, s. m. paragraph.
paraître*, v.n. appear, come in sight; come out; *faire* ~ publish.
parallèle, adj. & s. f. parallel.
paralysie, s. f. paralysis.
paralytique, s. m. f. paralytic.
parapluie, s. m. unbrella.

paratonnerre, s. m. lightning-conductor.
parbleu, int. indeed!
parc, s. m. park; fold.
parce que, conj. because, on account of.
parcourir, v.n. travel through, go over; cover; run over, look over.
parcours, s.m. course, run; distance; mileage.
pardessus, s. m. overcoat.
par-dessus, prep. above.
pardon, s. m. pardon; *je vous demande* ~! I beg your pardon!; pardon me!; excuse me!; ~? (I beg your) pardon?
pardonner, v.a. pardon.
pare-boue, . s.m. mudguard.
pare-brise, s.m. windscreen.
pare-choc, s. m. bumper.
pareil, -eille, adj. like, similar; such; same.
parent, s. m. f. relative, relation; ~s parents; relatives.
parer, v. a. adorn, trim; parry, ward off.
paresseux, -euse, adj. lazy, idle.
parfait, adj. & s. m. perfect.
parfaitement, adv. perfectly; ~! quite so!
parfois, adv. sometimes.
parfum, s. m. perfume.
parfumer, v. a. perfume.
parfumerie, s. f. perfumery.
parier, v. a. bet, stake.
parisien, -enne, adj. & s. m. f. Parisian.
parlement, s. m. parliament.
parlementaire, adj. parliamentary.
parler, v. n. & a. speak, talk; — s. m. speech, utterance; parlance.

parmi, *prep*. among.

paroi, *s. f.* wall, partition.

paroisse, *s. f.* parish.

parole, *s. f.* speech, utterance; language; word.

parquet, *s. m.* parquet.

part, *s. f.* part, share; side; *prendre ~ à* take part in, participate; *faire ~ à* inform (of), let know; *à ~* apart; *d'une ~ ... d'autre ~* on the one hand ... on the other (hand).

partager, *v.a.* divide, share out; share.

partenaire, *s. m. f.* partner.

parterre, *s. m.* flower-bed; pit.

parti, *s. m.* party; side.

participant, -e, *s. m. f. & adj.* participant.

participation, *s. f.* participation, share.

participe, *s. m.* participle; *~ passé* past participle.

participer, *v.n.* participate, take part (à in).

particulier, -ère, *adj*. particular, special, specific; peculiar; private; — *s. m. f.* private person; *en ~* in particular.

partie, *s. f.* part; match, game; party; *en ~* partly, in part.

partir*, *v. n.* start, leave, go (away), set out.

partisan, *s. m.* partisan, follower.

partition, *s. f.* score.

partout, *adv.* everywhere.

parure, *s. f.* ornament; set.

parvenir, *v. n.* attain (à to), reach.

pas¹, *s. m.* step, pace.

pas², *adv.* no, not, not any; *~ du tout* not at all; *~ nécessaire* unne-cessary.

passage, *s. m.* passing passage; corridor crossing; thoroughfare; *~ clouté* pedestrian crossing; *~ à niveau* level-crossing; *~ interdit* no thoroughfare.

passager, -ère, *adj*. passing, transient, fugitive; — *s. m. f.* passenger.

passant, -e, *adj. en ~* by the way, cursorily; — *s. m. f.* passer-by.

passe, *s. f.* pass, passage; channel; permit.

passé, *adj.* past; — *prep.* after, beyond.

passeport, *s. m.* passport.

passer, *v. n. & a.* pass; pass along, by; cross; go on, pass on; hand; pass away; omit; forgive; strain; *en ~ par là* submit to it; *~ un examen* take an examination; *~ la nuit* spend the night; *se ~* happen; disappear; do without.

passif, -ive, *adj.* passive — *s. m.* liabilities. *(pl.)*.

passion, *s. f.* passion.

passionné *adj.* passionate.

pastel, *s. m.* pastel.

pastille, *s. f.* pastille.

pâte, *s. f.* paste; dough.

pâté, *s. m.* pie, pasty; block (of buildings); blot.

patente, *s. f.* patent, licence.

patience, *s. f.* patience.

patient, -e, *adj. & s. m. f.* patient.

patin, *s. m.* skate.

patinage, *s. m.* skating.

patiner, *v.n.* skate.

patinoire, *s. f.* skating-rink.

pâtisserie, *s. f.* pastry; pastry-shop, cake-shop.

pâtissier, -ère, s. m. f. pastry-cook.

pâtre, s. m. shepherd.

patrie, s. f. country.

patriote, adj. patriotic; — s. m. f. patriot.

patron[1], -onne, s. m. f. patron; employer, boss.

patron[2], s. m. model, pattern.

patronage, s. m. patronage, support.

patronner, v. a. patronize, protect.

patrouille, s. f. patrol.

patte, s. f. paw, foot.

pâture, s. f. fodder, pasture.

paume, s. f. palm.

paupière, s. f. eyelid.

pause, s. f. pause, stop, break; rest.

pauvre, adj. poor.

pauvreté, s. f. poverty.

pavé, s. m. paving-stone; pavement; street.

paver, v. a. pave.

pavillon, s. m. pavilion, summer-house; flag.

payable, adj. payable, due.

paye, s.f. pay, wages pl.

payement, paiement, s. m. payment.

payer, v.a. pay; pay down, for, off; repay.

pays, s. m. country, land; home; nation; district, region.

paysage, s. m. landscape; scenery.

paysan, -anne, s. m. f. peasant, countryman; countrywoman.

peau, s.f. skin; hide; leather.

pêche[1], s. f. peach.

pêche[2], s. f. fishing; angling; ∼ à la ligne angling.

péché, s. m. sin, trespass.

pécher, v. n. sin, trespass.

pêcher, v. a. & n. fish, angle.

pécheur, -eresse, s. m. f. sinner.

pêcheur, s.m. angler, fisher.

pécuniaire, adj. pecuniary.

pédagogie, s. f. pedagogy.

pédale, s. f. pedal.

pédant, adj. pedant.

pédicure, s. m. pedicure.

peigne, s. m. comb.

peigner, v. a. comb.

peignoir, s.m. wrapper, dressing-gown.

peindre*, v.a. paint.

peine, s. f. punishment; pain, grief; trouble.

peintre, s. m. painter.

peinture, s. f. painting.

pêle-mêle, adv. pell-mell, in a muddle.

pelle, s. f. shovel, spade.

pellicule, s. f. film.

pelote, s. f. ball.

pelouse, s. f. lawn.

pelure, s. f. rind, peel.

pénalité, s. f. penalty.

penchant, s. m. slope, slant; bent, liking.

pencher, v. a. & n. incline, bend; stoop; lean (towards).

pendant[1], adj. hanging, pendent; — s. m. pendant; match.

pendant[2], prep. during; ∼ que while.

pendre, v. a. & n. hang (up), suspend; hang down; be hanging.

pendule, s. f. clock.

pénétrer, v. a. & n. penetrate, go through; search; see through.

pénitence, s. f. penitence.

pensée, s.f. thought, thinking; mind; pansy.

penser, v. n. & a. think.

pension, s.f. pension; board (and lodging);

boarding-house; board-
ing-school; life annui-
ty; ~ *et chambre(s)*
board and lodging; ~
pour étudiants hostel.

pensionnaire, *s.m.f.*
boarder; paying guest.

pensionnat, *s. m.* boarding-school.

pente, *s. f.* slope, descent;
en ~ downhill.

Pentecôte, *s. f.* Whitsun-
tide; *dimanche de la* ~
Whit Sunday.

pépier, *v.n.* chirp.

pépin, *s. m.* pip, stone.

perçant, *adj.* piercing.

perception, *s.f.* perception.

percer, *v. a. & n.* pierce,
bore; punch; tap.

percevoir, *v. a.* perceive,
understand.

perdre, *v. a. & n.* lose;
waste; be the ruin of;
se ~ get lost, disappear;
be ruined.

perdrix, *s. f.* partridge.

père, *s. m.* father.

perfection, *s.f.* perfection.

perforation, *s. f.* perforation.

perforer, *v.a.* perforate.

peril, *s.m.* peril, danger.

période, *s. f.* period, term.

périodique, *adj.* periodic,
periodical.

périr, *v. n.* perish.

perle, *s. f.* pearl, bead.

permanent, *adj.* permanent.

permanente, *s. f.* perm.

permettre, *v.a.* allow,
permit, let; *permettez-
moi de* allow me to;
vous permettez? may I?

permis, *s.m.* permit,
licence.

permission *s. f.* permission, leave (of absence).

perron, *s. m.* stair, steps
(pl.).

perroquet, *s. m.* parrot.

persan, -e (P.), *adj. &
s. m. f.* Persian.

persécuter, *v. a.* persecute.

persécution, *s. f.* persecution.

persil, *s. m.* parsley.

persister, *v.n.* persist.

personnage, *s. m.* person-
age, person.

personnalité, *s. f.* personality.

personne, *s.f.* person;
grande ~ grown-up;
— *pron.* any one;
anybody; no one.

personnel, -elle, *adj.* personal; — *s. m.* person-
nel, staff.

perspective, *s. f.* perspective, prospect, outlook.

persuader, *v. a.* persuade,
convince.

persuasion, *s. f.* persuasion, conviction.

perte, *s. f.* loss; ruin.

pertinent, *adj.* pertinent.

peser, *v. a.* weigh; ponder.

pessimiste, *s. m. f.* pessi-
mist; — *adj.* pessimis-
tic.

petit, *adj.* small, little.

petite-fille, *s.f.* granddaughter.

petit-fils, *s. m.* grandson.

pétition, *s.f.* petition,
request.

petits-enfants, *pl.* grand-
children.

pétrole, *s.m.* petroleum.

peu, *adv. & s. m.* little, bit,
few; ~ *à* ~ little by
little, bit by bit; *un
(petit)* ~ a (little) bit;
quelque ~ somewhat; ~
abondant scanty; ~
commun unusual; ~
confortable uncomfor-
table; ~ *nécessaire* un-
necessary.

peuple, *s. m.* people.

peur, *s. f.* fear; fright; *avoir* ~ *(de)* be afraid (of); *de* ~ *que* for fear that.

peut-être, *adv.* perhaps.

phare, *s. m.* lighthouse; headlight.

pharmacie, *s. f.* pharmacy, chemist's (shop).

pharmacien, -enne, *s. m. f.* chemist.

phase, *s. f.* phase.

phénomène, *s. m.* phenomenon.

philologie, *s. f.* philology.

philosophe, *s. m.* philosopher.

philosophie, *s. f.* philosophy.

philosophique, *adj.* philosophical.

phono(graphe), *s.m.* gramophone.

photo, *s. f.* photo, snap.

photographe, *s.m.* photographer.

photographie, *s. f.* photograph; photography.

photographier, *v. a.* photograph.

photographique, *adj.* photographic; *appareil* ~ camera.

phrase, *s. f.* phrase; sentence.

phtisie, *s. f.* consumption.

physicien, -enne, *s. m. f.* physicist.

physique, *adj.* physical; — *s. f.* physics; ~ *nucléaire* nuclear physics; — *s. m.* physique, constitution.

pianiste, *s. m. f.* pianist.

piano(forte), *s. m.* piano.

pièce, *s. f.* piece, part, bit, coin; play; room; joint.

pied, *s. m.* foot, leg; *à* ~ on foot; *aller à* ~ walk.

pierre, *s. f.* stone; rock.

piéton, *s. m.* pedestrian.

pieu, *s. m.* stake, post.

pieux, -euse, *adj.* pious.

pigeon, -onne, *s. m. f.* dove, pigeon.

pile, *s. f.* pile, heap; battery.

pilier, *s. m.* pillar, post, column.

piller, *v. a. & n.* pillage.

pilot, *s. m.* pile. ·

pilote, *s. m.* pilot.

piloter, *v.a.* pilot, guide.

pilule, *s. f.* pill.

pin, *s. m.* pine(-tree).

pince, *s. f.* pinch; pincers, pliers, tongs *(pl.)*.

pincer, *v. a.* pinch.

pipe, *s. f.* pipe.

piquant, *adj.* pungent, sharp; piquant.

pique, *s. f.* pike; *s. m. (cards)* spade.

pique-nique, *s. m.* picnic.

piquer, *v. a. & n.* prick, sting; lard; goad, spur.

piqûre, *s. f.* prick, sting; puncture; injection.

pirate, *s. m.* pirate.

pire, *adj.* worse.

pis, *adv.* worse.

piscine, *s. f.* swimmingpool.

piste, *s. f.* track; trace; runway.

pistolet, *s. m.* pistol.

pitié, *s. f.* pity.

placard, *s. m.* placard, poster; cupboard.

place, *s. f.* place; room; seat; square.

placement, *s. m.* placing; investment; *bureau de* ~ labour-exchange.

placer, *v. a.* place, put, set; invest; sell.

plafond, *s. m.* ceiling.

plage, *s. f.* beach.

plaider, *v. a. & n.* plead.

plaindre, *v. a.* pity, feel compassion for; *se* ~ complain.

plaine, *s. f.* plain.

plainte, *s. f.* complaint.

plaire*, *v. n.* please; *vous plaît-il de?* would you like to?; *s'il vous plaît* (if you) please; **se** ~ take pleasure, enjoy.

plaisant, *adj.* pleasant, pleasing.

plaisanterie, *s.f.* joke, jest; *par* ~ as a joke.

plaisir, *s. m.* pleasure.

plan, *s. m.* plan; design; plane.

planche, *s.f.* board, plank.

plancher, *s. m.* floor.

planer, *v. a.* plane.

plante, *s. f.* plant; sole.

planter, *v. a.* plant; set.

planteur, *s. m.* planter.

plaque, *s. f.* plate; slab; plaque; ~ *de police* number-plate.

plaquer, *v. a.* plate; lay on.

plastique, *adj.* plastic, — *s. f.* plastic art; figure; — *s. m.* plastics *pl.*

plastron, *s. m.* (shirt-)front; plastron; stiff shirt.

plat, *adj.* flat; plain; dull; — *s. m.* flat (part); blade.

plateau, *s.m.* tray; scale (of balance); plateau.

plate-bande, *s. f.* flowerbed.

plate-forme, *s.f.* platform.

plâtre, *s. m.* plaster.

plein, *adj.* full; filled; *en* ~ fully, entirely.

pleurer, *v. n.* cry, weep.

pleuvoir: *il pleut* it rains.

pli, *s. m.* fold, crease.

pliant, *adj.* flexible, pliant; folding.

plier, *v. a. & n.* fold (up), bend; **se** ~ submit *(a* to).

plisser, *v. a. & n.* plait, fold, tuck; wrinkle.

plomb, *s.m.* lead.

plombage, *s. m.* filling.

plombier, *s. m.* plumber.

plonger, *v. a. & n.* plunge, immerse, dip, dive.

pluie, *s. f.* rain.

plume, *s. f.* feather, plume, pen.

plupart, *s. f.* most, the greatest part, majority.

pluriel, *s. m.* plural.

plus, *adv.* more, most; further, longer; any more; *de* ~ *en* ~ more and more; *en* ~ *de* in addition to; *ne . . .*~ no more, no longer.

plusieurs, *adj.* several, many, some, a few; — *pron.* several people.

plutôt, *adv.* rather, preferably.

pluvieux, -euse, *adj.* rainy, wet.

pneu(matique), *s. m.* tyre.

pneumonie, *s. f.* pneumonia.

poche, *s. f.* pocket; pouch.

poêle[1], *s. m.* stove.

poêle[2], *s. f.* frying pan.

poème, *s. m.* poem.

poésie, *s.f.* poetry; poesy.

poète, *s. m.* poet.

poétique, *adj.* poetic(al).

poids, *s. m.* weight.

poignant, *adj.* poignant.

poigne, *s. f.* grip, grasp.

poignée, *s. f.* handle; hilt; handful.

poignet, *s. m.* wrist; cuff.

poil, *s. m.* hair; bristle; coat.

poinçon, *s.m.* punch, bodkin.

poinçonner, *v. a.* punch, clip; stamp.

poing, *s.m.* fist.

point, *s. m.* point, dot; full stop; *deux* ~s colon; ~ *et virgule* semicolon; *à* ~ just in time; *être sur le* ~ *de* be about to; ~ *de vue* point of view.

pointe, *s. f.* point, head, tip.

pointer, *v. a. & n.* point.

pointu, *adj.* sharp, pointed.

poire, *s. f.* pear.

pois, *s. m.* pea.

poison, *s. m.* poison.

poisson, *s. m.* fish.

poissonnier, -ère, *s. m. f.* fishmonger.

poitrine, *s. f.* chest, breast.

poivre, *s. m.* pepper.

pôle, *s. m.* pole.

poli, *adj.* polished; polite.

police, *s. f.* police; policy; *agent de* ~ policeman.

policier, *s. m.* policeman.

policlinique, *s. f.* out-patients' department.

polir, *v. a.* polish, refine.

politesse, *s. f.* politeness.

politicien, -enne, *s. m. f.* politician.

politique, *s. f.* politics.

polonais, -e (P.), *adj.* Polish; — *s. m.* Pole; *s. f.* Polish woman; polonaise.

pomme, *s. f.* apple; ~ *de terre* potato.

pommier, *s. m.* apple tree.

pompe¹, *s. f.* pomp, ceremony.

pompe², *s. f.* pump; ~ *à incendie* fire-engine; ~ *à essence* petrol pump.

pompier, *s. m.* fireman; *les* ~s fire-brigade.

ponctuel, -elle, *adj.* punctual.

pont, *s. m.* bridge; deck; ~ *suspendu* suspension-bridge; ~ *inférieur* lower deck.

populaire, *adj.* popular; vulgar, common.

popularité, *s. f.* popularity.

population, *s. f.* popula-

tion.

populeux, -euse, *adj.* populous.

porc, *s. m.* pig, hog; pork.

porcelaine, *s. f.* porcelain, china(ware).

pore, *s. m.* pore.

poreux, -euse, *adj.* porous.

port¹, *s. m.* harbour (sea-)port; *arriver à bon* ~ arrive safely.

port², *s. m.* bearing, gait; carriage; postage; ~ *payé* postage paid.

portable, *adj.* portable.

porte, *s. f.* door(way), entrance; ~ *d'entrée* front-door.

porte-cigarettes, *s. m. pl.* cigarette-case.

portée, *s. f.* litter; range, scope; *à* ~ within reach.

portemanteau, *s. m.* coat-stand; suit-case.

porter, *v. a. & n.* bear; carry; convey; wear, have on; hold; ~ *intérêt* yield interest; show interest; ~ *la santé de B* drink B's health; *se* ~ be worn, be carried; *comment vous portez-vous?* how are you?

porteur, *s. m.* porter, carrier; bearer.

portier, -ère, *s. m. f.* porter, door-keeper.

portière, *s. f.* door (on vehicle); (door-)curtain.

portion, *s. f.* portion, part, share; helping.

portrait, *s. m.* portrait.

portugais, -e (P.), *adj. & s. m. f.* Portuguese.

posemètre, *s. m.* light-meter.

poser, *v. a. & n.* place, lay down, put; state.

positif, -ive, *adj. & s. m. f.* positive.

position, *s. f.* position, situation; attitude.

posséder, *v.a.* possess.

possession, *s.f.* possession; property.

possibilité, *s.f.* possibility.

possible, *adj.* possible; *faire tout son* ~ do one's best.

postal, *adj.* postal; post; *carte* ~*e* post-card.

poste¹, *s. f.* post(-office), mail; *mettre à la* ~ post (a letter); *bureau de* ~ post-office; *timbre* ~ stamp; ~ *aérienne* airmail.

poste², *s. m.* post, station, office; police-station; receiver, set; ~ *de* T. S. F. wireless-set.

postulant, -e, *s. m. f.* applicant, candidate.

pot, *s. m.* pot, can, jug, vessel, pitcher.

potager, *s.m.* kitchen garden.

poteau, *s. m.* post.

poterie, *s. f.* pottery.

potin, *s. m.* noise; (piece of) gossip.

poubelle, *s. f.* dustbin.

pouce, *s.m.* thumb.

pouding, *s. m.* pudding.

poudre, *s. f.* powder, dust.

poudrier, *s. m.* compact.

poule, *s.f.* hen; fowl.

poulet, *s.m.* chicken, fowl.

pouls, *s. m.* pulse.

poumon, *s. m.* lung(s).

poupée, *s. f.* doll.

pour, *prep.* for; ~ *cent* per cent; ~ *que* in order that.

pourboire, *s. m.* tip.

pourquoi, *conj. & adv.* why; what for; for what reason.

poursuite, *s. f.* pursuit, chase; ~*s* suit, action.

poursuivre, *v. a.* pursue, chase, prosecute.

pourtant, *adv.* however, still.

pourvoir, *v. n. & a.* provide (*à* for), supply, cater (*à* for).

pousser, *v. a. & n.* push; shove; urge; impel; grow; utter.

poussière, *s. f.* dust

poussièreux, -euse *adj.* dusty.

pouvoir*, *v. a. & n.* be able, may; **se** ~ be possible; *cela se peut* that may be; — *s. m.* power.

pratique, *s. f.* practice, execution; experience; customers (pl.); — *adj.* practical, convenient.

pratiquer, *v. a.* practise, carry out; exercise.

préalable, *adj.* previous, *au* ~ first of all.

précédent, *adj.* precedent, previous; — *s. m.* precedent.

précéder, *v. a. & n.* precede; come before.

prêcher, *v.a. & n.* preach.

prêcheur, *s. m.* preacher.

précieux, -euse, *adj.* precious, valuable, costly.

précipice, *s. m.* precipice.

précipitation, *s.f.* precipitation, haste, hurry.

précipité, *adj.* hasty.

précipiter, *v.a.* precipitate; hasten, hurry.

précis, *adj.* exact, precise; — *s. m.* summary.

préciser, *v.a.* specify.

prédécesseur, *s. m.* predecessor.

prédire, *v.a.* foretell.

préfabriqué, *adj.* prefabricated.

préface, *s.f.* preface.

préférable, *adj.* preferable, better.

préférer, *v.a.* prefer; like

better.

préfet, *s.m.* prefect.

préjugé, *s. m.* prejudice, presumption.

prélat, *s.m.* prelate.

préliminaire, *adj.* preliminary.

premier, -ère, *adj.* first, former; ~ *plan* foreground; close-up; *de* ~ *ordre* first-rate; ~ — *s. m.* first floor.

première, *s. f.* first night; first class (in a carriage).

prendre*, *v. a.* take, take up, seize; receive, accept; put on, wear; charge; catch; ~ *place* take a seat: *à tout* ~ on the whole; ~ *pour* mistake for; ~ *du corps* put on weight; ~ *l'air* take a walk; se ~ be taken, be caught.

prénom, *s. m.* Christian name.

préoccuper, *v. a.* preoccupy, engross; worry; se ~ trouble oneself.

préparatifs, *s.m.pl.* preparations.

préparation, *s. f.* preparation.

préparer, *v. a.* prepare, make ready; read for; se ~ prepare oneself, get ready.

préposition, *s. f.* preposition.

prérogative, *s. f.* prerogative, privilege.

près, *adv.* & *prep.* near, close by, close to; nearly; *à peu* ~ nearly (so); *de* ~ closely.

prescription, *s. f.* prescription.

prescrire*, *v. ı.* prescribe.

présence, *s. f.* presence, attendance; *en* ~ *de* in the presence of.

présent[1], *s. m.* present, gift; *faire* ~ *de* give as a present.

présent[2], *s. m.* present (time); present tense; — *adj.* present, current *à* ~ at present; *jusqu'à* ~ till now, as yet; *pour le* ~ for the time being.

présentation, *s. f.* presentation, introduction.

présenter, *v. a.* present, offer; introduce; se ~ appear.

préserver, *v. a.* preserve.

président, *s. m.* president.

présomption, *s. f.* presumption; conceit.

presque, *adv.* almost.

pressant, *adj.* pressing.

presse, *s. f.* press; printing-press; haste; crowd.

pressé, *adj.* pressing; *être* ~ be in a hurry.

pressentiment, *s. m.* presentiment; misgiving.

pressentir, *v.a.* have a presentiment of.

presser, *v. a.* press, crush; hurry; *pressez-vous!* hurry up!; se ~ hurry (up).

pression, *s.f.* pressure.

pressurer, *v.a.* press, squeeze; oppress.

prestige, *s.m.* marvel; influence, prestige.

présumer, *v. a.* suppose, expect; presume.

prétendre, *v. a.* & *n.* pretend, claim; intend.

prétention, *s.f.* pretension, claim.

prêter, *v.a.* lend, attribute; se ~ lend oneself (to).

prétexte, *s. m.* pretext.

prêtre, *s. m.* priest.

preuve, *s. f.* proof; *faire*

~ *de* show.

prévaloir, *v .n.* prevail.

prévenir, *v. a.* anticipate, inform, let know.

préventif, -ive, *adj.* preventive.

prévention, *s.f.* bias, prejudice.

prévision, *s. f.* prevision, anticipation; forecast.

prévoir, *v.a.* foresee, anticipate, forecast.

prévoyance, *s. f.* foresight.

prier, *v. a.* pray, beg; ask.

prière, *s.f.* prayer; request.

primaire, *adj.* primary.

prime, *adj.* first, early.

primer, *v. a.* surpass, excel; award a prize to.

primeur, *s. f.* early vegetables *(pl.).*

primitif, -ive, *adj.* primitive, original.

prince, *s. m.* prince.

princesse, *s. f.* princess.

principal, *adj.* principal.

principalement, *adv.* principally, mainly.

principe, *s. m.* principle.

printemps, *s. m.* spring-(time); *au* ~ in spring.

priorité, *s.f.* priority.

prise, *s.f.* taking; capture, catch; ~ *de courant* (electric) plug.

prisme, *s. m.* prism.

prison, *s. f.* prison.

prisonnier, -ère, *s. m. f.* prisoner.

privation, *s. f.* privation.

privé, *adj.* private.

priver, *v. a.* deprive.

privilège, *s. m.* privilege.

prix, *s. m.* price, cost, charge; prize; *au* ~ *de* at the cost of; ~ *de la course* fare; ~ *par mille* mileage; ~*courant* market-price; ~ *fixe* fixed price.

probabilité, *s. f.* probability.

probable, *adj.* probable.

probablement, *adv.* probably.

problématique, *adj.* problematic(al).

problème, *s. m.* problem.

procédé *s. m.* proceeding.

procéder, *v. n.* proceed.

procédure, *s. f.* procedure.

procès, *s.m.* (law-)suit, trial; *faire un* ~ *u* bring an action against.

procession, *s.f.* procession.

prochain, *adj.* near(est), next. — *s. m.* neighbour

prochainement, *adv.* shortly, soon.

proche, *adj.* near, neighbouring, close at hand.

proclamer, *v. a.* proclaim.

procurer, *v. a.* procure.

procureur, *s. m.* attorney.

prodigieux, -euse, *adj.* wonderful, prodigious.

producteur, -trice, *s. m. f.* producer; — *adj.* producing.

production, *s. f.* production.

produire*, *v. a.* produce, bring forth, yield.

produit, *s. m.* produce; product.

professer, *v. a. & n.* profess; teach.

professeur, *s. m.* teacher; professor; lecturer.

profession, *s.f.* profession.

professionnel, -elle, *adj. & s. m. f.* professional.

profil, *s. m.* profile.

profit, *s. m.* profit, gain.

profitable, *adj.* pro'itable.

profiter, *v. n.* profit (by).

profond, *adj.* deep, profound.

profondeur, *s. f.* depth; *dix pieds de* ~ ten feet deep.

programme, *s. m.* program(me); scheme.

progrès, *s. m.* progress, improvement; *faire des* ~ make progress.

prohiber, *v.a.* prohibit.

projecteur, *s. m.* headlight; searchlight; projector.

projectile, *s. m.* projectile, missile.

projection, *s. f.* projection.

projet, *s. m.* project, plan; scheme; ~ *de loi* bill.

projeter, *v.a.* project throw; scheme, plan.

prolonger, *v.a.* prolong.

promenade, *s.f.* walk; promenade.

promener: se ~ *go* for a walk; *se* ~ *en voiture* go for a drive.

promesse, *s. f.* promise.

promettre, *v. a.* promise.

promotion, *s. f.* promotion.

prompt, *adj.* prompt.

pronom, *s. m.* pronoun.

prononcer, *v.a. &n.* pronounce; utter; deliver.

prononciation, *s. f.* pronunciation; delivery.

propagande, *s. f.* propaganda.

propager, *v.a.* propagate.

prophète, *s.m.f.* prophet.

prophétie, *s. f.* prophecy.

proportion, *s. f.* proportion; ratio.

propos, *s. m.* talk, remark; *à* ~ in good time; by the way.

proposer, *v.a.* propose, offer.

proposition, *s. f.* proposal, proposition.

propre, *adj* own, peculiar; proper, fit.

propriétaire, *s.m.f.* owner, proprietor; landlord, landlady.

propriété, *s. f.* ownership; property.

propulsion, *s. f.* propulsion; ~ *à réaction* jet propulsion.

prosaïque, *adj.* prosaic.

proscrire*, *v. a.* proscribe.

prose, *s. f.* prose.

prospectus, *s.m.* prospectus.

prospère, *adj.* prosperous.

prospérer, *v. n.* prosper, get on (well).

prospérité, *s.f.* prosperity.

protecteur, *s. m.* protector, patron.

protection, *s.f.* protection, support.

protéger, *v.a.* protect; patronize.

protestant, -e, *s. m. f. & adj.* Protestant.

protestation, *s.f.* protest(ation).

protester, *v. n. & a.* protest.

prouver, *v.a.* prove.

provenir, *v.n.* come (from), issue, arise.

province, *s. f.* province, country, district.

provincial, *adj.* provincial, country.

provision, *s. f.* provision.

provisoire, *adj.* provisional, temporary.

provoquer, *v. a.* provoke; stir up.

proximité, *s.f.* proximity.

prudence, *s. f.* prudence, caution.

prudent, *adj.* prudent, cautious.

prune, *s. f.* plum.

pruneau, *s. m.* prune.

prunelle, *s. f.* pupil.

psaume, s. m. psalm.

psychologie, s. f. psychology.

psychologique, adj. psychological.

public, publique, adj. public, common; — s. m. public, audience.

publication, s.f. publication.

publicité, s. f. publicity.

publier, v. a. publish.

puce, s. f. flea.

puer, v. n. stink.

puéril, adj. childish.

puis, adv. then, after that.

puiser, v. a. draw up, fetch up.

puisque, conj. as, since.

puissance, s.f. power, might, force.

puissant, adj. powerful, strong; tout ~ almighty.

puits, s. m. well; pit.

punaise, s. f. drawing-pin; bug.

punch, s.m. punch (drink).

punir, v. a. punish.

punition, s.f. punishment.

pupille, s.m.f. ward, pupil; — s. f. pupil (of the eye).

pupitre, s. m. desk.

pur, adj. pure, clean.

purée, s. f. mash, purée.

purement, adv. purely, merely.

pureté, s. f. purity.

purgatif, -ive, adj. & s. m. purgative.

purger, v. a. purge.

purifier, v.a. purify, cleanse.

puritain, -e, adj. & s. m. f. Puritan.

pyramide, s. f. pyramid.

Q

quai, s. m. quay; wharf; platform; billet de ~ platform ticket.

qualification, s. f. qualification.

qualifié, adj. qualified.

qualifier, v.a. qualify.

qualité, s.f. quality.

quand, adv. & conj. when; while; ~ même all the same.

quant à, prep. as for, with regard to.

quantité, s. f. quantity; amount; ~ de plenty of.

quarante, adj. & s. m. forty.

quart, s.m. quarter, fourth part; quart.

quartier, s. m. quarter; piece, slice; district; ~ général headquarters (pl.).

quatorze, adj. & s.m. fourteen.

quatre, adj. & s.m. four; fourth.

quatre-vingt-dix, adj. & s. m. ninety.

quatre-vingts, adj. & s. m. eighty.

quatrième, adj. & s. m. fourth; fourth floor; — s. f. third form.

quatuor, s. m. quartet(te).

que, qu', rel. pron. whom, which, that; of which, at which; — adv. how much, how many; — conj. that; than; as; if; as though.

quel, quelle, adj. what, which.

quelque, adj. some, any; a few; ~ chose something, anything; ~ part somewhere; ~ peu somewhat — adv. about, some.

quelquefois, adv. sometimes.

quelqu'un, -e, pron.

somebody; anybody.

querelle, s. f. quarrel.

quereller, v. a. & n. quarrel with.

question, s.f. question; point, matter, issue.

questionner, v.a. question, interrogate.

queue, s.f. tail; rear; queue; handle.

qui, rel. pron. who, whom; which; that; à ~ to whom.

quille, s. f. keel, skittle.

quincaillerie, s. f. hardware (shop).

quintal, s. m. hundredweight.

quinze, adj. & s. m. fifteen; fifteenth; ~ jours fortnight.

quittance, s. f. receipt.

quitte, adj. quit, free.

quitter, v. a. leave, give up, quit.

quoi, rel. pron. what, which; à propos de ~ what is it about?; ~ qu'il en soit at any rate.

quoique, conj. (al)though.

quotidien, -enne, adj. & s. m. daily.

R

rabais, s. m. reduction in price, rebate.

rabaisser, v. a. lower.

rabattre, v.a. beat down, pull down; reduce.

raccommoder, v. a. mend, repair.

raccourcir, v.a. & n. shorten, abridge.

raccrocher, v.a. hang up again.

race, s. f. race; stock; breed.

racine, s. f. root; prendre ~ take root.

raconter, v.a. tell, relate.

radar, s. m. radar.

radiateur, s. m. radiator.

radiation s. f. radiation.

radical, adj. radical.

radieux, -euse, adj. radiant, beaming.

radio, s. f. radio.

radio-actif, -ive, adj. radioactive.

radiodiffuser, v.a. broadcast.

radiodiffusion, s. f. broadcasting.

radiogramme, s. m. X-ray photograph; radiogram.

radiographie, s. f. X-ray photograph(y).

radioreportage, s. m. running commentary.

radioscopie, s. f. radioscopy.

radioscopique, adj. examen ~ X-ray examination.

radis, s.m. radish.

raffermir, v.a. strengthen, fortify.

raffinage, s.m. refining.

raffiné, adj. refined.

raffinement, s. m. refinement.

raffiner, v. a. refine.

rafraîchir, v. a. refresh, cool; se ~ cool down.

rafraîchissement, s.m. refreshment; ~s refreshments.

rage, s.f. rage, fury.

ragoût, s. m. ragout, stew.

raide, adj. stiff, rigid.

raidir, v. a. make stiff.

raifort, s.m. horse radish.

rail, s. m. rail.

railler, v.a. mock, rail at.

raillerie, s.f. raillery, mocking.

raisin, s. m. grape(s);

~ *sec* raisin.

raison, *s.f.* reason; judgement; *à ~ de* at the rate of; *avoir ~* be right.

raisonnable, *adj.* reasonable.

raisonnement, *s. m.* reasoning.

raisonner, *v. n. & a.* reason, argue.

ralentir, *v. a. & n.* slow down.

ramasser, *v.a.* gather up, pick up; take up.

rame, *s. f.* oar; prop.

ramener, *v.a.* bring back, take back.

ramer, *v. n.* row.

rampe, *s.f.* banister; footlights *(pl.)*.

ramper, *v.n.* crawl, creep.

rance, *adj.* rancid.

rancune, *s.f.* spite, grudge.

randonneur, -euse, *s. m. f.* excursionist, hiker.

rang, *s.m.* row, line; rank.

rangé, *adj.* tidy.

rangée, *s.f.* row, line, range.

ranger, *v. a.* put in order; arrange; range; *se ~* settle down; make room.

ranimer, *v.a.* revive, restore to life, refresh.

râpe, *s.f.* rasp, grater.

râpé, *adj.* shabby.

rapide, *adj.* rapid, fast; steep.

rapidité, *s.f.* rapidity, speed.

rappel, *s.m.* recall.

rappeler, *v. a.* recall, call back; bring back; *se ~* remember.

rapport, *s.m.* product, yield; report, account; connection, relation;

reference; *sous ce ~* in this respect.

rapporter, *v.a.* bring back; produce, yield; report, state; *se ~* relate to, refer to.

rapprochement, *s. m.* drawing closer.

rapprocher, *v. a.* bring closer; *se ~* draw nearer.

raquette, *s. f.* racket.

rare, *adj.* rare.

raser, *v. a.* shave, graze; pull down; bore; *v.n. se ~* shave.

rasoir, *s. m.* razor; *~ électrique* electric razor; *~ de sûreté* safety razor.

rassembler, *v. a.* gather, assemble, collect.

rassis, *adj.* settled; stale.

rassurer, *v.a.* reassure, comfort.

rat, *s. m.* rat.

râteau, *s. m.* rake.

râtelier, *s. m.* rack; set of false teeth.

rater, *v. n. & a.* miss fire; fail.

ratification, *s. f.* ratification.

ration, *s. f.* ration.

rattacher, *v.a.* tie up again, join.

rattraper, *v.a.* catch again; catch up; overtake.

rauque, *adj.* hoarse.

ravager, *v. a.* ravage, lay waste.

ravir, *v. a.* delight.

ravissant, *adj.* ravishing, charming.

rayer, *v. a.* scratch (out); cross out.

rayon, *s.m.* ray, beam; spoke; radius; shelf.

rayonnement, *s. m.* radiation; radiance.

rayonner, *v.n.* radiate, shine.

razzia, *s. f.* raid.

réacteur, *s.m.* reactor.

réactoin, *s.f.* reaction.

réagir, *v.n.* react.

réalisation, *s.f.* realization; carrying out.

réaliser, *v.a.* realize.

réaliste, *adj.* realistic.

réalité, *s. f.* reality; *en ~* in fact.

rebelle, *adj.* rebellious; — *s. m. f.* rebel.

rébellion, *s. f.*, rebellion.

rebord, *s.m.* edge, brim.

rébus, *s.m.* riddle.

récemment, *adv.* recently, lately.

récent, *adj.* recent.

récepteur, *s. m.* receiver.

réception, *s. f.* reception, receipt; at-home.

recette, *s.f.* receipt; recipe.

receveur, *s.m.* receiver; conductor *(bus).*

recevoir*, *v.n.* receive; admit, take in; accept; *v. n.* entertain; *aller ~ qn. à la gare* meet s.o. at the station.

rechange, *s. m. pièces de ~* spare parts.

recharge, *s. f.* refill.

réchaud, *s.m.* dishwarmer.

réchauffer, *v. a.* warm up again.

recherche, *s.f.* research; inquiry.

rechercher, *v. a.* look for, search for; research into.

récipé, *s.m.* recipe.

réciproque, *adj.* reciprocal, mutual.

récit, *s. m.* recital, account.

récital, *s. m.* recital.

récitation, *s. f.* recitation.

réciter, *v.a.* recite.

réclamation, *s. f.* claim, complaint.

réclame, *s. f.* advertisement; *faire de la ~ (pour)* advertise.

réclamer, *v.a.* demand, claim.

recommandation, *s. f.* recommendation.

recommander, *v. a.* recommend; introduce; request; register.

recommencer, *v. a. & n.* begin again.

récompense, *s. f.* reward.

récompenser, *v. a.* reward, repay.

réconcilier, *v. a.* reconcile.

reconnaissance, *s. f.* recognition, gratitude.

reconnaître, *v. a.* recognize, know; acknowledge; explore.

reconstruction, *s. f.* reconstruction.

reconstruire*, *v.a.* rebuild.

record, *s.m.* record *(sport etc.).*

recourir, *v. n. ~ a* have recourse to.

recouvrir, *v.a.* cover again, hide.

récréation, *s. f.* recreation, amusement, pastime.

recrue, *s. f.* recruit.

recteur, *s.m.* rector, chancellor.

rectifier, *v.a.* rectify, correct.

reçu, *s. m.* receipt; *au ~ de* on receipt of.

recueil, *s. m.* collection.

recueillir, *v.a.* collect; *se ~* collect oneself.

reculer, *v.a.* put back; *v. n.* draw back, recoil.

rédacteur, -trice, *s. m. f.* editor; writer.

rédaction, *s. f.* drawing up; composition; editorial staff.

rédemption, *s. f.* redemption.

rédiger, *v.a.* draw up; edit.

redingote, *s.f.* frock-coat.

redire, *v. a.* repeat, say again; *trouver à ~ à* find fault with.

redoubler, *v.a.* redouble.

redoutable, *adj.* formidable, dreaded.

redouter, *v.a.* dread, be afraid of.

redresser, *v. a.* & *se ~* straighten (up).

réduction, *s. a.* reduction, cut.

réduire*, *v. a.* reduce, cut down.

réduit, *adj.* reduced.

réel, **réelle**, *adj.* real, actual.

réélection, *s.f.* re-election.

réélire, *v. a.* re-elect.

refaire, *v.a.* do (over) again.

réfectoire, *s. m.* refectory, dining-hall.

référence, *s. f.* reference.

référer, *v. a.* refer; *se ~ à* refer to; *nous référant à* referring to.

réfléchir, *v.a.* reflect; consider, think over.

réflecteur, *s. m.* reflector.

reflet, *s. m.* reflection.

refléter, *v. a.* reflect.

réflexe, *adj.* reflex.

réflexion, *s. f.* reflection, consideration.

reflux, *s. m.* ebb.

réformation, *s.f.* reformation.

réforme, *s.f.* reform, improvement.

Réforme, *s. f.* Reformation.

réformer, *v. a.* reform.

refrain, *s. m.* refrain.

refréner, *v. a.* bridle, curb.

réfrigérateur, *s.m.* refrigerator.

réfrigérer, *v. a.* refrigerate.

refroidir, *v. a.* chill, cool.

refuge, *s. m.* refuge; lay-by.

réfugié, **-e**, *s. m. f.* refugee.

réfugier: *se ~* take shelter, take refuge.

refus, *s. m.* refusal, denial.

refuser, *v. a.* refuse, deny; *~ de connaître* ignore; *être refusé* fail.

regagner, *v.a.* regain, recover; return to.

regard, *s. m.* look.

regarder, *v. a.* look at; concern; regard.

régime, *s. m.* (form of) government; diet.

régiment, *s. m.* regiment.

région, *s. f.* region, area.

régional, *adj.* local.

régir, *v.a.* rule, administer.

régisseur, *s. m.* steward; stage-manager.

registre, *s.m.* register; record.

règle, *s. f.* rule; ruler.

réglé, *adj.* regular; punctual; steady; ruled.

règlement, *a.m.* rule, regulation.

régler, *v. a.* rule; regulate; time; settle.

règne, *s.m.* reign.

régner, *v.a.* reign.

regret, *s. m.* regret.

regretter, *v. a.* regret, be sorry for.

régulariser, *v. a.* regularize.

régularité, *s. f.* regularity.

régulateur, *s. m* regulator.

régulier, **-ière**, *adj.* regular; correct.

rein, *s.m.* kidney.

reine, *s.f.* queen.

reine-claude, *s. f.* green-gage.

rejeter, *v. a.* reject, throw out.

rejoindre, *v.a.* rejoin; overtake, catch up; se ~ meet.

réjouir, *v. a.* give joy to, cheer up, delight; se ~ rejoice.

relâche, *s. f.* relaxation; respite.

relâcher, *v.a.* slacken, loosen; relax; se ~ relax.

relatif, -ive, *adj.* relative; ~ à relating to.

relation, *s.f.* relation, connection; report; *entrer en* ~ *avec* get in touch with.

relever, *v. a.* lift, take up, pick up; set off; *v. n.* recover.

relief, *s.m.* relief.

relier, *v. a.* bind (a book); hoop (casks).

religieux, -euse, *adj.* religious; — *s. m.* monk; *s. f.* nun.

religion, *s.f.* religion.

relique, *s.f.* relic.

relire, *v.a.* read (over) again.

remarquable, *adj.* remarkable, noticeable.

remarque, *s. f.* remark, observation, notice.

remarquer, *v. a.* remark, notice, observe; *faire* ~ point out.

rembourser, *v.a.* repay, reimburse.

remède, *s.m.* remedy; medicine.

remerciement, *s.m.* thanks *(pl.)*.

remercier, *v.a.* thank *(de* for).

remettre, *v. a.* put back; put on again; post-pone; se ~ recover (oneself).

remilitariser, *v. a.* rearm.

remise, *s. f.* remittance; delivery; allowance; revival, restoration.

remonter, *v. n. & a.* go up, remount; bring up again; set up again.

remords, *s. m.* remorse.

remorque, *s. f.* tow(ing), trailer.

remorqueur, *s. m. (bateau)* ~ tug-boat.

remous, *s. m.* eddy(-water), whirl.

remplacer, *v. a.* replace, substitute.

remplir, *v. a.* fill; fill up; fulfil; carry out.

remporter, *v.a.* take away, carry off; get, obtain.

remuer, *v. a. & n.* move, fidget about; se ~ be busy, move.

rémunération, *s. f.* remuneration.

renaissance, *s. f.* renascence; revival; *la Renaissance* the Renaissance.

renaître, *v.n.* be born again, revive.

renard, *s.m.* fox.

rencontre, *s. f.* meeting, encounter; collision.

rencontrer, *v.a.* meet, meet with; come across; run into; se ~ *avec* meet, be met with.

rendement, *s. m.* output.

rendez-vous, *s. m.* appointment, rendezvous.

rendormir: se ~ go to sleep again.

rendre, *v.a.* give back, return; yield; render; convey; ~ *un arrêt* issue a decree; ~ *compte* render an account, realize; ~ *visite* pay a visit.

renfermer, v. a. lock up again, confine; contain, include.

renfler, v.a.&n. swell.

renforcer, v. a. strengthen, reinforce.

renfort, s. m. reinforcement; help.

renier, v. a. deny.

renom, s.m. reputation.

renommée, s. f. renown.

renoncer, v.n.&a. renounce, give up.

renouveler, v.a. renew, renovate.

renseignement, s. m. information; indication; bureau des ～s inquiry office.

renseigner, v. a. give information to; se ～ inquire, ask (sur about).

rente, s. f. income; rent.

rentrée, s. f. return; reopening.

rentrer, v. n. reenter, go in; get back, return home.

renversé, adj. reversed, upset.

renverser, v.a. upset; overthrow; turn upside down; se ～ be upset, tip over.

renvoi, s.m. return; (cross-)reference.

renvoyer, v.a. return; dismiss; refer.

réorganiser, v.a. reorganize.

répandre, v.a. pour; spread, scatter, diffuse.

réparation, s.f. repair, amends.

réparer, v. a. repair, mend; make up for.

repartir*, v.a. answer.

repas, s. m. meal.

repasser, v. n. pass again.

répéter, v. a. repeat; say again; rehearse.

répétition, s. f. repetition; rehearsal.

réplique, s. f. retort, reply, answer.

répliquer, v. a. & n. reply, answer.

répondre, v. a. & n. answer, reply; respond to.

réponse s.m. answer; response; ～ payée reply paid.

reporter, v. a. carry back, take back.

repos, s. m. rest; sans ～ restless.

reposer, v. a. lay again; v. n. rest, lie.

repoussant, adj. repulsive.

repousser, v. a. push back; repulse; drive back.

reprendre, v.a. & n. take back, get back; take up, go on; ～ sa parole go back on one's word.

représentant, -e, s. m. f. representative.

représentation, s. f. show, production; performance; display; representation.

représenter, v. a. represent; show, display.

reprise, s.f. renewal.

reproche, s. m. reproach, blame.

reprocher, v. a. reproach (with); blame for.

reproduction, s.f. reproduction.

reproduire*, v. a. reproduce.

républicain, -e, adj. & s. m. f. republican.

république, s. f. republic.

répulsion, s.f. repulsion.

réputation, s. f. reputation.

requête, s.f. request,

demand.

réserve, *s.f.* reserve; reservation; caution; *de* ~ spare; *mettre en* ~ lay by.

réserver, *v. a.* reserve, lay by; book (in advance).

réservoir, *s.m.* tank *(petrol etc.).*

résidence, *s. f.* residence, dwelling.

résident, *s. m.* résident.

résignation, *s. f.* resignation; submission.

résigner, *v. a.* resign; se ~ *à* resign oneself, make up one's mind.

résistance, *s. f.* resistance.

résister, *v. n.* resist.

résolu, *adj.* resolute.

résolution, *s. f.* resolution.

résonance, *s. f.* resonance.

résonner, *v. n.* resound, ring.

résoudre*, *v.a.* resolve; solve; settle; se ~ resolve, make up one's mind (to).

respect, *s. m.* respect.

respectable, *adj.* respectable, decent.

respecter *v. a.* respect.

respectif, -ive, *adj.* respective.

respectueux, -euse, *adj.* respectful.

respiration, *s. f.* respiration, breath(ing).

respirer, *v. n. & a.* breathe.

responsabilité, *s. f.* responsibility.

responsable, *adj.* responsible.

ressaisir, *v. a.* seize again.

ressemblance, *s. f.* resemblance, likeness.

ressemblant, *adj.* like, similar.

ressembler, *v* emble.

ressentiment, *s. m.* resentment, grudge.

ressentir, *v.a.* feel; resent; se ~ be hurt; feel still.

resserrer, *v.a.* tighten; bind.

ressort, *s.m.* spring; energy.

ressortir, *v. n.* come out again; stand out.

ressource, *s. f.* resource.

restaurant, *s. m.* restaurant; ~ *à libre service* self-service restaurant.

restaurateur, -trice, *s. m. f.* restorer; restaurant keeper.

restauration, *s.f.* restoration.

restaurer, *v. a.* restore.

reste, *s. m.* rest, remainder.

rester, *v. n.* remain, be left, keep; ~ *en arrière,* lag behind.

restituer, *v. a.* restore.

restreindre*, *v. a.* restrict.

restriction, *s. f.* restriction.

résultat, *s.m.* result, issue; *avoir pour* ~ result in.

résulter, *v. n.* result *(de* from).

résumé, *s.m.* summing up.

résumer, *v.a.* sum up.

rétablir, *v.a.* restore.

retard, *s. m.* delay; *être en* ~ be late; be overdue.

retarder, *v.a.* delay, retard.

retenir, *v.a.* keep back, hold back; hinder.

retirer, *v.a.* draw back, pull back; extract, get, derive; se ~ retire.

retomber, *v. n.* fall again, fall back; relapse.

retour, *s. m.* return; *en* ~ homeward bound; *être*

de ~ be back.

retourner, *v. n.* turn back; return, go back; se ~ turn round.

retracer, *v.a.* retrace; relate, tell.

retraite, *s.f.* retreat; retirement; *mettre à la* ~ superannuate.

retrancher, *v. a.* retrench.

rétrécir, *v.a.* contract; make narrower; shrink.

retrousser, *v. a.* turn up.

retrouver, *v. a.* find again, recover.

rétroviseur, *s. m.* (rear-vision) mirror.

réunion, *s.f.* reunion.

réunir, *v.a.* reunite; join again.

réussi, *adj.* successful.

réussir, *v. n.* succeed.

réussite, *s. f.* success.

revanche, *s. f.* revenge; return match; *en* ~ in return.

rêve, *s. m.* dream.

réveil, *s. m.* waking.

réveille-matin *s. m.* alarm-clock.

réveiller, *v.a.* & se ~ wake (up).

révéler, *v.a.* reveal; se ~ come to light.

revenir, *v. n.* return, come back; recur; cost.

revenu, *s. m.* income.

rêver, *v. n.* dream.

révérence, *s. f.* reverence; curtsey.

révérend, *adj.* reverend.

rêverie, *s.f.* reverie, fancy.

revers, *s. m.* back, reverse, wrong side.

revêtir, *v.a.* put on; clothe; cover.

révision, *s. f.* revision.

revivre, *v. n.* live again; *faire* ~ revive.

revoir, *v. a.* sec again,

look over; *au* ~ good-bye (for the present).

révolte, *s. f.* revolt.

révolter, *v. a.* revolt; se ~ revolt, rebel.

révolution, *s. f.* revolution; turn.

révolutionnaire, *adj.* & *s. m. f.* revolutionary.

revolver, *s. m.* revolver.

revue, *s. f.* review; magazine.

rez-de-chaussé, *s. m.* ground floor.

rhétorique, *s. f.* rhetoric.

rhum, *s. m.* rum.

rhumatisme, *s. m.* rheumatism.

rhume, *s. m.* cold (in the head).

ricaner, *v. n.* sneer, grin.

riche, *adj.* rich, well off.

richesse, *s.f.* wealth, riches *(pl.).*

ride, *s. f.* wrinkle.

rideau, *s. m.* curtain.

rider, *v. a.* wrinkle.

ridicule, *adj.* ridiculous; — *s. m.* ridicule.

rien, *pron.* nothing; not ... anything; trifle.

rigoureux, -euse, *adj.* rigorous, severe.

rigueur, *s. f.* rigour.

rime, *s. f.* rhyme.

rincer, *v. a.* rinse.

rire*, *v. n.* laugh; *pour* ~ for fun; — *s.m.* laugh(ing), laughter.

risque, *s. m.* risk.

risquer, *v.a.* risk, run the risk of.

rivage, *s. m.* beach, shore.

rival, -e, *adj.* & *s. m. f.* rival.

rivalité, *s. f.* rivalry.

rive, *s. f.* bank, shore, beach.

rivière, *s. f.* river, stream.

riz, *s. m.* rice.

robe, *s. f.* gown, dress,

frock; robe; ~ *de chambre* dressing-gown.

robinet, *s. m.* tap, cock.

robuste, *adj.* robust; strong, sturdy.

roc, *s. m.* rock.

roche, *s.f.* rock, boulder.

rocher, *s. m.* rock, crag.

roder, *v. a.* run in.

rôder, *v.n.* rove.

rogner, *v. a.* clip, pare.

rognon, *s. m.* kidney.

roi, *s. m.* king.

rôle, *s. m.* roll; part, rôle.

romain, -e (R.), *adj. & s. m. f.* Roman.

roman, *s. m.* novel; ~s fiction.

romancier, -ère, *s. m. f.* novelist.

romanesque, *adj.* romantic.

romantique, *s. m.* romantic.

romantisme, *s. m.* romanticism.

rompre, *v. a. & n.* break.

rond, *adj.* round; — *s. m.* round, circle.

ronde, *s. f.* round; patrol; *à la* ~ round about, around).

rondelle, *s. f.* ring, collar, washer.

ronfler, *v. n.* snore; roar.

ronger, *v.a.* gnaw, eat.

rose, *s. f.* rose; — *adj.* rosy, pink.

roseau, *s. m.* reed.

rosée, *s. f.* dew.

rosier, *s.m.* rose-tree, rose-bush.

rossignol, *s. m.* nightingale.

rôti, *s. m.* roast (meat).

rôtir, *v.a.* roast; toast; *faire* ~ roast, bake.

roucouler, *v. n.* coo.

roue, *s.f.* wheel; ~ *de secours* spare wheel; ~ *dentée* cog-wheel.

rouge, *adj.* red; — *s. m.* red (colour); *bâton de* ~ lipstick.

rougeur, *s.f.* redness, blush.

rougir, *v.n. & a.* turn red, make red; blush.

rouille, *s. f.* rust.

rouiller, *v. n. & a.* rust, get rusty.

roulage, *s.m.* rolling; carriage (of goods); haulage.

rouleau, *s.m.* roll; roller; scroll.

roulement, *s. m.* roll(ing), rotation; ~ *a billes* ball-bearings.

rouler, *v. a. & n.* roll; roll up, wind up; turn, revolve.

roulotte, *s. f.* ~ *(de camping)* caravan.

roumain, -e (R.), *adj. & s. m. f.* Rumanian.

route, *s. f.* road; highway; course; way; *en* ~ on the way; *en* ~ *pour* bound for; *code de la* ~ highway code.

routine, *s. f.* routine.

roux, rousse, *adj.* red-(dish).

royal, *adj.* royal.

royaliste, -e, *adj. & s. m. f.* royalist.

royaume, *s. m.* kingdom.

ruban, *s m.* ribbon; band.

rubis, *s m.* ruby.

ruche, *s. f.* hive.

rude, *adj.* rough, rude.

rue, *s. f.* street; ~ *barrée* no thoroughfare; ~ *de traverse* crossroad.

ruée, *s. f.* rush.

ruelle, *s. f.* lane.

ruer; se ~ rush, dash.

rugissement, *s. m.* roar.

ruine, *s. f.* ruin; wreck.

ruiner, *v.a.* ruin, destroy.

ruisseau, *s. m.* stream, brook; gutter.

ruisseler, *v.n.* stream, run, flow.

rumeur, *s. f.* noise; rumour.

ruminer, *v. a. & n.* ruminate, chew (the cud).

rupture, *s. f.* rupture.

ruse, *s. f.* craft, cunning.

rusé, *adj.* cunning, sly.

russe (R.), *adj. & s. m. f.* Russian.

russien, -enne (R.), *adj. & s. m. f.* Russian.

rustique, *adj.* rustic, rural.

rythme, *s. m.* rhythm.

rythmique, *adj.* rhytmical.

S

s' see se.

sa, *adj. poss.* his, her, its.

sable, *s. m.* sand.

sablonneux, -euse, *adj.* sandy.

sabre, *s. m.* sabre.

sac, *s. m.* bag, sack; ~ *a main* handbag; ~ *de couchage* sleeping-bag.

saccager, *v. a.* plunder.

sacré, *adj.* sacred, holy.

sacrement, *s. m.* sacrament.

sacrifice, *s.m.* sacrifice.

sacrifier, *v.a.* sacrifice.

sacristain, *s.m.* sexton.

sage, *adj.* wise, well-behaved.

sagesse, *s. f.* wisdom.

saignant, *adj.* bleeding; underdone.

saigner, *v. a. & n.* bleed.

saillant, *adj.* projecting.

saillir, *v. n.* stand out, project.

sain, *adj.* sound; ~ *et sauf* safe and sound.

saint, -e. *adj.* holy, sa-

cred; — *s. m. f.* saint

saisir, *v.a.* seize.

saison, *s. f.* season.

salade, *s. f.* salad.

salaire, *s. m.* wages *(pl.)*, pay, salary.

sale, *adj.* dirty, filthy.

saler, *v. a.* salt.

saleté, *s. f.* dirt.

salière, *s. f.* salt-cellar.

salir, *v. a.* soil, dirty.

salle, *s. f.* hall; assembly room; house; ~ *d'attente* waiting-room; ~ *de classe* schoolroom; ~ *(de cours)* auditorium; ~ *familiale,* ~ *de séjour* living-room.

salon, *s. m.* drawing-room; saloon; *petit* ~ sitting-room.

saluer, *v. a. & n.* bow to; greet.

salut, *s. m.* salvation; bow, greeting.

samedi, *s. m.* Saturday.

sanatorium, *s. m.* sanatorium.

sanction, *s. f.* sanction.

sanctuaire, *s. m.* sanctuary.

sandale, *s. f.* sandal.

sang, *s. m.* blood.

sanglier, *s. m.* wild boar.

sanitaire, *adj.* sanitary.

sans, *prep.* without.

santé, *s. f.* health.

sapin, *s. m.* fir(-tree).

sarcasme, *s. m.* sarcasm.

sarcastique, *adj.* sarcastic.

sardine, *s.f.* sardine.

satellite, *s. m.* satellite.

satire, *s. f.* satire.

satisfaction, *s. f.* satisfaction.

savoir*, *v. n.* know, be aware; be trained in; understand; be able to; — *s. m.* knowledge, learning.

savon, *s. m.* soap.

savourer, *v. a.* taste, relish.

savoureux, -euse, *adj.* savoury, tasty.

scandale, *s. m.* scandal.

scaphandre autonome, *s. m.* skin diver.

scaphandrier, *s. m.* diver.

scarabée, *s. m.* beetle.

sceau, *s. m.* seal.

sceller, *v. a.* seal; fix.

scénario, *s. m.* scenario.

scène, *s. f.* scène; scenery; *fig.* stage; *mettre en* ~ produce (a play).

sceptre, *s. m.* sceptre.

scie, *s. f.* saw.

satisfaire, *v. a. & n.* satisfy, please.

satisfaisant, *adj.* satisfactory.

satisfait, *adj.* satisfied.

sauce, *s. f.* sauce.

saucisse, *s. f.* sausage.

sauf, sauve, *adj.* safe; — *prep.* except, save.

saumon, *s. m.* salmon.

saut, *s.m.* jump, leap.

sauter, *v. n.* leap, jump; spring; *faire* ~ blow up.

sauvage, *adj.* savage, wild.

sauver, *v. a.* save, rescue; se ~ run away.

sauveur, *s. m.* Saviour.

savant, -e, *adj.* learned, clever; expert; — *s. m. f.* scholar.

saveur, *s. f.* savour, taste.

science, *s. f.* science, knowledge; *homme de* ~ scientist.

scientifique, *adj.* scientific.

scier, *v. a.* saw.

scolaire, *adj.* school; *année* ~ school year.

scooter, *s. m.* motor-scooter.

scrupule, *s. m.* scruple.

sculpter, *v. a.* carve,
sculpture.

sculpteur, *s. m.* sculptor.

sculpture, *s. f.* sculpture.

se, s' *pron.* himself, herself, itself; each other.

séance, *s. f.* sitting, meeting.

seau, *s. m.* pail.

sec, sèche, *adj.* dry, dried up.

sécher, *v. a. & n.* dry (up).

sécheresse, *s. f.* dryness.

second, *adj.* second.

secondaire, *adj.* secondary.

seconde, *s. f.* second.

seconder, *v. a.* back.

secouer, *v. a.* shake.

secourir, *v. a.* help.

secours, *s. m.* help, succour, aid; *au* ~ help!

secousse, *s. f.* shake, jolt, jerk.

secret, -ète, *adj. & s. m.* secret.

secrétaire, *s. m. f.* secretary; — *s. m.* writing-desk.

secrétariat, *s. m.* secretariate.

secteur, *s. m.* sector, section; ~ *(de courant)* mains.

section, *s. f.* section

sécurité, *s. f.* security.

sédatif, -ive, *adj. & s.m.* sedative.

sédiment, *s. m.* sediment.

séduire, *v. a.* seduce.

seigle, *s. m.* rye.

seigneur, *s.m.* lord, squire.

seize, *adj. & s. m.* sixteen; sixteenth.

seizième, *adj.* sixteenth.

séjour, *s. m.* stay, visit; (place of) residence.

séjourner, *v.n.* stay, sojourn.

sel, *s. m.* salt.

selle, *s. f.* saddle.

selon, *prep.* according to; after.

semaine, *s. f.* week.

semblable, *adj.* (a)like.

semblant, *s. m.* semblance; appearance.

sembler, *v. n.* appear, look, seem.

semelle, *s. f.* sole *(footwear)*.

semer, *v. a.* sow.

semestre, *s. m.* half year; semester.

séminaire, *s. m.* seminary.

sénat, *s. m.* senate.

sénateur, *s. m.* senator.

sens, *s. m.* sense; judgement, opinion; direction.

sensation, *s. f.* feeling; sensation.

sensé, *adj.* sensible, reasonable.

sensibilité, *s. f.* sensibility, feeling.

sensible, *adj.* sensible, perceptible; sensitive.

sentence, *s. f.* sentence.

senteur, *s. f.* scent, smell.

sentier, *s. m.* path.

sentiment, *s. m.* feeling, sense, sentiment.

sentimental, *adj.* sentimental.

sentinelle, *s. f.* sentry, sentinel.

sentir*, *v. a.* feel, perceive; experience; smell; se ~ feel.

séparation, *s. f.* separation.

séparer, *v. a.* separate, divide; se ~ part.

sept, *adj. & s. m.* seven; seventh.

septembre, *s. m.* September.

septième, *adj.* seventh.

sérénade, *s. f.* serenade.

sérénité, *s. f.* serenity.

sergent, *s. m.* sergeant.

série, *s. f.* series.

sérieux, **-euse**, *adj.* grave, serious.

serin, **-e**, *s. m. f.* canary.

seringue, *s. f.* syringe.

serment, *s. m.* oath.

sermon, *s. m.* sermon.

serpent, *s. m.* snake, serpent.

serpenter, *v. n.* wind, meander.

serre, *s. f.* claw; hothouse.

serré, *adj.* tight, close, serried.

serrer, *v. a.* press, crush, jam, tighten.

serre-tête, *s. m.* crash-helmet, headband.

serrure, *s. f.* lock.

serrurier, *s. m.* locksmith.

servante, *s. f.* servant.

service, *s. m.* service, duty; favour; set; *être de* ~ be on duty; *à votre* ~ at your disposal.

serviette, *s. f.* napkin; towel; briefcase.

servir*, *v. a. & n.* serve; be in the service of; ~ *à* be used for; *ne se* ~ *à rien* be of no use; *Mme est servie* dinner is ready; se ~ use, make use of, help oneself.

serviteur, *s. m.* servant.

servitude, *s. f.* servitude.

ses, *adj. poss.* his, her, its; one's.

session, *s. f.* session.

seuil, *s. m.* threshold.

seul, *adj.* alone, single, sole, only.

sévère, *adj.* severe, hard.

sévir, *v. n.* punish; rage.

sexe, *s. m.* sex.

sexuel, **-elle**, *adj.* sexual.

shampooing, *s. m.* shampoo.

si, *conj.* if, whether; — *adv.* so, so much, such.

siècle, *s. m.* century.

siège, *s. m.* seat.

sien, -enne, *poss. adj.* his, hers; its; one's.

siffler, *v. n.* whistle, hiss.

sifflet, *s. m.* whistle.

signal, *s. m.* signal; ~ *d'alarme* communication-cord.

signaler, *v. a.* signal.

signalisation, *s. f.* signals *(pl.); feux de* ~ traffic-lights.

signature, *s. f.* signature.

signe, *s. m.* sign.

signer, *v. a. & n.* sign.

significatif, -ive, *adj.* significant.

signification, *s. f.* signification; meaning.

signifier, *v. a.* signify.

silence, *s. m.* silence.

silencieux, -euse, *adj.* silent.

silhouette, *s.f.* outline, silhouette.

sillon, *s. m.* furrow.

simple, *adj.* simple.

simplicité, *s. f.* simplicity.

simplifier, *v. a.* simplify.

simultané, *adj.* simultaneous.

sincère, *adj.* sincere.

sincérité, *s. f.* sincerity.

singe, *s. m.* monkey.

singulier, -ère, *adj.* singular, strange.

sinon, *conj.* (or) else, otherwise.

sire, *s. m.* sir, lord.

sirène, *s. f.* siren; hooter, fog-horn.

site, *s. m.* site, place.

sitôt, *adv.* as soon; ~ *que* as soon as; ~ ... ~ no sooner... than.

situation, *s. f.* situation; state; office, position.

situer, *v. a.* place, locate.

six, *adj. & s. m.* six; sixth.

sixième, *adj.* sixth.

ski, *s. m.* ski; *faire du* ~ ski.

skieur, *s. m.* skier, ski-runner.

smoking, *s. m.* dinner-jacket.

sobre, *adj.* sober.

social, *adj.* social.

socialisme, *s. m.* socialism.

socialiste, *adj. & s. m. f.* socialist.

société, *s. f.* society; company; ~ *anonyme* limited liability company.

sœur, *s. f.* sister.

soi, *pron.* oneself; himself, herself; itself.

soi-disant, *adj.* so-called.

soie, *s. f.* silk.

soif, *s. f.* thirst; *avoir* ~ be thirsty.

soigner, *v. a.* take care of, look after.

soigneux, -euse, *adj.* careful.

soin, *s. m.* care; *prendre* ~ *de* take care of; *aux bons* ~s *de* c/o.

soir, *s. m.* evening.

soirée, *s. f.* evening (party).

soit, *conj.* say; suppose; either ... or; ~ *que* whether.

soixante, *adj. & s. m.* sixty.

soixante-dix, *adj. & s. m.* seventy.

sol, *s. m.* soil; ground.

soldat, *s. m.* soldier.

soleil, *s. m.* sun; *il fait du* ~ the sun is shining.

solennel, -elle, *adj.* solemn.

solennité, *s. f.* solemnity.

solidarité, *s. f.* solidarity.

solide, *adj.* solid.
solidité, *s. f.* solidity.
solitaire, *adj.* solitary.
solitude, *s. f.* solitude.
solliciter, *v. a.* solicit, entreat.
sollicitude, *s. f.* care.
soluble, *adj.* soluble.
solution, *s. f.* solution.
sombre, *adj.* dark; dim.
sombrer, *v.n.* founder, sink.
sommaire, *adj. & s. m.* summary.
somme, *s. f.* sum, a-mount.
sommeil, *s. m.* sleep; *a-voir ~* be sleepy.
sommeiller, *v. n.* slumber.
sommer, *v. a.* summon.-
sommet, *s. m.* top, summit.
sommier, *s. m.* spring mattress.
somnifère, *s. m.* sleeping-pill.
somnolent, *adj.* sleepy.
son¹, sa, *adj. poss. (pl. ses)* his, her, its; one's.
son², *s. m.* sound.
songe, *s. m.* dream.
songer, *v. n.* dream.
sonner, *v. a. & n.* ring, sound; *on sonne (à la porte)* there is a ring at the door.
sonnette, *s. f.* bell.
sonore, *adj.* sonorous.
sorcier, *s. m.* sorcerer, wizard.
sorcière, *s. f.* witch, sorceress.
sornette, *s. f.* nonsense.
sort, *s. m.* fate, lot.
sorte, *s. f.* sort, kind.
sortie, *s. f.* going out; way out, exit; *~ secours* emergency exit.
sortir*, *v. n.* go out, walk out, leave; *ne*

pas ~ keep indoors; *v.a.* take out, bring out.
sot, sotte, *adj.* foolish, silly.
sottise, *s. f.* foolishness, nonsense.
sou, *s. m.* sou, copper, penny.
souci, *s. m.* care, concern.
soucier: se ~ de care for.
soucieux, -euse, *adj.* full of care, anxious.
soucoupe, *s. f.* saucer.
soudain, *adj.* sudden; — *adv.* suddenly.
soude, *s. f.* soda *(chemical).*
souffle, *s. m.* breath.
souffler, *v.a. & n.* breathe; blow (out).
soufflet, *s. m.* box (on the ear); bellows *(pl.).*
souffrance, *s. f.* pain, suffering.
souffrir*, *v. a. & n.* suffer, bear.
souhaiter, *v. a.* desire.
soulever, *v. a.* lift, raise; *se ~* rise (in rebellion).
soulier, *s. m.* shoe.
souligner, *v. a.* underline.
soumettre, *v. a.* submit, subdue; *se ~* submit.
soumission, *s. f.* submission.
soupçon, *s. m.* suspicion.
soupçonner, *v. a.* suspect.
soupe, *s. f.* soup.
souper, *s. m.* supper; — *v. n.* have supper.
soupir, *s. m.* sigh.
soupirer, *v. n.* sigh; *~ après* long for.
souple, *adj.* supple, flexible.
source, *s. f.* source, spring.
sourcil, *s. m.* eyebrow.
sourd, *adj.* deaf.
sourd-muet, sourde-muette, *adj. & s. m. f.* deaf and dumb (per-

son).

sourire, *v. n.* smile.

souris, *s. f.* mouse.

sous, *prep.* under; beneath; before.

souscripteur, *s. m.* subscriber.

souscription, *s. f.* subscription.

souscrire, *v. a. & n.* sign, subscribe (to).

sousdéveloppé, *adj.* under-developed.

sous-marin, *s. m.* submarine.

soussigné, -e, *adj. & s. m. f.* undersigned.

sous-sol, *s. m.* basement.

sous-titre, *s. m.* subtitle, caption.

soustraction, *s. f.* subtraction.

soustraire, *v. a.* take away; subtract.

soutenir, *v. a.* support, sustain, maintain.

souterrain, *adj.* underground; — *s. m.* subway.

soutien, *s. m.* support.

soutien-gorge, *s. m.* bra.

souvenir*, *s. m.* remembrance; souvenir; memory; — *v. reflex.* se ∼ remember.

souvent, *adv.* often.

souverain, -e, *s. m. f.* sovereign.

spatial, *adj. vaisseau* ∼, *véhicule* ∼ space-craft, space-vehicle.

speaker, *s. m.* announcer.

speakerine, *s. f.* lady announcer.

spécial, *adj.* special.

spécialement, *adv.* specially, particularly.

spécialiser, *v. a.* specialize.

spécialiste, *s. m. f.* specialist.

spécialité, *s. f.* special(i)ty.

spécifier, *v. a.* specify.

spécifique, *adj.* specific.

spectacle, *s. m.* spectacle, sight.

spectateur, -trice, *s. m. f.* spectator, spectatress, onlooker; bystander.

spéculation, *s. f.* speculation.

spéculer, *v. n.* speculate.

sphère, *s. f.* sphere.

spirale, *adj.* spiral.

spirituel, -elle, *adj.* spiritual; witty.

splendeur, *s. f.* splendour.

splendide, *adj.* splendid.

spontané, *adj.* spontaneous.

sport, *s. m.* sport.

sportif, -ive, *adj.* sporting; sportsmanlike.

squelette, *s. m.* skeleton.

stade, *s. m.* stadium; *fig.* stage.

stalle, *s. f.* stall; box.

station, *s. f.* standing; stay; station, stop; ∼ *balnéaire* watering-place, spa.

stationnement, *s. m.* stationing; parking; ∼ *interdit* no parking.

stationner, *v. n.* stop; park.

station-service, *s. f.* service-station.

statistique, *s. f.* statistics; — *adj.* statistical.

statue, *s. f.* statue.

statut, *s. m.* statute.

sténographie, *s. f.* shorthand.

stérile, *adj.* sterile.

stimuler, *v. a.* stimulate.

stipuler, *v. a.* stipulate.

store, *s. m.* (Venetian) blind.

strabisme, *s. m.* squint-

(ing).

stratégie, *s. f.* strategy.

structure, *s. f.* structure.

studieux, -euse, *adj.* studious.

stupéfier, *v. a.* stupefy.

stupide, *adj.* stupid, dull.

stupidité, *s. f.* stupidity.

style, *s. m.* style.

stylo, *s.m.* ~ *à bille* ball(-point) pen.

stylo(graphe), *s. m.* fountain-pen.

suave, *adj.* soft, gentle.

subjonctif, *s.m.* subjunctive.

subjuguer, *v.a.* subjugate, overcome.

submerger, *v. a.* submerge, flood.

subordonné, *adj.* subordinate.

subordonner, *v. a.* subordinate.

subséquent, *adj.* subsequent.

subsistance, *s. f.* subsistence.

subsister, *v. n.* subsist.

substance, *s. f.* substance.

substantiel, -elle, *adj.* substantial.

substantif, *s.m.* substantive.

substituer, *v.a.* substitute.

substitution, *s. f.* substitution.

subtil, *adj.* subtle.

subvention, *s. f.* subvention, subsidy.

succéder, *v. n.* succeed (*à* to), follow; *se* ~ follow one another.

succès, *s. m.* success; result.

successif, -ive, *adj.* successive.

succession, *s. f.* succession.

sucer, *v. a.* suck (in).

sucre, *s. m.* sugar.

sucré, *adj.* sweet(ened).

sud, *adj. & s. m.* south; *du* ~ southern; *au* ~ southward.

sud-est, *adj. & s. m.* south-east.

sud-ouest, *adj. & s. m.* south-west.

suédois, -e, (S.), *adj.* Swedish; — *s. m. f.* Swede; Swedish (language).

suer, *v. n. & a.* sweat.

sueur, *s. f.* sweat.

suffire*, *v.n.* be sufficient, be enough.

suffisamment, *adv.* sufficiently, enough.

suffisant, *adj.* sufficient, enough; conceited.

suffoquer, *v.a. & n.* suffocate, choke.

suggérer, *v.a.* suggest, propose.

suggestion, *s. f.* suggestion, hint.

suicide, *s. m.* suicide.

suisse (S.), *adj. & s. m.* (*f.* Suissesse) Swiss.

suite, *s. f.* retinue; suite, sequence, result; *a la* ~ after; *tout de* ~ at once, directly; *par* ~ consequently; *par* ~ *de* due to.

suivant, *adj.* following, next; — *prep.* according to.

suivre*, *v.a. & n.* follow; *comme suit* as follows; *ce qui suit* the following.

sujet, -ette, *s. m. f.* subject; *s. m.* subject.

superficie, *s. f.* surface, area.

superficiel, -elle, *adj.* superficial.

superflu, *adj.* superfluous.

supérieur, *adj.* superior, upper.

supériorité, s. f. superiority.

supermarché, s. m. supermarket.

supersonique, adj. supersonic.

superstitieux, -euse, adj. superstitious.

superstition, s. f. superstition.

suppléer, v.a. supply; substitute, do duty for; v. n. make up for.

supplément, s. m. supplement; extra charge; excess.

supplémentaire, adj. supplementary, extra.

suppliant, -e, adj. suppliant; — s. m. f. supplicant.

supplier, v.a. beseech.

support, s.m. prop; support.

supporter, v.a. bear, support.

supposer, v. a. suppose.

supposition, s. f. supposition, conjecture.

suppression, s. f. suppression.

supprimer, v. a. suppress, abolish, do away with.

suprême, adj. supreme.

sur, prep. on; over; concerning.

sûr, adj. certain, sure; secure, safe; pour ~l to be sure!

surcharger, v.a. & n. overload; weigh down.

sûrement, adv. surely, certainly.

sûreté, s. f. safety; security.

surface, s.f. surface.

surgir, v. n. arise, spring up, emerge.

surmonter, v.a. surmount, overcome.

surnaturel, -elle, adj. supernatural.

surpasser, v. a. surpass, outdo.

surpeuplé, adj. overcrowded.

surplus, s.m. surplus, excess.

surprendre, v. a. surprise.

surprise, s.f. surprise.

surseoir*, v.n. & a. postpone, delay, put off.

surtaxe, s. f. surtax.

surtout, s. m. overcoat.

surveillance, s. f. supervision.

surveiller, v.a. supervise.

survenir, v. a. arrive unexpectedly; happen, occur.

survivant, -e, s.m.f. survivor.

survivre, v.n. survive, outlive.

susceptible, adj. susceptible.

suspect, adj. suspicious, suspect.

suspendre, v· a. hang up; suspend.

suspension, s. f. suspension.

svelte, adj. slender, slim.

syllabe, s. f. syllable.

symbole, s. m. symbol.

symétrie, s. f. symmetry.

symétrique, adj. symmetrical.

sympathie, s. f. sympathy.

symphonie, s.f. symphony.

symptome, s. m. symptom.

synagogue, s.f. synagogue.

syndical, adj. trade.

syndicat, s. m. syndicate; trade-union; ~d'initiative tourist information office.

synthétique, adj. synthetic(al).

systématique, adj. systematic.

système, *s. m.* system.

T

tabac, *s.m.* tobacco; *bureau de ~* tobacconist's (shop).

table, *s. f.* table; board; food; *~ des matières,* table of contents.

tableau, *s.m.* picture; scene; board, panel.

tablette, *s. f.* tablet.

tablier, *s.m.* apron; dash-board.

tabouret, *s. m.* stool.

tache, *s. f.* spot, stain; *sans ~* spotless.

tâche, *s. f.* task, job.

tacher, *v.a.* spot, stain.

tâcher, *v.n.* try.

tact, *s. m.* touch.

tactique, *s.f.* tactics.

taille, *s.f.* cut; height, stature, size; waist.

tailler, *v.a.* hew, trim; cut.

tailleur, *s. m.* tailor.

taire*, *v.a.* be silent about, conceal; *se ~* be quiet.

talent, *s. m.* talent, attainment(s).

talon, *s. m.* heel; counterfoil.

talus, *s. m.* slope, bank.

tambour, *s. m.* drum.

tamis, *s. m.* sieve.

tamiser, *v. a.* sift, sieve.

tampon, *s. m.* plug; tampon.

tamponner, *v. a.* plug.

tandis que, *conj.* whereas, while.

tangible, *adj.* tangible.

tant, *adv.* so much, so many, such, so.

tante, *s. f.* aunt.

tantôt, *adv.* shortly, by and by; *~ ... ~* now ... now.

tapage, *s. m.* noise, fuss.

taper, *v.a. & n.* tap, strike, knock; type.

tapis, *s. m.* carpet, rug.

tapisser, *v. a.* upholster.

tapisserie, *s. f.* tapestry.

tapissier, *s. m.* upholsterer.

tard, *adv.* late.

tarder, *v.n.* delay, put off; be long.

tardif, -ive, *adj.* late.

tarif, *s.m.* tariff, rate; price-list; fare.

tarte, *s. f.* tart.

tas, *s. m.* heap, pile; mass; crowd.

tasse, *s. f.* cup.

tâter, *v.a. & n.* feel, taste, handle.

tâtonner, *v.n.* grope.

taureau, *s.m.* bull.

taux, *s.m.* price, rate (of exchange); tax.

taverne, *s. f.* tavern.

taxe, *s. f.* tax.

taxer, *v. a.* tax, rate.

taxi, *s. m.* taxi; *station de ~s* taxi-rank.

tchèque (T.), *adj. & s. m. f.* Czech.

te, *pron.* you; to you.

technicien, -enne, *s. m. f.* technician.

technique, *adj.* technical; *s. f.* technique, technics.

technologie, *s. f.* technology.

teindre*, *v.a.* dye, stain.

teint, *s. m.* complexion; dye.

teinte, *s. f.* tint, shade.

teinter, *v. a.* tint.

teinture, *s. f.* dye; tincture.

teinturerie, *s.f.* dye-works, dyer.

tel, telle, *adj.* such, like, similar.

télécommunication, *s.f.* telecommunication.

téléférique, *s.m.* ropeway.

télégramme, *s.m.* telegram, wire.

télégraphe, *s.m.* telegraph.

télégraphie, *s.f.* telegraphy.

télégraphier, *v.a. & n.* wire.

télégraphique, *adj.* telegraphic.

télémètre, *s.m.* rangefinder.

téléphone, *s.m.* telephone.

télescope, *s. m.* telescope.

téléspectateur, -trice, *s. m. f.* (tele)viewer.

téléviser, *v. a.* televise, telecast.

téléviseur, *s.m.* television-set.

télévison, *s. f.* television.

télex, *s. m.* telex.

tellement, *adv.* so (much).

témoigner, *v.a. & n.* testify; give evidence.

témoin, *s.m.* witness; testimony.

tempe, *s.f.* temple *(forehead)*.

tempérament, *s. m.* temper(ament), constitution.

température, *s.f.* temperature.

tempête, *s. f.* storm.

temple, *s. m.* temple, church; chapel; lodge.

temporel, -elle, *adj.* temporal, transient.

temps¹, *s. m.* time; opportunity; *à* ~ in time; *pendant ce* ~ *l* in the meantime; *en* ~ *voulu* in due time; *combien de* ~? how long?; *la plupart du* ~ mostly; *de* ~ *en* ~ at times.

temps², *s.m.* weather; *prévisions du* ~ weather-forecast.

tenaille, *s.f.* pincers, pliers, tongs *(pl.)*.

tendance, *s.f.* tendency, trend.

tendon, *s.m.* tendon, sinew.

tendre¹ ¹*adj.* tender, soft.

tendre², *v.a.* stretch; strain; bend; hang.

tendresse, *s. f.* tenderness.

tendu, *adj.* tense, taut.

ténébreux, -euse, *adj.* dark, gloomy, dismal.

tenir*, *v. a. & n.* hold; get hold of; hold on; take, contain; keep; **se** ~ stay, remain.

tennis, *s. m.* tennis.

tension, *s.f.* tension.

tentation, *s. f.* temptation.

tentative, *s. f.* attempt.

tente, *s. f.* tent.

tenter, *v.a.* attempt; try; tempt.

ténu, *adj.* thin, slender.

tenue, *s. f.* holding; session; behaviour.

terme, *s. m.* term; expression; goal, aim.

terminer, *v. a.* terminate, end, close; **se** ~ (come to an) end.

terminus, *s. m.* terminus.

terne, *adj.* dull, dim.

terrain, *s. m.* soil, earth; site; ground; ~ *de jeux* sports-ground.

terrasse, *s.f.* terrace.

terre, *s.f.* earth, land.

terreur, *s.f.* fear.

terrible, *adj.* terrible.

terrifier, *v.a.* terrify, frighten.

territoire, *s. m.* territory.

testament, *s.m.* will, testament.

tête, *s. f.* head.

têtu, *adj.* stubborn.
texte, *s.m.* text; type.
textile, *s.m.* textile.
textuel, -elle, *adj.* textual.
texture, *s. f.* texture.
thé, *s. m.* tea.
théâtral, *adj.* theatrical.
théâtre, *s.m.* theatre, stage; drama; *pièce de* ~ play.
théière, *s. f.* tea-pot.
thème, *s. m.* theme, topic; prose.
théologie, *s. f.* theology.
théologique, *adj.* theological.
théorie, *s. f.* theory.
théorique, *adj.* theoretic, theoretical.
thermal, *adj.* thermal.
thermomètre, *s. m.* thermometer.
thermos, *s. f.* thermos.
thèse, *s. f.* thesis.
thon, *s. m.* tunny.
tien, -enne, *poss. adj.* yours.
tiers, tierce, *adj.* third; — *s.m.* third party.
tige, *s. f.* stem, stalk.
tigre, *s. m.* tiger.
tigresse, *s. f.* tigress.
timbre, *s. m.* bell; sound; (postage-)stamp.
timbre-poste, *s. m.* postage-stamp.
timide, *adj.* timid, shy.
timidité, *s. f.* timidity.
tir, *s.m.* shooting.
tirage, *s.f.* draught, pull(ing); impression; issue.
tire-bouchon *s. m.* corkscrew.
tirer, *v. a. & n.* draw, pull, drag; extract; derive; fire, shoot; print.
tiroir, *s.m.* drawer.
tison, *s.m.* brand.
tisonnier, *s.m.* poker.

tisser, *v.a.* weave.
tisserand, *s.m.* weaver.
tissu, *s. m.* texture, fabric; tissue.
titre, *s. m.* title; heading; right.
titrer, *v.a.* give a title to.
toast, *s. m.* toast.
toi, *pron.* you.
toile, *s. f.* linen; cloth.
toilette, *s.f.* dress, clothes *(pl.);* dressing-table; *faire sa* ~ dress; *cabinet de* ~ dressing-room.
toison, *s. f.* fleece.
toit, *s. m.* roof.
tolérance, *s. f.* tolerance, toleration.
tolérer, *v.a.* tolerate, bear.
tomate, *s.f.* tomato.
tombe, *s. f.* tomb, grave.
tombeau, *s. m.* tomb.
tombée, *s.f.* fall.
tomber, *v.n.* fall, fall down; tumble; decay; ~ *sur* meet, run into; *faire* ~ push down; *laisser* ~ drop.
tome, *s. m.* volume.
ton¹, ta, *poss. adj. (pl.* tes) your.
ton², *s. m.* tone; colour; manner.
tondeuse, *s.f.* lawn-mower.
tondre, *v.a.* shear, clip, mow.
tonnage, *s. m.* tonnage.
tonne, *s. f.* barrel, tun; ton.
tonneau, *s.m.* barrel.
tonner, *v.n.* thunder.
tonnerre, *s.m.* thunder-(bolt).
toqué, *adj.* crazy.
torche, *s. f.* torch.
torcher, *v.a.* wipe, rub.
torchon, *s.m.* duster; dish-cloth.
tordre, *v. a.* twist, wring

(out).

torpille, s. f. torpedo.

torrent, s. m. torrent.

tort, s. m. wrong, harm, injury; *avoir* ~ be wrong.

tortue, s. f. tortoise.

torture, s. f. torture.

torturer, v. a. torture.

tôt, adv. soon, quickly; early.

total, adj. total, whole.

totalement, adv. totally, entirely.

touchant, prep. about.

touche, s. f. touch; key; hit.

toucher, v. n. & a. touch; feel; strike, hit; concern; — s. m. touch; feeling.

touffe, s. f. tuft.

toujours, adv. always, ever; still.

toupet, s. m. tuft, lock.

tour¹, s.f. tower.

tour², s.m. turn; tour, trip; feat, trick; (turning-)lathe; revolution; ~ à ~ in turns; à son ~ in turn; *faire le* ~ *de* go round.

tourelle, s. f. turret.

tourisme, s. m. tourism; touring; *faire du* ~ *à pied* hike.

touriste, s. m. f. tourist, hiker.

tourment, s. m. torment, torture.

tourmenter, v. a. torment; se ~ worry.

tournant, adj. turning; — s. m. turn(ing).

tourné, adj. turned; sour.

tournée, s. f. tour, walk; circuit.

tourner, v. a. turn, twist, wind; turn round; v. n. turn, revolve; turn out; turn sour.

tournevis, s.m. screw-driver.

tournoi, s.m. tournament.

tournure, s.f. shape, figure; turn; cast; appearance.

tous see tout.

tousser, v.n. cough.

tout, -e, adj. (pl. **tous, toutes**) all, every, any, whole, full; ~ le monde everybody; ~ son possible one's utmost; à ~e force at any cost; — adv. wholly, entirely; ~ coup suddenly; ~ fait thoroughly; ~ de suite directly; ~ à l'heure just now; ~ au moins at least; — pron. & s.m. everything, all; pas du ~ not at all.

toutefois, adv. yet, nevertheless, however.

tout-puissant, adj. almighty.

toux, s. f. cough.

tracas, s. m. bustle, stir; worry.

tracasser, v. n. & a. worry.

traduction, s. f. translation.

traduire*, v. a. translate.

trafic, s. m. traffic; trade, commerce.

trafiquer, v.n. traffic; ry, bother; fuss; se ~ worry.

trace, s. f. trace, track; footprint.

tracer, v. a. trace, draw; lay out.

tracteur, s. m. tractor.

traction, s.f. traction, pull.

tradition, s. f. tradition.

traditionnel, -elle, adj. traditional.

traducteur, -trice, s. m. f. translator.

trade, deal.

tragédie, s. f. tragedy.

tragédien, -enne, s. m. .f. tragedien.

tragique, adj. tragic.

trahir, v. a. betray; deceive, mislead.

trahison, s. f. treason, treachery.

train, s.m. pace, rate; train; ~ couloir corridor-train; ~ direct through train; ~ de marchandises goods train.

traîne, s.f. train (of a dress).

traîneau, s. m. sledge.

traîner, v.a. drag, draw; lead (to); delay; v.n. drag; lie about; lag behind.

train-poste, s.m mail-train.

traire*, v.a. milk.

trait, s.m. arrow; dart; flash; line; trait, feature.

traite, s.f. journey; stretch; export; draft, bill.

traité, s. m. treaty.

traitement, s. m. treatment; usage; reception; salary.

traiter, v.a. treat, use, deal with; call; entertain.

traître, s. m. traitor; — adj. treacherous.

trajet, s.m. passage, journey, course, crossing.

tram, s.m. tram(-car).

trammer, v. a. weave; plot; devise.

tramway, s. m. tram.

tranchant, adj. sharp, keen.

tranche, s. f. slice, chop, steak.

trancher, v.a. & n.

cut; cut off; carve; break off.

tranquille, adj. quiet, calm; soyez ~! don't worry!

tranquilliser, v. a. soothe, calm; se ~ keep calm.

transaction, s. f. compromise, transaction.

transalpin, adj. transalpine.

transatlantique, adj. transatlantic; — s. f. deckchair.

transfert, s. m. transfer.

transformation, s. f. transformation, change.

transformer, v.a. transform, convert.

transfusion, s.f. transfusion.

transistor, s. m. transistor.

transit, s.m. transit.

transition, s.f. transition.

transmettre, v. a. transmit; forward; pass on.

transmission, s. f. transmission.

transparent, adj. transparent.

transpiration, s.f. perspiration.

transpirer, v. n. perspire.

transport, s. m. transport, conveyance; enterprise de ~ forwarding agency.

transporter, v.a. transport, convey; transfer; enrapture.

trappe, s. f. trap; trapdoor.

travail, s. m. (pl. -aux) work, job, employment; task; piece of work; workmanship; petits travaux odd jobs; sans ~ unemployed.

travailler, v.n. & a. work, labour; take pains.

travailleur, -euse, *s. m. f.* worker, workman, workwoman.

travers, *s. m.* breadth; *à* ~ across, through; *au* ~ *de* through; *en* ~ across.

traverse, *s. f.* traverse; obstacle; crossing.

traversée, *s. f.* crossing, passage.

traverser, *v. a.* traverse, cross, go through; run through.

trayeuse, *s. f.* milking-machine.

trébucher, *v. n.* stumble; turn the scale.

tréfle, *s. m.* clover; club *(cards)*.

treille, *s. f.* vine arbour.

treize, *adj. & s. m.* thirteen;

tremblant, *adj.* tembling, shaky.

tremblement, *s. m.* trembling, shaking; ~ *de terre* earthquake.

trembler, *v. n.* tremble, shake.

tremper, *v. a.* soak, wet; dip; *il est tout trempé* he is wet through.

tremplin, *s. m.* springboard.

trentaine, *s. m.* thirty.

trente, *adj. & s. m.* thirty; thirtieth.

très, *adv.* very, most, very much; ~ *bien* very well; all right.

trésor, *s. m.* treasure.

trésorie, *s. f.* treasury.

trésorier, *s. m.* treasurer

tresse, *s. f.* plait, tress, braid.

trève, *s. f.* truce, rest; *faire* ~ stop, cease.

triangle, *s. m.* triangle.

tribu, *s. f.* tribe.

tribunal, *s. m.* tribunal, law-court.

tribune, *s. f.* tribune, platform; grand-stand.

tributaire, *adj.* tributary.

tricher, *v. n. & a.* cheat; trick (s.o. out of).

tricot, *s. m.* (knitted) jersey.

tricoter, *v. a. & n.* knit.

triomphant, *adj.* triumphant.

triomphe, *s. m.* triumph.

triompher, *v. n.* triumph.

triple, *adj.* triple.

tripot, *s. m.* gambling-den.

triste, *adj.* sad.

tristesse, *s. f.* sadness.

trivial, *adj.* trivial.

trois, *adj. & s. m.* three; third.

troisième, *adj. & s. m.* third.

trolley, *s. m.* trolley (-pole).

trolleybus, *s. m.* trolley-bus.

trompe, *s. f.* trumpet, horn.

tromper, *v. a.* deceive, cheat, take in; *se* ~ mistake, be mistaken; be wrong; *se* ~ *de train* take the wrong train.

trompette, *s. f.* trumpet; trumpeter.

tronc, *s. m.* trunk; stock; collecting box.

trône, *s. m.* throne.

trop, *adv.* too; too much.

trophée, *s. m.* trophy.

tropical, *adj.* tropical.

tropique, *s. m.* tropic.

trot, *s. m.* trot.

trotter, *v. n.* trot.

trottoir, *s. m.* pavement; footway.

trou, *s. m.* hole; gap; opening.

trouble, *s. m.* disorder; confusion; misunderstanding; dispute; — *adj.* troubled; muddy.

troubler, *v. a.* stir up,

disturb; make muddy; muddle; confuse, perplex; upset; trouble.

troué, *s. f.* opening, gap.

trouer, *v. a.* make a hole in; pierce; bore.

troupe, *s. f.* troop, band.

troupeau, *s.m.* herd, drove; flock.

trouvaille, *s. f.* find(ing)

trouver, *v. a.* find, discover; find out; think; contrive; se ~ be, be found to be, prove; turn out, happen; *je me trouvais là* I happened to be there.

truite, *s. f.* trout.

trust, *s. m.* trust.

T.S.F., *s. f.* (=*télégraphie sans fil*) wireless (set).

tu, toi, *pron.* you.

tube, *s. m.* tube; pipe; ~ *de télévision* TV tube.

tuberculose, *s. f.* tuberculosis.

tuer, *v. a.* kill; slay.

tuile, *s. f.* tile.

tumeur, *s. f.* tumour.

tunnel, *s. m.* tunnel.

turbine, *s. f.* turbine.

turbopropulseur, *s. m.* turbo-prop aircraft.

turboréacteur, *s.m.* turbo-jet engine.

turc, turque (T.),*adj.* Turkish (language), Turk.

tuteur, -**trice**, *s.m.f.* guardian, trustee.

tutoyer, *v. a.* to 'thee-and thou' s. o.

tuyau, *s. m.* pipe, tube; flue; ~ *d'échappement* exhaust-pipe.

tympan, *s. m.* ear-drum.

type, *s. m.* type.

typique, *adj.* typical.

typographie, *s. f.* typography; printing.

tyran, *s. m.* tyrant.

tyrannie, *s. f.* tyranny.

tyranniser, *v. a.* tyrannize (over); oppress.

U

ulcère, *s. m.* ulcer.

ultérieur, *adj.* ulterior; further.

ultime, *adj.* ultimate, last, final.

ultra-violet-, -**ette**, *adj.* ulra-violet.

un, une, *art. & pron.* a, an; any, some; one; *l'*~ *ou l'autre* either one or the other; *ni l'*~ *ni l'autre* neither one; *l'*~ *et autre* both; ~*e fois* once; ~ *à* ~ one by one.

unanime, *adj.* unanimous.

uni, *adj.* smooth, even, level; united.

unification, *s. f.* unification.

unifier, *v. a.* unify; unite.

uniforme, *adj.* uniform.

union, *s. f.* union; agreement: match, marriage.

unique, *adj.* unique, sole, only.

uniquement, *adv.* solely, only.

unir, *v.a.* unite; level, smooth; s'~ join.

unité, *s.f.* unity; unit.

univers, *s. m.* universe.

universel, -**elle**, *adj.* universal; world-wide.

universitaire, *adj.* academic, university.

université, *s.f.* university.

urbain, *adj.* urban.

urgence, *s.f.* urgency; *d'*~ urgent; *en cas d'*~ in case of emergency.

urgent, *adj.* urgent, pressing.

uriner, *v. n. & a.* urinate.

urne, *s. f.* urn.

usage, *s. m.* use, custom;

habit, way; wear; d'∼ usual, habitual; en ∼ in use.

usé, adj. worn-out, shabby.

user, v. n. & a. use, make use of; wear out; use up; — s.m. wear, service, use; être d'un bon ∼ wear well.

usine, s. f. factory, works.

ustensile, s. m. utensil; implement, tool.

usuel, -elle, adj. usual, customary.

usure[1], s. f. usury.

usure[2], s. f. wear (and tear).

usurper, v.a. usurp.

utile, adj. useful, of use, profitable; être ∼ ( ) be of use.

utilisation, s.f. utilization.

utiliser, v.a. utilize.

utilité, s. f. utility, use.

V

va int. agreed!, indeed.

vacance, s. f. vacancy; (pl.), holiday(s), vacation; être en ∼s be on holiday.

vacant, adj. vacant.

vacarme, s.m. noise, uproar.

vaccin, s.m. vaccine.

vacciner, v. a. vaccinate.

vache, s.f. cow.

vaciller, v.n. vacillate; reel; waver.

vacuum, s. m. vacuum.

vagabond, s. m. trampe.

vague[1], adj. vague.

vague[2], s.f. wave.

vaillant, adj. valiant.

vain, adj. vain; empty; en ∼ in vain.

vaincre*, v. a. & n.

conquer, defeat.

vainqueur, s.m. conqueror, victor; — adj. conquering, victorious.

vaisseau, s. m. vessel; ship.

vaisselle, s. f. plates and dishes, table-service; laver la ∼ wash up the dishes; lavage de ∼ washing-up.

valet, s. m. valet; knave, jack.

valeur, s. f. value, worth; price; courage; ∼s securities.

valide, adj. valid; able-bodied.

validité, s.f. validity.

valise, s. f. valise, (travelling-)bag; suitcase; ∼ diplomatique dispatch-box, diplomatic bag.

vallée, s. f. valley.

valoir*, v.n. & a. be worth, be as good as; deserve; procure; yield.

valse, s.f. waltz.

vanille, s.f. vanilla.

vanité, s.f. vanity.

vaniteux, -euse, adj. vain, conceited.

vanter, v. a. extol, cry up; se ∼ boast.

vapeur[1], s.f. steam; vapour.

vapeur[2], s.m. steamer.

vaporeux, -euse, adj. vaporous.

vaquer, v. n. be vacant.

variable, adj. variable, changeable.

variante, s.f. variant.

variation, s.f. variation.

varier, v. n. & a. vary; ∼ de ... a range from ... to.

variété, s. f. variety.

vase, s. m. vase; vessel.

vaseline, s. f. vaseline.

vassal, s. m. vassal.

vaste, *adj.* vast; spacious.
vautour, *s. m.* vulture.
veau, *s. m.* veal; calf.
vedette, *s.f.* mounted sentinel; motor-boat; (film) star.
végétal, *s. m.* vegetable; plant.
végétation, *s. f.* vegetation.
végéter, *v. n.* vegetate.
véhémence, *s. f.* vehemence.
véhément, *adj.* vehement.
véhicule, *s. m.* vehicle.
véhiculer, *v. a.* transport.
veille, *s. f.* waking; vigil; eve.
veiller, *v. n.* sit up, keep watch; *v.a.* watch.
veine, *s. f.* vein; luck.
vélo, *s.m.* bike.
vélocité, *s.f.* velocity.
velours, *s.m.* velvet.
velouté, *adj.* velvety, soft.
velu, *adj.* hairy.
venaison, *s.f.* venison.
vendange, *s.f.* vintage, grape-harvest.
vendeur, **-euse**, *s. m. f.* salesman, shop assistant; saleswoman.
vendre, *v. a.* sell; *à* ~ for sale.
vendredi, *s. m.* Friday; *le* ~ *saint* Good Friday.
vénéneux, **-euse**, *adj.* poisonous.
vénérable, *adj.* venerable.
vengeance, *s. f.* vengeance, revenge.
venger, *v.a.* avenge, revenge; *se* ~ avenge oneself.
venin, *s.m.* poison.
venir*, *v. n.* come, arrive; grow; occur; arise; ~ *de* come from; ~ *à bout de* manage.
vent, *s. m.* wind; *grand* ~ gale; ~ *alizé* trade-wind.

vente, *s. f.* sale; auction; *en* ~ for sale.
venteux, **-euse**, *adj.* windy.
ventilateur, *s. m.* ventilator.
ventilation, *s. f.* ventilation.
ventre, *s. m.* belly.
venue, *s.f.* coming, arrival.
ver, *s.m.* worm.
verbal, *adj.* verbal, oral.
verbe, *s.m.* verb.
verdeur, *s.f.* greenness; harshness.
verdict, *s.m.* verdict.
verdure, *s.f.* verdure; greenness.
verger, *s.m.* orchard.
vergue, *s.f.* yard.
vérification, *s.f.* verification; check(ing).
vérifier, *v.a.* verify; check; confirm.
vérité, *s.f.* truth.
vermicelle, *s.m.* vermicelli.
vernir, *v. a.* varnish; polish.
vernis, *s.m.* varnish; polish.
verre, *s.m.* glass.
verrou, *s.m.* bolt.
verrouiller, *v.a.* bolt.
vers[1], *s.m.* line; verse.
vers[2], *prep.* towards, to; about.
verser, *v. a.* pour (out) spill, upset; *v. n.* overturn.
version, *s. f.* translation; version.
vert, *adj.* green; hearty; sharp.
vertical, *adj.* vertical, upright.
vertige, *s. m.* dizziness.
vertu, *s.f.* virtue.
vessie, *s.f.* bladder.
veste, *s. f.* coat, jacket.
vestiaire, *s. m.* cloakroom.

vestibule, *s.m.* lobby, hall; *grand* ~ lounge.

veston, *s. m.* coat; *complet* ~ lounge-suit.

vêtement, *s.m.* clothes *(pl.);* ~*s de dessous* underwear, underclothes.

vétéran, *s.m.* veteran.

vétérinaire, *s. m.* veterinary surgeon, vet.

vêtir*, *v. a.* clothe, dress.

véto, *s.m.* veto.

veuf, *s.m.* widower.

veuve, *s.f.* widow.

vexer, *v. a.* vex, annoy.

via, *prep.* via.

viaduc, *s. m.* viaduct.

viande, *s. m.* meat; ~ *réfrigérée* chilled meat.

vibration, *s. f.* vibration.

vibrer, *v. n.* vibrate.

vicaire, *s.m.* curate.

vice, *s.m.* vice, evil.

vice-, *prefix* vice-

vicieux, -euse, *adj.* vicious; faulty.

vicomte, *s. m.* viscount.

victime, *s.f.* victim.

victoire, *s.f.* victory.

victorieux, -euse, *adj.* victorious.

victuailles, *s. f. pl.* victuals.

vide, *adj.* empty; void; vacant; — *s.m.* space.

vider, *v. a.* empty; drain.

vie, *s.f.* life.

vieillard, *s.m.* old man.

vieillesse, *s.f.* old age.

vieillir, *v.n.* grow old.

vierge, *s. f.* virgin, maid.

vieux, vieil, vieille, *adj.* old.

vif, vive, *adj.* live; quick; lively; full of life; bright, vivid; fiery, ardent.

vigilant, *adj.* watchful.

vigne, *s.f.* vine; vineyard.

vignoble, *s.m.* vineyard.

vigoureux, -euse, *adj.* vigorous.

vigueur, *s.f.* vigour force.

vilain, *s. m.* villain, cac

village, *s.m.* village.

ville, *s. f.* town, city; *hôtel de* ~ town hall.

vin, *s. m.* wine.

vinaigre, *s. m.* vinegar.

vingt, *adj.* & *s.m.* twenty; twentieth.

vingtième, *adj.* twentieth.

violation, *s.f.* violation.

violence, *s.f.* violence.

violent, *adj.* violent; excessive.

violer, *v. a.* violate, ravish.

violette, *s.f.* violet.

violon, *s.m.* violin.

violoncelle, *s. m.* (violon-) cello.

violoniste, *s. m f.* violinist.

vipère, *s.f.* viper.

virgule, *s.f.* comma; *point et* ~ semicolon.

virtuose, *s. m. f.* virtuoso.

vis, *s. f.* screw.

visa, *s.m.* visa, visé.

visage, *s. m.* face.

vis-à-vis, *prep.* opposite; facing.

viser, *v.a.* aim (at); aspire to.

viseur, *s. m.* view-finder.

visibilité, *s. f.* visibility.

visible, *adj.* visible.

vision, *s.f.* sight.

visite, *s. f.* visit; *faire* ~ *à* pay a visit to, call on.

visiter, *v. a.* visit; ~ *les curiosités* go sightseeing.

visiteur, -euse, *s. m. f.* visitor.

visser, *v. a.* screw (down, in).

visuel, -elle, *adj.* visual.

vital, *adj.* vital.

vitalité, *s.f.* vitality.

vitamine, _s. f._ vitamin.

vite, _adj._ fast; swift; — _adv._ fast, rapidly.

vitesse, _s. f._ speed; rate (of speed); gear; _à toute_ ～ at top speed; _boîte de_ ～ gear-box; ～ _de croisière_ cruising speed.

vitrail _s. m._ church window.

vitre, _s. f._ pane.

vitrier, _s.m._ glazier.

vivant, _adj._ alive, living; full of life; _de mon_ ～ in my lifetime.

vivement, _adv._ quickly, fast.

vivre*, _v. n._ live, be alive.

vocabulaire, _s. m._ vocabulary.

vocation, _s.f._ vocation, calling.

vœu, _s. m. (pl. -x)_ wish, desire; vow.

vogue, _s. f._ vogue, fashion; _avoir la_ ～ be in vogue.

voici, _prep._ here (is); _le_ ～_!_ here he is!

voie, _s.f._ way, road; route; line, track; means, channel.

voilà, _prep._ there (is).

voile¹, _s.m._ veil.

voile², _s.f._ sail.

voiler, _v.a._ veil, cover, hide.

voilier, _s. m._ sailing-ship.

voir*, _v. a._ see; look at; view; _faire_ ～ show; _ne pas_ ～ miss.

voire, _adv._ even.

voisin, _adj._ neighbouring, adjoining, next (door).

voisinage, _s.m._ neighbourhood.

voiture, _s.f._ vehicle, conveyance; carriage; car; coach; van; wagon; _aller en_ ～ drive.

voiture-ambulance, _s. f._ ambulance(-car).

voix, _s. f._ voice; sound; _à haute_ ～ aloud.

vol¹, _s. m._ flying, flight.

vol², _s. m._ theft, robbery.

volaille, _s.f._ poultry, fowl.

volant, _s.m._ steering-wheel.

volcan, _s.m._ volcano.

volée, _s.f._ flight.

voler¹, _v. n._ fly; run at top speed.

voler², _v. a. & n._ steal, rob.

volet, _s.m._ shutter.

voleur, _s. m._ thief, robber.

volontaire, _adj._ voluntary; — _s. m. f._ volunteer.

volonté, _s. f._ will; _à_ ～ at will.

volontiers, _adv._ willingly.

volt, _s.m._ volt.

voltiger, _v.n._ flutter about, fly about.

volume, _s. m._ volume; bulk.

voluptueux, -euse, _adj._ voluptuous.

vomir, _v. a. & n._ vomit, be sick.

vos, _adj. poss._ your.

vote, _s. m._ vote; voting.

voter, _v. n._ ～ _& a._ vote.

votre, _adj._ yours.

vouer, _v. a._ vow; dedicate.

vouloir*, _v. a._ want, require, demand; ～ _bien_ be willing; _je voudrais + inf._ I should like to; _comme vous voulez_ as you please.

vous, _pron._ you; to you.

vous-même, _pron._ yourself.

voûte, _s.f._ vault, arch.

voyage, _s.m._ journey; voyage; _bon_ ～_!_ a pleasant journey (to you)!; *partir en* ~ set off on a journey; *fair e un* ~ make a journey.

voyager, *v.n.* travel, make a trip.

voyageur, -euse, *s. m. f.* traveller, passenger.

voyelle, *s.f.* vowel.

voyou, *s.m.* hooligan.

vrai, *adj.* real, true, right; *être* ~ hold (good); — *s. m.* truth; *être dans le* ~ be right.

vraiment, *adv.* truly, really; indeed.

vraisemblable, *adj.* likely, credible, probable.

vu, *prep.* considering.

vue, *s. f.* sight; vision; view; *à* ~ at sight; *en* ~ *de* with a view to; *point de* ~ point of view; *avoir la* ~ *courte* be short-sighted; *être en* ~ be in the limelight.

vulgaire, *adj.* vulgar; common; coarse.

W

wagon, *s. m.* coach, carriage, car.

wagon-lit, *s. m.* sleeping-car.

wagonnet, *s.m.* tub; truck.

wagon-poste, *s. m.* mail-van.

wagon-restaurant, *s. m.* dining-car.

water-closet, *s. m.* W. C.

water-polo, *s. m.* water-polo.

wattman, *s.m.* tram-driver.

week-end, *s.m.* week-end.

whisky, *s.m.* whisky.

X

xérès, *s. m.* sherry.

xylographie, *s. f.* xylography.

xylophages, *s.m.* *pl.* xylophages.

Y

y, *adv.* here, there; *il* ~ *a* there is, there exists; *s'* ~ *connaître* well informed.

vacht, *s. m.* yacht.

yeux *see* œil.

yogourt, yoghourt, *s. m.* yoghourt, yaourt.

yougoslave, *adj.* Yugoslav.

youyou, *s.m.* dinghy.

Z

zèbre, *s.m.* zebra.

zébrer, *v.a.* stripe.

zèle, *s.m.* zeal.

zélé, *adj.* zealous.

zénith, *s.m* zenith.

zéro, *s.m.* zero.

zézayer, *v.n.* lisp.

zigzag, *s.m.* zigzag.

zinc, *s.m.* zinc.

zone, *s.f.* zone, belt.

zoo, *s.m.* zoo.

zoologie, *s.f.* zoology.

zoologique, *adj.* zoological.

zut, *int.* ~ *!* damn it!